ENGLISH LANGUAGE TEACHING TECHNIQUES

영어교수기법

박상옥 편저

신아사

ENGLISH LANGUAGE TEACHING TECHNIQUES

머리말

〔제2판〕

이 책은 사범대학 영어교육과 학생들과 그밖에 영어를 가르치고자 하는 사람, 그리고 현재 영어를 가르치는 교사들에게 영어지도기법을 소개하여 지도에 직접 활용할 수 있게 하려는 목적으로 쓰여졌다.

필자는 지난 20여년 동안 영어교육과 학생들에게 실질적인 영어교수기법을 가르쳐 왔다. 주로 원서를 사용하고 영어로 강의를 했으며 micro-teaching과 실제 수업 참관기회도 줌으로써 이론과 실제의 괴리를 좁히기 위해 많은 노력을 해왔다. 또한 학습지도안 작성, 교과서 평가 작업들도 해보면서 교사가 되기 위한 준비를 나름대로 충실히 해주려고 하였다.

이러한 노력을 하면서도 한 가지 아쉬운 점은 적당한 교재를 찾을 수 없었다는 것이다. 영어습득론, 영어교수법을 별도로 택하는 학생들에게 각 기능별 지도기법이 중심이 되면서 수업참관, 학습지도안 작성, 영어교과서 평가 등을 다루는 두 학기 정도에 소화할 분량의 교재를 필요로 했기 때문이다. 결국 주 교재 이외에 많은 관련 유인물과 우리말 부교재를 사용해야만 했었다.

이 책은 지금까지 필자가 사용한 자료 중에서 적절하다고 판단된 것들을 모은 것이다. 발음지도, 문법지도, 말하기 지도, 듣기 지도, 읽기 지도, 쓰기 지도, 문화지도, 평가, 교수분석, 수업계획, 교과서 평가 등 열 한 개의 장르로 분류하여 순서를 배열하였으며 주로 영문으로 되어 있지만 우리말의 논문도 소수 포함시켰다.

각 장은 관련 논문들을 읽기에 앞서 전체적인 이해에 도움이 될 수 있는 간단한 배경설명 부분이 있고 이어서 각 논문에 대한 요약이 있다. 과목의 성격과 허용된 시간 그리고 학생의 수준에 따라 순서나 분량에 있어서 융통성 있게 사용할 수 있을 것이다.

ENGLISH LANGUAGE TEACHING TECHNIQUES

한편, 이 책의 내용을 기초로 하여 우리말로 영어교수 기법을 정리한 '한국인을 위한 영어학습지도'는 상호 보완을 해 줄 수 있을 것이다.

교육의 목적이 다 그러하듯이 이 책을 통하여 영어교수기법에 관해 일방적인 지식을 전달하려는 것이 아니다. 중요한 것은 배운 지식을 토대로 독자 나름대로 자신의 상황에 가장 적합하게 기법들을 고안할 수 있는 창의적 능력을 키워주는 것이다. 그래서 필자는 각 장이 끝날 때마다 가상의 또는 실제의 학생들을 대상으로 직접 교수하게 한 후 이를 녹화하여 자체 평가하는 기회를 주었다. 즉 micro-teaching을 해오고 있다. 학기말에 학생들이 가장 유익한 경험 중 하나로 언급하는 부분이다.

좀 더 많은 시간적 할애가 된다면 국내외 영어교육 관련 학술지에서 관심 있는 영어교수기법 관련 논문을 적어도 한편씩 찾아 읽고 영어(국내 학술 논문) 또는 우리말(국외 학술 논문)로 요약하여 발표하는 기회를 제공하기를 원한다. 끊임없이 자기 개발을 하는 영어교사가 되기 위해 필요할 것이다.

마지막으로 이 책이 되어 나오기까지 격려와 조언을 주신 영어교육과 동료교수와 특별히 컴퓨터와 오랜 시간 씨름을 하며 땀을 흘린 제자 김말희에게 감사한다. 그리고 출판을 흔쾌히 허락해 주신 신아사 정현걸 사장님께 고마움을 표한다.

2009년 2월

편저자

CONTENTS

PART ONE

TEACHING PRONUNCIATION

언어교육 목표의 변화와 언어습득 이론의 발달은 제2언어 및 외국어 발음지도 목표에도 큰 변화를 가져왔다. 이제는 더 이상 개별음소의 정확한 발음을 모든 학습자에게 기대하지 않고 대신 원어민의 말을 이해하고 동시에 원어민에 의해 말이 이해되는 정도의 발음이 목표로 설정된다. 즉 'We want our students to be able to understand the native speech and to be understood by the native speaker'이다. 따라서 intelligibility 또는 comprehensibility가 발음교육의 목표라고 한마디로 축약할 수 있겠다.

첫 번째 논문에서 Pennington과 Richards는 전통적으로 언어능력의 한 요소로 간주되었던 발음이 오늘날 의사소통 능력의 요소로 간주되게 되면서 발음교육이 어떻게 새로운 의미를 지니게 되었는가, 그리고 그것이 발음교육에 시사하는 바는 무엇인가를 논한다. 다음으로 Wong의 'Does pronunciation teaching have a place in the communicative classroom?'은 구체적으로 발음의 어떤 요소들에 의해서 원어민과의 의사소통에 문제가 발생하는가를 보여주면서 명확하게 논문 제목의 질문에 'yes'라는 답을 해준다. 그렇지만 여기에 따르는 문제는 이처럼 의사소통에 방해가 되는 발음의 요인들을 가르칠 수 있는 교수자료가 없다는 것이므로 적절한 교재개발이 필요하다고 덧붙인다.

다음으로 최소 대립쌍(minimal pair)을 이용한 발음연습은 전통적으로 가장 많이 사용되었던 교수기법중 하나이고 지금도 어떤 특정한 소리로 인하여 의사소통에 방해를 받게 될 때 사용하면 효과적이다. 그래서 구체적으로 개별 단어가 최소 대립쌍이 되게 하여 연습시키는 방법을 소개한 Spaventa의 논문 내용은 우리에게 익숙한 것이고, 이어서 소개된 Donald의 문맥화를 통한 최소 대립쌍 발음연습은 자연스럽고 의미 있는 상황에서의 언어교육 방법으로서 발음지도뿐 아니라 영어교육의 모든 분야에서 이용되어야 하는 교사들의 기본 태도까지 제시하고 있다.

1. PRONUNCIATION REVISITED

While pronunciation has in the past occupied a central position in theories of oral language proficiency, the view of pronunciation embodied in traditional approaches to language teaching trivializes its true nature. In older methods such as audiolingualism, pronunciation has been largely identified with accurate production of isolated sounds or words, and this view is reflected in more contemporary methods such as the Silent Way. The Contrastive Analysis Hypothesis (Lado, 1957) regards pronunciation as central to second language proficiency, but it likewise largely restricts the domain of pronunciation to the segmental level.

The goals of language teaching have changed under the impact of communicative views of language and interactive theories of language learning. Pronunciation, traditionally viewed as a component of linguistic rather than communicative competence or as an aspect of accuracy rather than of conversational fluency, has come to be regarded as of limited importance in a communicatively oriented curriculum.

Recent changes in perspective in TESL/TEFL methodology have produced uncertainty about the role of pronunciation. In view of this uncertainty, there is a need to assess and clarify the current status of the teaching of pronunciation.

While phonology has not occupied as central a position as syntax in second language acquisition research, some important characteristics of the phonological learning process have been isolated. These include the extent to which the second language phonological system is influenced by the phonological system of the first language, the role of universal acquisition processes in the development of L2 phonology, psychosocial and individual factors, and the context of language learning and use.

The Influence Of The First Language

Language transfer has always been recognized as basic to any theory of second language phonological development (Lado, 1957). The notion of interlanguage acknowledges the role of language transfer (Selinker, 1972), and current views of the nature of interlanguage consider the learner's phonological representations as constituting a system intermediate between the native language and the target language (Flege, 1980, 1981).

Other researchers argue that the phenomenon of transfer extends beyond the level of individual phonemes to include syllable structure (Hecht & Mulford, 1982; Johansson, 1973; Macken & Ferguson, 1981; Tarone, 1980) as well as prosodic and voice-setting features

(Esling & Wong, 1983). Faerch, Haastrup, and Phillipson (1984) report the transfer of the following mother tongue intonation patterns in the speech of Danish learners of English:

1. A tendency to pitch the unstressed syllables higher than the preceding stressed ones (the normal pattern in Copenhagen Danish), creating a weaving or lilting impression.
2. Instead of full [intonational] glides (falls, rises, fall-rises), flattening them out (as is the case in Danish) and consequently making them less clearly marked. (p. 125)

Gumperz (1982), in his studies of cross-cultural interactions, demonstrates that transfer of voice-setting and prosodic features of the first language can lead to serious intercultural misunderstanding in the target culture.

Acquisition Processes In L2 Phonology

Second language acquisition (SLA) research has confirmed that many other processes interact with language transfer in shaping the L2 (second language) phonological system. Some of these acquisition processes are similar to those found in first language phonological development and may be interpreted as a reactivation of first language development strategies. For example, children acquire voiceless consonants before voiced consonants (Macken & Ferguson, 1981), and the same order of acquisition has been observed in second language phonological development, even when the learner's native language possesses voiced final consonants (Hecht & Mulford, 1982). Mulford and Hecht (1980) stress the interrelation of transfer and universal developmental processes in determining the particular range of persistent sound substitutions that occur in the acquisition of second language phonology.

The course of acquisition, both in terms of rate and order, has been a focus of SLA studies, though most of these studies have addressed L2 syntactic rather than phonological development. In first language learning, however, there has been a considerable amount of research on the rate and order of L1 phonological development (Macken & Ferguson, 1981), and L2 phonology needs to be examined from a similar perspective.

Another phenomenon cited as a developmental process in first and second language acquisition is simplification (e. g., of syllable structure, as in Tarone, 1978, 1980; however, see Hodne, 1985, and Sato, 1984). Large-scale simplification of the target language by nonnative speakers has been seen as a kind of pidginization (Ferguson, 1971; Schumann, 1978). For second language learning the pidginization model predicts that a learner's interlanguage forms will either fossilize at some distance from the target or go through a process of de-creolization to approximate the target phonology over time (Anderson, 1983; Schumann, 1975, 1978).

The development of L2 phonology can be viewed as a dynamic process involving cognitive, psychomotor, linguistic, and interactive factors. Markedness theory has been invoked to account for the fact that certain phonological features are more difficult for second language learners to acquire than other features (Eckman, 1977). It has also been suggested that part of the problem of pronunciation is psychomotor.

The development of phonological representations, or schemata, for the target language (i.e., second language phonological competence), through opportunities to hear and to speak the language, appears to be a long-term cognitive process which may not develop at the same rate as the corresponding motor skills required for articulation (i.e., second language phonological performance). As a consequence, perception and production may not develop in parallel (Leather, 1983; Neufeld, 1977; Neufeld & Schneiderman, 1980; Sheldon & Strange, 1982).

Other features of second language acquisition are similar to processes found in the context of language change and variation. As in the case of first language phonological change, in second language learning a new item or rule is not acquired categorically: Learners do not immediately begin to use a new phonological rule or feature in all its contexts or in all its appropriate phonetic variants. Rather, learners acquire variants of target language features and gradually refine the range of contexts in which the variants are used. At the same time, they add new features to their repertoire, which at an earlier time they may have avoided altogether (Celce-Murcia, 1977).

L. J. Dickerson (1975) shows that Japanese learners of English, in acquiring the phoneme /z/, produce a higher percentage of target variants for the phonemes in initial than in medial or final positions. As learning proceeds, they gradually produce more target variants in medial and final positions.

W. B. Dickerson (1976), drawing on sociolinguistic variation theory (e.g., Cedergren & Sankoff, 1974; Labov, 1972), describes the process of acquiring new environments for target language rules as a wave mechanism in which rules are learned in specific contexts and then spread throughout the learner's interlanguage. Through this wave mechanism, phonological features learned in the context of specific lexical items, phrases, or grammatical constructions may be applied by analogy to additional items, phrases, and constructions.

Lacking from the SLA studies, however, has been a thorough examination of interactional effects in connected spoken discourse, including the universal and language-specific mechanisms for highlighting and de-emphasizing information, and how these affect the acquisition and spread of new phonological features in interlanguage development.

Psychosocial And Individual Factors

Pronunciation is a central component of face-to-face interaction and is consequently part of the process by which speakers present an image of themselves to others. The concept of language ego (Guiora, Beit-Hallahmi, Brannon, Dull, & Scovel, 1972) may help to explain the fact that phonological features are among the most salient linguistic dimensions used by speakers to create a sense of personal identity,

Certain first language phonological features may be consciously retained as markers of ethnic or group identity (Giles, Bourhis, & Taylor, 1977), and so

> caution should be exercised in regarding [phonological] intrusions simply as instances of interlingual interferences, particularly in the cases of second and third generations of immigrants, as they may often be adopted by them deliberately as ethnic speech markers to establish a distinctive linguistic identity. (Giles, 1979, p. 260)

Some learners, wishing to integrate actively into the target culture and to be identified with its speakers, may be motivated to try to attain a native accent in the foreign language. Others, in contrast, may not have a strong integrative motivation toward the target culture and so may consciously or unconsciously seek to maintain a distinctive accent.

The fact that pronunciation is intimately associated with a person's identity may also explain why considerable individual variation is found in rates and ultimate levels of achievement in phonology (Leather, 1983; Macken & Ferguson, 1981). Personality variables such as introversion, extroversion, or sociability have been suggested to explain differences among individuals in phonological attainment (Busch, 1982). Individual language aptitude (e.g., the ability to mimic sounds) has also been cited as a contributing factor. Leather (1983) reports findings which support the view "that it is individual perceptual ability which remains in principle the limiting factor in developing second-language pronunciation" (p. 206).

The age factor remains an unresolved issue in language acquisition research. Some studies have shown a biological advantage for younger learners (Scovel, 1969; Seliger, Krashen, & Ladefoged, 1975), while others have shown no such advantage (Olson & Samuels, 1973; Snow & Hoefnagel-Hohle, 1977). Lowenthal and Bull (1984) suggest that these contradictory findings "suggest not a critical period of language development but, rather, that the way in which language is processed can change throughout the course of development" (Menyuk, 1978, p. 154). There is evidence that retention of the native accent by adult second language learners may be the result of the use of a speech-processing strategy--based, perhaps, on motor speech perception (Liberman, Cooper, Shankweiler, & Studdert-Kennedy, 1967)--established in childhood (Menyuk, 1978; Menyuk & Anderson, 1967). However, adults do not necessarily lose the linguistic capabilities which were present at earlier stages of development (Leather, 1983), and "dormant" capabilities could possibly be elicited in adults through "germane experience" (Menyuk, 1978, pp. 156-157).

The Context Of Learning And Use

The context and conditions for learning and using the language may also affect levels of attainment in phonology. The degree and type of exposure to the second language in classroom and naturalistic settings may in part determine eventual outcomes in phonology.

Traditionally, explicit instruction in phonology (e.g., via minimal pair drills) was thought to influence the student's ability to articulate new sounds and to improve the learner's capacity for self monitoring (Acton, 1984; Morely, 1979). Currently, acquisition or communication-based methodologies do not assign a central role to direct instruction in pronunciation, nor do many bilingual education models, which set the goal as intelligibility rather than native-like phonology. It is assumed in these models that target-like pronunciation will eventually result from interaction with native speakers in naturalistic settings and cannot be achieved through formal instruction.

A number of research studies have investigated the effects of instruction on the learning of pronunciation, but the results are inconclusive. While Suter (1976) and Madden (1983) find no positive effect for formal training on achievement in pronunciation, two studies report positive effects for phonetic training of adults. Murakawa (1981) shows that a 12-week program of phonetic training can produce significant changes in the articulation of individual phonemes by adult learners of English. Similar results are reported by Pennington (1984) after six instructional sessions incorporating training in both articulation and listening discrimination. Positive effects on production or perception are also reported for training in prosodic features by Gilbert (1980), Neufeld and Schneiderman (1980), de Bot (1983), and de Bot and Mailfert (1982). Differences in results in the reported studies appear to be due to the great variation in their experimental design, particularly in the type of training which was provided.

Phonological performance in the target language is affected by the communicative demands of the situation or task in which the learner is engaged. Some aspects of L2 phonological learning can be viewed from the perspective of information processing, which describes the learning of any complex task or form of behavior as the integration of a number of subskills. Initially, the use of these become routinized and are performed without conscious attention, through what is referred to as automatic processing (McLaughlin, Rossman, & McLeod, 1983).

Under certain circumstances--for example, in a public presentation--performance conditions may inhibit access to automatic processing. In such cases the learner may have to resort to the domain of conscious processing and so plan and monitor speech more closely. Thus, a learner's phonological performance may differ in the controlled and automatic modes of processing. In particular, performance may suffer when it must be consciously maintained under stressful conditions.

Implications For Teaching

The model of pronunciation as a context-dependent and dynamic interaction of segmental, voice-setting, and prosodic features has a number of implications for language teaching. This view leads to the articulation of goals different from those set forth for traditional approaches to the teaching of pronunciation.

Accuracy at the segmental level is no longer the fundamental aim of teaching, since it is now known that accurate production of segmental features does not in itself characterize native-like pronunciation, nor is it the primary basis for intelligible speech:

> In view of the fact that segmental information in the acoustic signal may well be of limited scope and reliability, it is of the greatest importance that the learner's attention is directed to non-segmental information. (Dirven & Oakeshott-Taylor, 1984, p. 333)

As the emphasis moves away from a narrow focus on segments to a broader focus on stretches of speech, the effects of voice setting, stress and intonation, as well as coarticulatory phenomena such as shortenings, weakenings, and assimilations, assume greater importance for teaching.

This top-down perspective on pronunciation highlights the overarching role of context in determining phonological choices at all three levels--segmental, voice-setting, and prosodic features. Teaching isolated forms of sounds and words fails to address the fact that in communication, many aspects of pronunciation are determined by the positioning of elements within long stretches of speech, according to the information structure and the interactional context of the discourse as determined by speaker and hearer.

The research we have reviewed on the learning of pronunciation also supports a different focus in teaching. Intervention by the teacher may not be able to alter the learner's path of development in mastering second language phonology. Learning is a gradual process involving successive approximations to the target language system over time and a progression from controlled to automatic processing.

In addition, the learner's performance and competence may not develop in synchrony; that is, lower level motor skills may develop at a different rate from their higher level corresponding mental representations. Immediate results from pronunciation training may not be achieved if the learner has not reached an appropriate stage in phonological development and so lacks the developmental prerequisites for what is being taught. Such training may, however, assist in the development of new articulatory habits and contribute to the reorganization of higher level systems, or schemata, eventually resulting in a change in performance. For the same reason, immediate improvements in pronunciation resulting from direct training may take time to become a part of spontaneous language use. In the domain of pronunciation, then, there is not likely to be a one-to-one relationship between teaching and learning.

These conclusions support the following general recommendations regarding pronunciation and its place in second language teaching:

1. The teaching of pronunciation must focus on longer term goals; short-term objectives must be developed with reference to long-term goals.
2. The goal of any explicit training in pronunciation should be to bring learners gradually from controlled, cognitively based performance to automatic, skill-based performance.
3. Teaching should aim toward gradually reducing the amount of native language influence on segmental, voice-setting, and prosodic features but should not necessarily seek to eradicate totally the influence of the native language on the speaker's pronunciation in the second language.
4. Pronunciation ought to be taught as an integral part of oral language use, as part of the means for creating both referential and interactional meaning, not merely as an aspect of the oral production of words and sentences.
5. Pronunciation forms a natural link to other aspects of language use, such as listening, vocabulary, and grammar; ways of highlighting this interdependence in teaching need to be explored.

■ References

Acton, W. (1984). Changing fossilized pronunciation. *TESOL Quarterly, 18*, pp. 71-85

Anderson, R. (1983). *Pidginization and creolization as language acquisition*. Rowle, MA: Newbury House.

de Bot, K. (1983). Visual feedback of English intonation, I: Effectiveness and induced practice behavior. *Language and Speech, 26,* pp. 331-350.

de Bot, k., & Mailfert, K. (1982). The teaching of intonation: Fundamental research and classroom applications. *TESOL Quarterly, 16,* pp. 71-77.

Brazil, D., Coulthard, M., & Johns, C. (1980). *Discourse intonation and language teaching.* London: Longman.

Brown, G. (1977). *Listening to spoken English*. London: Longman.

Brown, G., & Yule, G. (1983a). *Discourse analysis.* Cambridge: Cambridge University Press.

Brown, G., & Yule, G. (1983b). *Teaching the spoken language*. Cambridge: Cambridge University Press.

Busch, D. (1982). Introversion-extraversion and the EFL proficiency of Japanese students. *Language Learning, 32,* pp. 109-132.

Cedergren, H. J., & Sankoff, D. (1974). Variable rules: Performance as a statistical reflection of competence. *Language, 50,* pp. 333-355.

Celce-Murcia, M. (1977). Phonological factors in vocabulary acquisition: A case study of a two-year-old English-French bilingual. *Working Papers in Bilingualism, 13,* pp. 27-41.

Clark, H. H., & Clark, E. V. (1977). *Psychology and language*. New York: Harcourt Brace Jovanovich.

Dickerson, L. J. (1975). The learner's interlanguage as a set of variable rules. *TESOL Quarterly, 9,* pp. 401-408.

Dickerson, W. B. (1976). The psycholinguistic unity of language learning and language change. *Language Learning, 26,* pp. 215-232.

Dirven, R., & Oakeshott-Taylor, J. (1984). Listening comprehension (Part 1). State of the art article. *Language Teaching, 17,* pp. 326-343.

Eckman, F. R. (1977). Markedness and the contrastive analysis hypothesis. *Language Learning, 27,* pp. 315-333.

Esling, J. H., & Wong, R. F. (1983). Voice quality settings and the teaching of pronunciation. *TESOL Quarterly, 17,* pp. 89-95.

Faerch, C. K., Haastrup, K., & Phillipson, R. (1984). *Learner language and language learning.* Clevedon, England: Multilingual Matters.

Ferguson, C. A. (1971). Towards a characterization of English foreigner talk. *Anthropological Linguistics, 17,* pp. 1-14.

Flege, J. E. (1980). Phonetic approximation in second language acquisition. *Language Learning, 30,* pp. 117-134.

Flege, J. E. (1981). The phonological basis of foreign accent: A hypothesis. *TESOL Quarterly, 15,* pp. 443-455.

Gilbert, J. B. (1980). Prosodic development: Some pilot studies. In R. C. Scarcella & S. D. Krashen (Eds.), *Research in second language acquisition* (pp. 110-117). Rowley, MA: Newbury House.

Gilbert, J. B. (1984). *Clear speech.* New York: Cambridge University Press.

Giles, H. (1979). Ethnicity markers in speech. In K. R. Scherer & H. Giles (Eds.), *Social markers in speech* (pp. 251-290). Cambridge: Cambridge University Press.

Giles, H., Bourhis, R. Y., & Taylor, D. M. (1977). Towards a theory of language in ethnic group relations. In H. Giles (Ed.), *Language, ethnicity and intergroup relations* (pp. 307-348). London: Academic Press.

Guiora, A., Beit-Hallahmi, H., Brannon, R., Dull, C., & Scovel, T. (1972). The effects of experimentally induced changes in ego states on pronunciation ability in a second language: An exploratory study. *Comprehensive Psychiatry, 13,* pp. 421-428.

Gumperz, J. J. (1982). *Discourse strategies.* Cambridge: Cambridge University Press.

Haycraft, B. (1971). *The teaching of pronunciation: A classroom guide.* London: Longman.

Hecht, B. F., & Mulford, R. (1982). The acquisition of a second language phonology: Interaction of ransfer and developmental factors. *Applied Psycholinguistics, 3,* pp. 313-328.

Hodne, B. (1985). Yet another look at interlanguage phonology: The modification of English syllable structure by native speakers of Polish. *Language Learning, 35,* pp. 405-422.

Johansson, F. A. (1973). *Immigrant Swedish phonology*: A study in multiple contact analysis. Lund, Sweden: CWK Gleerup.

Labov, W. (1972). *Sociolinguistic patterns.* Philadelphia: University of Pennsylvania Press.

Ladefoged, P. (1982). *A course in phonetics* (2nd ed.). New York: Harcourt Brace Jovanovich.

Lado, R. (1957). *Linguistics across cultures.* Ann Arbor: University of Michigan Press.

Laver, J. (1980). *The phonetic description of voice quality.* Cambridge: Cambridge University Press.

Leather, J. (1983). Second-language pronunciation learning and teaching. State of the art article. *Language Teaching, 16,* pp. 198-219.

Liberman, A., Cooper, F., Shankweiler, D., & Studdert-Kennedy, M. (1967). Perception of the speech code. *Psychology Review, 74,* pp. 431-461.

Lowenthal, K., & Bull, D. (1984). Imitation of foreign sounds: What is the effect of age? *Language and Speech, 27,* pp. 95-98.

MacCarthy, P. (1979). *The teaching of pronunciation.* Cambridge: Cambridge University Press.

Macken, M. A., & Ferguson, C. A. (1981). Phonological universals in language acquisition. *Annals of the New York Academy of Sciences, 379,* pp. 110-129.

Madden E. (1983). The effect of training on pronunciation. *ORTESOL Journal*, 4, pp. 69-80.

McLaughlin, B., Rossman, T., & McLeod, B. (1983). Second language learning: An information processing perspective. *Language Learning, 33,* pp. 135-159.

Menyuk. P. (1978). *Language and maturation.* Cambridge, MA: The M.I.T. Press.

Menyuk, P., & Anderson, S. (1969). Children's identification and reproduction of /w/, /r/ and /l/. *Journal of Speech and Hearing Research, 12,* pp. 39-52.

Morely, J. (1979). *Improving spoken English.* Ann Arbor: University of Michigan Press.

Mulford, R., & Hecht, B. F. (1980). Learning to speak without an accent: Acquisition of a second-language phonology. *Papers and reports on child language development, 18,* pp. 16-74.

Murakawa, H. (1981). *Teaching English pronunciation to Japanese adults.* Unpublished doctoral dissertation, University of Texas, Austin.

Neufeld, G. (1977). Language learning ability in adults: A study on the acquisition of prosodic and articulatory features. *Working Papers in Bilingualism, 12,* pp. 45-60.

Neufeld, G., & Schneiderman, E. (1980). Prosodic and articulatory features in adult language learning. In R. C. Scarcella & S. D. Krashen (Eds.), *Research in second language acquisition* (pp. 105-109). Rowley, MA: Newbury House.

Olson, L. L., & Samuels, S. J. (1973). The relationship between age and accuracy of pronunciation. *Journal of Educational Research, 66,* pp. 263-268.

Parish, C. (1977). A practical philosophy of pronunciation. *TESOL Quarterly, 11,* pp. 311-317.

Pennington, M. (1984, March). *Can pronunciation be improved by instruction in pronunciation?* Paper presented at the 18th Annual TESOL Convention, Houston.

Sato, C. J. (1984). Phonological processes in second language acquisition: Another look at interlanguage syllable structure. *Language Learning, 34,* pp. 43-57.

Schumann, J. H. (1975). Affective factors and the problem of age in second language acquisition. *Language Learning, 25,* pp. 209-235.

Schumann, J. H. (1978). *The pidginization process: A model for second language acquisition.* Rowley, MA: Newbury House.

Scovel, T. (1969). Foreign accents, language acquisition and cerebral dominance. *Language Learning, 19,* pp. 245-253.

Selinger, H. W., Krashen, S., & Ladefoged, P. (1975). Maturational constraints in the acquisition of second language accent. *Language Sciences, 36,* pp. 20-22.

Selinker, L. (1972). Interlanguage. *International Review of Applied Linguistics, 10,* pp. 209-232.

Sheldon, A., & Strange W. (1982). The acquisition of /r/ and /l/ by Japanese learners of English: Evidence that speech production can precede speech perception. *Applied Psycholinguistics, 3,* pp. 243-261.

Snow, C. E., & Hoefnagel-Hohle, M. (1977). Age differences in the pronunciation of foreign sounds. *Language and Speech, 20*, pp. 357-365.

Stevick, E. W. (1978). Toward a practical philosophy of pronunciation: Another view. *TESOL Quarterly,*

12, pp. 145-150.

Suter, R. W. (1976). Predictors of pronunciation accuracy in second-language learning. *Language learning*, *26,* pp. 233-254.

Tarone, E. (1978). The phonology of interlanguage. In J. C. Richards (Ed.), *Understanding second and foreign language learning* (pp. 15-33). Rowley, MA: Newbury House.

Tarone, E. (1980). Some influences on the syllable structure of interlanguage phonology. *International Review of Applied Linguistics*, *18,* pp. 139-152.

From Pennington, M. C. & Richards, J. C. (1986). Pronunciation revisited, *TESOL Quarterly*, *20,* pp. 207-225.

2. DOES PRONUNCIATION TEACHING HAVE A PLACE IN THE COMMUNICATIVE CLASSROOM?

It was not very long ago that pronunciation teaching was the sine qua non of the second language curriculum. Today, however, it seems to be regarded as a luxury which many programs that teach English to nonnative speakers in the U. S. find unaffordable. This is an assumption that requires examination, because the neglect of pronunciation may have serious consequences for second language learners in the U.S., as well as in other English-speaking contexts. I would like to begin this examination by considering three factors which have contributed to the declining interest in teaching pronunciation.

First of all, instruction has apparently had a minimal effect on students' pronunciation, leading many teachers to conclude that pronunciation development is impervious to instruction. Studies such as the ones done by Suter (1976) and Purcell and Suter (1900) seem to corroborate this belief. Additionally, the debate over whether there is a critical period, beyond which learners cannot achieve an accent-free level of proficiency, has helped to weaken the position of pronunciation in the classroom (Scovel 1969; Oyama 1976; Flege 1981). In view of this resistance or inability to develop pronunciation, some teachers have turned to admittedly unorthodox methods, including hypnosis (Schumann et. al. 1978; Action 1984). Others have abandoned the *ship* and the *sheep* altogether.

A second factor which has shaken the foundation of pronunciation teaching is a change in the goal of language teaching from a focus on language form to a concern for language function, which Higgs and Clifford have labeled, a "push toward communication" (1982). In this view, pronunciation is seen as a skill with little communicative value. Unfortunately, most of the instructional materials we have for teaching pronunciation seem to confirm this assumption, since they generally promote attention to language form apart from language use.

A third factor which has influenced the current attitude toward pronunciation is the change in assumptions about language learning. One well-known view, that of Krashen's (1981), advises that language learning develops not through conscious study of the language but through a subconscious acquisition process, which is facilitated by exposure to comprehensible input. The teacher's energies, therefore, must be redirected from the specifics of language to the more general task of providing this comprehensible input to the learners. Pronunciation work has no place in this approach.

That pronunciation instruction has failed in the past does not mean that it cannot be done or that it is dispensable. It only means that our assumptions about what is important to teach and the methods that we have used to teach it may be at fault. While the shift to communicative goals is a welcomed one, I believe that pronunciation teaching is not irrelevant to these goals. In fact, if we look closely at the components of the communicative process, we will see that pronunciation is one of the more important means by which we achieve our communicative objectives. What I would like to do, then, is to show how nonnative pronunciation directly affects the communication process and what specific pronunciation factors affect this process. I will also show why pronunciation teaching has been generally unsuccessful and process what directions we must take in order to promote the communicative effectiveness of nonnative speakers by developing their pronunciation skills.

The communicative importance of pronunciation is most clearly seen beyond the classroom walls and from the perspective of the nonnative speakers themselves. Let us take a look at how pronunciation affects five groups of nonnative speakers. The first group consists of nonnative speakers whose pronunciation is so unintelligible that there is no question that some pronunciation teaching is essential. A good example of this type of speaker can be found in the community of recent Vietnamese refugees. While teachers of second language learners are noted for their ability to comprehend the interlanguage of nonnative speakers, even they have expressed frustration over the unintelligibility of many Vietnamese speakers. This group poses a major challenge to language teachers.

The second group consists of foreign students in American universities, who, while in language courses, may have apparently adequate communication skills. However, when they are assigned as teaching assistants, their students complain that they cannot understand them (Bailey et al. 1984).

The third group consists of long-term residents in the U. S., many of whom have lived here for five or ten years or even longer. Many of these nonnative speakers, often graduates of the U. S. educational system, having entered the workforce, now find that their communication skills are inadequate to meet the demands of their jobs.

The problems of the foreign teaching assistant and the nonnative professional are significant enough that universities have responded by establishing special training courses for the teaching assistants, and corporations have set up in-house courses for their nonnative employees (Bailey et. al. 1984; Browne and Huckin 1985; Eaton et al. 1985).

The fourth group comprises all those nonnative speakers who have experienced difficulty establishing and maintaining relationships with native-speaker schoolmates, co-workers, colleagues or neighbors because their communication skills are inadequate or because their pronunciation marks them as outsiders.

The fifth and last group is composed of the nonnative speakers of English living in other countries, who, for political, business, educational or social reasons need to interact with Americans. I include also in this group the speakers of nonnative varieties of English, for example, Indian English, Singapore English, Philippine English and Nigerian English. For the purpose of communicating with American-English speakers, the members of this last group need to identify those areas of English use which are most likely to affect communicative clarity.

These real world needs present a dilemma for language teachers, which is complicated by the fact that (1) many nonnative speakers in the U. S. have spoken English for many years without attention to pronunciation; (2) speakers of nonnative varieties of English may not perceive that there are differences between their English and American English; and (3) many teachers are uncertain about how to address these needs. In today's confusion over pronunciation teaching and its value, solutions have ranged from adhering to the known techniques of consonant and vowel exercises to exploring more general aspects of the communication process, such as cross-cultural comparisons of the structure and dynamics of the American classroom or the American corporate culture. While I would not want to say that these activities are not valid for specific groups of learners, I believe that major aspects of the spoken language system itself are being overlooked, aspects which play a major role in communicative interaction. These aspects are stress, rhythm and intonation and they should be a part of any second language curriculum that purports to teach oral communicative competence because they influence communication in very real ways.

First of all, everyday judgments of speakers are often made on the basis of these features. To illustrate, let me read you the comments of three native speakers of English, who were asked, "What's wrong with your voice?" for a column called Question Man published recently in the San Francisco Chronicle.

"I'm from Newcastle," said the first man, "a working class area, and it's the heavy Geordie accent. It's a class thing in England. It's important to talk right. Correctly. An accent tends to be looked down on." The second man responded by saying, "I'm disappointed that I still have a New York accent which is associated with a certain kind of person — pushy, aggressive and not necessarily trustworthy — and I left New York for all those reasons." The third man said, "I'd like it lower. I talk more through my nose rather than my mouth and diaphragm. I feel it's not as masculine as a man's voice should be. I try to lower it in mixed company" (S. F. Chronicle 6/1/85). For these three men, pronunciation communicates class distinctions, as well as characteristics related to personality and masculinity. So, on one level, pronunciation is viewed as a means of identifying in-groups and out-groups, us vs. them. Such attitudes have consequences for nonnative speakers. If their speech is distinctively different, it leaves them open to so many more judgments of this type and may keep them as outsiders.

We have seen a sample of how English speakers judge the pronunciation differences of speakers of the same language. How would they evaluate the pronunciation differences of nonnative speakers? In an article in this month's Washingtonian, writer Michael Weiss describes a Ghanaian cabbie's English as "syncopated" (July 1985). Another writer, Andrea Lee, in her book Russian journal describes the effect a Russian speaking English had on her in this way:

> His voice was loud and hoarse, with a peculiarly irritating, insistent edge to it. I had never heard such an accent and intonation: a haphazard mixture of American and British pronunciation, bound together by a heavy monotonous stress on every syllable, which after a few sentences began to strike my ears like the thud of a boot. (1984: 27)

Irritating, insistent, monotonous, like the thud of a boot, — these words vividly describe the potential effect of nonnative rhythm on American ears and in this case, this nonnative rhythm is so disruptive to the listener that she no longer processes the sounds as language but as noise. The noise has caused communication to come to a grinding halt.

Communication may also be affected by nonnative ways of using stress because stress, as a feature of rhythm, and rhythm itself are believed to provide a structure for the way we understand the spoken message. Lenneberg described rhythm as "an organizing principle for the timing of articulations and as a grid against which we match our perceptions" (Ladd 1978: 25). Thus, if a nonnative speaker fails to employ this pattern, the mismatch between the nonnative pattern and the expected English pattern will interfere with comprehension and communication.

What Andrea Lee described as a *heavy, monotonous stress on every syllable* and Washingtonian writer Weiss as syncopated rhythm is noticeable because it differs from the alternating patterns of stressed and unstressed syllables found in English, and it is typical of many varieties of nonnative speech.

Because this pattern of syllables of equal duration is characteristic of many language, such as French, Spanish, Tagalog and Indonesian, speakers of such languages are expected to have the most difficulty with English rhythm. However, speakers of so-called stress-timed language, like English, languages such as Arabic and Russian, also seem to have similar difficulties as Taylor (1981), of the University of Leeds, has observed. Taylor points out that the explanation lies in the nature of English syllables, some of which can bear stress while others cannot. As this tendency is specific to English, and the written language offers few clues, all nonnative speakers, who wish to speak English regardless of language background, have to learn how these syllables behave.

Stress is also important because it is one of the identifying characteristics of words. That stress patterns function in the word recognition process is substantiated by evidence which shows that listeners who do not hear a word clearly will substitute words with identical stress patterns. For example, in a study by Bansal (in Cutler 1984), when Indian English speakers incorrectly pronounced words with the stress on the second syllable instead of the first, for example, atMOSphere for ATmosphere, British English speakers misidentified what the Indian speakers said. The English speakers heard:

YESterday as STUdy
CHAracter as diRECtor
WRItten as reTAIN

Conversely, when words were incorrectly stressed on the first syllable instead of the second, they identified:

preFER as FEARful
corRECT as CARried
aBOUT as COME out

In my own class, I once heard a student say what I thought was *two more*. As it turned out, he was trying to say *tumor*, but he had stressed the second syllable instead of the first and pronounced what should have been a reduced vowel as a full vowel. In another instance, a student told our secretary that he needed *insulin*. It took several exchanges before she realized that what he was asking for was *insurance*. His problem was compounded by the substitution of /s/ for /š/ and /l/ for /r/ and he had also deleted the final /s/ of *insurance*. Despite these segmental problems, if he had stressed the correct syllable, inSUlin, I suspect that our secretary would have identified the word *insurance* more quickly from the context.

Stress, then, contributes to the characteristic rhythm of English and to word identification. In addition, stress serves to mark what a speaker considers to be the important words in a sentence. Because British and American-English speakers expect the important words to be more prominently articulated, they can listen selectively for those words. But if nonnative speakers fail to employ stress properly, their listeners will be lost in a sea of syllables. Since stress plays such an active part in word identification, in organizing the flow of information and in directing the listener's attention to what is important in that flow, it should clearly occupy a place in the communicative syllabus. In fact, Gillian Brown has said that, "It is this aspect of spoken English, more than any other, which the teacher of English to foreign students should concentrate on. From the point of view of production the correct pronunciation of /θ/, /ŋ/, and /ə/ fades into insignificance beside the ability to produce correct stress patterns on words" (1977:52).

Having briefly considered stress and rhythm, let us look at intonation and its role in communicative interaction. We know that intonation helps to convey how speakers feel about what they are saying and of equal importance, how they feel about the people they are talking to. The New Yorker who associated the New York accent with pushiness or aggressiveness may have based this evaluation in part on intonational cues. Likewise, Saudi Arabian businessmen have been judged to be abrasive by American managers, again an evaluation that may have been made partially in response to intonational cues (Adelman and Lustig 1981). The intonation of Danes is suggested to give English listeners the impression that they are hesitant, apathetic and sombre (Phillipson, cited in Albrechtsen et al. 1980:366).

How are these perceptions formulated? Possibly in the way suggested by the now familiar example from Gumperz (1982), which illustrates so well how cross-cultural stereotypes may germinate from misinterpretations of intonation. Indian women, newly hired to work in a British airport cafeteria, were having problems with their supervisors and their customers, both of whom felt that the women were surly and uncooperative. The Indian women, on their part, were perplexed by the reactions that they were getting and consequently felt discriminated against. From the tape recordings of the interactions, Gumperz observed that when customers who had ordered meat were asked whether they wanted gravy, the Indian workers would say gravy with a falling intonation. As Tannen has pointed out, this would be heard by the British English speakers as "This is gravy. Take it or leave it" (Tannen 1984). When the Indian and British workers examined the tape with Gumperz, the Indian workers could not see any difference in the way they made the offer of gravy from the way the British employees did. It was only after he had called their attention to the way British employees made the same offer by using a rising intonation *gravy*? that they could see the source of the problem. The British supervisors, on the other hand learned that the Indian women had not intended to be rude; their falling intonation was simply a carryover from their native language.

If Gumperz had not intervened, the British supervisors may have begun to formulate a stereotype of Indians as surly and uncooperative and as a result, conveyed their dissatisfaction toward the Indian employees, who in turn, would have felt permanently discriminated against. Because intonation operates on a subconscious level, cross-cultural miscommunications, such as the one in this example, may occur without either party knowing its true roots. Consequently, all concerned would be helpless to resolve problems or to prevent them from reoccurring.

In addition to communicating speaker attitudes, intonation plays a part in the structure of conversations, for example, as a cue to turn taking and to topic shifts. Gillian Brown and her colleagues (1980) observed that, among Scottish English speakers, high pitch was used when a speaker began a new topic. Generalizing from this observation, if a nonnative speaker does not recognize this signal or understands it to have a different meaning in conversation, it could result in miscommunication. In fact, such an instance of miscommunication was observed by Gumperz (1982). He reports that an Indian English speaker, who was a part of a conversation with British English speakers, frequently interrupted the other participants and was herself interrupted more frequently than the others. In discussing the conversation with the participants, Gumperz learned that neither the Indian-English speaker nor the British-English speakers had intentionally interrupted each other. They each thought the other had finished speaking before taking their turn. Gumperz identified the problem as stemming from a misinterpretation of the function of pitch. Whereas in British and American English, a rise in pitch is used to mark a shift in focus or to introduce new information, as Brown and her colleagues observed, in Indian English, speakers mark new information with low pitch. Thus, when the Indian English speaker heard the rise in pitch, she identified it as carrying not new but old information and felt that she could begin to take her turn. The British-English speakers assumed that her low pitch carried old information and would begin to take their turn. Both groups felt frustrated because each would be interrupted just before they were about to make a new point.

We have seen from these examples how cross-cultural miscommunication can occur because conversational participants misinterpret intonation signals as rudeness or other forms of negative behavior. Conversations may lurch along because intonational signals for turn-taking are not shared. Communication may be frustrated or prematurely curtailed because listeners cannot identify important words or even recognize words at all if nonnative speakers do not use stress properly. Stress, rhythm and intonation, then, are important components of the communication process; yet pronunciation teaching has not focused on these components sufficiently and specifically with respect to the way they function in communication. It is for this reason that pronunciation teaching has not met communicative goals. What must be done? The two areas that require immediate attention are: (1), the need for explicit pronunciation instruction and (2), the need for new instructional materials. The long term effects of neglecting pronunciation are most dramatically exemplified by the accountants, programmers, police officers, telephone operators and engineers in "accent improvement" and "effective communication" courses. They now have to pay a high price to untangle the linguistic morass that is strangling their ability to communicate at the level demanded by their jobs. These long-term residents and citizens of the U. S. demonstrate that pronunciation is not simply picked up through interaction with English speakers. Moreover, instead of linguistic improvement, interaction with native speakers can sometimes lead to serious miscommunications, as the example of the Indian cafeteria workers show. Where language learning takes place formally in classrooms, the only native-speaker interaction that occurs is with the teacher, whose pronunciation cannot always be taken as illustrative of natural speech because it is often more characteristic of foreigner talk (Hatch et al. 1978). When learners have progressed beyond the initial stages of language learning, explicit pronunciation instruction will be essential. The rhythm of English, which depends on the employment of stressed and unstressed syllables, was found by Taylor to be diffiicult for nonnative speakers to incorporate into their speech, regardless of whether or not the rhythm of their native language resembles that of English, and these were foreign teachers of English! The Indian cafeteria workers were unaware of intonation and so, had not noticed any difference in the way they offered gravy and the way the British workers did, until Gumperz pointed out the difference to them explicitly. The phenomena of stress, rhythm and intonation, as these examples show, are invisible not only to nonnative speakers but also to many language teachers. We know so little about how they function.

The second area requiring immediate attention is that of instructional materials. What we have now in the U. S. describe only the most elementary details of stress, rhythm and intonation. For example, our textbooks tell students that there are just three intonation patterns: a sentence final rise, a sentence final fall and a non-sentence final rise. The rise is applied to yes/no question, the fall to statements and wh-questions. The non-final rise applies between phrases and clauses within sentences. The rules that are given are typically hedged: "Stress *usually* falls on content words." "Phrasal stress *usually* falls on the stressed syllable of the last content word." "Compound nouns *usually* bear stress on the first noun." But how are we to explain the exceptions? No American texts that I know of cover the cases not addressed by these rules, which generally analyze stress on the basis of syntax rather than on the basis of meaning. As Bolinger's work suggest, stress placement might be more adequately explained by looking at what speakers want to express (Bolinger 1965). Our texts also need to show how stress and intonation operate at the discourse level and in interactions, so that nonnative speakers do not get into the kinds of fixes I have described. What we have now focuses mainly on the sentence level, with some limited exchanges off dialogue. Clearly, we need textbooks that can demonstrate how stress and intonation operate in functional discourse, that can answer questions such as: how is sentence stress really determined? How does intonation connect parts of texts? How does intonation signal the beginning of new topics? How does intonation distinguish background information from new information? How does it communicate attitude and emotions? Are there specific contours which convey specific meanings, for example, is there a contradictory contour, a contour of concession, a contour of deference? Until texts include such information, what we can offer students is sketchy at best and will continue to create the misleading impression that the role of pronunciation in communication is peripheral.

■ References

Action, William. (1984). Changing fossilized pronunciation, *TESOL Quarterly, 18,* 1, pp. 71-85.

Adelman, Mara B. and Myron W. Lustig. (1981). Intercultural communication problems as perceived by Saudi Arabian and American managers, *International Journal of Intercultural Relations, 5,* pp. 349-363.

Albrechtsen, Dorte et. al. (1980). Native speaker reactions to learners' spoken interlanguage, *Language learning, 30, 2,* pp. 365-396.

Bailey, Kathleen, Frank Pialorsi and Jean Zukowski/Faust (eds.) (1984). *Foreign teaching assistants in U. S. universities.* Washington, D. C: NAFSA.

Bolinger, Dwight. (1965). *Forms of English*, ed. by Issamu abe and Tetsuya Kanekiyo, Cambridge: Harvard University Press.

_______. (1965) (1957-58). Intonation and grammar. Forms of English, ed. by Isamu Abe and Tetsuya Kanekiyo, Cambridge: Harvard University Press. Originally published in *Language Learning, 9, 1/2,* pp. 31-38.

_______. (1982). Intonation and its parts, *Language, 58, 3,* pp. 505-533.

Brown, Gillian. (1977). *Listening to spoken Engllish*, London: Longman Group Ltd.

______. Karen L. Currie and Joanne Kenworthy. (1980). *Questions of intonation.* London: Croom Helm Ltd.

______. and George Yule. (1983). *Teaching the spoken language.* New york: Cambridge University Press.

Browne, Sandra and Thomas Huckin. (1985). *Four problems in spoken English for non-native professionals.* Paper given at TESOL '85, New York.

Cutler, Anne. (1984). *Stress and acccent in language production and understanding, Intonation, accent and rhythm: studies in discourse phonology,* ed. by Dafydd Gibbon and Helmut Richter. Berlin: Walter de Gruyterr.

Flege, James E. (1981). The phonological basis of foreign accent: a hypothesis, *TESOL Quarterly, 15, 4,* pp. 443-345.

Gilbert, Judy B. (1984). *Clear speech.* New York: Cambridge University Press.

Gumperz, John J. (1982). *Discourse strategies.* New York: Cambridge University Press.

Hatch, E., R. Shapira, and J. Wagner-Gough. (1978). Foreign talk discourse. ITL: *Review of Applied Linguistics*, pp. 39-60.

Higgs, Teodore and Ray Clifford. (1982). *The push toward communication. Curriculum, competence and the foreign language teacher* ed. by Theodore Higgs. Skokie, Ill: National Textbook Company.

Krashen, Stephen. (1982), *Principles and practice in second language acquisition.* Oxford: Pergamon Press.

Ladd, D. Robert Jr. (1978). *The structure of intonational meaning.* Bloomington: Indiana University Press.

Lee, Andrea. (1984,1979). *Russian Journal.* New York: Vintage Books.

Liberman, Mark and Ivan Sag. (1974). *Prosodic forms and discourse function.* CLS 10, 416-27.

Morley, Joan. (1979). *Improving spoken English.* Ann Arbor: University of Michigan Press.

Oyama, Susan. (1976). A sensitive period for acquisition of a nonnative phonological system. *Journal of Psychological Research 5, 3,* pp. 261-283.

Pike, Kenneth L. (1945). *The intonation of American English.* Ann Arbor: University of Michigan Press.

Prator, Clifford H. and Betty Wallace Robinett. (1972). *Manual of American English pronunciation.* New York: Holt, Rinehart and Winston, Inc.

Purcell, Edward and Richard Suter. (1980). Predictors of pronunciation accuracy: a reexamination. *Language Learning, 30, 2*, pp. 271-288.

Schumann, John H. et. al. (1978). Improvement of foreign language pronunciation under hypnosis: a preliminary study. *Language Learning, 28, 1,* pp. 143-148.

Scovel, Tom. (1969). Foreign accents, language acquisition and cerebral dominance. *Language Learning, 19*, pp. 245-254

Suter, Richard. (1976). Predictors of pronunciation accuracy in second language learning. *Language Learning, 26, 2,* pp. 233-254.

Tannen, Deborah. (1984). *Conversational style: analyzing talk among friends.* Norwood, New Jersey: Ablex Publishing Company.

Taylor, D. S. (1981). *Non-native speakers and the rhythm of English.* IRAL *19, 3*, pp. 219-226.

From a paper presented at the 1985 Georgetown University round talk on language and linguistics, June 27-29, by Rita Wong.

3. MINIMAL PAIR TECHNIQUES

OVERVIEW

The minimal pair is a tool of the linguistic researcher which has been of some use in the language classroom in helping students to become aware of sound contrasts in the target language, especially those contrasts which do not exist in the students' native language. A minimal pair is a pair of utterances which are different in meaning because of a single difference between two sounds which occupy the same position in the utterance.

Example: pig big

are a minimal pair of words because it is only the difference between the first or *initial sound* in both words that signals their meaning difference to an English speaker. Here are some other minimal pair words which have their difference in initial position:

to do
came game

A meaning difference can occur because of sound differences in the middle or *medial* position of a word.

Example: simple symbol
sighting siding
decree degree

Up to this point, our examples have all shown a voicing contrast between the sounds /p/ and /b/, /t/ and /d/, or /k/ and /g/. These consonants are the six stop sounds of English. Vowels may also signal meaning differences as we see in these examples. (It may help to say the sounds out loud to prove to yourself that the difference is only in one slot or position in the word).

Initial: ill eel
Between Consonants: liver leaver

The last position in a word is called *final position.* Here are some minimal pairs.

how	who
boy	buy
bet	bed
loose	lose
leaf	leave

Some teachers of English as a foreign language use a phonemic notation system to make clear the difference in sound against the difference in spelling. Loo*se* and lo*se* illustrate why some teachers feel that teaching a phonemic writing system helps the student to concentrate on the sound system rather than the writing system or *orthography*, since in this pair of words the sound /s/ and /z/ are represented by the same *-se* spelling. Other teachers feel that teaching a phonemic writing system just gives the student one more memorization task. Whatever your feeling is about phonemic notation, it is a good idea to focus attention on the sound/orthography correspondence by underlining the appropriate part of each word in the minimal pair.

Example: rate and late would be underlined
rate late

WHEN TO USE MINIMAL PAIR TECHNIQUES

(1) When a problem arises in class which needs immediate attention because it is impeding classroom communication
(2) As a part of a systematic treatment of the sound system of English incorporated into a curriculum
(3) In contrasting the sounds of the native language with English (for example, the French /l/ and /r/ are not different in the same way that English /l/ and /r/ are).

CLASSROOM TIME

The minimal pair exercises should generally be short (5 minutes or less) and done with a certain liveliness of pace.

HOW TO DO A MINIMAL PAIR EXERCISE

The following classroom procedures can be done one after the other or stopped after each section.

Introduce a group of minimal pair words through:
(1) writing a prepared list of 4 or 5 pairs of items on the blackboard or

Example: (to practice /s/ and /z/)

Sue	zoo
sipper	zipper
seal	zeal
sink	zinc
sewn	zone

(2) showing drawings of vocabulary items that students already know.

Example: ax ox

In either case there should be about 4 pairs or more.
In introducing the minimal pairs, you should model the words in a clear and natural voice, while pointing to each.

Sound Identification Drill 1

Tell the students that you are going to pronounce two words from the list. Ask them to respond by saying *same*, if the words sound the same to them, or *different* if they do not. After the students' or student's response, repeat the model and give the answer.

Example:
Teacher: Sue Sue
Student: "same"
Teacher: Sue Sue "same"

Example:
Teacher: Sue sew
Student: "different"
Teacher: Sue sew "different"

It is usually better, as in most class activities, to start with the larger group and move to the individual last. However, this is not a rule, only a suggestion.

Sound Identification Drill 2

Tell the students that you are going to call the first column, "I," (one), and the second column, "2" (two). Then ask them to listen to a series of three words, giving you the numbers in order.

Example:

/s/ words = 1	/z/ words = 2
Sue	zoo
sipper	zipper
seal	zeal
sink	zinc
sewn	zone

Teacher: Sue zoo zoo
Student: 1 2 2
Teacher: (pointing to the words)
Sue zoo zoo
1 2 2

Sound Identification Drill 3

This time pronounce only one word from both columns, one and two. Ask the students to tell you which column the word is from.

Example:

Teacher: zinc
Student: 2
Teacher: zinc
2

Example:

Teacher: sink
Student: 1
Teacher: sink
1

Example:

Teacher: zoo
Student: 2
Teacher: zoo
2

FOLLOW-UP

At this point the listening practice is completed. Further activities can be:
(1) having students suggest rhyming words for each sound if they are vowels

Example: sit
Student: wit hit lit

or words that have the same sound in the same position in the case of consonant sounds

Example: class
Student: ice loss less face

(2) having students pronounce the contrasting pairs at a rapid pace
(3) giving students a prepared quiz sheet with instructions to circle the word that has the same sound as the given word

Example: zone (a) measure
(b) assist
(c) as
(d) azure

or the word whose underlined sound is different from the others

Example: (a) cistern
(b) messy
(c) rise
(d) us

(4) having students pronounce minimal sentences and create contexts for them

Example: (a) Feel these teeth.
(b) Fill these teeth.

Context: (a) Two people are in a natural history museum; one of them is touching the teeth of a mounted shark and asking the other to try doing it.
(b) An impatient patient orders a dentist to begin work on his teeth.

SUMMARY AND REFERENCES

Minimal pair practice can be an aid to students in mastering English sound discrimination if it is done at the appropriate time and at a light and lively pace. Recent trends in EFL methodology have attributed a great deal of the learner's difficulty with English sounds to psychological factors and group identification. Consequently, the minimal pair exercise as a child of habit theory/structural linguistics//audio-lingualism has been paid less attention than in the past. However, it remains a useful reference for the teacher and point of comparison for the student. Below is a list of some common minimal pair contrasts in English.

VOICELESS VERSUS VOICED CONSONANTS IN ENGLISH

/p/	/b/	pill	bill
/t/	/d/	tan	Dan
/k/	/g/	could	good
/f/	/v/	fine	vine
/θ/	/ð/	thigh	thy
/s/	/z/	sounds	zounds
/č/	/j/	choose	Jews

SIMPLE VERSUS COMPLEX AMERICAN ENGLISH VOWEL SOUNDS

/i/	/ay/	Mick	Mike
/i/	/iy/	mitt	meat
/e/	/ey/	pen	pain
/u/	/uw/	full	fool

From Spaventa, L. J. *Listening: practice with minimal pairs,* Selected from a continuing monograph series for the overseas teacher of English as a foreign language which were used in a lecture at Indiana Univ., Bloomington in 1977.

4. CONTEXTUALIZING PRONUNCIATION PRACTICE IN THE ESOL CLASSROOM

The teaching of pronunciation in ESOL classes has not always been as successful as other aspects of English teaching, possibly because pronunciation has been considered a seperate skill and has not been well integrated in language courses. If pronunciation can be presented in meaningful contrasts and in situations that are both relevant and interesting to the students — in other words, if instruction in pronunciation can be contextualized — perhaps achievement can be improved. Productive contextualization suggests: (a) pronunciation features and contrasts should carry meaning with minimum redundancy that will offer additional clues affecting interpretation; i. e., the student should have to rely on what s/he hears (and produces) rather than on an intelligent estimate of what the situation calls for; (b) situations should be meaningfully related to student interest and/or experience; (c) the repetition of specific drills and situations should be minimized; (d) the language and style of pronunciation exercise material should be convincingly natural and realistic; and (e) at least some exercises should be designed to give practice when the students' attention is on the content rather than the form of the message.

Some thirty years ago, foreign language classes in the United States were largely concerned with teaching students to read. Pronunciation was a low priority skill, usually presented by a quick run through the alphabet to illustrate the characteristic sound or sounds associated with each letter. It did not really matter if the sounds of the new language were not authentically produced, since any contact with the foreign culture would be almost exclusively through reading, using the familiar visual symbols of a Roman alphabet. In fact, pronunciation hints were not offered in terms of the new language sound system, but framed in terms of the native language in such instructions as: pronounced like the *i* in *machine*, or like the *g* in *get*.

Today the purposes of language teaching more often include face-to-face contact with live speakers. Indeed oral communication has come to be one of the central purposes of language study, and the philosophy on which classroom activities are based has correspondingly changed to reflect the present oral emphasis. The Audiolingual Method of foreign language teaching accords pronunciation a central role in pedagogy, and the mystery of an adequate command of the spoken language is a goal seriously taken.

With respect to linguistic theory, pronunciation enjoyed an estimate of maximum importance as the phonology component of language analysis of structural linguistics, which flourished in the 1940s and 1950s. Later, when transformational analysis caught the imagination of the theorists, phonology was relegated to a minor role. The linguistic primitives were syntactic or perhaps semantic units, which were interestingly and creatively controlled, manipulated, and combined to encode a message, after which a relatively uninteresting set of morpho-phonemic rules were applied to produce a sequence of spoken sounds. These rules are less interesting to the theoretical linguist because they are applied automatically and mechanically once the underlying syntactic elements are in place.

This new theoretical alignment has not so far had a significant effect on pedagogy. In the contemporary classroom, pronunciation has not experienced the same diminished interest as has phonology in linguistic theory. Pronunciation remains the entree to the linguistic system of a new language, and a student cannot be said to have mastered a second language unless s/he has a command of its spoken symbols. The ideal is to be able to pronounce and speak with native-like competence, though in most classrooms and with most students this remains an ideal, a goal to shoot at, the approximation to which serves as a measure of student achievement. In actual practice the teaching of pronunciation has been a frustrating experience. Pre-puberty-aged students need only a model and an incentive to follow that model to acquire an authentic native-speaker pronunciation. A well-planned pronunciation component in the foreign language course is unnecessary. Post-puberty students are essentially unsuccessful when they attempt to speak like natives. A pronunciation component is usually quite unproductive of satisfactory results.

Most frustrating is the observation that when mature students try seriously to imitate a foreign pronunciation model, and when the expertise is available to offer technical assistance, they will demonstrate the physical capacity for a quite satisfactory production. But the minute the students' attention is diverted to the content of the message, the pronunciation control loosens, and native language influence reappears to produce a heavy speech accent. Adult learners seem to have their cultural identification firmly implanted, and their language follows this identification. Only rarely does one find an adult student of unusual language acquisition aptitude who is the exception to this rule.

What are the implications for language teachers in this observation of the difficulty of teaching native speaker proficiency in pronunciation? Should we abdicate formal responsibility, given the prediction that full success is highly unlikely? Or should we conclude that "man's reach must exceed his grasp," and use native speaker competence only as an ideal to guide students of limited aptitude toward whatever approximation to the model they are capable of achieving?

My own belief is a retreat to eclecticism, taking the best of each theoretical possibility in a compromise. For most adult students a reasonable goal is the ability to communicate orally with ease and efficiency, but without expecting to achieve a competence in pronunciation that would enable them to conceal their own different language background.

At the same time it should be possible to achieve a consistent production of the basic contrasts of the sound system, to speak fluently and understandably in a form that requires minimum adjustment on the part of one's listeners. And of course students must be capable of understanding native pronunciation under normal circumstances of production, and not require of their interlocutors a special style. They should, for example, be capable of understanding two native speakers addressing each other in informal speech.

It is my opinion that improvements can be made in the teaching of the pronunciation component in a language course. It is my further opinion that one way to effect an improvement would be to find a means of better integrating pronunciation instruction with other elements of instruction.

In too many language classes the teaching of pronunciation is something that is done with an approach that identifies pronunciation as something to be taught separately. It is traditionally advised that the "pronunciation lesson," that segment of the full lesson to be devoted to pronunciation, should be limited to about five minutes, moving then to other aspects. But when attention is shifted, gains disappear.

It is true that there are different aspects to a language lesson, that a teacher must devote attention to grammatical forms, to the sequence of words, to the transformation of patterns, and to the meaning of related sentences used to transmit a message. But perhaps there is a way of incorporating some of these elements in a lesson segment designed to improve pronunciation. I suggest an effort to contextualize the pronunciation lesson. What I mean by this should become clear with the discussion and examples that follow.

Pronunciation instruction has been presented in various ways. First there is model and imitation. The teacher (or a recording playback device) sets a model which the student attempts to reproduce. If this were adequate, no problems would appear. But experience has shown that habits of one's first language will interfere in ways that can be explained by a knowledge of the specific differences in the pronunciation patterns of the first and second languages.

A second technique for teaching pronunciation is explanation. The teacher tries to guide the student by telling him or her how to produce troublesome sounds, how to manipulate his or her speech organs, or what characteristics the sounds should have when produced. This method may help some students, but many fail to respond, either because the explanations tend to be esoteric or because students have no effective experience in controlling speech production on the basis of instructions. Another possible limitation is that explanations usually involve labels, so that sounds can be referred to and discussed. Often these labels will be the names of letters used to represent the sounds. But since letter names may in fact repeat the minimal difference of the sounds in a pair of words, they can pose the same problem of identification. It is not very enlightening to differentiate the two words *base* and *vase* by saying that one begins with a *b* and the other with a *v*.

A third technique is practice. Applications are seen in example sentences that provide multiple opportunities to produce a sound, such as the famous *Erre con erre cigarro* example for the Spanish trilled rr. It has never been satisfactorily explained how a sound difficult to produce becomes any easier when it appears in multiple form. If one *rr* is a problem, surely the solution is not a series of twelve. In my opinion the tongue-twister approach to problem sounds is wholly without merit.

A fourth technique is comparison and contrast — an application to pedagogy that has been recognized as the analytical tool par excellence of phonological research. Two similar but significantly contrasting sounds are taught together, with an effort to highlight the feature that differentiates them. Thus *p* and *b* are contrasted by voicing (voiceless vs. voiced), d and g by point of articulation (alveolar vs. velar), and *sh* and *ch* by manner of articulation (fricative vs. affricate). This kind of comparison helps pinpoint the difference, but doesn't always guarantee efficient acquisition of the two contrasting sounds. If the contrast is a new aural experience, the fact of contrast will not necessarily become simple to interpret and produce. Let me illustrate by offering a contrast from Tagalog, the two words *bata* meaning *bathrobe* and *bata* meaning *child.* Most American speakers of English experience difficulty even hearing this distinction, let alone understanding, producing, and assimilating it. Yet for Tagalog speakers the distinction is every bit as clear as the one in the English pair *cart* and *card.*

The contrast can be made clear by a fifth technique, which I'll refer to as a combination (of modeling, explanation, comparison, mimicry, and practice). A model of *bata-bata* has been given. The explanation is that one ends in an aspirate, the other in a glottal closure (conveniently not shown in the spelling, but illustrable in a special transcription, as /bata^h bataʔ/. A comparison would perhaps involve the closest native language phenomenon, in this case English uh huh and *uh uh*, transcribable as /ʔəhə–ʔəʔə/, calling attention to the fact that the contrast occurs syllable initially in English but syllable finally in Tagalog; and this is precisely the reason why English speakers have perception difficulties: they have no experience with a meaningful contrast involving these sounds in final position. Finally, with this explanation as guidance, students would attempt to mimic and practice.

But this procedure (combining the techniques of modeling, explanation, contrast, comparison, mimicry and practice) more often than not fails to internalize the new habits to make them actually part of the students' new language pronunciation. When they listen, they'll fail to consistently produce the contrast (unless close attention exaggerates the distinction). Why this difficulty internalizing a new contrast? I think it is to a significant extent because the presentation has been disembodied from a meaningful context.

Obviously there are problems of motivation involved. When communication is possible, why strive for perfection? Or as a Japanese student once confided to me: "I get along, with some difficulty to be sure, but why should I invest a tremendous effort in an attempt to sound like an American when I'm really Japanese?" Motivation can be materially heightened by increasing the chance of success.

We need reasonable and realistic goals, and these need to be tied to students' views of their own objectives. A Basque-speaking student from Spain working under my supervision once reported experiencing, while on a date, a headache that was so severe she went into a drugstore and asked the manager if he had any aspirin. He answered that he did, and asked how many she wanted, to which she answered two. The manager invited her and her boy friend to be seated. In two minutes he reappeared with two dishes of rice pudding. In reporting this event the next day, this young woman demonstrated a very strong motivation to improve her command of English pronunciation.

The young Basque woman was motivated by a context that demonstrated rather vividly that she could be misunderstood. How can we build a similar motivation into our classroom presentations? I believe that we should seek to introduce contextualization into pronunciation teaching and that it is quite possible to do so. The remainder of this paper is devoted to examples that will hopefully illustrate at least some of the ways this can be done, how drill activities can be devised that will reinforce the pronunciation aspects of what has been termed "communicative competence."

The minimal pair concept has been widely applied to teaching pronunciation contrasts that have been found empirically to cause trouble for students in specific first and second language situations. Typically a contrast is illustrated, such as *base-vase*, possibly explained, and then presented for identification by the students. Usually they are asked to do something overt to signal their reaction to the pair. Two words will be given, sometimes alike (base-base) and sometimes *different* (base-vase). Students will be asked to respond same or different. Or the words will be given one at a time, with instructions to raise the left arm if base is heard, the right arm if vase. Or the identification can be made by saying A or B, or one or two, or by raising one or two fingers, etc. Or three pronunciations can be given, with the students instructed to identify by number (one, two, or three) the word that is different from the other two. Later students practice the contrast by imitating the teacher: *base-vase* (*base-vase*), *bile-vile* (*bile-vile*), *ban-van*, (*ban-van*), *boat-vote* (*boat-vote*), etc.

There may be other activities used in a typical minimal pair drill, including production of the words in illustrative sentences, such as: They are going to vote on the boat. One might say this is a form of contextualization, but if so it is not a very powerful example, since there is no indication of who is going to vote, what the occasion of the vote is, why a boat should be voted on (or, since the sentence is grammatically ambiguous, why people should be on a boat when they vote), etc. In other words, this is meaningless context, and it will not serve to fix the contrast in the mind or habits of the student. Minimal-pair sentences are sometimes employed, such as *This is a base. This is a vase.* These may be a little better, especially if the concepts are picturable and appropriate pictures can be shown. Pictorial illustration can be difficult — which interpretation of base should be pictured, for example? Even when pictures are appropriate, the context is still minimal, and identification frames are not really very interesting. This pattern is typically used to teach vocabulary, not pronunciation. Of course there may be other frames than the identification *This is a ...*, but rarely are effective ones employed in a classroom.

I suggest that the context for the minimal pair should be an entire situation, supported and reinforced by reasonable and credible visual images, and placed in a setting that can hope to provide a measure of intellectual stimulus and interest. The dull recitations that characterize most pronunciation lessons need to be markedly upgraded if there is to be any hope of solid improvement in classroom performance and any promise of carry-over in out-of-class competence.

The following sequence of activities describes a pronunciation lesson I have used several times as a demonstration. I begin by asking if any one in the class is good at drawing. If no one responds immediately, I ask who is the best artist in the class, hoping somebody will volunteer, either him- or herself or another student. When an artist is finally identified, I invite him or her to the front of the class and whisper my first request in his or her ear — to draw a horse. Not letting the other students know what s/he is to draw usually builds a bit of interest, and I ask class members to tell me as soon as anyone can guess what the volunteer is drawing. Depending on the skill of the artist they may say *dog* or *cow* or something, but we finally arrive at horse. Then I whisper a second instruction: fire. We go through the same process, with guesses such as *grass*, *bush*, and eventually *fire*. I thank my collaborator and then I draw a horse shoe. (This is safely within my artistic competence; I might do all the drawing myself if I were more talented.) I ask if anyone can identify what I have drawn and then, if the class level permits, have a brief discussion of what a *horse shoe* is, why it is used, how it is affixed to the horse's hooves, etc. As this is given, or as I give it, I am drawing a picture of a *hammer*. Then I explain how the metal shoe can be heated to white hot on a forge and bent by pounding so it will fit the horse. Together we identify the profession of the person who does this job — the blacksmith. This detail can be omitted, with a general reference *he* or *she* if the new vocabulary load seems to be getting too high. (We will refer to the blacksmith simply as *he* throughout this example.)

I show that the blacksmith first heats the shoe, then pounds it with a hammer to shape it. Then I ask the class to identify the means the blacksmith uses for each of two tasks:

He's heating the shoe.
With a fire.
He's hitting the shoe.
With a hammer.

I now have the statement and rejoinder to serve as model and response for a meaningful identification drill. I have purposely not put the contrasting sound pair in sentence-final position where they will get the extra emphasis of sentence stress, because I want the students to have practice with the minimum of differentiation that will be presented in a real-life use, where rarely will there be an overt, specific contrast (that is, with *both* of the contrasting sentences in the same conversation or situation). Note that both interpretations are reasonable in an overall context; one does not overshadow the other in probability of occurrence.

(This balance of probability is very important. Consider for a moment an example of minimal-pair sentences that lack balance. The sentence frame is He came back from Paris on a ... with *ship-sheep* as candidates for the blank. In this example *ship* is infinitely more likely than *sheep.* In cases like this one, students and native speakers alike will correct *sheep* to *ship* in their own interpretation if the wrong stimulus is offered, since people expect language to make sense. Lack of balance is a common weakness of minimal-pair sentences used for pronunciation drills, and students usually pay scant attention to the crucial features if the probabilities make one interpretation silly. And if they are not listening, they do not learn.)

After I've produced the full sentence several times — *He's heating the shoe with a fire. He's hitting the shoe with a hammer* — I then give just the first part of the sentence and ask the class to give the final phrase as a rejoinder. If, as often happens, there is a disagreement, I stop and ask for a show of hands: *How many say fire? How many say hammer?* Then I announce which one I said by indicating which response I expected. As confidence builds, I get a volunteer to come to the front of the room and work with me. I make my statement, and s/he offers his or her rejoinder. Then I ask how many in the class agree with him or her; then announce what my intention was.

Then I ask the class to produce the statement in chorus, following my cue as I point alternately to the pictures of the fire and the hammer. Often it is difficult to tell if the production is accurate, so I ask individuals to produce the appropriate rejoinder on cue. If there is any doubt in my mind as to the accuracy of the production, I ask the class if they agree. After a few experiences they are conditioned to consider my query as evidence that I do not agree, so I recapture initiative by questioning a production that is perfectly satisfactory. I find this introduction of the unexpected into a class routine an excellent way to keep interest and attention. Students soon come to know "that I can't be trusted" and they are encouraged to keep a more careful check, which is of course just what I want.

Finally I ask for another volunteer, who comes to the front of the room. I mark a figure 1 over the fire and a figure 2 over the hammer. Then I go to the back of the room where only the volunteer can face me. I insist that other students face front, away from me. Then with arms folded or extended I briefly signal an intention to the volunteer. If I flash one finger, s/he is to say *He's heating the shoe*; If two fingers, *He's hitting the shoe.* The class is to respond with the appropriate rejoinder. In this way I retain the initiative, I decide the intention. After the rejoinder of the class indicates their interpretation, I ask the volunteer if s/he agrees. I'm then in a very strong position to judge his or her performance. I know what s/he was instructed to say, and I can agree or disagree with the interpretation of the class. In case of a mismatch of statement and rejoinder, if I agree with the volunteer (assuming s/he confirms my signaled intention), the mistake is one of aural interpretation (by the class). If I agree with the class, the mistake is one of production (by the volunteer).

This last step doesn't always go right, since it depends for success on a good performance by the volunteer. S/he is expected to take an abstract symbol (one or two, gathered from seeing one finger or two) and convert it into a performance based on an arbitrary association. S/he may get confused. If the student is apt, the procedure usually goes well. But note that this is the only point at which an arbitrary meaning association is introduced, and it comes after logical associations have been established: *heating with fire, hitting with hammer.* This is much less an artificial signal than the left hand/right hand or A/B so frequently used in minimal-pair identifications. And the use I propose is purposeful. Even this last bit of arbitrariness could be avoided if one prepared a couple of flash cards with a fire and a hammer to use in the back of the room, or these two items could quickly be drawn on the rear blackboard with signals given by pointing to one or the other.

One might observe that this technique gives production practice to only one student, and that in a large class there will not be time to repeat the sequence for each student. Even if several repetitions were feasible, there is some question about the advisability of repeating the same procedures; it is possible that the loss in motivation is greater than the gain from additional practice. But the problem remains of how to generalize effective practice. Production is an individual matter, and if meaningful guidance to students is to be offered, choral practice has serious limitations beyond a very general kind of tongue-loosening activity. Students must perform one at a time with the techniques discussed here, or with any others I am familiar with. Options are (a) to repeat the last phase of the exercise with different students, or (b) to follow the exercise as described with other activities that involve individual performance. As an example of the second alternative I suggest a short reading passage that embeds the pronunciation problem in various ways, preferably ways not fully expected. This makes it possible to maximize variety and to avoid excessive repetition of the elaborate procedure described earlier. As students read, individually and audibly, they can be recorded for subsequent review and analysis as a separate class activity. Rehearsing a sentence or phrase or word is helpful in case there is disagreement on just what pronunciation was used. Brief discussion following the recorded readings can answer queries on interpretations and possible misinterpretations.

A suggested selection which students can take turns reading into a recording microphone, a sentence or two at a time, is as follows:

> If a blacksmith wants to shoe a horse, he must first heat the shoe over a hot fire. Then he will put it on an anvil and hit it with a large hammer. He must heat the shoe before he hits it so the metal will be soft enough to shape. If he hits it first, the cold shoe will not take a new shape, and after hitting it, there's no point in heating it. So after first heating the shoe, he will beat it into the right shape, in case it's a little bit too big or too little. Then the shoe can be attached to the horse's hoof. The blacksmith does this by driving several long nails through the shoe into the hoof. He probably uses a smaller hammer to hit the nails than he did on the heated shoe. In any event, we'll easily see that it's a lot of work, and a blacksmith needs to be very strong to do his job.

The aim in preparing this reading is to produce something that is natural-sounding English prose, but that still incorporates the teaching points. It should also be reasonably interesting in content. It is quite likely that the class will notice that forms of *heat* and *hit* (five each) appear in the reading and that a special effort will be made to produce these forms correctly. These are distributed as follows:

> If a blacksmith wants to shoe a horse, he must first *heat* the shoe over a hot fire. Then he will put it on an anvil and *hit* it with a large hammer. He must *heat* the shoe before he *hits* it so the metal will be soft enough to shape. If he *hits* it first, the cold shoe will not take a new shape, and after *hitting* it, there's no point in *heating* it. So after first *heating* the shoe he will beat it into the right shape, in case it's a little bit too big or too little. Then the shoe can be attached to the horse's hoof. The blacksmith does this by driving several long nails through the shoe into the hoof. He probably uses a smaller hammer to *hit* the nails than he did on the *heated* shoe. In any event, we'll easily see that it's a lot of work, and a blacksmith needs to be very strong to do his job.

There is of course no objection to this attention to the forms of *heat* and *hit*. Not only is it desirable that they be learned and produced accurately, but they serve as a temporary screen to other, more important items in the reading, that test and practice the same contrast of /iy/ and /I/ in other words. There are 53 of these, 21 for /iy/ and 32 for /I/. There are two minimal pairs fully represented, beat-bit and we'll-will, and four minimal pairs partially represented, eat-it, eats-it's, deed-did, he's-his. The other examples of one or the other sounds occur in words that do not occur as minimal pairs. The relevant syllables are marked in the version of the reading that follows:

> If a black***smith*** wants to shoe a horse, ***he*** must first *heat* the shoe over a hot fire. Then he **will** put **it** on an an**vil** and *hit* **it with** a large hammer. **He** must *heat* the shoe before **he** *hits* **it** so the metal **will be** soft enough to shape. **If he** *hits* **it** first, the cold shoe will not take a new shape, and after *hitting* **it**, there's no point **in** *heating* **it.** So after first *heating* the shoe, **he will beat it in**to the right shape, **in** case **it's** a **little bit** too **big** or too **little**. Then the shoe can **be** attached to the horse's hoof. The black**smith** does **this** by dri**ving** several long nails through the shoe **in**to the hoof. **He** proba**bly** uses a smaller hammer to *hit* the nails than **he did** on the *heated* shoe. **In** any event, **we'll easily see** that **it's** a lot of work, and a black**smith needs** to **be** very strong to do **his** job.

In using a reading of this kind to check (and encourage) the contrast that is being taught, good use should be made of juxtapositions of two words with different members of the contrast. In the reading the following opportunities occur: *he will, will be, if he hits, in heating it, he will beat it, he did, in any, smith needs.* Also useful are sequences of several examples of the same sound, to check for consistency: in case it's a little bit too big or too little, in any event we'll easily see.

In spite of the relatively large number of examples of the sounds being drilled and learned (66 if everything is counted), it is important not to overload the reading question, or at least not to give the impression of overloading. When a contrast drill becomes too conspicuous it is felt to be ridiculous, and this damages the atmosphere for efficient learning. As an example of something that would be too overloaded to be used effectively, consider the following portion:

> The blacksmith did the deed so that the horse shoes would fit the feet of the horse. He takes the shoe, first heats and then hits it. He usually has to beat it a bit. This is what he does to eat; it is his job.

This is too forced, and the contrasts are unnatural. The fact that the contrasts are conspicuous means that special attention may be given to them, and the conditions of generalization are violated: that accuracy of pronunciation be extended to language use where the student's attention is on the message rather than the form. Even if the student could do the above segment satisfactorily, there is no assurance that a carryover would improve his or her general use of the language.

My experiences with the techniques described and illustrated above have been that they capture and hold class interest. I have no controlled, experimental evidence that they teach pronunciation, but at least that first giant step toward learning is taken: getting the ears and eyes of the students focused on a problem, since when there is no attention, there is no learning.

Many pronunciation problems can be handled by the techniques of contextualized pronunciation practice: all that is necessary is a bit of imagination and ingenuity to devise an appropriate situation, one that is (a) meaningful, (b) picturable, (c) balanced, and (d) if possible, relevant to the experience and/or interest of the students. I can suggest two or three possibilities. A pedagogue and a cook complain that:

This pen leaks.
Then don't write with it.
This pan leaks.
Then don't cook with it.

Pedagogues write and cooks cook, and neither likes a leaky utensil. The differentiaters *write* and *cook* are clearly distinct, and will serve to identify members of the pair *pen-pan*. All concepts are concrete and readily picturable. Both pens and pans fit the instrumental use after the preposition with and both have been known to leak. This contrast drills the vowel pair /ɛ–æ/, which causes difficulties for students of English as a second language with many language backgrounds.

Another contrast is:

What's this pool for?
For swimming.
What's this spool for?
For sewing.

This pair illustrates and drills two features: (a) a single vs. a double *s*, signaled by length, and (b) the presence and absence of aspiration with the voiceless stop consonant *p*. The feature of a lengthened consonant occurs only across word boundaries in English. The aspiration is present when the /p/is initial in the word *pool*, but absent when /p/ follows /s/ in the word *spool*. This pair is perhaps a little weaker pedagogically, since while spools of thread are certainly associated with sewing, the sequence *spool —for sewing* is not quite as convincing as *pool —for swimming*. However, it's not a bad match, and the balance, picturability, and relevance are satisfactory.

A pair that illustrates a stress contrast is:

Where can I buy côld créam?
At the dairy.

Where can I buy cóld crèam?
At the drugstore.

In this pair a normal adjective-noun sequence is compared with a noun compound or construct. The minimal stress contrast influences the pitch pattern by placing the highest pitch on the syllable with the strongest stress: *cream* in the first sentence and *cold* in the second:

côld créam vs cóld crèam.

A possible difficulty with these two concepts is their picturability. *Cream* may come in a bottle or a paper carton, or perhaps in an aerosol can, and the student may not be personally familiar with the container. *Cold cream* is a women's cosmetic product that might not be commonly known to men students. If this disadvantage of being unfamiliar is too great, there are many other pairs illustrating the same stress contrast that can be used:

What's a hêad dóctor?
He's an administrator.

What's a héad dòctor?
He's a psychiatrist.

or to produce a more easily handled rejoinder:

A hêad dóctor works
at a desk.

A héad dòctor works
at a couch.

If you disagree with the levity implicit in the use of an informal designation *head doctor* for a psychiatrist, pick another pair. There are plenty of them available.

This, then, is an example of contextualized pronunciation practice. Students work with familiar (or specifically learned but relevant and reasonable) concepts, which are associated with easily distinguished clues. The activities carry messages that are not arbitrary, and the sequence has been demonstrated to hold the interest of a wide variety of students. This, hopefully, is a step toward making all of our language teaching activities more meaningful and relevant to the lives, interests, and experience of our students.

Perhaps there are other ways of using meaning and meaningful communication to make teaching more effective; that is, perhaps there are other ways of contextualizing teaching materials. We know that schools do not provide the most productive language learning, that learning in an immersion situation, where a need for communication is strongly felt and sympathetic encouragement is offered, is much more efficient. In such an environment every utterance ever heard or used is meaningful and relevant to the situation it is used in. It is, to use the word I have chosen, contextualized.

I have indicated one way to contextualize a pronunciation presentation. Perhaps there are other, maybe better ways. Surely something must be done to win and hold the attention of students, to organize materials for learning in a way that is compatible with the development of skills needed for communication. Our record of success in the schools is not an enviable one. Perhaps we can do better.

From Bowen, J. D. (1972). Contextualizing pronunciation practice in the ESOL classroom. *TESOL Quarterly*, 6, pp. 83-94.

PART TWO

TEACHING GRAMMAR

문법은 간단히 말해서 어순 (word order)이다. 즉 어떻게 단어가 형성되고 형성된 단어들이 구나 문장을 만들기 위해 어떻게 배열되는가에 관한 규칙이라고 할 수 있다. 그렇다면 문법에는 구어표현에 필요한 문법 (grammar for oral English), 문어표현에 필요한 문법 (grammar for written English)이 별개로 존재하고 따라서 학교 교육에서 이들을 모두 가르쳐야 할 것이다.

혹자는 예전의 문법 번역 식 교수방법에서는 문법설명이 외국어 교육의 중심을 차지했었으나 의사소통 교수법은 문법규칙에 관한 지식은 수업에서 다룰 필요가 없으므로 처음부터 자연스런 대화문을 듣고 말하게 해야 한다는 것을 주장한다. 그리고 그들은 문법은 이제 더 이상 중요하지 않다고 말할지 모른다. 그러나 이는 잘못된 견해이다. 우리는 언어 교육의 목표가 의사소통 능력 (communicative competence)의 배양이라는 사실을 결코 부정하지 않는다. 그리고 이 의사소통 능력은 다시 표현해서 언어를 정확하고 (accurately), 적합하게 (appropriately) 사용할 수 있는 능력을 의미한다. 정확하게 사용한다는 뜻은 'form' 또는 'usage'로서 linguistic competence를 가리키며 문법적으로 틀리지 않는 언어사용 능력이다. 그리고 적합하게 사용한다는 것은 'meaning'과 'function' 또는 'use'로서 sociocultural competence를 가리키며 실제로 그 언어가 사용되는 사회에서 용납되는 언어를 구사하는 능력을 뜻한다. 또 다른 말로 전자는 정확성, 그리고 후자는 유창성이라고 표현할 수 있을 것이다. 간단히 말해서 문법은 언어 교육에서 매우 중요한 부분이고 반드시 가르쳐져야 하겠다.

Celce-Murcia는 첫 번째 논문에서 영어 교육에 있어서 문법이 어느 정도까지 다루어져야 하는지에 관해 학습자 변인과 교수 변인에 따라 결정되어야 한다는 충고를 하고 문법을 좀 더 효과적으로 지도하는 방법을 그렇지 못한 방법과 대조시켜 제시한다.

두번째 글은 유명한 Paulston의 문형연습 (pattern drill)의 세 가지 유형이며 이어서 Bruder와 Paulston이 함께 고안한 다양한 종류의 구두사용을 위한 문형연습들이 제시되어 있다. 각각의 연습방법이 Paulston의 세 가지 유형 중 어디에 속하는 지 분류해 보면 좋을 것이다.

마지막으로 한 가지 문어표현을 위한 문법의 실제 교수 절차를 통하여 어떻게 문법 사항이 선택되고 의미 있게 제시된 후 연습되는가를 살펴보고 각자 시범 수업을 할 수 있기를 제안해 본다.

5. MAKING INFORMED DECISIONS ABOUT THE ROLE OF GRAMMAR IN LANGUAGE TEACHING

There are currently two extreme positions in ESL concerning the teaching of English grammar. At one extreme, the proponents of audio-lingualism (Lado, 1964) and methodologists such as Gattegno (1972, 1976) argue that we must make grammar the core of our language instruction and that we must correct all student errors. At the other extreme, methodologists such as Krashen and Terrell (1983) tell us not to teach grammar explicitly and not to correct any learner errors.

Given such conflicting professional advice, many ESL teachers are understandably confused and frustrated. What should they do? Who should they believe?

When ESL teachers ask me which of the two extreme positions I prefer, I like to begin by reminding them of the tale about the four blind men of Hindustan. As you will recall, when the four blind men came upon an elephant, each one touched a different part. The first one felt the tail and concluded, "It's a rope." The second felt the side and said, "It's a wall." The third, after touching the ear, announced, "It's a fan." Finally, the fourth one felt the trunk and decided, "It's a tree."

Like the four blind men many of us in ESL have very limited "feeling" for the role of grammar in language teaching because we have dealt primarily with a certain type of learner and with specific and limited instructional objectives. Yet we are surprised when other ESL teachers express a completely different "feeling" regarding the role of grammar in language teaching. In other words, we have not appreciated the fact that other teachers might be working with a different type of learner and focusing on other instructional objectives.

In reality there are many different types of language learners and many different purposes for learning ESL (Strevens, 1977). Each teaching-learning context deserves its own answer to the question of whether or not grammar should be emphasized. There is no single right or wrong position to take. Also, rather than two extreme choices, there is a continuum along which grammar becomes increasingly more important or less important depending upon a number of learner variables and instructional variables that each ESL teacher must carefully consider.

It is perhaps somewhat misleading to state the issue as one of deciding whether or not to teach grammar. The issue is whether accuracy of form is more important or less important for the learner. In those cases where accuracy of form is required, it is important for the ESL teacher to know how to focus on form and to know how to correct errors.

LEARNER VARIABLES

An observant ESL teacher does not need to be told that students learn in different ways. Research in educational psychology (see Cronbach and Snow, 1977, and Witkin et al., 1977) suggests that there are at least two distinct ways in which people can learn anything — including second or foreign languages. Some learners, consciously or unconsciously, have an analytic style and learn best by formulating and testing hypotheses or "rules." Other learners have a holistic style and learn best by experiencing relevant data and doing little or no analysis. Young children, for example, tend to be more holistic in their approach to learning than adults. Also, when one is beginning to learn something completely new and different, one tends to initially approach the new "object" holistically for a time before feeling ready to do any meaningful analysis.

This suggests that learner variables such as age can be very important in helping the ESL teacher decide whether or not it will be of any use to focus on form. If your ESL students are young children, the most likely answer is "No." If your students are adolescents or adults, the answer is "Maybe." Proficiency level is also a factor. If your ESL students are beginners, there is little point in focusing on form regardless of their age. However, if your students are at the intermediate or advanced level, It may well be necessary for you to do some correction.

The educational background of your ESL students is another noteworthy factor. If they are pre-literate with little formal education, then it is a waste of time and effort to focus on form. On the other hand, if your students are literate and well educated, they may become frustrated and annoyed if you do not provide adequate opportunity for them to focus on the formal aspects of English.

INSTRUCTIONAL VARIABLES

The need to focus on form also changes according to the objectives that the ESL teacher must address. If one is teaching a receptive skill, i. e., listening or reading, then it is distracting and irrelevant to emphasize grammar since these receptive skills require competence primarily in the area of semantic processing. However, if you are teaching the productive skills (i. e. speaking and, in particular, writing), then formal accuracy can become an important concern. Furthermore, for the productive skills, register and medium are additional factors. If you are teaching a conversation class, then accuracy of form is much less an issue than it is if you are teaching a class in formal expository writing.

The final factor to consider is the learner's need: what will the learner have to be able to do in English? If the learner's immediate goal is survival communication, formal accuracy is of negligible value; on the other hand, if the learner wants to function as an academic, a diplomat, or a business executive, then a high degree of formal accuracy is essential.

LEARNER AND INSTRUCTIONAL VARIABLES

Given all of the learner variables and instructional variables we have discussed, I would like to suggest that it is a bit complicated but certainly not impossible for ESL instructors to decide whether or not it is appropriate for them to focus on form with a given group of students. I have found that a grid such as the following is useful in helping me come to a sound decision: the more factors I identify on the left side of the grid, the less important it is for me to focus on form; the more factors I identify on the right, the more essential it is that I focus on form.

	Focus on Form		
	Less Important		**More Important**
Learner Variables			
1. Age	children	adolescents	adults
2. Proficiency	beginning	intermediate	advanced
3. Educational	pre-literate; no formal education	semi-literate; some formal education	literate; well educated
Instructional Variables			
4. Skill	listening, reading	speaking	writing
5. Register	informal	consultative?	formal
6. Need/Use	survival communication	vocational	professional

This grid helps you to decide, for example, when you are teaching beginning level adults who are pre-literate and are in need of survival communication skills, that focus on form is not important. On the other hand, when you are teaching literate young adults in college who are at the high intermediate level, then the grid tells you that focus on form is essential if you want to help them successfully complete their composition requirement.

EFFECTIVE WAYS TO FOCUS ON FORM

By drawing on recent improvements in language teaching methodology, we can isolate at least six different dimensions that can guide preparation of activities that will effectively focus our students' attention on form when this is necessary: It is not easy to be consistently on the right side of this grid when teaching grammar; however, the more we can follow the suggestions on the right, the more successful we will be in getting our students to focus on form while at the same time experiencing language in context.

Ways to focus on Form

Less Effective	More Effective
manipulative drills	communicative activities
context-free practice	context-embedded practice
sentence-based exercises	text-based exercises
cognitively undemanding activities	cognitively demanding activities
contrived materials	authentic materials
dull or neutral content	interesting and motivating content

One example of an activity primarily on the right side is the use of a pet store as the context for focusing the attention of adolescent students on the form of yes-no questions. Using pictures or small figures of 10 or 12 animals that are possible pets (e. g., a dog, a cat, a pony, a goldfish, a turtle, a canary, a parrot, a hamster, a monkey, a snake), the teacher has one student come to the front of the class and secretly "buy" one of the pets. Then the classmates must guess which pet the student has purchased by asking yes-no questions until someone guesses the correct pet. (Note that different question forms are possible):

Classmate 1: Did you buy the monkey?/ Is it the monkey?
Student: No.
Classmate 2: Did you buy the dog?/ Is it the dog?
Student: No.
Classmate 7: Did you buy the pony?/ Is it the pony?
Student: Yes.

The classmate who guesses the right pet can then go to the front and make the next secret purchase. This can continue as long as such practice is useful. The activity can be made more demanding by also requiring the class to guess the price of the pet.

EFFECTIVE WAYS TO CORRECT ERRORS

From classroom research we know that there are more effective and less effective ways of correcting ESL students when formal accuracy is desirable. At least five dimensions should be kept in mind when you are doing correction. (Such adtivities can be planned in advance or occur spontaneously as the need arises.) Again one should attempt to stay to the right of this grid as much as possible.

Teacher Correction Strategies

Less Effective	**More Effective**
teacher lectures, gives rule, or explains	teacher elicits information from class
teacher corrects directly	teacher elicits peer or self correction
teacher gives indirect, diffuse cues on type and location of correction needed	teacher gives focused, specific cues as to what correction is needed and where
teacher conducts mechanical drill of problematic form	teacher conducts meaningful practice of problematic form
teacher corrects everything	teacher corrects selectively

For example, if an ESL teacher wants to focus on the fact that several students in an intermediate college-level writing class are using infinitives where gerunds are required, the teacher might start by putting some of the students' errors on the board:

- I enjoy to see French movies.
- I stopped to smoke because it's bad for my health.

The teacher then asks for corrections, and in the unlikely event that the class cannot make the corrections, the teacher can write the correct form next to the incorrect form and say "That's how I write these sentences. What's the difference?" Once the class decides that the student sentence uses infinitives rather than gerunds (or *to* forms rather than *-ing* forms), the teacher can elicit partial lists from the class, showing which verbs take only infinitives, which take only gerunds, and which take both forms. If they cannot do this from experience, they should be given some authentic texts rich in examples of all three possibilities and asked to develop the lists as a group activity.

1 **Infinitive only**	2 **Gerund only**	3 **Infinitive/Gerund**
want	enjoy	try
expect	avoid	like
hope	finish	remember
plan	admit	forget
.	.	.
.	.	.
.	.	.

The teacher can then ask questions about lists 1 and 2:

T: Which verbs refer more to past or current facts?
Ss: Those in list 2.
T: Which refer more to future or hypothetical events or states?
Ss: List 1.

The teacher can then ask the students to use what they know about the differences between List 1 and List 2 verbs to explain the difference in meaning in pairs of sentences like these:

(1) a. I tried to open the window.
    b. I tried opening the window.
(2) a. I remembered to lock the door.
    b. I remembered locking the door.

After some discussion, students generally agree that in (1) the first sentence can imply an unsuccessful attempt, while the second sentence signals a successful one. In (2) they see that in the first sentence *remember* occurs before *lock* in the sequence of events, while in the second sentence *remember* occurs after *lock*, which is a past fact.

The students can then be asked to work in pairs and do a role play involving a university student and his/her advisor. Their role play should draw on a list of verbs supplied by the teacher:

admit, advise, anticipate, encourage, enjoy, expect, force, forget, induce, justify, like, motivate, permit, plan, postpone, remember, try, urge, want

In the course of doing the role plays, there can be discussion, if necessary, as to whether a given verb takes an infinitive or a gerund and why. Following the oral roleplaying, there might be one or two volunteer performances. Then, for homework each pair writes a dialog or short composition based on the role play. The teacher will follow up on the written assignment if any further errors are made in the use of infinitives and gerunds. In any event, there should be recycling of this point several weeks later in another context to check for retention.

CONCLUSION

Whatever your methodological preference may be with respect to teaching ESL, I would argue that you need to know the rules of English grammar to carry out the following responsibilities adequately:

1. Integrate form, meaning, and content in syllabus design and lesson planning;
2. Selectively identify student production errors in need of correction (consider learner variables and instructional variable);
3. Prepare appropriate activities for getting students to focus on form when needed;
4. Develop effective strategies that raise students' awareness of their own errors and enhance their ability to self correct;
5. Answer students' questions about English grammar.

As a caveat, it should be noted that ESL learners never truly attend to form unless they want to and are able to do so. One of the best times for them to attend to form is after comprehension has been achieved and in conjunction with their production of meaningful discourse (perhaps spoken but more particularly written discourse).

It must be recognized that grammar is but one of many important aspects of language teaching. To be optimally effective an ESL teacher also must be able to use the target language (English) well, must have methodological expertise and classroom management skills — not to mention reasonable teaching materials, proper facilities and motivate students.

To conclude, let me return briefly to the moral of the tale of the four blind men of Hindustan. I do not recommend that any ESL teacher take an extreme inflexible position (i. e., always teach grammar, never teach grammar) based on limited experience with one small part of the total ESL teaching-learning spectrum. I recommend that the ESL teacher consider all the relevant variables, and then arrive at an informed decision for each distinct teaching situation he or she faces. The teacher must, of course, also have acquired or be willing to develop the necessary knowledge of English grammar along with the pedagogical skills to apply that knowledge effectively.

■ References

Celce-Murcia, M. and D. Larsen-Freeman (1983) *The Grammar Book: An ESL/EFL Teacher's Course.* Rowley, Mass.: Newbury House.

Cronbach, L. J. and R. E. Snow (1977) *Aptitudes and Instructional Method: A Handbook for Research in Intersections.* New York: Halstead Press.

Gattegno C. (1972) *Teaching Foreign Languages in Schools: The Silent Way.* New York: Educatiooal Solutions, Inc.

Gattegno, C. (1978) *The Common Sense of Teaching Foreign Languages.* New York: Educational Solutions, Inc.

Joos, M. (1962) The Five Clocks, *IJAL Publication No. 22 Vol. 23,* Part 2.

Krashen, S. and T. Terrell (1983) *The Natural Approach: Language Acquisition in the Classroom.* Hayward, CA: The Alemany Press.

Lado, R. (1984) *The Effect of Morphological and Syntactic Errors on the Holistic Scores of Native and Non-native Compositions.* Unpublished M. A. thesis in TESL. UCLA.

Strevens, P. (1977) New Orientations in the Teaching of English Witkin, H. A., C. A. Moore, D. R. Goodenough, and P. W. Cox (1977) Field · dependent and field-independent cognitive styles and their educational implications. *Review of Educational Research. Vol. 47.* 1-85.

From Celce-Murcia, M. (1985). Making informed decisions about the role of grammar in language teaching, *TESOL Newsletter, 19, 1,* pp. 4-5.

6. A CLASSIFICATION OF STRUCTURAL PATTERN DRILLS

I have recently attempted in an article called "Structural Pattern Drills: A Classification" to suggest such a conceptual framework; that is, a classification, which recognizes that language learning is partly but not only habit formation, which proposes to put meaning and communication into classroom activities, and to do so in a consistent and orderly procedure. This paper is an attempt to further expand and clarify this proposition for classifying drills. We need such a classification for grading and sequencing drills in order to obtain a systematic and more efficient progression in the classroom from mechanical learning to the internalizing of competence. I believe with John Carroll, Wilga Rivers and others in our field that "there is no reason to believe that the two positions (language teaching as formation of language habits versus the establishment of rule governed behavior) are mutually exclusive." Rivers points out in a fascinating footnote that many of the language features which are most efficiently taught by drills (person and number inflections, gender agreements, formal features of tense, etc.) "are excluded by Chomsky from his system of rewrite rules and are included in the lexicon as parts of complex symbols."

If, as the evidence seems to suggest, language involves more than one level and there are at least two types of learning, then this should be reflected in the nature and types of drills. Both Stevick and Titone conceive of language learning as a three stage process, but as Prator points out, there is no way of accurately assigning a drill to a specific stage. My contention is that there are three classes of drills: mechanical, meaningful, and communicative and that we may distinguish these three classes from each other if we analyze the drills in terms of (1) expected terminal behavior, (2) degree of response control, (3) the type of learning process involved, and (4) criteria for selection of utterance response.

TESTING DRILLS AND TEACHING DRILLS

But before I proceed to a discussion of the criteria for classifying drills, we need to consider an important aspect of drills, which cuts across this classification. Many have recognized a basic division in kinds of drills. Etmekjian refers to them as teaching drills and testing phase, and Fries spoke of patterns produced "on the level of conscious choice." What is involved is the difference between drills that serve primarily to help the student memorize a pattern with virtually no possibility for mistake and the drills which test or reinforce the learning of that pattern. The concord of person and verb in the Romance languages serves as a good example for a teaching drill:

Model: andar (tú) R: andas
cantar (tú) cantas
Continue the drill:
Cue: trabajar (tú) R:
pasar (tú)
hablar (tú)

This is a memorizing drill, where even the reader who does not know (or understand) Spanish can complete the drill correctly. But as soon as we change the cues to include all persons, that is, to change the cues so as to require an answer of more than minimal items, we require that the student know all the verb endings for the *ar*-verbs, present tense, and by his response we know whether he does or not. The response depends on the conscious choice of the student:

Model: andar (tú) R: andas
cantar (Vd.) R: canta
Continue the drill:
Cue: trabajar (el) R:

Only the student who has previously memorized these patterns can complete the drill successfully. I have constructed a tentative design to clarify the overall division of drills. (See Figure 1.)

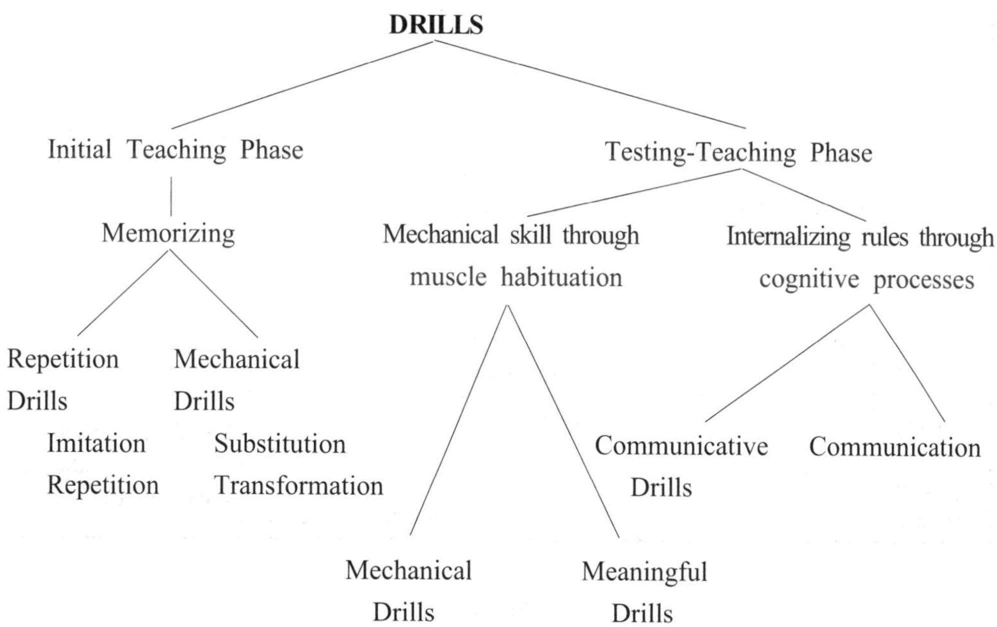

Figure 1

Drills are basically divided into teaching (memorizing, habituation) drills and testing (feedback, quizzing) drills. There are two types of drills to help the student memorize: repetition drills and mechanical drills which basically tend to be substitution drills but transformation drills are also possible. The testing drills in turn can be divided according to purpose: acquiring mechanical skill through muscle habituation on the one hand and on the other internalizing of rules through cognitive processes. The mechanical skill drills subdivide into mechanical and meaningful drills while the internalizing of competence drills subdivides into communicative drills and actual communication. It can thus be seen that it is possible for mechanical drills to be either testing or teaching drills, depending on their breakdown into minimal items. I mention this before discussion of the three classes — mechanical, meaningful, and communicative — of drills because this duality of mechanical drills troubled me for a long time and contributed to some confusion in my other article.

The chart in Figure 2 may make the following discussion somewhat clearer.

	MECHANICAL DRILLS	MEANINGFUL DRILLS	COMMUNICATIVE DRILLS
Expected terminal behavior	Automatic use of manipulative patterns — formation of habits	Automatic use of manipulative patterns — formation of habits still working on habit formation	Normal speech for communication — free transfer of patterns to appropriate situations
Degree of Control	Complete	Less control but there is a "right answer" expected	No control of lexical items — some control of patterns. Answer cannot be anticipated
Learning process involved	Learning through instrumental conditioning by immediate reinforcement of correct response ANALOGY	Learning through instrumental conditioning by immediate reinforcement of correct response ANALOGY trial-and-error ANALYSIS	PROBLEM SOLVING ANALYSIS
Criteria for selecting response	Teacher	Teacher, Situation, Readings (knowledge common to the class)	Student himself (new information about real world)

Figure 2

MECHANICAL DRILLS

A mechanical drill is defined as a drill where there is complete control of the response, where there is only one correct way of responding. Because of the *complete* control, the student need not even understand the drill although he responds correctly, as in the first Spanish Drill. One might possibly consider repetition drills as the most extreme example of this class of drill. Substitution drills lend themselves particularly well to this. Here is another mechanical drill that all readers can complete because it has been broken down to minimal items. It is a memorizing drill on the subject-adjective word order in Thai:

Example:$^{+}$ $\overset{3}{\text{poom}}$: $\overset{+}{\text{nakrian}}$ poom

$\overset{+}{\text{suun}}$: $\overset{3}{\text{nakrian}}$ $\overset{+}{\text{suun}}$

$\overset{2}{\text{əuan}}$: $\overset{3}{\text{nakrian}}$ $\overset{2}{\text{əuan}}$

Continue the drill:

1. $\overset{+}{\text{naaw}}$
2. $\overset{3}{\text{roon}}$
3. dii
4. $\overset{2}{\text{suay}}$

The following drill is also a mechanical drill but unless you have studied (and memorized) the various classifiers you will not be able to complete it. It is a mechanical testing drill and (apart from the choice of numeral) there is only one correct answer:

Complete the sentence with a numeral and a classifier.

Example:$^{+}$ $\overset{3}{\text{Kaw}}$ $\overset{3}{\text{suu}}$ roon Taaw

$\overset{+}{\text{Kaw}}$ $\overset{3}{\text{suu}}$ roon $\overset{3}{\text{Taaw}}$ soon$\overset{2}{\text{Kuu}}$

Continue the drill:

1. $\overset{+}{\text{Kaw}}$ $\overset{3}{\text{suu}}$ $\overset{2\ \ 2}{\text{Paanun}}$
2. $\overset{2}{\text{Poo}}$ $\overset{1}{\text{Puuk}}$ $\overset{3}{\text{nekTay}}$
3. $\overset{2}{\text{maeae}}$ $\overset{1}{\text{say}}$ $\overset{2}{\text{soyKoo}}$
4. $\overset{3}{\text{noon}}$ $\overset{3}{\text{sak}}$ $\overset{2}{\text{sua}}$

8. $\overset{3}{\text{nakrian}}$ $\overset{1}{\text{say}}$ $\overset{2\ \ +}{\text{suanaaw}}$
9. Kruu $\overset{3}{\text{suu}}$ roon $\overset{3}{\text{Taaw}}$
10. $\overset{2}{\text{Pii}}$ $\overset{3}{\text{sak}}$ kaankeen
11. $\overset{1}{\text{dek}}$ $\overset{2\ \ +}{\text{Puuyin}}$ $\overset{1}{\text{say}}$ $\overset{+}{\text{waeaen}}$

The difference between a mechanical memorizing drill and a mechanical testing drill lies in the ability of the student to respond, which again depends on how well he has memorized certain patterns, but understanding what he is saying is not a necessary requisite. It is perfectly possible to supply a verb with a correct ending in, e. g., Spanish, without necessarily knowing what the verb means: given Cue: *gratar*(*nosotros*) any docile student will respond with *gratamos* and he no more than I will know the meaning of that nonsense word. I remember perfectly well drilling classifiers in Thai without knowing the lexical meaning of the words; I just divided the words in terms of fruits, containers, and people, but what kind of people or fruits I did not need to know. The ability to drill mechanical drills without necessarily understanding them is an important criterion in distinguishing them from meaningful drills.

Transformation drills may be mechanical:

> John kicked the door.
> The door was kicked by John.

All the student need memorize is the structural change and he can complete such a drill without understanding exactly what he is saying. Response drills, which so frequently are being masqueraded forth as communication, can be some of the easiest mechanical drills for the student:

> Which would you prefer, tea or coffee?
> wine or beer?
> nectar or ambrosia?

I know very well that the student is going to answer *ambrosia* without the foggiest notion of what it is.

The expected terminal behavior of such drills is the automatic use of manipulative patterns and is commensurate with the assumption that language learning is habit formation. It involves the classical Skinnerian method of learning through instrumental conditioning by immediate reinforcement of the right response. Learning takes place through analogy and allows transfer of identical patterns. This is clearly the mechanical level of learning, and this class of drills provides practice in mechanical associations such as adjective-noun agreement, verb-endings, question-forms and the like. This is a very necessary step in language learning, and as long as the student is learning, he won't mind the mechanical nature of the drill. The teacher needs to remember that the student can drill without understanding and to make sure that in fact he does understand. Because of the response-control, it is eminently suited for choral drills.

The student knows how to select his utterance response on the basis of the teacher's cue, be it oral or pictorial, but the teacher is the sole criterion for supplying the correct response. This becomes an important distinction between meaningful and communicative drills.

MEANINGFUL DRILLS

Much of the criticism of the audio-lingual method is based on the mechanical drill or rather the overuse to which it has been put. There are a number of psychological studies which demonstrate that there is a limit to the efficiency of mechanical drills in language learning. While not denying the need for mechanical drills, we may note that on the mechanical level alone the student certainly cannot yet express his own ideas fluently. He next needs to work through a set of meaningful drills:

1. Teacher: for five years	Student: How long did he (study)?
2. Teacher: during March	Student: When did he (register)?
3. Teacher: until four o'clock	Student:

In a meaningful drill there is still control of the response although it may be correctly expressed in more than one way and as such is less suitable for choral drilling. There is a right answer and the student is supplied with the information necessary for responding, either by the teacher, the classroom situation or the assigned reading, but in all cases the teacher always knows what the student ought to answer. Everyone is always aware that these drills are only language exercises and that any answer will do as well as another as long as it is grammatically correct and conforms to the information supplied. The student cannot complete these drills without fully understanding structurally and semantically what he is saying. I have attempted very hard to exclude lexical meaning from structural in the definition of meaningful drills, but I doubt that it is either possible or desirable. With the new license for mentalism I shall include both. The result is that some pattern drills come very close to being vocabulary drills. Compare the above "Which would you rather have, tea or coffee?" with "Which would you rather be, rich and healthy or sick and poor?" In other words, some meaningful drills may have the check for feedback that the student really understands the pattern built into the lexical components.

Comprehension type questions and answers based on assigned readings fall in this class of drills:

Teacher: What time did John come to school?
Student: John came to school at 9 o'clock.

as well as much "situational" teaching as in this drill on post-nominal modification using prepositional phrases, where the students were instructed to describe each other.

> Teacher: Which boy is in your class?
> Student: The thin boy with long sideburns.
> The handsome boy with black hair. etc.

It will be noticed that in the question-answer drill above, the long answers were given. The expected terminal behavior is the same as for mechanical drills. We still want an automatic use of language manipulation; we are still working on habit formation, although for the language teacher, who is fluent in the target language, it may be difficult to appreciate the enormous difference in difficulty in these two classes of drills.

This is not to deny that a response like "The man was bitten by the dog," albeit in a mechanical drill, is much more difficult for the learner than a single lexeme substitution drill. Language learning is also the ability to control increasing amounts of language in mechanical manipulation, and we need to consider the difficulty level within the "amount range" as well.

But the method is different. Mechanical drills by their nature can be drilled without grammatical analysis with the students left to "analogize" the pattern on their own. This is not possible with meaningful drills. Unless the student understands what he is doing, i. e., recognizes the characteristic features involved in the language manipulation, he cannot complete the drill. Politzer reports on an interesting experiment in "The Role and Place of the Explanation in the Pattern Drill" and points out that an early introduction of the explanation seems to be a more effective treatment than its postponement or omission and that it is preferable to show the application and relevance of the new material in some sort of context before explaining it. The place for the explanation then is following the mechanical drills; those students who grasped the analogy will be rewarded with positive reinforcement and those who did not will be helped to understand the specific characteristics of that language structure. The learning process varies depending on the structural pattern drilled, and while there may still be instrumental conditioning involved, there is very often a trial-and-error process involved in finding the correct response.

COMMUNICATIVE DRILLS

At this point, however, there is still no real communication taking place. Students have a tendency to learn what they are taught rather than what we think we are teaching. If we want fluency in expressing their own opinions, then we have to teach that. The expected terminal behavior in communicative drills is normal speech for communication or, if one prefers, the free transfer of learned language patterns to appropriate situations.

The degree of control in a communicative drill is a moot point. I originally stated that there is no control of the response, that the student has free choice to say whatever he wants. However, this turns out not to be true. All classroom teachers, using this system of sequencing drills, have reported back saying that there is indeed control, not of lexical items as we had at first thought but of structural patterns. The difficulty lies just in retaining this control so that the students indeed practice what they have learned; they themselves lose track of the fact that they are drilling and become engrossed in exchanging information. But it is a drill rather than free communication because we are still within the realm of the cue-response pattern. Communication "requires interpersonal responsiveness, rather than the mere production of language which is truthful, honest, accurate, stylistically pleasing, etc. — those characteristics which look at language as language rather than as behavior, which is the social purpose of language. Our end product is surely getting things done, easing social tensions, goading ourselves into doing this or that, and persuading others to do things. Communication arises when language is used as such interpersonal behavior, which goes beyond meaningful and truthful manipulation of language symbols." To recapitulate, the differences between a meaningful drill and a communicative drill lie in the expected terminal behavior (automatic use of language manipulation versus free transfer of learned language patterns to appropriate situations) and in response control. But the main difference between a meaningful drill and a communicative drill is that in the latter the speaker adds new information about the real world. All of us have seen a meaningful drill turn communicative when the student suddenly took the question or cue personally and told us something about himself that we did not know from the classroom situation: "I have three sisters" is communicative, but "My shirt is red" is merely meaningful; that information is supplied by the situation, and I can see it as well as the student.

Language teachers have always used communicative drills in the classroom (where else is one asked such personal questions as "Did you brush your teeth this morning?"), but my point is that there should be an orderly progression from mechanical drilling through meaningful to communicative drills, that the teacher should know one from the other, and that one should not rely on chance that the students will turn a drill into communicative activity.

Communicative drills are the most difficult to arrange within the classroom. They can, of course, never be drilled chorally. Still, if we want fluency in expressing personal opinion, we have to teach that. One way of working with communicative drills is to structure the classroom activity so that it simulates the outside world of the students and to work within this situation. Need I point out that running through a memorized dialogue with accompanying gestures and action is not communicative drill nor necessarily language learning; nonlanguage teachers refer to such activity as acting. Another, simpler way of working with communicative drills is simply to instruct students to answer truthfully.

Example:

1. What is your responsibility?
   My responsibility is to (learn English).
   (learning English).
2. What's your hobby?
   My hobby is to (make models).
   (making models).
3. What's your favorite pastime?
4. What are your lab instructions?
5. What will your occupation be?
6. What are your interests?
7. What is your advice to (Ahmed)?

Gone is the instrumental conditioning; there is no facilitating of the correct response. What we have is John Carroll's "'problem-solving' situation in which the student must find ... appropriate verbal responses for solving the problem, 'learning' by a trial-and error process, to communicate rather than merely to utter the speech patterns in the lesson plan." We are clearly working within a level of language that involves thought and opinion and teaching it in a way that necessitates an understanding of the essential elements of what is being learned. It is a very different experience from mechanical drilling. It is indeed practice in performance by practice in generating new utterances in order to internalize the rules of grammar so that competence will not be defective. I am not saying that language teaching should be concerned solely with communicative type drills, but I am suggesting that any amount of mechanical drills will not lead to competence in a language, i. e., fluency to express one's own opinions in appropriate situations.

To summarize, in language teaching we ought to classify the drills we use into three classes: mechanical, meaningful, and communicative in order to reach free communication. We then need to proceed systematically, not leaving out any one step. Mechanical drills are especially necessary in beginning courses and in learning languages markedly different from the native tongue, such as Thai is for me. I do not believe that this is the only way of teaching languages because it patently is not. Rather, given what we know about languages and learning today, this classification of drills will provide for more efficient language learning.

From Paulston, C. B. (1970). Structural pattern drills: A classification. *Foreign Language Annals*, 4, pp. 187-193.

7. A TYPOLOGY OF STRUCTURAL PATTERN DRILLS

What follows is a discussion of our typology of structural pattern drills. The basic criterion for assigning drills to the various types is in terms of the types of restructuring.

Here is an overview of the total typology:

Ⅰ. Repetition Drills
- A. Verbatim repetition
- B. Open-ended repetition
- C. Dialogue repetition

Ⅱ. Discrimination Drills
- A. Pattern recognition
- B. Context recognition
- C. Function coding

Ⅲ. Alternation Drills
- A. Morpho-lexical Drills
  1. Single slot substitution
  2. Double slot substitution
  3. Multiple slot substitution
  4. Moving slot substitution
  5. Correlative substitution
     - a. simple
     - b. complex
- B. Syntactic Drills
  1. Expansion
  2. Completion
  3. Reduction
  4. Transformation
  5. Integration

Ⅳ. Reply
- A. Two Stage Drills
  1. Short answer
  2. Comprehension questions
  3. Rejoinder
  4. Comment
  5. Free response
- B. Three Stage Drills

Ⅰ. REPETITION DRILLS

Repetition drills are just what they sound like, plain repetition of the cue. By varying the nature of the cue, one can achieve different subtypes of repetition drills.

One might well question the justification for including mindless parroting in a language class. In the first place, the teacher must make very sure that it is not mindless parroting. Students can do some of these drills without understanding them and the teacher therefore has to make extra sure that they do understand. As for justification, these drills serve two purposes. At the beginning stages of language learning, repetition drills are very useful in building up "kinetic memory," i. e., for the traininng of the perceptual motor skills. We have forgotten the rules for the word order of the French oblique personal pronouns but we can still use them correctly, the tongue trips along its memorized path, as it were. We suspect that the function of kinetic memory in language learning is more important than what it presently is given credit for being, and repetition drills are excellent for its development.

As Francis Johnson has pointed out, part of language learning is also the ability to control increasing amounts of language in mechanical manipulation. Beginning students can remember and repeat only relatively short sentences. Repetition drills of steadily increasing lengths are very useful for developing auditory memory, for increased competence in recognition and recall of long utterances of language.

A. Verbatim Repetition

The students repeat the cue exactly as given. The drills are useful in teaching subject-verb agreement, adjective-noun order and word order in general.

NP + BE + adjective

Repeat: The campus is confusing.
The boy is handsome.
The house is white.
The car is small.

There + BE + NP

Repeat: There's a good restaurant down the street.
There's a drug store in the next block.
There are some new students in the class.

Verbatim repetition tends to be very boring for more advanced students; but by increasing the length of the utterances as the students increase in proficiency, the students' memory is challenged and the drills seem to be regarded as games.

Perfect modals — negative
Listen: I didn't see Judy at the party.
Repeat: She may not have been there — she had to finish a paper.
Listen: John wasn't in class when it began.
Repeat: He might not have been on time — he overslept this morning.
Listen: I got up late, so I didn't go to the store for a New York Times.
Repeat: They might not have had any during the truckers' strike.

B. Open-ended Repetition (Chain Drills)

These drills are done individually and each student repeats all the responses prior to his own and adds his own piece of information. Since the students tend to regard them as games, they work well for extra practice on complicated patterns when verbatim repetition might be rejected. The drills also require the students to listen to each other, and attention is diverted from the fact that they are drilling and toward actual use of the language.

going to future
Teacher presents situation: You have $50.00. The stores are having "end-of-season" sales. What are you going to buy?
S1: I'm going to buy (a coat).
S2: I'm going to buy a coat and (a hat).
S3: I'm going to buy a coat and a hat and (a scarf).

In the previous example, the concord between subject and verb can be practiced by expanding the drill to include the other students' full statements. (She's going to buy a coat, he's going to buy a hat, and I'm going to buy a scarf.)

The following example is a variation of a chain drill in that each student repeats only part of the previous student's answer as he adds to the information concerning the proposed situation.

Conditional
T: Imagine a situation where it is possible for you to go to New York.
Make a series of statements, each of which is based on the preceding one.
S1: If we receive some money, we will go to New York.

S2: If we go to New York, we will go by plane.
S3: If we go by plane, we will arrive at Kennedy Airport.
S4: If we arrive at Kennedy Airport. . .

Chain drills can be varied by altering the pattern of student responses. At first the students should answer in order around the class so as to reduce the number of elements they must remember (pattern, item, order); later the teacher can call on students at random and finally, the student himself can choose the next to answer. We make it a rule in our classes that no one is allowed to write down the items because the challenge of remembering seems to be important to the success of the drills.

C. Dialogue Repetition Drills

In these drills a sequence of specified patterns is repeated with minor variations. They are excellent for practice in the changing of tenses, formation of questions and changing word order, as well as for practice in conversational exchanges. The students concentrate on the exchange and forget they are drilling.

Irregular past
T: He teaches the class every day.
S1: Then he taught the class yesterday.
S2: No, he didn't teach it yesterday.
S1: Why not?
S2: (He was sick.)
S1: When did he teach it?
S2: He taught it (the day before yesterday).
T: She makes a cake every week.
S1: Then she made a cake last week.
S2: No, she didn't make one last week.
S1: Why not?
S2: (She was busy.)
S1: When did she make one?
S2: She made one (the week before last).
T: Bill catches up on his sleep every Saturday.
Nancy has a date every weekend.
Chen makes a long distance phone call every Sunday.

If the drills are to be used for conversational exchanges, care must be taken to make the language as "natural" as possible. In the example above, use of the pronouns *it* and *one* make the dialogue much more realistic even though they increase the complexity of the drill considerably.

It is important to recognize drills of this type for what they are, i. e., simply repetitions. However, well done they look impressive and can easily delude an observer into thinking that actual communication is taking place.

II. DISCRIMINATION DRILLS

Discrimination drills are by nature testing drills, i. e., drills where the correct answer (there is only one) depends on conscious choice by the student. Discrimination drills are useful when introducing new patterns which vary only slightly from previous patterns (e. g., singular/plural; third person; present perfect/present continuous), and the students must recognize subtle differences for accurate encoding. Very little time should be spent on this type of drill since the students are talking about language rather than using it. However, these drills do reduce the necessity for grammatical explanations; they assure student' grasp of the function of the pattern; and they give valuable practice in listening comprehension in that they serve to focus the students' attention on syntactic cues.

A. Pattern Recognition

The "same-different" responses are most often found in pronunciation exercises but can be helpful in determining discrimination of grammatical patterns as well. More common in grammar drills are those in which the student is required to identify the patterns on the basis of some specified feature.

BE — singular/plural

T: If you hear a sentence in the singular, raise one finger; if plural, raise two fingers.

The girl is tall.	S: (1)
The girls are tall.	(2)
The boys are lost.	(2)

In order to avoid the linguistic terminology, examples of the patterns are sometimes written on the board and labeled A and B. The students then respond by saying the appropriate letter.

Adjective/Noun

A	B
He's an American.	He's American.
You're Brazilians.	You're Brazilian.

She's a Thai.	She's Thai.
We're Arabs.	We're Arab.

B. Context Recognition

Similar surface structures may have different underlying deep structures, i. e., similar sounding words and phrases may have different meanings, for example, *Whose/who's*. These drills ascertain whether the students have grasped the various functions of such words and phrases, a determination not always possible in drills requiring encodings.

Who's/whose

T: Whose book is this?	S: Possession
Who's going downtown?	Person
Whose is this?	Possession
Who's a doctor?	Person
Whose is the VW?	Possession

Could

T: Could you tell me the time?	S: Request
Could you speak English before you came?	Ability
Could you go tomorrow?	Possibility
Could he come later?	Possibility
Could she cook before she was married?	Ability
Could you lend me a dime?	Request

Uses of *If* clauses

T: If you have time, I'd like some suggestions.	S: Request
T: If he has a test, he studies for three days.	S: Habit
T: If you've learned the acronyms, you've learned the language.	S: Generalization
T: If my friend is late, I try to to cover up for her.	S: Habit
T: If you've read one English book, you've read them all.	S: Generalization

C. Function Coding

Modal verbs

T: go to our friends' party (possibility) — S: We might go to our friends' party.

T: write to my parents (good idea) — S: I should write to my parents.

T: pay his bills by Monday (obligation) — S: He has to pay his bills by Monday.

These drills might be said to be the reverse of the context recognition drills. Rather than decoding a specific function, the student here has to encode it. Our students find them useful for sorting out the meanings of the various modals.

Modal *have to*/causative *have*

T: cut the grass (necessity) — S: (1) have to cut the grass.

T: cut the grass (cause) — S: (I' going to) have the grass cut.

T: type the term paper (cause)
wash the windows (necessity)
fix the car (cause)
type the letters (necessity)

III. ALTERNATION DRILLS

These are the drills familiar to all who have used the audio-lingual texts; substitution, transformation, expansion drills, and so on. They are all encoding drills which provide the students with practice with the rules of the grammar where the purpose is to internalize the structure by practicing the pattern.

A. Morpho - Lexical Drills

The teaching point of these drills focuses on morphological structure or lexical items like frequency adverbs, prepositions, etc. Some drills combine practice of more than one grammatical feature, and such drills are much more difficult. All of these drills involve manipulation of a single sentence utterance where the constituents (i. e., slot and filler in the tagmemic sense) remain in the same order and of the same number as in the model utterance.

1. Single slot substitution

Negative modal
Repeat: I might not go to class today.
Substitute: go shopping — S: I might not go shopping today.
do the laundry
finish the lesson
see John
have time to do the assignment

Only one constituent is changed throughout the drill. The drills are useful for practicing the word order of difficult patterns or for function words like the frequency adverbs. They also lend themselves to teaching vocabulary. At the beginning stages of language learning, the substituted constituent is likely to be a single word, but the drills should steadily be made more difficult by increasing the length of the constituent.

If clauses — condition
Repeat: John would help the students if he knew the answers to their questions.
Substitute: if he could — S: John would help the students if he could.
Substitute: if he had time — S: John would help the students if he had time.
Substitute: if he didn't have so much to do — S: John would help the students if he didn't have to much to do.
Substitute: if he wanted to
if someone asked him to
if he could understand their English

2. Double slot substitution

Count nouns
Repeat: We don't smoke many cigarettes.
Substitute: eat/vegetables — S: We don't eat many vegetables.
use/eggs
read/books

In these drills the student changes two constituents from the model. The drills are useful for practicing comparison, and for highlighting many structural contrasts.

Comparison (*the same* NP *as*)
Repeat: My coat is the same size as yours.
Substitute: city/size S: My city is the same size as yours.
book/price
hat/shape
car/color

BE-past + *going to* + verb
T: fly to Paris/fly to London
S: I was going to fly to Paris; I'm going to fly to London instead.
T: study English/study French
S: I was going to study English; I'm going to study French instead.
T: read a novel/read a biography
buy a VW/ buy a Chevrolet
work all day/sleep all day

3. Multiple slot substitution

Three or more constituents are replaced in the model with each student response. These drillls are excellent for practicing comparisons and can be used as problem-solving activities even for quite advanced students, especially if the order of the cues is different from that expected in the response.

Comparison (the same NP as)
T: VW/Volvo (size) S: My VW is the same size as her Volvo.
hat/coat (color) My hat is the same color as her coat.
novel/short story (length)
Ford/Oldsmobile (width)

4. Moving slot substitution

With each student response one constituent is changed but it is a different constituent in each response. The drills are very useful for extended practice on verb tenses or virtually any pattern on which the students need extra practice, since the drills are usually regarded as games.

Going to future
Repeat: He's going to buy a new car.

Substitute: radio — S: He's going to buy a new radio.
get — He's going to get a new radio.
I — I'm going to get a new radio.
house

Past continuous
Repeat: I was watching TV at 10:00 last night.
Substitute: we — S: We were watching TV at 10:00 last night.
sleeping
11:00
yesterday
the children

Past perfect continuous
Repeat: I'd been travelling for three months when I met him.
Substitute: working — S: I'd been working for three months when I met him.
Substitute: two months — S: I'd been working for two months when I met him.
Substitute: saw — S: I'd been working for two months when I saw him.
Substitute: her — S: I'd been working for two months when I saw her.
Substitute: we — S: We'd been working for two months when we saw her.
Substitute: studying
two days
them

5. Correlative substitution

The cue triggers a morphological or syntactic correlative change in the pattern. The drills are excellent for testing the students' ability to encode grammatical relationships such as subject-verb agreement, indefinite article choice, count-mass nouns, pronoun forms — in short, any structure which contrasts minimally in its various patterns. All correlative drills are by nature testing drills.

a. Simple : These drills are single slot substitutions which require the students to make some adjustment in another part of the pattern in order to respond correctly.

Indefinite article
Repeat: The girl is a student
Substitute: teacher — S: The girl is a teacher
artist — The girl is an artist.
actress
spy

Reflexive pronouns

Repeat:	I'd rather do it by myself.	
Substitute:	she	S: She'd rather do it by herself.
	he	
	we	
	you and Joe	

Conjunction *but*

Repeat:	We don't understand the game, but Jack does.	
Substitute:	We didn't see the game.	S: We didn't see the game, but Jack did.
Substitute:	We saw the game.	S: We saw the game, but Jack didn't.
Substitute:	We aren't having a picnic.	
	We can understand the rules.	
	We won't have time.	

b. Complex: If the student must replace two or more constituents, correlative changes add greatly to the complexity of producing the expected response. In the following example, note that a lexical change is also required :

Relative clauses

Repeat:	The boy who is coming is my brother.	
Substitute:	boys	S: The boys who are coming are my brothers.
	girl	The girl who is coming is my sister.
	girls	The girls who are coming are my sisters.
	woman	
	man	

In the following example the students must know the semantic relationship between the items in order to do the drill successfully.

Comparison (*like/the same as*)

T: Pepsi/Coke	S: Pepsi is like Coke.
autumn/fall	Autumn is the same as fall.
frozen water/ice	Frozen water is the same as ice.
VW/Volvo	A VW is like a Volvo.

In the next example, Student 1 must infer from the double cue the expected response in order to postulate the correct question form.

Question words and time expressions.

T: Paris/three weeks	S1: How long were you in Paris?
	S2: I was in Paris for three weeks.
Paris/1965	S1: When were you in Paris?
	S2: I was in Paris in 1965.
Paris/April 5	S1: When were you in Paris?
	S2: I was in Paris on April 5.
London/July 14	
Caracas//a month	

Modal verbs-present/past

Repeat: I could have looked up the words yesterday.

Substitute: today	S: I could look up the words today.
my friends	S: I could look up my friends today.
yesterday	S: I could have looked up my friends yesterday.

B. Syntactic Drills

In syntactic drills the student manipulates either the number or the order of the constituents in the cue. The teaching point of these drills tends to involve syntactical relationships of features such as question formation, formation of negative statements, word order, changes from phrase to clause and from clause to phrase.

1. Expansion

Frequency adverbs

T: The baby cries. (often)	S: The baby often cries.
He's hungry. (always)	He's always hungry.
There's a nurse in the hall. (usually)	There's usually a nurse in the hall.
The girls fight. (never)	The girls never fight.

Adjective phrase

T: The napkins are on the table.	S: The napkins are on the table.
T: two	S: The two napkins are on the table.
T: paper	S: The two paper napkins are on the table.
T: pretty	
yellow	

The student's response contains more constituents than does the model but their relative word order remains the same. These drills are useful for practice on word order in adjective phrases and of frequency adverbs, and for tag questions.

Expansion drills can combine with various kinds of substitution drills, as in the following example, in which the student is required to expand the basic Noun Phrase + BE + Noun Phrase pattern by adding an adjective of his choice to each NP.

Adjective + noun

T: man/lawyer	S: The (big) man is a (bad) lawyer.
women/students	The (thin) women are (good) students.
women/actresses	
men/hairdressers	
children/actors	

There-subject

T: some letters on the desk	There are some letters on the desk.
a good restaurant near here	There's a good restaurant near here.
a phone call for John	
some bills for you	

2. Completion

As with the expansion drills, the student's response will contain more constituents than the cue, but in these drills the cue is always just part of an utterance which the student must complete.

Since/ago + time expression

T: They had an election ______________.	S: They had an election (a year ago).
T: They haven't had an election ______________.	S: They haven't had an election (since 19_____).
T: She hasn't smoked a cigarette ______________.	
We saw the new movie ______________.	
Nancy has read three books ______________.	

Conjunctions

T: He smiled but ______________.	S: He smiled but (refused).
T: They were laughing and ______________.	S: They were laughing and (telling jokes).

T: He usually eats here or ______________. S: He usually eats here or (in a restaurant).

T: I'll take sugar but ______________.
She went to the door and ______________.
We'll see you on Thursday or ______________.

These drills are useful for moving the student away from the extremely structured nature of most of the preceding types of drills to a point where he can begin to express his own thoughts. Completion drills can be used with virtually any pattern, but they are particularly useful for contrasting such structural patterns as conjunctions and time expressions which occur with specific tenses. In the preceding examples, note that the teaching point of the first drill is the structural relationship, in the second the semantic relationship of the features in the pattern.

Here are two more examples of completion drills, one from a beginning lesson and one quite advanced:

Count/noncount nouns

T: Carlos uses a few ______________. S: Carlos uses a few (eggs).
Jim doesn't smoke many ______________. Jim doesn't smoke many (cigars).
Jane wants a little ______________.
Bill doesn't use much ______________.
Paul spends a little ______________.

Transitive verb + complement

T: I feel it is my duty to ______________. S: I feel it my duty to (tell you that you're wasting your time).
T: We call it failure when ______________. S: We call it failure when (you don't accomplish your objective).
T: I find it impossible to ______________. S:
They regard it as an insult that ______________.
Do you consider it correct to ______________?

3. Reduction

These drills are the converse of expansion drills. That is, the order of the constituents remains the same, but the number is fewer in the response than in the cue. They are most common in the practice of pronoun forms and are frequently accompanied by correlative changes as in the second of the following examples.

Subject pronouns

T: The car is small.	S: It's small.
The girl is beartiful	She's beautiful.
The man is tall.	He's tall.
The house is big.	It's big.

Indefinite pronouns

T: All of the people are coming	S: Everyone is coming.
All of the people like Coke.	Everyone likes Coke.
All of the people want clean air.	Everyone wants clean air.

4. Transformation

In transformation drills the order of constituents in the cue is changed in the response. The number of constituents in the cue may also vary from that in the response. The drills can be used to practice tense, question, and negative formations as well as many noun modifications.

BE — question formation

T: You're lost.	S: Are you lost?
He's a good student.	Is he a good student?
She's lost.	Is she lost?
They're good instructors.	Are they good instructors?

Noun modification

T: the club for the faculty	S: the faculty club
a room in the dormitory	a dormitory room
delivery of the mail	
the people in the office	
a frame for the picture	

Irregular past

T: They're beginning the program promptly at six today.	S: (Yesterday) they began it at five.
T: She's singing with an orchestra this time.	S: (Last time) she sang with (only a piano).

T: The bells usually ring every Sunday at eleven.
This semester he's sitting in the front of the room.
They're throwing a big party at their place this weekend.

Relative clause formation

T: Do you know any superstitious people?	S: Do you know any people who are superstitious?
T: Do you like exciting stories?	S: Do you like stories which are exciting?
T: Does the store have any cheap paperbacks?	S: Does the store have any paperbacks which are cheap?

Of all the types of structural pattern drills, transformation drills vary the widest in degree of difficulty, from very easy ones as in the examples above to the very difficult (from the students' point of view) question formation types found in most audio-lingual texts on any language.

It seems fairly obvious that the degree of difficulty is directly proportional to the number of changes performed on the cue in order to arrive at the response. Consider the following examples from drills on WH question formation:

a. One change required (Movement of the WH word)
T: Did John drive somewhere?
S: Where did John drive?
b. Two changes required (Formation of past question; movement of WH word)
T: John drove somewhere.
S: Where did John drive?
c. Three changes required (Formation of past question; supply and movement of the WH word.)
T: John drove home.
S: Where did John drive?

In all three examples the student response is the same, but the last is the most difficult because it involves the most operations. In our experience, when a transformation drill has gone astray, it has been because the number of transformations is beyond the ability or training of the students.

5. Integration

All of the previous types of drills have involved a single sentence utterance; integration drills require the students to combine two utterances into one, a manipulation which frequently requires some transformation or correlative change in the pattern. Integration drills are useful in practicing conjunction and subordination, relative clause formation, and other rather complex structures.

BE + adjective/adverb + present participle

T: Is he busy? Is he doing his assignment? S: Is he busy doing his assignment?
T: Are they in the kitchen? Are they eating? S: Are they in the kitchen eating?
T: Is she outside? Is she waiting? S: Is she outside wating?
T: Is he sitting? Is he reading?
Are they at the bank? Are they cashing a check?
Is she back home? Is she watching TV?

Adjective phrase

T: This apartment is cheap. She can rent it. S: This apartment is cheap enough for her to rent.
T: This car is big. ( ) can't drive it. S: This car is too big for ( ) to drive.
T: These chairs are heavy. We can't lift them. S: These chairs are too heavy for us to lift.

Relative clause formation

T: The man broke his leg. He's in my class. S: The man who broke his leg is in my class.
T: The women are studying computer science. They're waiting to see the professor. S: The women who are studying computer science are waiting to see the professor.
T: The man came to dinner. He stayed for three weeks. S: The man who came to dinner stayed for three weeks.

IV. REPLY

We consider all types of drills which consist of a conversation-like exchange to belong to this category. With these drills it is especially important to keep the class of the drill in mind for it is easy to mistake mechanical manipulation for communicative activity. (This type of drill does, however, lend itself well to communicative drills.) The drills are important in training the students to interact with others in the foreign language.

A. Two Stage Drills

In two stage drills, the exchange is completed by the teacher cue and the student response. The cue may consist of a question or a statement which requires an appropriate controlled or free reply by the student. The reply types of drills are grouped according to the nature of the expected response and the degree of control by the teacher.

1. Short Answer

Much natural language exchange consists of partial utterances or short answers in responses to inquiries. The students must be trained in this usage if they are to sound natural in real conversation and not as if they are still doing language classroom drills.

Tag question responses

T:	S:
T: Big cars increase pollution, don't they?	S: Yes, they do.
He has a VW, doesn't he?	Yes, he does.
You come from Libya, don't you?	Yes, I do.
The weather gets hot, doesn't it?	Yes, it does.

Conjunctions

T	S		
T: Do you have to make a lot of money?	S:	Yes, I do.	But (I can't). / And (I will).
		No, I don't.	But (I hope to). / And (I won't).
T: Do you overeat?	S:	Yes, I do.	But (I shouldn't). / And (I like to).
		No, I don't.	But(they're always encouraging me to). / And (I don't ever expect to).

T: Do you ever eat in American homes?
Did you enjoy yourself?
Did they go out of their way to give you a good time?

2. Rejoinder

These drills are useful for training the students in the use of phatic language — the conversational formulas which serve as introductions, leave takings, change of topics, etc.

"By the way"

T	S
T: With an F visa you have a Temporary Entry Permit.	S: By the way, (will they order us to do military service?
T: Jim Barlett wrote me a nice letter.	S: By the way, (I saw his wife's name in the paper).
T: (Christmas) will soon be here.	
I have to see my advisor tomorrow.	

3. Guided Comment or Reply

The student replies to a comment or a question by the teacher using a specified structure.

Prenominal Modification

T: What's a service for cashing checks?	S: It's a check-cashing service.
T: What's an operation that consumes time?	S: It's a time consuming operation.
T: What's an operating cost that's high?	S: It's a high operating cost.

T: What's an expert in reading minds?
What's a display that catches the eye?

Comparison

T: She's 35, but he's 45.	S: He's older than she is.
T: The Hudson is an important river, but the Mississippi is very important.	S: The Mississippi is more important than the Hudson.

T: He made some progress, but she made a lot of progress.
It's easy to go by train, but it's very easy to go by bus.

Modals (perfect) — *must*

T: John slept in until 10:00 this morning.	S: (He must have stayed out late last night.) (He must have been tired.)
T: Bill and Jim had to break a window to get into their apartment.	S: (They must have lost their key.)

T: When the professor returned the exams, Jane looked sad.
Nancy's mother was angry with her.

4. Comprehension Questions

Questions which test the student's understanding of material read or heard are usually more common in reading exercises, but they can be used in the grammar class to check on the comprehension of a dialogue or narrative used to introduce the grammar patterns.

Grammar drills which contain alternative questions are really tests of the student's comprehension.

In order to/for

T: What do you go to the post office for, stamps or envelopes? S: You go to the post office for stamps.

T: What do you go to the bank for, to take out money or to have a good time? S: You go to the bank to take out money.

T: What do you go to school for, an education or a good time?
What do you study English for, to get a better job or to be able to communicate?

5. Free Response

Free response drills are just that — the student is free to respond as he wants. They lend themselves particularly well to being communicative; although such drills are designed to practice a specific pattern, there is no guarantee that the student will actually use the target pattern in his response.

BE-present

T: Describe the capital of your country. S: (It's a beautiful city.)

T: Describe the people of your country. (They're friendly people.)
Describe a big university in your country.
Describe the leader of your country.
Describe the houses in your country.

Reflexives

T: What kinds of things do you like to do by yourself? S: (I like to study alone, but I don't like to eat by myself.)

T: Do you always type your own papers?
Did you come here by yourself?
Do you live alone or do you have a roommate?

Have-Causative

T: Do you wash and iron your clothes yourself? S: (Yes, I do.)
(No, I don't. I have them done at the laundry down the street.)

T: Where do you have your clothes cleaned?
Does your roommate cut your hair?
Do you polish your shoes yourself?
If you tear your shirt, do you fix it yourself?

B. Three Stage Drills

The cue, either a question or a statement by the teacher, sets up a conversational exchange among the students. The most common of these are the directed dialogues, the "Ask him..." type of exercise. These tend to be in the meaningful and communicative classes of drills, but it is possible by using pictures or objects to construct mechanical-testing drills of this type.

Tenses/time expressions

always	Student A: Is he always thirsty?
	Student B: No, he isn't always thirsty.
now	Student A: Are they busy now?
	Student B: No, they aren't busy now.
last night	Student A: Was he hungry last night?
	Student B: No, he wasn't hungry last night.
tomorrow	
always	
now	
last night	

The relative difficulty of these drills depends on the nature of the manipulation from the cue to the first response. The example above is an expansion, but note the increased complexity caused by the required transformations in the next example.

Subordinators

T: Was (Cecelia) standing near the door when you came in?	S1: (Jose,), (do you recall) whether (Cecelia) was standing near the door when we came in?
	S2: I (didn't notice) whether she was or not.

T: Did today's weather report say anything about rain?
Were you sitting in the right laboratory booth yesterday?
Do New York City and Long Island have different area codes?

Communicative drills result when the structures for the exchange are not specified in the model. Students get the information by use of any patterns at their command.

Simple past

T: Find out when (Ali) called long distance and what kind of call it was?	S1: (When did you call long distance?)
	S2: (Last weekend I called Iran.)
	S1: (Did you call person-to-person?)
	S2: (No, station-to-station.)

T: Find out when ( ) called long distance and who dialed the number, ( ) or the operator.
Find out if ( ) ever called a wrong number long distance and what happened.

Modal *have to*/causative *have*

T: Find out if ( ) has to do something today.	S1: (What do you have to do today?) (Do you have to do something today?)
	S2: (Nothing. I'm free all day.) (I have to finish my research paper.)
T: Find out if ( ) has something done every week.	S1: (Do you have your laundry done every week?
	S2: (No, I do it myself at the laundromat.)

T: Find out if ( ) and ( ) had to do something last week.
Find out if ( ) and ( ) will have something done this afternoon.
Find out if ( ) had to go somewhere last weekend.

CONCLUDING REMARKS

We presume that drills can be found which do not fit exactly into any of the categories discussed, but if so, we are reasonably certain that such drills will be combinations of the basic types in this typology.

Typologies are boring, but so is writing supplementary drills for a bad text. In this section it has been our intention to alert teachers to potential troublespots in different types of drills so that such drills can be avoided or changed, and to provide models for facilitating the writing of supplementary drills.

From Paulston, C. B. & Bruder, M. N. (1976). *Teaching English as a second language,* Cambridge, Mass: Winthrop Publishers, Inc, pp. 10-33.

8. PREPARATION FOR THE GRAMMAR LESSON

The first step in preparing a grammar lesson is to consult a variety of grammar reference books and ESL texts in order to establish how a structure is formed, when it is used, and whether there are any particular rules or exceptions governing its use. For exemple, in her English grammar reference, Frank (1972) says of the passive:

> The active voice is used in making a straightforward statement about an action....In the passive voice, the same action is referred to indirectly; that is, the original "receiver" of the action is the grammatical subject and the original "doer" of the action is the grammatical object of the preposition *by*. Because the grammatical subject of a passive verb is the original object of an active verb, *only a transitive verb may be used in the passive voice*. (p. 56)

Frank lists the situations in which the passive voice would be chosen over the active voice, including:

1. when attention is being drawn to the "receiver" rather than the "doer" of the action (e. g., *My dog was hit by a car*), and
2. when the "doer" of the action is unimportant or not known.

Another point Frank makes is that get or become can be used instead of be as a passive of transition

(e. g., *They're getting married tomorrow*).

In another source, Leech and Svartvik (1975) describe the passive as "the type of verb phrase which contains the construction *be* + past participle: *was killed, was seen*, etc." (p. 257). The authors go beyond Frank in saying that not all verbs taking objects have a passive, such as *have* in *I have a Fiat* (but not *A Fiat is had by me*) and *hold* in *This jug holds two pints* (but not *Two pints is held by this jug*). Leech and Svartvik say the agent in the *by*-phrase is retained only in specific cases; in fact, about four out of five English passive clauses do not have an agent. Despite this information, the authors do not enumerate the cases in which the agent is required. They do deal with the *get* passive, but characterize it as belonging to "informal style and in constructions without an agent" (p. 259). However, the following examples come to mind in response to their claim that the *get* passive doesn't normally take an agent: *Tom got hit by a truck,* and *Maurice gets stung by a bee every single summer*. In American English, it seems, *get* passives can retain the agent.

Azar, in her grammar book (1981), mentions that only transitive verbs are used in the passive and that usually the *by*-phrase is omitted, since the agent is generally understood.

She also says that the passive ranges over all tenses and she gives the form for the present, past, future, progressive perfect, and simple tenses.

Additional aspects of the passive are given by Celce-Murcia and Larsen-Freeman (1983); they disagree with Frank's claim that the passive is the same action as the active referred to indirectly. As proof, they cite the famous example from Chomsky (1965) which shows that active and passive pairs are not necessarily synonymous: *Everyone in the room speaks two languages* (i.e., any two languages per person) and *Two languages are spoken by everyone in the room* (i.e., two specific languages that everybody speaks). To this we would add an example given to us by Ed Keenan: *Every politician kissed a baby* (i.e., different politicians kissed different babies) and *A baby was kissed by every politician* (i.e., every politician kissed one, specific baby).

Celce-Murcia and Larsen-Freeman also counter Azar's claim that only transitive verbs take a passive with examples that show there are some passives which do not have active transitive counterparts: *Mehdi was born in Teheran* (but not *Someone bore Mehdi in Teheran*) and *It is rumored that he will get the job* (but not *Someone rumored that he will get the job*). Thus, they conclude that whether a verb is compatible with the active voice, the passive voice, or both is a property of the verb.

Another aspect noted by Celce-Murcia and Larsen-Freeman is that most passives do not have an agent. They cite a usage study conducted by Shintani which suggests that since 85 percent of all passives will not retain an agent, we should teach our students when and why to retain an agent in a passive, rather than teach when to omit an agent. Shintani's study (1979) includes a list of those situations in which a *by*-phrase is retained:

1. when the agent is a proper name designating an artist, inventor, discoverer, innovator, etc., who is too important to omit in the context (e. g., *The Mona Lisa was painted by da Vinci.)*
2. when the agent is an indefinite noun phrase (i. e., new information) and is retained to provide the listener or reader with the new information (i. e., *While Till was walking down the street, her purse was snatched by a young man.)*
3. when the agent is an inanimate noun phrase which is retained because it is unexpected... (we usually expect an agent to be animate, e. g., *All the lights and appliances in the Albertson household are switched on and off daily by an electrical device.*

Celce-Murcia and Larsen-Freeman also mention different kinds of passives. In addition to the *get* passives already mentioned, they introduce a complex passive with *have*: *Alice had her purse snatched while shopping downtown.* They explain the differences in meaning among a simple passive, the *get* passive, and the complex passive with *have*, as well as stative passives in which the participles function more like predicate adjectives than passive verbs.

Finally, Celce-Murcia and Larsen-Freeman talk about the circumstances under which the passive is used. Besides the two situations provided by Frank, these include:

1. when the agent is obvious and, therefore, not expressed (e. g., *Grapes are grown in the Napa Valley.)*
2. when the writer wants to sound objective (e. g., *It is assumed/believed that this was among the most significant policy decisions of the decade.*)
3. when the writer wishes to retain the same grammatical subject in successive clauses (e. g., *Rene Arredondo beat Lonnie Smith, but he was beaten by Gato Garcia.)*
4. when the theme is shared information, but the agent is new (e. g., *What a beautiful picture! Isn't it? It was painted by one of my students.*)

Having looked at just two grammar references, one ESL text, and one TESL training text, we already see problems. All of the texts provide interesting and helpful information. However, none is 100 percent complete. Therefore, it is necessary to consult more than one text when preparing to teach a grammar point for the first time. Since not all of the sources will agree, and not all will agree with what we have learned through our own experiences, questions which arise during preparation need to be resolved to some degree before the lesson is presented, since some bright and articulate student will probably notice a discrepancy and ask about it.

THE GRAMMAR LESSON

The second step or stage is the grammar lesson, which consists of four parts:

1. Presentation, in which we introduce the grammar structure, either inductively or deductively. There are a variety of techniques and resources that can be used during this step. Selection should be made according to teacher strengths, student preferences, and the nature of the structure (e. g., What is the structure-language-factor match?)

2. Focused practice, in which the learner manipulates the structure in question while all other variables are held constant. The purpose of this step is to allow the learner to gain control of the form without the added pressure and distraction of trying to use the form for communication. The teacher should not proceed to the next phase until most students have mastered at least the form of the structure.

3. Communicative practice, in which the learner engages in communicative activities to practice the structure being learned. According to Morrow and Johnson (1981), a communicative task incorporates the actual processes of communication; the more of these features an exercise incorporates, the more communicative it is.

- *Information gap.* In the course of doing the activity, one participant should be in a position to tell one or more other people something that the others do not yet know.

- *Choice.* The speaker must have some role in deciding exactly what he will say and how he will say it. (Options can be presented in advance by the teacher.) This also means that there should be some uncertainty in the mind of the listener(s) about what the speaker will say next.
- *Feedback.* What the speaker says to the person(s) he is communicating with depends not only on what the other person(s) says, but also on what the speaker wants to accomplish via the conversation.

4. Teacher feedback and correction. Although this is usually considered a final step, it must take place throughout the lesson. We also feel that a teacher's correction strategy should probably change according to the phase of the lesson. For example, during the second part of the lesson, correction should be predominantly straightforward and immediate. During the third part, however, communication should not be interrupted. Instead, the teacher should take note of errors and deal with them after the communicative execises. There is one element of correction, however, that we feel should remain constant; regardless of when correction is made, teacher feedback should always attempt to engage the student cognitively rather than to simply point out the error and provide the appropriate target form. In any case, the match in language factors, technique, and resources will be used in each part of the lesson.

Because review is essential in our program (like many adult schools, our imaginary school has a policy of open enrollment, so that students may enter our class at any time during the semester), we will teach the passive voice after reviewing the major tenses and aspects. As we cycle through each tense to review over the next few weeks, we will include the passive voice for that particular tense and aspect. In other words, we will introduce the passive in present and past tense now, but when we review the present perfect some weeks hence, we will introduce the passive voice of the present perfect. In this way, we will be able to cover the passive voice with various verb tenses and aspects once the basic concept has been understood and mastered, and we will not have to give students so much initial data that they lose sight of the general picture.

Since we have established that the active and passive versions of a sentence are not always as closely tied as we had first imagined, we will not teach the passive sentences by simply transforming active ones. We will teach passive in its own right, not as a structure derived from an active sentence. We will start out by teaching the passive *without* the agent *by*-phrase because naming the agent through a *by*-phrase is unusual — not commonplace — in the passive voice. Only later will we teach the exceptions that allow students to retain the agent.

Finally, for this lesson we should keep in mind that not all passives have an active, transitive counterpart, and we will therefore teach "passivization" as a property of the verb (i. e., some verbs can be used in passive sentences and some cannot; whether a given verb can or not is not a function of transitivity, but rather a property of the verb, although, of course, there is a strong correlation between verbs that are transitive and verbs that passivize).

Now that we have made the basic preliminary decisions, we will describe an actual lesson we observed in an adult school in terms of the steps outlined above. We visited the class of an experienced teacher who had excellent rapport with her class, which consisted of fifty-one students, predominantly from Latin America, about evenly divided between male and female. The teacher was comfortable with the number of students, as well as with the subject matter and the techniques used. The techniques were appropriate for the structure she was teaching and worked well for her, but they are not necessarily appropriate for everyone. It is important for each of us to explore and develop techniques which are compatible with our personalities and philosophies. Recall that we have suggested that any grammar lesson has four parts: (1) presentation, (2) structured, focused practice, (3) communicative practice, and (4) feedback and correction. We will begin by describing the observed teacher's presentation.

Presentation

The teacher's first objective was to focus students' attention on the structure in a natural context for the passive. Her second aim in the presentation phase was to elicit the rule for forming the passive from the students rather than simply telling them the rule. Her technique was a roleplay/storytelling combination. She began by selecting a student from the class and having her come to the front of the room with her purse. She whispered to the student briefly, explaining what was going to happen so that the student would not be startled or upset. She then selected another student to play the role of a thief. She directed the second student to run by the first student, grab her purse, and run to the back of the room. The teacher assured us that most students love a role play, and that she had never seen students take this one seriously or become upset or agitated by it. We would caution, however, that if you think the students you are working with would not respond well to this situation, you might want to select another context in which the focus will naturally be on the one who receives rather than the one who performs the action, such as being invited to the movies by a famous person.

The teacher felt that by the time students reach an intermediate level, they should be proficient at both hamming it up and participating as an audience. Her narration of the scene for the class follows:

"You know, last night Luisa was walking home from her friend's house when suddenly something terrible happened."

At this point, the second student was cued to run by and steal the purse.

"Her purse was stolen! Oh my goodness! That was terrible! Luisa, what happened?"

The teacher then allowed Luisa to enjoy her role by giving the class as much detail about the incident as she wanted, and involved the other students as much as they wanted. As soon as everything settled down, the teacher helped Luisa to her seat and said:

"You poor thing! That's too bad! Here, let me help you to your seat."

Then the teacher said to the class:

"Wasn't that awful? Luisa is going to call the police right away, and what is she going to tell them?"

Then the teacher elicited answers from the class and wrote on the board,

My purse was stolen.

She then shifted the class's attention to the student at the back of the room with the purse, who had been forgotten in all the excitement. Her narration continued:

"Well, here's the thief. Carmen. Let's see what happened to her. She was chased all over the city by the police."

The teacher acted as both narrator and police officer, chasing Carmen around the room and giving commentary on the action in the passive voice. After everyone had enjoyed the action, the teacher shouted, "Halt!" and then continued:

"Finally Carmen was caught. She was frisked and then she was handcuffed, and finally she was taken to jail. And what happened to Luisa's purse? It was given back to her."

The teacher returned Luisa's purse, thanked the students for participating, and asked everyone to be seated. Returning to the chalkboard, she said:

"Now, what happened to Carmen?"

She wrote each statement on the board after eliciting it from a student. Not all of the suggestions were grammatically correct, but when students couldn't provide the form exactly, the teacher accepted appropriate content and put the grammatically correct form on the board in order to give feedback:

She was chased, she was caught...

After all the forms were written on the board, the teacher proceeded as follows:

"Now this is sort of interesting. We have a new grammatical form here. Does anyone know what this is called?"

No student could provide the name of the form, so she said:

"This is called the passive voice."

Then she explained why the context demanded use of the passive voice. Her explanation was more like a dialog with the students than a lecture. It went something like this:

"What is important to Luisa?"

The students responded, "Her purse."

"That's right. Luisa is interested in her purse. She doesn't even know the person who took it. The thief isn't interesting. If Luisa calls you on the phone to tell you about her experience, what are you interested in?"

Again, the students responded, "Her purse."

"That's right. And that's why Luisa is talking about her purse, not the person who took it. Sometimes we're more interested in what receives the action than what does the action. In this case, the person who did the action is a stranger. We're not interested in her. We want to talk about what's important to us. So this is one time we would use the passive voice in English."

She then wrote the rule on the board, under the heading *Passive Voice.*

The next focus of attention was form. Referring to the sentences she had written on the board, the teacher asked:

"Can you see what the pattern is? How do we make the passive voice?"

She worked with the students until the correct rule of *be* + past participle was arrived at. Technically, the passive is formed with a passive participle, but for all intents and purposes, it is identical to the past participle, so the teacher used the term "past participle" to draw on what her students already knew. At this point, she then reviewed exactly what the forms of the verb *be* are, writing each on the board:

"Now what is the verb *be* again? *Am, are, is, was, and were*, and when do I use *am*? *Are*?" (etc.)

She put the pronouns by the verb so that she finally had the paradigm, *I am, you are, he/she/it is*, etc. on the board, and then reviewed past participles as the "third part of the verb" and went through several verbs, writing the base form, simple past, and past participle on the board. After this mini-review, she turned to the passive sentences her students had formed about the scene their classmates had performed and pointed out and underlined the verb *be* and the past participle in each example, as well as the rule for its production that had been elicited from the class. She then erased the sentences about Luisa and the fate of the thief and called a young man to the front of the class.

"Everyone knows Ali. Ali, say hello to everyone."

Ali hammed it up.

"You know, a few months ago, Ali did something very wonderful. He helped a lot of poor people in this city, which was a very fine and important thing to do. In fact, it was so wonderful that the mayor held a special ceremony for Ali last week. Did you know that? Ali, is it true?"

Once again, Ali did his part.

"Let me tell you what happened at that ceremony. Ali was given... what's this called?"

Someone supplied the term a medal. The teacher pinned a paper medal she had made on Ali's chest and asked:

"What happened to Ali? Everyone write it down on your paper, but don't say it. Give everyone a chance to get it."

She waited a few minutes and then asked the class:

"What happened to Ali?"

A student volunteered the answer, "Ali was given a medal," and the teacher wrote it on the board, repeating it as she wrote. She then went over each element of the sentence and asked:

"How many people got this right?"

Several students raised their hands. She acknowledged them and then continued with Ali's story, using the same procedure for each main point:

"And he was congratulated by a lot of important people. His picture was taken."

Here the teacher again simulated the action and had the students try to write on their papers before she provided the narration for the event:

"and he was given the key from the city."

The teacher presented a "key," with a brief side discussion about what it meant to receive the key from the city. At each step the teacher asked for a show of hands of how many students had gotten the sentence correct. She told us she was using this as an informal evaluation process, and she would continue the story of Ali or begin a new story until about 80 percent of the class was correctly producing the passive on their papers. As an additional verification, she walked around the room as she told the story, informally checking papers during the pauses when students were writing. When she was satisfied, she addressed the class, standing by a very proud Ali,

"Don't you feel proud just to know him? Let's give him a hand."

All the students applauded. The teacher then returned to the line of reasoning begun before.

"Now, what are we interested in, the person who gave Ali the medal or our friend, Ali? What's more interesting to us, the person who took his picture or Ali?"

At each point the students responded properly and the teacher said:

"That's right, and that's why we say..."

She again reviewed the context for the passive and the rule for constructing it, and then she moved into the second phase of the lesson.

Focused Practice

Recall that in this part of a grammar lesson students are asked simply to manipulate the structure under consideration. To accomplish this task, the teacher asked the students to imagine they were writing home about their classmate, Ali, and his award ceremony. She put these sentences on the board and asked students to fill in the appropriate form of the verb.

Dear _______ ,

Last night an award ceremony (hold) for my friend, Ali. He is a real hero in this city, and last night he (give) a medal for his bravery. Everyone (impress). After the ceremony, his picture (take) with the mayor and everyone wanted his autograph. Later there was a party at a fancy restaurant to celebrate. We all (invite). It was fantastic! We danced and drank champagne until two in the morning. Truly, all had a good time. I'll write more later. Bye for now.

Love,

Students copied the letter from the board and filled in the blanks with the passive form (*was* or *were* and the past participle of the verb in parentheses). As students were working, the teacher walked around the room, answered questions, and worked individually with students who were having trouble or who asked for help.

When everyone had finished, the teacher selected a volunteer to fill in the blanks on the board. Members of the class then took turns reading aloud from the board. The teacher corrected any errors immediately with the help of students. Finally, she asked students to check their work against the examples on the board. During this phase of the lesson, the teacher gave careful attention to correction. She was circulating in the room, correcting errors as she found them. Her last step was to ask how many students had gotten all the answers correct, only one wrong, only two wrong, etc. As students raised their hands, she looked around and acknowledged each.

This concluded her presentation and focused practice of the passive. Her lesson lasted about thirty-five minutes. Each day for about one and a half weeks she planned to review the previous day's work and introduce a new context and some structured practice for the passive voice.

Communicative Practice

The teacher didn't really give the class any communicative exercises (the third phase of a grammar lesson) until about a week after introducing the passive, when she was confident that most students could at least manipulate the form and use it in a controlled context. For her first communicative activity, the class was divided into pairs. One member of each pair was sent to an adjoining room, and the door was closed so they could not see what was going to happen. Then an aide, Alan, whose help had been solicited before class, came to the front of the room. The students laughed while a silly hat was put on Alan, a mustache was drawn, a fingernail was painted green, etc. While the victim retreated to clean himself up, the second members of the pairs were called back to the room. The teacher explained that students who had stayed in the room had to tell their partners what had happened to Alan, using the passive voice. During the communicative exercises, no corrections were made, but the teacher circulated around the room, noting errors in her notebook.

Feedback And Correction

The next day's grammar lesson began with the teacher writing several errors she had overheard the day before on the board. She said to the class, "Yesterday during our lesson I heard someone say this. What do you think about this sentence?" She then elicited the correct form from the class and did a very quick focused review, much like the structured, focused exercises mentioned in our description of the presentation phase of the lesson. Next she moved into another communicative exercise and alternated between phases two and three until she was satisfied with her students' mastery of the structure.

Lesson Summary

Because we have decided the most frequent and natural context for the passive voice is written discourse, more advanced or sophisticated students might respond better or more comfortably to some of the exercises for the passive. We have explained what we observed one adult-school teacher do successfully, but of course presentation, focused practice, communicative practice, and correction and feedback procedures will vary according to the natural inclinations and preferences of the teacher and students.

In addition to the lesson we saw and the teacher's projected lessons, we would suggest a lesson toward the end of the unit illustrating when the agent *by*-phrase is retained in a passive sentence and another one on verbs that occur only in the passive (e. g., *to be born).*

Conclusion

We looked up the passive in two reference texts, an ESL text, and a TESL text. We noticed similarities and differences among the texts and compared them to our own experience and common sense. Then we summarized our findings. Our next step was to determine the match between structure, language factors, techniques, and resources so that we could select appropriate techniques and resources for the lesson.

Finally, we described in detail an actual thirty-five minute grammar lesson for teaching the passive voice and the sequencing the teacher planned to follow over a period of time as she moved through the four phases of teaching grammar:

- presentation
- focused practice
- communicative practice
- feedback and correction

From Celce-Murcia, M. & Hilles, S. (1988). *Techniques and resources in teaching grammar.* Oxford, England: Oxford University Press.

PART THREE

TEACHING SPEAKING

듣기가 말하기로 전이하고 읽기도 말하기로 전이한다는 주장이 어느 정도 설득력이 있고 특별히 듣기와 말하기의 직접적인 상관관계는 어린아이가 모국어를 습득하는 과정에서 분명히 나타나기 때문에 제 2언어나 외국어 지도에 적용되어 왔다. Total physical response는 교사의 명령을 듣고 그에 따르는 행위를 보게 하여 언어를 가르치는 교수법이고 Natural approach에서 주장하는 이해할 수 있는 입력(comprehensible input) 가설에서도 듣기를 통하여 입력이 충분히 제공되면 말이 자연스럽게 나타난다(speech emerges)고 역설한다. 그렇지만 영어사용이 학교에서의 영어 수업시간 중 극히 일부에 국한되어 있는 우리의 영어교육 환경에서는 이러한 이론을 적용하는 것이 불가능하다. 따라서 어차피 모국어를 이미 상당 수준까지 배운 초등학교 이상의 학생들에게 영어를 가르치는 상황에서 우리는 어떻게 하면 영어를 많이 사용하여 말할 기회를 줄 수 있을까 에 관심을 기울여야 하겠다. 'We learn to speak by speaking.'의 진리를 부정할 사람은 없기 때문이다. 그리고 말하기 지도에 있어서 목표는 학생들이 정확하고 적절한 영어를 사용하여 자신의 생각을 표현할 수 있게 한다는 것일 것이다. 그런 의미에서 앞의 문법지도에서 다룬 내용들이 말하기 지도와 그대로 연계가 되겠다. 단 전자의 경우에는 문법적인 형식을 따르는 것이 우선이므로 표현에 많은 제한이 있고 후자에 있어서는 학생의 영어 사용 능력에 따라 차이가 있기는 하지만 비교적 자유롭게 자신의 의견을 이야기 할 기회가 부여된다.

Gebhard는 자신의 경험을 토대로 학생들의 말하기 능력 향상을 위해 교사가 취해야 할 기본적인 태도에 대해 말한다. 두 번째 논문에서 Bassano는 다양한 형태의 말하기 연습을 위한 집단학습 방법을 구체적으로 소개하고 있고 다음으로 Doff가 소개한 몇 가지 의사소통 활동(communicative activities)은 의사소통을 위한 연습(communicative drills)에 포함되는 것들이다. 이어서 Papalia는 특별히 진정한 의사소통(true communication)을 유도하는 데 필요한 교사의 역할을 기술하면서 자신의 의사를 솔직하게 표현하게 할 수 있는 학습 활동들을 묘사한다. 무엇보다도 그의 학습 활동에서는 학생들이 스스로의 생각을 전달하기 위해 필요한 어휘를 알고 싶어 하고 서로 관심 있게 경청하는 모습이 관찰되었다고 실제로 참여했던 외국어 교사들의 말을 빌려 결론짓는다. 마지막으로 유창한 말하기 능력 향상을 위한 효과적인 교수 활동으로 꼽히는 역할 극(role-play)에 대해 그것의 종류, 교실에서의 제시 절차, 한계점, 효과, 그리고 교육적 가치에 관해 Raz가 전반적인 토론을 하고 있다.

9. SOME SUGGESTIONS FOR THE EFL CONVERSATION CLASS

In teaching and observing conversation classes in EFL, I have found many problems, and to solve them I have developed, through the years, the following suggestions:

1. Speak the language being learned.
2. Help the students understand how they can acquire the language.
3. Avoid talking about the language.
4. Draw on the passive knowledge of your students.
5. To draw on their passive knowledge, get the students involved.
6. Strive for a classroom atmosphere with a community spirit geared towards learning to communicate in the foreign language.

1. Speak The Language Being Learned

Learning to converse in a foreign language requires frequent practice in speaking and listening. Thus, the first priority for both students and teacher should be using the language.

I have observed, however, that too often this is not the case. Students find security in reverting frequently to their mother tongue. Often the teacher feels pressured to explain things (e. g., instructions, rules, a point of grammar, a function) in the students' mother tongue. While working in a teacher-training program for nonnative (and native) speakers, I was faced with such statements (spoken in beautiful English) as "The students can't understand unless I explain it in my native language," "It takes too long to explain what I want them to do," and "I'm the same nationality. They expect me to speak in our language." My answer to statements like these is from Diller:

> To get a person to think in the language and to use it for communication, we must provide the student with something serious to think about. We must provide something challenging. There is nothing more challenging in a foreign language than trying to learn something new while using the language. If the teacher reverts to the student's native language every time he has something serious to say, then he loses his best opportunities to get the student to concentrate and to think in the foreign language. (1978:77)

2. Help The Students Understand How They Can Acquire The Language

Students bring with them expectations and attitudes from past learning experiences. Many students have studied in programs that were based on such premises as these: (1) language learning is a habit - forming process, and "correct" language should be drilled into the student by the teacher; and (2) students cannot learn from their mistakes. An incorrect response is seen as the beginning of an incorrect habit (Diller 1978:49).

Teaching based on such premises often results in defensive learning.

> Such learning sees the foreign language as a vast set of sounds and words and rules and patterns that are to be transferred from the teacher or textbook into the mind of the student. In this view, the teacher is seen as hurling darts at the learner. If a dart strikes an unprotected area (that is, if the learner makes a mistake in speaking or understanding), the experience is painful. (Stevick 1976:110)

If a student has experienced, and perhaps suffered through, this type of learning, (1) he will probably not be willing to speak a great deal, (2) he will expect the teacher to lead the exercises, (3) he may not be aware that he can learn from mistakes, and (4) he won't be aware that he can learn from his classmates.

To counteract such tendencies I try to teach the students that (1) to acquire the language, especially speaking skills, you need to speak a lot; (2) to acquire the language, you have to initiate the process and raise questions within yourself and search out the answers for yourself (the teacher can only provide you with information, feedback, and encouragement); (3) to acquire the language, you have to go through a process that includes making mistakes (if you make a mistake, this is good, because if you actively pay attention to your mistakes and especially the corrections, you can learn very rapidly); and (4) to acquire the language, you need people with whom to share its use. Native speakers can, of course, share the language with you. However, so can your classmates. Since each member of the class has his own unique experiences in learning, each one will know different things. If you listen, and ask for and accept feedback from other class members, you will learn a great deal.

3. Avoid Talking About The Language

It is easy to talk about language. In fact, you can even talk about talking about language, as I am doing now. However, many students who, for many years, have heard the teacher talk about how to use the language cannot communicate even simple ideas. The students must discover how to use the language through their own experience. This does not mean the teacher should say nothing. The teacher can introduce functions, wisely correct usage, and guide the students through exercises. If this is done simply and with few words, the students can gain a great deal. If it is done in an overly detailed manner, the students will only gain more passive knowledge.

4. Draw On The Students' Passive Knowledge, And Help Them To Make It Active

Since many students have studied the language in a passive setting, they often enter a conversation class unable to express themselves in it. However, they usually have at least two important assets: an abundant store of knowledge about grammar and language in general, and their own unique experience. The teacher can draw on these assets by giving the students as many chances to speak as possible. In other words, "It's not our job to cram the student's head full of new facts, but to take what he/she knows and help him/her to expand it" (McLean 1980:19). We should try to make the students' passive knowledge active.

5. To Draw On The Students' Passive Knowledge, Get Them Involved

To get the students involved, the teacher needs to "do exercises where the students are actively searching out, discovering, and depicting" (Stevick 1976:25). This includes doing exercises in which the students speak much more than the teacher.

Many types of approaches and exercises can fulfill this purpose. Strip stories, Via's technique using plays, role playing and simulation exercises, problem-solving exercises, community-language learning, and the silent way all get the students involved in their own and each other's learning process.

As to which approach the teacher should choose, I agree with Mullins (1980), who suggests that the successful foreign-language teacher — the one who is self-confident professionally — is the one who can eclectically choose his techniques on the basis of his own personality, the students' personalities, and the local situation.

6. The Teacher Should Consciously Maintain Control Of The Exercises

How successful an exercise is often depends on how well it is presented. Facilitators have long known the importance of consciously thinking about and organizing an exercise before presenting it to a group.

To *facilitate* means to make learning easier. This concept is certainly relevant to teaching EFL skills. If I can make the process of learning easier for the students, I am doing my job. Our job as teachers is not only to present information, exercises, and a means for the students to get feedback, but also to help them learn as quickly and easily as possible. Learning should and can be easy, and the way the teacher presents an exercise has much to do with how easy it is for the students to acquire the language.

Pfeiffer and Jones (1972) present a model for facilitating an exercise so that it is clear for the learner. It consists, basically, of three stages: (1) brief, (2) do, and (3) debrief.

To *brief* means to frame the exercise or define exactly what task is expected of the learner. This includes directions, time limits, rules, etc. In EFL it is important that the students know exactly what they are to do. They should also know, in most cases, what the exercise is designed to teach them (e. g., how to request, when to apologize, or to understand the behavior differences between accepting a gift in their culture and, say, American culture).

To *do* means to carry out the instructions given. It is important for both students and teacher to comply with the instructions.

To *debrief* means to go over what happened during the exercise, and to discuss what was difficult or easy. If the exercise is a problem-solving exercise with only one possible solution, it is a time to help the students discuss how well they did and the reasons for their success or failure. Unfortunately, many teachers ignore this step. I think it is important, as it often acts as a catalyst in helping students realize their abilities, their weaknesses, and what they need to learn within themselves. It also serves as an opportunity for the teacher to maintain his authoritarian role as well as provide motivation for the students.

7. Strive For A Classroom Atmosphere With A Community Spirit Geared Towards Learning To Communicate In The Foreign Language

The teacher can best understand his own limits in creating such an atmosphere by understanding what motivates the students. Each student will be motivated differently, depending on his experience. The foreign language teacher often discovers that primary motivation for students is "instrumental" (Lambert 1963). Many students study the language in order to pass a test, obtain a degree, get a good job, or to go abroad for university study. Often these far-off goals lack immediate relevance for the students. Creating a community spirit, in the sense of having the students help one another acquire the language, is difficult under such circumstances. Students who are "integratively" (Lambert 1963) motivated tend to help one another more by providing feedback, raising questions, and generally encouraging one another.

An "integrative" motivation is based on such factors as general interest in the language, attitudes toward the teacher, and ability to strive toward goals (Stevick 1976: 48). The talented teacher, through his own personality, can help to encourage students to become more integratively motivated. For example, if the teacher creates a favorable and realistic image of himself, of the language he is teaching and the culture to which it relates, the students will tend to be more attracted toward the language and its culture than if these are presented in an unfavorable way. The teacher can also make the language as interesting as possible through the types of exercises he uses.

Much of this has to do with the teacher's own personality and behavior, which he needs to be constantly aware of and which he must change if necessary. A teacher who is defensive and over-critical, who lacks candor and has little empathy for the students' opinions and feelings, will not be able to create a climate favorable for learning beyond the "instrumental" level (e. g., a grade). In such an environment, a community spirit will never evolve, unless it's against the teacher!

If, however, a teacher builds what Barnlund (1968) calls "a constructive communicative relationship" with the students, a more favorable climate for learning results. To do this, the teacher (1) must be willing to become involved with the students, and to show a positive regard for them; he should not try to manipulate them into doing what he wants, nor should he try to stop them from saying things that displease him; (2) must be empathetic toward the students' problems and feelings, being especially careful not to project his own perceptions onto the student; (3) must allow a permissive psychological climate, sharing feelings and withholding judgment (students who feel they are being judged every time they speak are not going to speak a great deal); (4) must listen openly to the students, focusing on the things they say through inflections and nonverbal behavior as well as through words, and not answering until they have finished speaking; (5) must be genuine and consistent in dealing with the students — being honest with them, and making sure the things he says and does accurately reflect his real thoughts and feelings.

From Gebhard, J. G. (1982). Some suggestions for the EFL conversation class, *English Teaching Forum, 20, 2,* pp. 14-16.

10. DEVELOPING SUCCESSFUL CONVERSATION GROUPS

Ask any student of English as a second language what it is that he or she wants from the language class experience and nine times out of ten the answer will be, "More conversation practice." We have thought about this request frequently and have wondered just what our students mean. If students are living and studying in the United States, don't they have plenty of opportunity to practice their English? Isn't the free conversation experience waiting for them daily just out of the classroom door?

We believe that students are, in fact, asking for more opportunity to become themselves in the new language. They want to become enthusiastically and authentically involved. They want to know that they are genuinely respected and treated as individuals by their teachers and classmates. It is so easy for our classes to become mechanistic and dull for the students. It is certainly easier to provide rote drills and endless pattern practice for them than it is to devise meaningful and relevant communication! We may be giving them ample opportunities to manipulate their new language, but too little time to become truly involved.

Outside of class, our students may have the chance to interact with the clerk in the market, the postmaster or the bus driver, but personal communication is often only available with friends from the same native language background. Many times real conversation with native speakers of English is severely limited.

Being aware of the input students receive both in and out of the classroom, we have often experimented with the free conversation session. Sometimes we succeed and we are able to touch our students in just the right spot and they "take off." Sometimes we see our great plans fall flat! It often seems like a case of good or bad luck — no guarantees. Many times we put our students in a circle, give them a topic for discussion that we think is particularly stimulating and we see them just sit and look at one another in an embarrassing silence, constrained, nervous, and tense. We end up bailing out the group and carrying the bulk of the dialogue ourselves! Often, too, there is one aggressive student who seems to feel a need to be the center of attention at all times, a student who shows little awareness of functional group interaction patterns, and even less self-discipline. Other times, we have one or two students who are either too shy to participate or who have such low self-esteem that they feel they have nothing of interest to offer the group. (What do I have to contribute? Who could possibly be interested in what I have to say?)

Another very real problem is that most of our foreign students come to us from an academic background that is typified by straight rows of desks, all eyes to the front on the teacher who is directing each classroom activity like a conductor leading an orchestra. They have had no experience in directing their own classroom use of language, and consequently fall apart when left to their own devices. Many subconsciously assume that learning is not possible without the teacher present.

We have come to believe that when conversation groups fail it is neither the fault of the activities presented, nor due to the lack of creativity or energy expended on the part of the teacher. Hours are spent conscientiously developing and designing activities and topics to cue exciting and effective conversation among the students. Our hearts are in the right place! Rather, the problem lies with unrealistic expectations. We put a room full of strangers into a circle, and we expect them to act as close friends before they even know or trust each other. We expect them to be well versed in the dynamics of group process such as turn talking, interrupting, active listening, etc. We expect them to know how to deal with the more vocal members and draw out the more timid or self-conscious ones. They are expected to know how to conduct themselves as a cohesive entity with no previous experience at self-direction in the classroom. Too often we give them topics that are too hot to handle —topics that require a great deal of personal disclosure.

What we propose as a solution to these problems is a progressive format or *sequencing* of strategies in the conversation class which carefully prepares students, that systematically breaks down student stereotypes of classroom procedure and allows them to begin interacting democratically and independently. Through this approach, students learn step-by-step, functional interaction techniques at the same time the group spirit or trust is being built. By careful sequencing of strategies, plenty of attention can be given to the boisterous students in an acceptable manner and the quiet, retiring ones can be drawn into action in a painless procedure. All interpersonal activities should move from low-risk, non-personal content, such as games, information gathering, reporting, problem solving, etc., to activities which ask for the sharing of personal values, beliefs and feelings.

Through classroom experimentation, we have identified and worked with six activity categories or strategies.[1] We call them: restructuring, one-centered, unified group, dyads, small group, large group. Each one of the hundred or so activities we introduce to our conversation classes fits into one of these strategies. The objectives and formats are as follows:

1) The six strategies were originally developed for a workshop entitled "A Structural Approach to the Conversation Class" for TESOL '80 in San Francisco, presented by Karl J. Krahnke, Mary Ann Christison, and Thomas Schroeder.

Restructuring

1. To break down expected classroom structures.
2. To create opportunities for supportive behavior.
3. To dispel fears and anxieties.
4. To relax both the student and the teacher.

Restructuring activities usually require the students to get up and out of their chairs, to interact physically as a group. There is minimal participation by the teacher. Often the communication is done non-verbally, through action, drawings, or quick-written statements, and is usually non-personal.

One-Centered

1. To provide each student with individual attention and acceptance from the entire group.
2. To increase the likelihood of contributions in the discussions which will follow later.

One-centered activities always put one student in the spotlight for a short time on a voluntary basis. Content can be either personal or non-personal, and, depending on the student's self-confidence, may entail maximum or minimum verbalization, from the front of the class or in his or her seat.

Unified Group

1. To develop co-operation among group members.
2. To emphasize each group member's value to the group.
3. To provide opportunities for group success.

Unified group activities require the participation of each group member. No one may bow out. Each person's contribution is essential to completion of the activity. The teacher is only minimally engaged in the activity, and content may be both personal or non-personal.

Dyads

1. To get students accustomed to dealing openly with their own feelings, sensitivities, and emotions.
2. To provide opportunity for simple interaction with only one other class member at a time.
3. To develop sincere interpersonal communication in the second language.

Paired activities include both personal and non-personal content. Time is usually given to gather thoughts individually before sharing with the partner. Often these activities are followed up with a short written assignment or journal entries.

Small Group

1. To develop in each individual a growing sense of commitment to the group.
2. To develop trust and cooperation among group members.
3. To develop group interaction techniques that facilitate fair interaction.

Group activities require patience and good listening patterns. They require attention sharing, turn-taking, and fair interruptions. The teacher is usually facilitator and participator.

Large Group

The objectives for large groups are the same as for small groups. The only difference is the inclusion of a wider range of individuals whom the student has learned to trust.

We include here 12 sample activities, two for each strategy, to illustrate how the objectives are met. As you read them, consider what activities you personally have done in your conversation classes that might fit into each category or strategy.

STRATEGY TYPE: RESTRUCTURING

Title: Everybody Votes

Hang large newsprint sheets around the room, each sheet having as a heading a conversation topic — politics, religion, family, fun and recreation, work, love and romance, friendship, etc. Ask students to consider what their personal favorite conversation area is, and to signify their choice by going over and standing by the chart. After all have noticed the balance of interests, ask them to move and go stand by the chart that is their least favorite topic of conversation. After all have gotten a feeling for who is in the class and what some of their interests might be, give them all colored pens and ask them to mill about the room considering each chart and ask them to write some graffiti — a comment, a statement or a question they might personally have regarding each topic. Let this activity continue until all have had a chance to write something and to read what others have written.

To process or complete this restructuring activity, you might ask the group as a whole how they felt doing this exercise, what they noticed, what they heard. Or they might sit down in small groups and comment on what they were compelled to write or on something they read that they didn't agree with.

Title: Introductions

Give each student a piece of colored paper (12 x 18) and some colored pens. Ask them to do the following:

Make a picture of yourself that shows us how you feel today, something you have, something you like to do, something you need or want. Under the picture, write three words that end with-ing that tell us three things you do very well. Over the picture write your first name.

Allow five or six minutes for this activity, then have the students pin the drawing to the front of their shirts and have them mill about silently for a few minutes — ask them to get acquainted — to learn a little bit about each other only with their eyes. After they have done this, ask them to stop where they are and think about:

Did you see anything similar to your drawing?
Did you see something very different from your drawing?
What did you see that interested you?
Whom do you think you would like to talk with?
Was there anything you didn't understand?

Now, ask them to mill about again, this time asking questions or making comments or pointing out similarities or differences. After this activity, you might want to ask each student to choose a partner to sit down with and find out a little more about that person.

STRATEGY TYPE: ONE-CENTERED

Title: What Am I?

Prepare 20 three by five cards with the name of an animal or a thing written on each one. These items can range from easy ones like *tree, cat, dog, elephant*, and *book* to more complicated ones like *glue, coca-cola*, and *matches*. The teacher asks for a volunteer from the class to be the first participant. If you don't get a volunteer, pick one of the more aggressive students. The student is then asked to come to the front of the class and sit on a chair.

Instructions. Ask for a volunteer from the class. Have the student come forward and turn around with his or her back to the rest of the class. Now show the class one of the three by five cards with the name of an animal or thing written on it. Pin the card on the student's back. The student now becomes that thing or animal, i. e., *dog, cat, soap*, etc. The volunteer student does not know what he is, but the class does. The only way for the volunteer student to find out what he is, is to ask the class questions. Class members give only the information asked for. Each volunteer is allowed to ask 10 questions of 10 different class members. After five questions, the student may ask one of the class members for a hint. If the student does not get the correct answer after 10 questions, the class may give him hints until he or she finds the answer. Make certain all class members understand the rules before the activity begins.

Instructions. For the shyer, less verbal student, turn the activity around. Let the spotlighted person know what the card says, but not the rest of the class. The class members must ask the questions to find out what is on the card, the focus person only has to answer yes or no! This is, obviously, a very painless, low risk way to be the star of the show.

Title: In the Spotlight

Thought Gathering: Give each student a copy of a list of possible interview questions and allow them a few minutes of quiet reflection — a chance to think about how they might answer the questions.

Sharing. Ask a volunteer to come up to the front of the class and sit comfortably in a chair. Allow group members to ask questions from the list or their own original questions to the volunteer. The one being interviewed has the right to say " I pass," on any question that she or he can't or doesn't want to answer. She or he also has the opportunity after eight minutes of interviewing to ask back to members of the group any question that was posed to him or her. Be sure that the group understands that there is a time limit, a right to pass, and an opportunity to ask the three questions back.

STRATEGY TYPE: UNIFIED GROUP

Title: Line Ups

Ask your students to line up in the room according to a certain pattern (listed examples below). In order to form their lines, it will be necessary for them to speak with each other to determine their relative positions.

Use these ideas and invent your own!

1. Alphabetical order according to last names.
2. Alphabetical order according to native country name.
3. How long have you been in the United States?

4. How long have you studied English?
5. How many brothers and sisters do you have?
6. How many people do you know in this town that are from your native country?
7. What time did you get up this morning?
8. What time did you go to bed last night?
9. How old are you?
10. How tall are you?
11. How many different girlfriends/boyfriends have you had?
12. How long is your hair?
13. Who is wearing the brightest color clothing?
14. How much money do you have in your pocket right now?

Title: Strip Story

Find a short story or make up a story with a very simple plot. Divide the story into parts equal to the number of students in the class. Type each part on a separate piece of paper. Give each student a part of the story in random order. The task is for the class to put the story back together again. Students will have to understand what is contained in each part and will have to ask each other questions in order to discover where the part they have fits into the main plot of the story.

Instructions. You have just been given a slip of paper with a sentence on it. This sentence is part of a larger story. Each member of your group has one sentence from the story. You will now have 5 minutes to memorize the sentence on your paper. After you have memorized your sentence, give the paper to me.

Now give the students 20 minutes to put the story back together again from memory. After the students feel they have the correct order, have them tell the story to the rest of the class. Each individual in the group must remember his or her portion of the story in order for it to be successful.

STRATEGY TYPE: DYADS

Title: Where Do I Put It?

The following two activities involve one student giving directions to his or her partner. A screen of some sort is set up between the two students who sit facing each other so that they can see each other's face and hear each other clearly but cannot see each other's paper or materials. A manila file folder opened out and set on edge works fine for a screen or barrier.

Activity 1. One student has a blank sheet which he or she folds into nine squares and then opens out to use as a game board. The partner has a sheet that has nine squares with a small simple illustration in each square. The illustrations might be something like a cup and saucer, a cat, a tennis racket, an old car, a woman's shoe, a garbage can, a flag, a brush, and a flower. The student with the illustrated sheet must tell his partner what to draw and where to draw it with as much detail as possible. He or she may not use his or her hands and may not show the drawings to the partner. When they are finished, they should compare papers. You might have them then switch roles, using another prepared sheet with different illustrations.

Activity 2. Give all students a piece of paper and have them fold it into nine squares and open it out to form a game board. Give both of the partners an identical set of nine picture cards. Tell the students they must place the pictures on the game board in exactly the same positions, but they must not look at each other's board or pieces. Have one student decide to be the speaker, the other, the listener. The speaker describes the pictures and tells the listener where to place them. When all the pieces are in place, have the students compare and then switch roles.

STRATEGY TYPE: SMALL GROUP

Title : Pictures! Pictures! Pictures!

Divide students into two or three groups with no more than five to a group. Each group will receive 20 pictures to pass around and look at. These should be a variety of pictures from magazines and should be mounted on 8 1/2 x 11 colored construction paper.

Instructions. Your group has just been given 20 pictures to pass around and look at. It will be the responsibility of your group to find things that these pictures have in common and place them in groups. Use your imagination and creativity. For example, let's say I have a picture of a bear, a cat, a dog, and an elephant. These pictures belong in the same group because they are all *animals*. This is something they all have in common. Appoint a secretary for the group. Have that individual write the number or letter of each picture which belongs in the group. Make certain that each picture belongs in a group.

After each group has finished, ask them to come up to the front of the class and display their pictures by groups. The class must see if they can guess what the pictures have in common.

Title: Word Search

Divide the class into groups of three to five. Write a polysyllabic English word on the board, e. g., *Encyclopedia* or *Translation.*

Instructions. I have just written the word _______ on the board. Your group will now have three minutes to make as many words as possible from the letters in this word. Possible words from *Encyclopedia*, for example, would be *can, an, loan*, and *pedal*. Words from *Translation* would be *train, sit, rat,* etc. (Write on board.) Your group will receive a score equal to the number of correct words. Each group should have a secretary. Only the secretary can write words within the group. If you think of a word, tell the group secretary and she or he will write it down. Your group may challenge any of the other groups or correct words. If you do not believe the word they have is correct, you say *challenge*. Look up the word in the dictionary. If you do *not* find the word, you get their point. If you find the word, they get the point. Make certain all class members understand the instructions before going on with the activity.

STRATEGY TYPE: LARGE GROUP

Title: Grab bag

Ask each student in the class to bring a small personal item to class. Tell them what they bring should be a secret. They should not let anyone else in the class know what they are bringing. It's a good idea to tell the students to bring items which are small and which will not break. Show them an average size grocery bag and tell them that all the items from the class must fit in the bag. After you have collected one item from every individual in the class, you are ready to start the activity. (Sometimes it takes several days to get *one* item from everyone, so plan ahead!) Have a volunteer student come up to the front of the class and pick out an object and show it to the class. The class will offer suggestions as to whose object it is and why they believe it is true. After one or two minutes of discussion the student who drew the item should find out if the class was correct.

From Bassano, S. K. & Cristison, M. A. (1987). In *Methodology in TESOL,* Long, M. H. & Richards, J. C. (eds.). Rowley, MA: Newbury House Publisher, pp. 201-207.

11. COMMUNICATIVE ACTIVITIES

1. GUESSING GAMES

A. Guess the picture

(1) The teacher demonstrates a guessing game using a picture.

i) Tell the students that you have a picture (but do not show it to them). In the picture there are a man, a woman and a train. They must find out exactly what the picture looks like by asking questions. You can only answer 'Yes' or 'No' — but you can help them by giving hints (e. g. 'You still don't know where the train is').

ii) When they have a clear idea of the picture, they should try to draw it.

iii) Finally, show them the picture.

— Hiding the picture gives students a genuine reason to ask questions: there is information they need to find out. They also have to listen carefully to the answers, so that they can draw the picture.

— Although the activity as a whole is controlled by the teacher, the students are mainly asking questions that *they* want to ask, not ones the teacher tells them to ask.

(2) The teacher has a set of flashcards with simple pictures (e. g. clothes, food, places, actions). He or she chooses one card, but does *not* show it to the class. They must guess what it is by asking questions, e. g.:

T: Guess how I went to X.
Ss: Did you go by car?
Did you go by bus?
Did you walk?

B. Guess the sentence

The teacher writes a sentence on a piece of paper or card. He or she does not show the sentence, but writes the basic structure on the board, e. g.:

I went (somewhere) to (do something).

Students must guess the exact sentence by asking questions, e. g.:

Did you go to the park?

Did you go to school?
Did you go to the stadium?
Did you play football?

C. Mime

The teacher calls a student to the front and secretly gives her a sentence written on a piece of paper, which describes a simple activity. The student mimes the activity. The other student try to guess the situation.

In any guessing game, it is a good idea for the teacher to stand aside and let students take over the activity.

Guessing games can also be organised with students working in small groups. The teacher gives a picture or a sentence to one student in each group, and the others in the group try to guess it. The pictures or sentences can be circulated from one group to the next, so it is not necessary to produce very many copies.

Some games which are widely used in English language classes:

— *Famous people*: One student pretends to be a famous person (alive or dead) who is known to the others. They try to guess who the person is, by asking questions, e. g.:

Are you alive or dead? (*alive*)
Are you English? (*yes*)
Are you a writer? (*no*)
etc.

— *What's my line*?: One student chooses a job, and mimes a typical activity which it involves. The others try to guess the job by asking questions either about the activity or the job, e. g.:

Were you mending something?
Were you digging?
Do you work outside?
etc.

— *What and where?*: The teacher sends two students out of the room. The other students hide an object. The two students come back and guess what the object is and where it is hidden, by asking questions, e. g.:

Is it made of wood?
Is it a pencil?
Is it on this side of the room?
Is it high or low?
etc.

2. 'INFORMATION GAP' EXERCISES

Many communicative activities are designed to be done by students working in pairs. To create a need to communicate, the two students in each pair are given *different* information. The activity can then work in various ways:

— One student has some information, and the other student has to find it out by asking questions.

— One student has some information and tells it to the other student.

— Both students have different information, and they tell each other.

Here are some exercises for pairwork. In each pair, the two students are given different information.

A.

STUDENT X

This evening	
Tomorrow morning	
Tomorrow Afternoon	
Tomorrow evening	

STUDENT Y

Tonight Kim is going to stay at home, because he wants to write a letter to a friend. Tomorrow morning he has classes as usual at college; but he has the afternoon free, so he's going to help his father repair the roof on their house. In the evening he's been invited out to a party.

Procedure: Students sit in pairs. In each pair, Student X has an empty grid, and Student Y has the text, which he or she does not show to Student X. Student X completes the grid by asking questions, e. g.:

What's he going to do tomorrow afternoon?

B.

STUDENT X

Shopping list
2 packets tea
1 kilo sugar
1 can orange juice
2 kilos rice
1 kilo beans
1 kilo oranges

STUDENT Y

You sell:
tea - 50p a packet
sugar - 30p a kilo
rice - 20p a kilo
orange juice - 25p a can

Procedure: Students sit in pairs. In each pair, Student X is a customer, and has a shopping list. Student Y is a shop assistant, and has a list of items in the shop and their prices. They do not look at each other's list. Student X tries to 'buy' the things on his or her list, e. g.:

A: Have you got any tea?

B: Yes, I have.

A: How much does it cost?

B: 50p a packet.

C: Find ten important differences.

Procedure: The two students in each pair have pictures which are identical except for ten important differences. They do not look at each other's pictures, but try to find the differences by describing their picture, e. g. 'In my picture there's a boy lying in bed.' When they find a difference, they mark it on the picture.

They provide intensive and interesting language practice. Although the exercises are quite controlled and use simple language, the students are really exchanging information and using language communicatively.

3. EXCHANGING PERSONAL INFORMATION

One of the easiest and most interesting forms of communicative activity in the classroom is for students to tell each other about their own lives, interests, experiences, etc. When students talk about themselves, there is a natural 'information gap' because everybody has something slightly different to say.

Work in pairs. Ask your partner questions about his or her daily routine.

Get up?	
Breakfast?	
School?	
Lunch?	
Evening?	
Go out?	

From Doff, A. (1988). *Teach English*, Cambridge: Cambridge University Press, pp. 211-220.

12. TECHNIQUES FOR PROMOTING CONVERSATION IN THE FOREIGN LANGUAGE CLASSROOM

Modern language teachers have a particularly good opportunity for stimulating interaction in the classroom, promoting students' self-awareness, and for developing in pupils more positive self-concepts because the second language can be used for communicating personal concerns, interests and values. However, in order for real communication to take place, teachers should:

— provide a meaningful context in the classroom which involves students' feelings and concerns;

— allow students to learn the words for the things they want to know, rather than insist on teaching structure before vocabulary;

— allow students to respond to certain stimuli without immediately correcting their errors. Let us remember that "error" comes from the Latin word "errare" meaning "to wander";

— cooperate with students to create classroom situations in which there is opportunity for self-expression and where language becomes the tool of communication;

— evaluate how successfully the student engaged in the transaction and not only how well he applied certain structures.

A large number of techniques exist for achieving these goals and have been freely borrowed and adapted by many teachers to encourage discussion in the language classroom and to supplement dialogues and drills. These strategies provide the tools for moving from manipulative drill to communicative language.

The following exercises emanated from the works listed in the *Annotated Readings* and are useful for promoting communication and self-expression in the classroom. Students should not have to participate if they prefer not to do so, nor answer questions they consider too personal. Teachers should also expect to answer questions under the same conditions.

· ***The Interview***. The group interviews one student. This activity gives the student volunteer interviewed a sense of satisfaction and a feeling of importance that comes from being the focus of attention, and it gives the teacher a vehicle for getting students to know each other better. It is of course essential for this activity that there be acceptance, security and mutual respect in the group. There should be no judging or ridicule.

The rules are simple. Members of the group prepare written questions containing a designated structure suggested by the teacher and then take turns asking them. The interviewee answers as many questions as he wishes. If he doesn't want to answer a question, he may exchange roles with his questioner by saying "your answer" and repeating the question. The student who asked the question must now reply and he now becomes the person interviewed by the class. It is understood that a student may only ask a question he would be willing to answer himself.

Specific structures can be practiced.

· ***"You and I".*** This is a variation of the Interview. Students are paired so that they can alternately ask teacher assigned questions of each other. One student asks his partner a question such as "What will you do tomorrow?" (Que haras manana?) and receives an answer. He repeats the same question six times. His partner must give a different answer each time. Then roles are reversed.

· ***Values Continuum.*** The teacher provides students with a worksheet containing a series of belief statements. Students complete the worksheets individually, first from the point of view of an American, then from the point of view of a native whose language they are learning.

This strategy forces students to examine how strongly they feel about certain issues or certain roles that people play and it generates topics of interest for classroom discussion.

1. Parents' authority should be accepted at all times without question.

Strongly Agree	Agree Somewhat	Disagree Somewhat	Strongly Disagree
________	________	________	________

2. Fifteen year old boys are more mature than 15 year old girls.

Strongly Agree	Agree Somewhat	Disagree Somewhat	Strongly Disagree
________	________	________	________

3. Money is more important than friendship.

Strongly Agree	Agree Somewhat	Disagree Somewhat	Strongly Disagree
________	________	________	________

4. It's not important what you do but rather how much money you make.

Strongly Agree	Agree Somewhat	Disagree Somewhat	Strongly Disagree
________	________	________	________

5. Woman have a place in politics.

Strongly Agree	Agree Somewhat	Disagree Somewhat	Strongly Disagree
________	________	________	________

· ***Values Voting.*** Values voting is a quick and simple procedure that enables students to affirm their beliefs on a number of topics. Controversial statements are read to the class in the modern language. Students then indicate their reactions. Those who agree with the statement raise their hands. Those who disagree point their thumbs down. Those who are undecided fold their arms. And those who want to pass do not make any action at all.

This technique can be used to identify areas of controversy and cultural dissimilarities that might profitably be discussed at a later time. Some possible areas of voting and discussion:

1. A girl should not go out alone after 10:00 p.m.
2. Friends should go out in groups to social functions rather than alone or in couples.
3. It is fair for you to be in charge of your younger brothers and sisters.
4. Your parents should approve of your dates.
5. Girls should pay for their part of a date.

. ***Rank order***. Rank order is appropriate strategy for many levels of language instruction. It provides students with practice in choosing from among alternatives and in publicly affirming and explaining their choices. Three or more choices are proposed and students must rank them in order of preference. Beginning students can simply state a choice. More advanced students may defend their preferences if they choose.

1. Would you rather go to ______________?
   a) a football game
   b) a soccer game
   c) a baseball game
2. Where do you like to meet your friends?
   a) at home
   b) at school
   c) at party
3. On Sunday afternoons would you prefer to ______________?
   a) take a walk in the park
   b) watch the football game
   c) listen to a concert

4. Do you prefer your biggest meal of the day ______________?
   a) in the afternoon
   b) in the morning
   c) late evening
5. Which do you prefer for your dessert?
   a) fruit
   b) pies
   c) ice cream

· ***Value Sheets***. Value sheets contain a provocative statement or paragraph and a series of questions designed to lead students through the steps of value clarification. Content may be based on current news stories, cultural selections or on reading selections.

Ideas emanating from cultural topics are particularly fruitful:

1. Money: how it is apportioned and treated.
2. Friendship: how people relate to each other.
3. Love: how people deal with intimate relationships.
4. Religion and morals: personal beliefs.
5. Leisure: how it is used.
6. Politics and social organization: how they affect the individual.
7. Work: attitudes towards work.
8. Family: relationships and roles in the family.
9. Maturity: goals worth striving for.
10 Character traits: how they affect behavior.

Because valuing is an individual matter each student should complete his own answers before discussing them in small groups. Later, teacher and students may select viewpoints which illuminate the issue and make comparisons with the target culture.

Some suggested topics:

A. When greeting one another, close friends kiss each other on each cheek.

Personal Questions:

1. How do you greet your friends?
2. Do you kiss your friend on each cheek when you greet?
3. When do you see men embrace each other?
4. How does a male greet a female friend here?
5. Does your greeting depend on how old you are?

B. Women with children should not work outside the home.

Personal Questions:

1. Should married women seek employment outside the home?
2. Should the husband make the final decision?
3. Should young children (2-5) go to day-care centers?
4. Whose responsibility is child rearing?
5. Why do women choose to work outside the home?
6. Do they all choose for the same reason?

C. Grandparents belong in nursing homes.

Personal Questions:

1. Would you like your grandparents to live with you all the time?
2. Would they interfere with your life? If so, how?
3. Do you think your grandparents would prefer to live with people their own age or with your family?
4. Do you find more value in your grandparents' advice, or in that of your friends?
5. In what ways could your grandparents make your life easier and more enjoyable?

D. Good looks are more desirable than intelligence.

Personal Questions:

1. What is your definition of beauty? (Give five adjectives)
2. What is your definition of intelligence? (Give five adjectives)
3. Which would be more of an advantage to have and why?
4. Which would you prefer your boyfriend or girlfriend to have?
5. Which would you rather possess?

· ***Twenty Things I Like to Do***

The student is asked to list in the modern language twenty activities he likes to do. The purpose is to allow students to decide whether the life they lead is consistent with their values system and to enable them to express their likings in the modern language.

· ***Incomplete Sentences***. Students are given a list of sentence stems that they complete in their own words either orally or in writing. This technique can be effectively used for practicing newly learned grammar and topical vocabulary.

Some sentence stems for reviewing vocabulary and grammar:

1. I am going to visit a farm and I am going to see . . .
2. When I go to a restaurant I like to eat . . .

3. I am going shopping and I am going to buy . . .
4. Before I go to school in the morning I . . .
5. In winter I . . .

· ***Role Playing***. Students act out in various roles. Through this activity students often develop greater insight about their own and other people's problems and behaviors.

1. Setting: Motorist and a policeman.
   A motorist is trying to talk his way out of getting a ticket.
2. Setting: Traveler or tourist and a lost and found clerk.
   A traveler is trying to locate lost baggage at an airline terminal (train station, etc.)
3. Setting: A waiter and a customer.
   The customer is inquiring as to what some of the dishes are. The waiter is explaining.
4. Setting: A gas station attendant and tourist.
   The tourist is trying to get directions.

· ***Variations for Role Playing***. A student is presented with, or chooses a certain setting and has to develop a monologue. Tasks can be assigned to practice specific language features.

1. You arrive at school and find it closed. What do you do?
2. You have just won a contest. The prize is a trip abroad. What four cities will you visit and why?
3. You have a chance to select your next year's teacher. What characteristics does the ideal teacher have?
4. List five places you could hide. (Use of prepositions in, behind, under, etc.)

· ***Advertising***. Students produce an advertisement either similar to those on TV or a satire of them.

· ***Inanimate Object's Point of View***. Students select an inanimate object and have that object tell its story.

For example: "A Day in the Life of a Pen", "a Floor" or "a Piece of Chewing Gum."

· ***Captions and Quotes***. Cut out pictures from the newspaper or magazines. Then have students provide captions and quotes for the pictures.

Communicative exercises are not recreational activities, they are designed to help students to learn and to achieve specific objectives in an active rather than a passive climate. They invite student involvement and concentration. They provide opportunities for effective and needed interpersonal relations and activities and, above all, they promote real communication in the classroom.

Spanish and French high school teachers enrolled in the course, Seminar of Teaching Foreign Languages, at SUNY buffalo implemented the exercise in their classrooms for four weeks. They reported that they used one communicative activity daily for about five to eight minutes of the class time and that students enjoyed talking about cultural similarities, dissimilarities, and about things which were relevant and meaningful to them. In addition, they noticed that students were eager to learn vocabulary necessary to express their thoughts and listened to each other with interest.

From Papalia, A. (1976). Techniques for promoting conversation in the foreign language classroom, *Language Association Bulletin*, pp. 13-16.

13. ROLE-PLAY IN FOREIGN LANGUAGE LEARNING

ROLE-PLAY — A VERSATILE TECHNIQUE

Role-play is used in various ways for various purposes: As an integral part of *Creative Drama*, it promotes personal growth through the release of spontaneity and creativity. In the classroom situation, simultaneous group or pair work is the most effective, leading to every child's maximum involvement. There is no audience and the quality of acting is irrelevant. This method is the most appropriate for the foreign language classroom, since it dispels the inhibitions of diffident and anxious learners. Obviously, our emphasis is on verbal expression, not on pantomime, frequently used in Creative Drama. However, in beginners' classes and especially with young children, pantomime can be very useful, with the language input being provided by the teacher in a dramatic tone of voice, 'the total physical response' helping to imprint the language in the memory.

Role-play is also used *for social values*, the aim being the improvement of human relations, the solving of specific problems in the group. Several pupils enact the situation, usually based on a problem story. Discussion follows and alternative solutions are acted out. Although the audience is actively involved, this method is less suitable for the EFL classroom. However, the educational value of basing role-play on such problem stories, of empathizing with others — stepping into other people's shoes — may well guide our choice of stimuli for role-play.

In *Sociodrama,* the emphasis is on social roles. It is widely used in the training of social workers, youth guides, doctors, teachers and army personnel, the aim being the fostering of social and professional skills. This type of role-playing has been found useful in ESP course, as part of the communicative approach. It is often extended into Simulation Games which include role-play within a more structured framework.

When role-play is used in *Psychodrama*, the aim is basic attitude change. Under the guidance of trained therapists, role-play enables patients to express their tensions and gain insight into deep personal problems. Teachers using role-play in EFL classes need not be afraid they are dabbling in Psychodrama. If the learners are given a wide choice of situations, they themselves will shy away from potentially risky topics. Throughout our experiment, no such problems were reported by the teachers.

The various types of role-play overlap to some extent. The quality they all have in common is the involvement of the whole person in a dramatic situation with 'ordinary life at a standstill.' Man's deep-seated urge or need to express himself through drama, seen both in the primitive ritual and in the dramatic play of the young child, makes role-play a powerful technique. Since the use of language is an integral part of dramatic expression it has been found to foster language development, both in the mother tongue and in foreign language learning.

THE STUDY

In order to verify the above assumptions, a study (Raz, 1980) was carried out in six schools in Israel, involving 200 learners, and investigated the potential effects of role-play on communicative competence, on motivation and on under-achieving foreign language learners. The rationale provided guidelines for experimentation with adolescent EFL learners at the intermediate stage. The teachers were chosen randomly and trained in special workshops. Role-play was used in the experimental classes once a week over a period of 14 weeks.

Communicative Competence Tests, administered before and after the experiment, demonstrated the effectiveness of the technique: on the post-tests the Experimental Group scored significantly higher than the Control Group on all parts of the test. The influence of role-play on motivation was investigated by way of Attitude Questionnaires. These revealed the beneficial effect of role-play on intrinsic motivation, on self-concept and the expectations of success of the learners and on their anxiety when speaking the language.

Besides focusing on individual learners, the case-study approach was used to reveal, with the help of observers, why in certain classes role-play was more successful than in others. This enabled us to draw conclusions as to the conditions necessary for the successful implementation of the technique, summed up in the form of implications for the regular use of role-playing in the classroom.

IMPLICATIONS FOR THE CLASSROOM

Suggested Procedure

The choice of stimulus is extremely important. It must be appropriate to the particular group of learners, of real concern to them, and presented effectively. A teacher who knows his class well can insert role-play frequently, in an unobtrusive way, for instance, during the study of a story, a poem or a song, exploiting the theme and getting the students to suggest situations or encounters for role-play. Other effective stimuli are: Large simple drawings of dramatic situations; snatches of ambiguous dramatic dialogues on tape, objects triggering off dramatic situations (such as keys, diaries, maps, jewellery, letters, newspapers); news items and readers' letters, discussed in class; problem situations based on incidents occurring in the school or community. The introduction can take anything from a few minutes to several lessons.

The students move into role-play, often sitting in their seats, turning to their neighbours or creating groups of three or four; the class may also use available floor-space to move about, as in a park situation, where many themes can be exploited, such as young and old people meeting. The students usually choose their roles from a number of alternatives, or create their own. No role cards are needed, no detailed descriptions of the roles are given. It is a truly learner-centred activity.

The teacher moves about the class, helping out where necessary (for instance when a group cannot get started), but keeping a low profile and *not* correcting mistakes. Work on corrections can be done in another lesson, 'anonymously'. The students switch roles when appropriate, whenever they are ready to do so. The teacher stops the role-play well before it peters out — this may be after just a few minutes or an hour. Even a few minutes of intensive role-play can be extremely valuable.

The teacher may then ask volunteers to say briefly 'what happened' in their group, *not* to enact the scene. Showing off by confident actors tends to inhibit those learners who 'need' role-play most. The reporting should be very brief.

Pre-requisites And Limitations

The kind of role-play recommended in this article is appropriate for intermediate and advanced learners. Some role-playing can be attempted even with a minimal knowledge of the language, as an extension of short dramatic dialogues. If necessary, the teacher should have a say in the way students pair up or form groups. It is important to pair up weak students with more advanced ones, provided they are patient and willing to help. Many weak students enjoy drama, and make good progress even when their knowledge of the language is minimal. When first experimenting with role-play, it is advisable to do so in a class where there is a relaxed, supportive atmosphere. Later, role-play can be used by a confident and experienced teacher to improve the atmosphere in a problematic class.

Pupil expectations may have to be dealt with. Learners who are used to very formal methods must be helped to understand the value of spontaneous personal expression in the foreign language and the inhibiting effect of on-going teacher correction. The teacher's own belief in the value of role-play is crucial, as is the ability to explain its beneficial effects in order to convince people whose doubts might hinder its benefits.

It is advisable for the teacher to take part in role-playing activities before introducing it in the classroom. At the Oranim Teachers' College Creative Drama is taught as an integral part of teacher education and in-service workshops are provided. This also gives teachers the opportunity to observe how role-play is best introduced and to become aware of the role of the teacher as facilitator.

Role-play should become an integral part of study, a regular component, used when the occasion arises, rather than an element injected artificially. The material studied thus provides the necessary linguistic basis for role-play and the students will be exploiting all they have learnt for self-expression.

The Positive Effects Of Role-playing

During role-play, learners are motivated to exploit all their latent knowledge of the foreign language, all they have absorbed through listening and reading. They become more fluent and confident. Their emotional involvement acts as a powerful stimulus.

Macnamara(1973) maintains it is *the need* to use the language which accounts for the speed with which it is learnt in 'nurseries and streets' as compared to classrooms; this is the key that makes 'the linguistic magic' work. When the learner is deeply involved in the conflict situation, he has an inner urge to express himself. Stevick(1976) stresses the effect of emotional involvement on retention. Moreover, some conflict situations are also cognitively challenging; problem-solving is known to be intrinsically motivating. So is the creative element in dramatic expression, which is emotionally very rewarding.

Role-play is perceived by the learner as a rehearsal for real life and therefore as relevant to his aims in learning the language (provided he wishes to be able to speak it). He becomes aware of the usefulness of what he has been learning and of the need to learn more in order to be able to express himself better. Thus his total attitude to learning the language is affected.

The language practised through role-play is easily transferable to real-life situations. This rehearsal also has the effect of 'psychological inoculation,' reducing anxiety and inhibitions when the learner has the opportunity to use the language outside the classroom. Concentration on the problem-situation is in itself liberating and quickens the mind.

The crucial role of self-concept in any learning situation is now fully recognized. Successful communication in the foreign language, however limited, has a beneficial effect on the student's self-concept as a learner of the language. Positive reinforcement by peers and the non-evaluative atmosphere during group-work are contributory factors.

The Educational Value Of The Use Of Role-play

The kind of role-playing described here is obviously different from conventional dialogue work, which is often based on undesirable stereotyping. Many textbooks use the term 'role-play' for structured exercises that are not all personally involving. For maximum language learning to take place, the situations must involve 'real' people expressing 'real' feelings in conflict situations, initiated, as far as possible, by the learners.

This is indeed a learner-centred approach. The teacher abandons her directive role and the frontal set-up disappears. The learners widen their experience by being helped to see problems from different points of view. This is particularly valuable in fighting prejudices of all kinds, for prejudice is one of the greatest evils prevalent in the world. Role-play is also beneficial to the individual: insightful learning and self-expression contribute to personal growth. We have found inhibited adolescents expressing feelings in a way that they would avoid in their mother tongue — English seemed to act as a convenient mask. This also seems to be the reason for their not slipping into their mother tongue, as they might in other heated discussions. In short, role-play helps to make foreign language learning more than just the acquisition of a tool; by arousing a concern for values, it helps to put foreign language teaching on the educational map.

From Raz, H. (1985). Role-play in foreign language learning, *System*, vol. 13, pp. 225-229.

PART FOUR

TEACHING LISTENING

듣기는 언어의 네 가지 기능으로 간주되는 듣기, 말하기, 읽기, 쓰기 중에서 말하기와 함께 구두 언어(oral language)라고 부르기도 하고 읽기와 함께 이해기능(receptive skill or decoding skill)이라고 하기도 한다. 특히 이해기능으로서의 듣기는 한때 수동적 기술(passive skill)로 간주되기도 했으나 hearing과 구별되는 개념으로서의 listening(comprehension)은 분명히 능동적 기술(active skill)로서 역할이 여러 가지이다. 즉, hearing을 한다는 것은 단순히 어휘, 발음, 문법과 같은 언어의 개별적 요소를 인식하는 것이기 때문에 내용의 이해와는 별개인데 반하여 listening은 반드시 이해를 수반한다. 따라서 우리는 hearing을 하면서도 listening은 안 하는 경우를 항상 경험하고 있다. 가까운 예로 TV뉴스를 시청 할 때 소리를 hearing하면서도 listening은 안 하기 일쑤다. 왜냐하면 자신이 관심 있는 부분만 주의해서 listening하기 때문이다. 그리고 이때도 들리는 새로운 정보를 그대로 수용하는 것이 아니라 이미 알고 있는 다른 관련정보(schema, script)와 연관시켜 재구성하게 된다. 따라서 listening은 능동적 기술인 것이다. 그리고 듣기교육의 목적은 자연스러운 상황에서 원어민의 말을 이해할 수 있도록 하는 것이라고 말할 수 있다.

이 장에서는 이와 같은 듣기기능의 지도에 있어서 듣기에 관한 이론과 지도의 실제가 여러 논문을 통해 제시되고 있다. 먼저 'Listening: Problems and Solutions'에서 Yagang은 듣기의 정의를 내리고 듣기에 있어서 문제가 되는 요인들과 이들을 해결하는 방안의 제시와 함께 다양한 듣기 지도 활동들을 단계별로 나열하고 있다.

두번째, 듣기를 화산에 비유한 Burbidge는 'Looking at Volcanoes and Listening Comprehension'에서 모국어에서 듣기를 할 때 특징이 되는 것들, 그리고 이 특징 각각이 듣기를 교수할 때 암시하는 것들을 차례대로 적고 있다. 이어서 시각자료를 이용한 듣기학습 활동들을 구체적인 예와 함께 제시한다.

다음으로, Spaventa는 듣기가 왜 능동적 과정(active process)인가를 설명하고 교실에서 듣기 지도에 사용되는 언어자료가 실제의 그것과 어떻게 다른 지를 보여주면서 몇 가지 듣기활동을 소개하고 마지막으로 Rathet는 듣기지도에서 그림 그리기를 이용할 수 있는 여러 가지 방법들을 보여준다.

14. LISTENING: PROBLEMS AND SOLUTIONS

In teaching listening comprehension we must be careful not to go to extremes, either by being concerned too exclusively with theories without thinking about their application to teaching, or by obstinately following frozen routines — opening the textbook and explaining new words, playing the tape recorder, and asking/answering questions. It is essential for a teacher to have an overall understanding of what listening is, why it is difficult for foreign-language learners, and what some solutions may be. The vital question is how to bridge the gap between an analysis of listening and actual classroom teaching.

WHAT IS LISTENING?

Listening is the ability to identify and understand what others are saying. This involves understanding a speaker's accent or pronunciation, his grammar and his vocabulary, and grasping his meaning (Howatt and Dakin, 1974). An able listener is capable of doing these four things simultaneously. Willis (1981: 134) lists a series of micro-skills of listening, which she calls *enabling skills*. They are:

- predicting what people are going to talk about
- guessing at unknown words or phrases without panicking
- using one's own knowledge of the subject to help one understand
- identifying relevant points; rejecting irrelevant information
- retaining relevant points (note-taking, summarizing)
- recognizing discourse markers, e. g., *Well; Oh, another thing is; Now, finally*; etc.
- recognizing cohesive devices, e. g., *such as* and *which*, including link words, pronouns, references, etc.
- understanding different intonation patterns and uses of stress, etc., which give clues to meaning and social setting
- understanding inferred information, e. g., speakers' attitude or intentions

WHAT ARE SOME LISTENING PROBLEMS?

The evidence that shows why listening is difficult comes mainly from four sources; the message to be listened to, the speaker, the listener, and the physical setting.

The Message

Content: Many learners find it more difficult to listen to a taped message than to read the same message on a piece of paper, since the listening passage comes into the ear in the twinkling of an eye, whereas reading material can be read as long as the reader likes.

The listening material may deal with any area of life. It might include street gossip, proverbs, new products, and situations unfamiliar to the student. Also, in spontaneous conversation speakers frequently change topics.

The content is usually not well organized.

In many cases listeners cannot predict what speakers are going to say, whether it is news report on the radio, an interviewer's questions, and everyday conversation, etc.

Messages on the radio or recorded on tape cannot be listened to at a slower speed. Even in conversation it is impossible to ask the speaker to repeat something as many times as the interlocutor might like.

Linguistic Features: Liaison (the linking of words in speech when the second word begins with a vowel, e. g., an *orange* /ənɔrɪnʤ / and *elision* (leaving out a sound or sounds e. g., *suppose* may be pronounced /spəuz/ in rapid speech) are common phenomena that make it difficult for students to distinguish or recognize individual words in the stream of speech. They are used to seeing words written as discrete entities in their textbooks.

If listening materials are made up of everyday conversation, they may contain a lot of colloquial words and expressions, such as *stuff* for *material*, *guy* for *man*, etc., as well as slang. Students who have been exposed mainly to formal or bookish English may not be familiar with these expressions.

In spontaneous conversations people sometimes use ungrammatical sentences because of nervousness or hesitation. They may omit elements of sentences or add something redundant. This may make it difficult for the listener to understand the meaning.

The Speaker

Ur (1984: 7) points out that "in ordinary conversation or even in much extempore speech-making or lecturing we actually say a good deal more than would appear to be necessary in order to convey our message. Redundant utterances may take the form of repetitions, false starts, re-phrasings, self-corrections, elaborations, tautologies, and apparently meaningless additions such as *I mean* or *you know*." This redundancy is a natural feature of speech and may be either a help or a hindrance, depending on the students' level. It may make it more difficult for beginners to understand what the speaker is saying; on the other hand, it may give advanced students more time to "tune in" to the speaker's voice and speech style.

Learners tend to be used to their teacher's accent or to the standard variety of British or American English. They find it hard to understand speakers with other accents.

Spoken prose, as in news broadcasting and reading aloud written texts, is characterized by an even pace, volume, pitch, and intonation. Natural dialogues, on the other hand, are full of hesitations, pauses, and uneven intonation. Students used to the former kinds of listening material may sometimes find the latter difficult to understand.

The Listener

Foreign-language students are not familiar enough with cliches and collocations in English to predict a missing word or phrase. They cannot, for example, be expected to know that *rosy* often collocates with *cheeks* nor to predict the last word will be something like *rage* when they hear the phrase *he was in a towering* .... This is a major problem for students.

Lack of sociocultural, factual, and contextual knowledge of the target language can present an obstacle to comprehension because language is used to express its culture (Anderson and Lynch, 1988).

Foreign-language learners usually devote more time to reading than to listening, and so lack exposure to different kinds of listening materials. Even our college students majoring in English have no more than four hours' regular training per week.

Both psychological and physical factors may have a negative effect on perception and interpretation of listening material. It is tiring for students to concentrate on interpreting unfamiliar sounds, words, and sentences for long periods.

Physical Setting

Noise, including both background noises on the recording and environmental noises, can take the listener's mind off the content of the listening passage.

Listening material on tape or radio lacks visual and aural environmental clues. Not seeing the speaker's body language and facial expressions makes it more difficult for the listener to understand the speaker's meaning.

Unclear sounds resulting from poor-quality equipment can interfere with the listener's comprehension.

SOME SOLUTIONS

What can teachers do to help students master the difficulties?

Not all the problems described above can be overcome. Certain features of the message and the speaker, for instance, are inevitable. But this does not mean that the teacher can do nothing about them. S/he can at least provide the students with suitable listening materials, background and linguistic knowledge, enabling skills, pleasant classroom conditions, and useful exercises to help them discover effective listening strategies. Here are a few helpful ideas:

The Message

1. Grade listening materials according to the students' level, and provide authentic materials rather than idealized, filtered samples. It is true that natural speech is hard to grade and it is difficult for students to identify the different voices and cope with frequent overlaps. Nevertheless, the materials should progress step by step from semi-authenticity that displays most of the linguistic features of natural speech to total authenticity, because the final aim is to understand natural speech in real life.

2. Design task-oriented exercises to engage the students' interest and help them learn listening skills subconsciously. As Ur (1984: 25) has said, "Listening exercises are most effective if they are constructed round a task. That is to say, the students are required to do something in response to what they hear that will demonstrate their understanding." She has suggested some such tasks: expressing agreement or disagreement, taking notes, marking a picture or diagram according to instructions, and answering questions. Compared with traditional multiple-choice questions, task-based exercises have an obvious advantage: they not only test the students' listening comprehension but also encourage them to use different kinds of listening skills and strategies to reach their destination in an active way.

3. Provide students with different kinds of input, such as lectures, radio news, films, TV plays, announcements, everyday conversation, interviews, storytelling, English songs, and so on.

Brown and Yule (1983) categorize spoken texts into three broad types: static, dynamic, and abstract. Texts that describe objects or give instructions are static texts; those that tell a story or recount an incident are dynamic texts; those that focus on someone's ideas and beliefs rather than on concrete objects are abstract texts. Brown and Yule suggest that the three types of input should be provided according to the difficulties they present and the students' level. They draw the figure shown below, in which difficulty increases from left to right, and, within any one type of input, complexity increases from top to bottom.

STATIC	DYNAMIC		ABSTRACT
description	description / instruction	storytelling	opinion-expressing
few elements which may be difficult to distinguish			
many elements which may be difficult to distinguish			

← less difficult more difficult →

(adapted from Brown and Yule, 1983: 107)

4. Try to find visual aids or draw pictures and diagrams associated with the listening topics to help students guess or imagine actively.

The Speaker

1. Give practice in liaisons and elisions in order to help students get used to the acoustic forms of rapid natural speech. It is useful to find rapidly uttered colloquial collocations and ask students to imitate native speakers' pronunciation. Listed below are a few of these from Ur (1984: 46):

let's have	/'letsəv/
there isn't any	/'ðrizndeni/
you shouldn't have	/'ju:'ʃudndəv/
you and me	/'ju:ən'mi:/
tell him, tell her	/'telm, 'telə/

2. Make students aware of different native-speaker accents. Of course, strong regional accents are not suitable for training in listening, but in spontaneous conversation native speakers do have certain accents. Moreover, the American accent is quite different from the British and Australian. Therefore, it is necessary to let students deal with different accents, especially in extensive listening.

3. Select short, simple listening texts with little redundancy for lower-level students and complicated authentic materials with more redundancy for advanced learners. It has been reported that elementary-level students are not capable of interpreting extra information in the redundant messages, whereas advanced listeners may benefit from messages being expanded, paraphrased, etc. (Chaudron 1983).

The Listener

1. Provide background knowledge and linguistic knowledge, such as complex sentence structures and colloquial words and expressions, as needed.
2. Give and try to get, as much feedback as possible. Throughout the course the teacher should bridge the gap between input and students' response and between the teacher's feedback and students' reaction in order to keep activities purposeful. It is important for the listening-class teacher to give students immediate feedback on their performance. This not only promotes error correction but also provides encouragement. It can help students develop confidence in their ability to deal with listening problems. Student feedback can help the teacher judge where the class is going and how it should be guided.
3. Help students develop the skills of listening with anticipation, listening for specific information, listening for gist, interpretation and inference, listening for intended meaning, listening for attitude, etc., by providing varied tasks and exercises at different levels with different focuses.

A TYPOLOGY OF ACTIVITIES FOR A LISTENING LESSON

In the following I suggest a variety of exercises, tasks, and activities appropriate to different stages of a listening lesson (pre-listening, while-listening, and post-listening). Good classroom activities can themselves be effective solutions to listening problems.

The list covers a wide range of listening activities from simple to more sophisticated. Some teachers, accustomed to following exactly the exercises and tasks provided in the textbook without thinking about whether they are suitable for their students or not, might look on these activities as extra work and a burden. I would like to point out that it is a pleasure and a positive experience to try various exercises, tasks, and classroom activities, for successful lessons depend on the teacher's knowing and using a variety of teaching methods. Teachers should have at their fingertips a set of exercises, tasks, and activities that they can use with their classes whenever they may be needed.

STAGES	ACTIVITIES	EXPLANATION/DEMONSTRATION
PRE-LISTENING	warm-up exercises 1. elicitation/discussion about the topic (perhaps based on visuals, title)	a. to elicit something associated with the topic b. to encourage students to exchange ideas/opinions about the topic
	2. brainstorming	a. word-star: ask students to predict the words and expressions likely to appear in the passage. Teacher writes them on the blackboard. b. expressing hypotheses about the content of the passage, based on previous knowledge, by writing notes down
	3. games	a. for warming-up relaxation b. for training in basic listening skills, e.g., miming words and expressions heard; minimal-pair distinctions
	4. guiding questions	· teacher asks/writes questions that help students exploit passages
WHILE-LISTENING	1. comparing	· to compare passage with prediction in pre-listening
	2. obeying instructions	· students are given instructions and show comprehension by physical movement, finishing a task, etc.
	3. filling in gaps	· e.g., students hear the utterances of only one of the participants and are asked to reconstruct those of the others
	4. repetition	· students are asked to repeat short phrases or complete utterances recorded
	5. detecting differences or mistakes	· students listen to passages, responding only when they come across something different or wrong
	6. ticking off items (bingo)	· students listen to a list of words and tick off or categorize them as they hear them
	7. information transfer	· maps/plans/grids/forms/lists/pictures, etc.
	8. paraphrase	· students are asked to focus on certain sentences and paraphrase them
	9. sequencing	· e.g., students are asked to give the right order for a series of pictures
	10. information search	· students listen to a passage and take notes on the segments that answer a particular question
	11. filling in blanks	· students are given the transcript of a passage with some words missing and must fill in the blanks while listening
	12. matching	· e.g., students are asked to match items that have the same meaning as those they hear
POST-LISTENING	1. answering to show comprehension of messages	· e.g., multiple-choice or true/false questions
	2. problem solving	· students hear all the information relevant to a particular problem and then set themselves to solve it
	3. summarizing	· students are given several possible summary-sentences and asked to say which of them fits a recorded text
	4. jigsaw listening	· different groups of students listen to different but connected passages, each of which supplies some part of what they need to know. Then they come together to exchange information in order to complete a story or perform a task
	5. writing as follow-up to listening activities	· e.g., letters/telegrams/postcards/ messages, etc., related to passages
	6. speaking as follow- up to listening activities	· e.g.,debate/interview/discussion/roleplay/dramatization, etc., associated with the passages heard

CONCLUSION

Some teachers think that listening is the easiest skill to teach, whereas most students think it is the most difficult to improve. This contradiction tells us that there are some things about teaching listening that need to be explored. Perhaps those who say it is "the easiest to teach" mean that it does not require much painstaking lesson preparation and all they need to do is play the tapes and test the students' comprehension. But is there nothing more to teaching listening than testing? We must find out all we can about how listening can be improved and what activities are useful to this end and then use this knowledge and these activities in our own classroom.

■ References

Anderson, A. and T. Lynch. (1988). *Listening*. London: Oxford University Press.

Brown, G. and G. Yule. (1983). *Teaching the spoken language*. Cambridge: Cambridge University Press.

Chaudron, C. (1983). Foreign talk in the classroom — An aid to learning? In *Classroom oriented research in second language acquisition*, ed. H. Seliger and M. H. Long. Rowley, Mass.: Newbury House.

Howatt, A. and J. Dakin. (1974). *Language laboratory materials*, ed. J. P. B. Allen, S. P. B. Allen, and S. P. Corder.

Ur, P. (1984). *Teaching of English as a second or foreign language.* Cambridge: Cambridge University Press.

Willis, J. (1981). *Teaching English through English.* London: Longman.

From Yagang, F. (1993). Listening: problems and solutions. *English Teaching Forum*, Jan. pp. 16-19.

15. LOOKING AT VOLCANOES AND LISTENING COMPREHENSION

If you wish to know the relationship between looking at volcanoes and listening comprehension immediately, you might refer to this article's last two paragraphs, which also contain the essence of what I am trying to say here. In this way you can kill two birds with one stone because you can skip the rest of the article if you are pressed for time.

I would like to point out six characteristics of listening for a native speaker and their implications for teaching. I will then indicate nine exercise types that can be used for listening comprehension with examples from commercial materials. Finally, I will describe some listening exercises developed for video lessons made by myself and my colleagues, Maurice Clapisson, Virginia Fox, Elizabeth Kahn and Laura Layton, for the United Nations Staff Language Programme.

There are six things we can say about listening in the real world (Brown, 1978, Porter and Roberts, 1981, Brown and Yule, 1983) :

(1) The spoken language and the written language are very different. Typically spoken language is not very well organized; does not consist of complete sentences; is full of hesitations, ums and ahs, interruptions and repetition; and does not necessarily contain a lot of information. Written language on the other hand, is more coherent and better organized, consists of complete sentences, has no ums and ahs and is very dense in information (at least we hope!).

The implication for teaching listening is that perhaps we should expose students to a lot of *authentic speech* as opposed to artificial dialogues or written language read aloud. One interesting technique suggested by Peggy Anderson of the University of Wichita is to have students record an interview from a magazine having seen only a skeleton of the interview, on the basis of which they could ad lib and thus produce quite a bit of natural speech.

(2) When we are listening we usually get a lot of *visual help*, which facilitates understanding. We can see the people who are speaking — their faces, their expressions, their gestures. We also see the situation we are in, the location, the background.

The implication for teaching listening would seem to be to use a lot of visuals to help our students understand. The ideal, of course, is to invite native speakers to the classroom and have conversations with them or to show videos of native speakers talking. This is not always possible, but we can make liberal use of slides, photos, pictures, maps, graphs and realia to fill in the visual details instead of using only a tape recorder. While it is true that when listening to the radio, a telephone conversation, an announcement or a record, we do not get visual help, these may be higher-level listening skills to be introduced gradually and carefully.

(3) Frequently when listening, native speakers have *expectations* about how the conversation might go, what they are going to hear, what their interlocutor is going to say. Based on our *knowledge of the world* we can *predict* the kind of things that might be said. For example, if you call up to rent a car, you have some idea about how the conversation will go, about the kind of questions you will be asked, the kind of information you will give. You would be surprised if the agent started to talk about the latest movie or asked after your family.

What is the implication for teaching listening? It might be that *pre-listening activities* are very important, so that our students are prepared for what they will hear, so that they have expectations and can predict. For example, if the students are going to listen to an interview the teacher has recorded, the teacher could invite the interviewee to the class to talk to the students first or to answer questions. Other pre-listening activities could take the form of pictures or maps, a quiz, a reading text, a check-list or simply a discussion about what is to be heard. It might be that such pre-listening activities are more important for helping our students to understand than post-listening exercises.

(4) When we listen as native speakers we have a lot of *contextual knowledge* about both the speakers and the situation we are in. We often know the age, sex, rank, and job of the speakers, and what attitudes they might have. We also have information based on prior knowledge of the setting and whether it is formal or informal, and we act accordingly.

The implication here is that in pre-listening activities we should probably make sure that our students are privy to contextual information before listening. This can be done with pictures or discussion or by encouraging students to guess attitudes, roles, register and settings

(5) Very often we have a *purpose* for listening. We do not necessarily want or need to hear everything that is said. We typically listen for specific pieces of information and, once we have hit the target, may well tune out. For example, as I listen to the news each morning, I do not hear everything; I am listening for the weather forecast so I'll know whether to wear my long jeans or not.

The implication here, I think, is not to expect our students to do what we do not do ourselves. Rather let us give them a *reason* for listening and ask them to listen for something specific. This would imply *while-listening activities* rather than post-listening exercises. Such tasks could be checking off things they hear on a list, locating something on a map or matching pictures with what is heard.

(6) A lot of spoken language is simply for *social interaction* and not for the exchange

of information. It is often to exchange pleasantries and maintain relationships with people. Sometimes we do not listen to what a person says but just wait our turn politely to say, and the other person does the same — a kind of turn-taking ritual.

The implication for teaching listening is perhaps not to have students listening for facts all the time, but to encourage them to attend to attitudes, feelings, gestures, expressions, body language. And also how people keep conversations going and take turns with phrases such as "By the way," "That reminds me," "That's interesting"(although it may not be), and all the ums and ahs.

Having looked at six characteristics of listening, I would now like to describe nine types of exercises which can be used to help our students understand (Richards, 1983). And I will show examples from commercial textbooks, some of which have been shortened for presentation here, which take into account some of these characteristics. All of these books contain visuals and both pre- and while-listening activities.

(1) **Matching** is to match what you hear with some pictures or with a series of sentences.

(2) **Transferring** is putting what you hear into a non-linguistic medium, such as drawing a picture, locating something on a map or making a graph.

(3) **Transcribing** is simply writing what you hear. The most traditional form of this exercise is of course straight dictation, but there are variations of this, for example, the cloze-type dictation.

note	trip
widower	fools around
neighborhood	pay attention
behavior	agree

LISTENING COMPREHENSION

A. Fill in. Listen to these sentences. Fill in the new vocabulary words from the list above.

1. He was away for three days on a business ________________.
2. When a student ________________ in class, the teacher seats the student alone in a corner.
3. No, he isn't divorced. He's a ________________.
4. Please ________________ when I give the directions.
5. If this ________________ continues, the teacher is going to call her parents.
6. I ________________ with you. He's an excellent student.

(4) **Scanning** is listening for specific details only, instead of trying to understand everything at once.

Read the second part of Terry's journal and listen to the conversation between Kim and Ray about someone they met at the airport.

▶ Terry and Kim have a different opinion about this person. What's the difference? Circle the correct answer.

1. Terry is/isn't suspicious of the man who gave them a ride.
2. Kim is/isn't suspicious of the man who gave them a ride.
3. Ray agrees with Kim/Terry.

(5) **Condensing** is summarizing what you hear or making an outline. This can be conveniently done in a chart.

Carolyn, Mary and Bart and Robin are talking about the places they have been to and what they did there.

1. Listen to the tape and write as much information in the chart as you can:

	Carolyn	Bart	Mary	Robin
Countries visited				
Food				
Drink				
Sights				
Other Activities				

(6) **Extending** is going beyond what you hear and trying to fill in the missing details. For example, students listen to one side of a conversation and have to guess the other sides.

This is Tom's side of a telephone conversation with Catherine.

As you listen. . .

Try to imagine what Catherine is saying during the pauses.

After you listen. . .

Write some possible reponses that Catherine could have given after Tom said:

1. Why are you going to be late?
2. I guess you don't love me anymore.
3. I know I'm not making much money, but that's not the point.
4. There's a lot of work for photographers in Los Angeles. Why don't we move there?

(7) **Recalling** is trying to remember details of a factual kind.

After listening to this documentary you should expect to know how the Talking Books for the Blind scheme works as well as understanding some of the technical details about the equipment that is used.

(8) **Inferring** is making inferences or evaluating what you hear.

Recognizing and interpreting attitudes

This time, listen to the woman's remarks about each item. Can you recognize and interpret her attitude from the words and tone she uses. Listen to the tape and identify the remarks in the grid below. Write next to the remark the number which corresponds to the attitude taken by the woman. You may consider that her remark can be interpreted by more than one of the attitudes listed below. If so, note down the other numbers and after listening, discuss your selection with your partner and teacher.

Attitudes:

Sarcasm 1 Reluctant acceptance 2 Acceptance with understanding 3 Objection 4 Patience 5 Irritation 6

	Goods	Remarks	Attitude number
i)	Cream	'Ooh dear! Well I, well I suppose yes I can beat it up. . .'	
ii)	Strawberries	'Well, all right. O. K.'	
iii)	Chicken	'Well, I suppose if it was the best you could get, it was the best you could get.'	
iv)	Tomatoes	'Well thank you for putting them under the chicken.'	
v)	Onions	'No dear! They're pickling onions.'	
vi)	Rice	'Yes dear, I wanted long grain rice.'	

(9) **Predicting** is making guesses and deductions on the basis of information you have heard.

Unit 8 One-upmanship

Pre-listening

1. Before listening to the tape, look carefully at the notes below. They were made by the director of a chain-store company who is interviewing candidates for a junior managerial post. In them he has noted down the qualities etc. he is looking for. Make sure you understand them before going on to the listening. It will be helpful for you to discuss them with a partner. Try to form a mental picture of the ideal candidate

Memo for interview, junior manager's post

Experience
At least 3 yrs in management of small family business or small store or similar.

Age
Late 20s early 30s.

Status
Single/no family problems.
Need for free transferability through U. K.

Personal qualities
Honesty.
Energy.
Loyalty to the firm.
Tact.
Must get on well with people.

Salary
Negotiable £2500 ~ £3500 according to experience.

Listening

2. a) Now listen to conversation on the tape. You will hear two of the candidates talking to each other after the interview. From what you hear and the way you interpret it, what can you deduce about them regarding the points the manager was looking for?

Some of the information is present in the conversation, that is, it is stated by the speakers. Much of it, however, you will have to make guesses about on the basis of the attitudes/qualities you feel are being expressed. You will need to listen to the conversation more than once.

b) Now compare your ideas in groups of three. Then check them with another group.

Points to look for	Candidate A	Candidate B
Experience		
Age		
Status		
Personal qualities — honesty — energy — loyalty to firm — tact — getting on well with people		
Salary		

What is the relationship between looking at volcanoes and listening comprehension? Well, looking a volcanoes is a very *visual* experience for me, and there is also a lot of *context* around to feed my eyes on. However, when I look at volcanoes I also listen and, based on my *knowledge of the world*, I have *expectations* about what I will hear. I have a *purpose* in listening. And if my *prediction* is right and I hear a certain rumbling sound beneath me, I do not sit around listening to every specific detail; the main idea is enough and I run like the dickens!

In brief, I am making an appeal for pre-listening and while-listening activities with lots of visuals, and indeed other non-linguistic and para-linguistic media, to help our students understand what they hear.

■ References

Anderson, K. H., K. Bruegging and J. Lance. (1983). *Missing person*, New York; Longman.

Blundell, L. and J. Stokes. (1981). *Task listening*. Cambridge; Cambridge University Press.

Brown, G. 1978. Understandinng spoken language. *TESOL Quarterly*, 12(3); pp. 271-283.

Brown, G. and G. Yule. (1983). *Teaching the spoken language*. Cambridge; Cambridge University Press.

Foley, B. H. (1984). *Now hear this*. Rowley, Massachusetts; Newbury House.

Maley, A. and S. Moulding. (1981). *Learning to listen*. Cambridge; Cambridge University Press.

Mumford, S. (1983). *Conversation pieces*. Oxford; Pergamon Press.

Porter, D. and J. Roberts. (1981). Authentic listening activities. *ELT Journal*, 36(1): pp. 37-47.

Richards, J. C. (1983). Listening comprehension; approach, design and procedure. *TESOL Quarterly*, 17(2): pp. 219-240.

Rost, M. and J. Lance. (1984). *PAIRallels*. Tucson, Arizona; Lingual House.

Scarbrough, D. (1984). *Reasons for listening*. Cambridge; Cambridge University Press.

Schecter, S. (1984). *Listening tasks*. Cambridge; Cambridge University Press.

From Burbidge, B. (1986). Looking at volcanoes and listening comprehension, *TESOL Newsletter*, 20, pp. 7-10.

16. LISTENING: LISTENING COMPREHENSION

The place of listening comprehension in an English language course has changed as theories of language learning have come into currency and declined. The behavioral psychology which underlay much language instruction in previous years gave a certain passive character to listening. Listening was considered an activity of either simple or overly complicated mechanism. In either case, listening was secondary to the "active" process of speaking and it was much ignored. Some years ago there was a shift; the dominant school of psychological theory applied to language learning became cognitivism. Because cognitive psychology, psycholinguistics, and neurolinguistics have added information to our picture of the language learning process, listening is now regarded as an active process.

Both of these words, *active* and *process*, are crucial to the current view of listening and to the application of listening practice in the classroom. The listener works at listening. The listener does not merely hear what is said, but constructs a message that is part of a matching process. For example, if I say to someone, "Nice day, isn't it?" his or her reaction is not merely a response to this audible stimulus and the chain of associations it bring forth, but a complex network of mental operations based on some of the following factors:

1. knowledge of English phonology, syntax, lexicon, register, style
2. knowledge of the real world shared with me
3. familiarity with the subject discussed
4. acquaintance with or assumptions about my personal attitudes and interests
5. observation and interpretation of the circumstances of the utterance, including what has preceded it
6. understanding of the cultural context
7. reading of paralinguistic cues
8. syntactic and rhetorical expectations about what is to come.

Clearly, listening is not as simple a process as we once believed it to be. To return to our salutation, "Nice day, isn't it?" let us suppose I have said it to the following people in the following situations:

1. To an attractive member of the opposite sex while standing in a long line in a bank
2. To a very big and mean-looking person who has just sat down beside me in a subway car in which we are the only passengers

3. To a friend of mine whom I had agreed to meet for a dawn outing on a stormy day.

The possibilities for interpreting this simple bit of language are numerous and varied. For the nonnative speaker of a language, the sheer diversity of possible interpretation is both an opportunity for approximating the message and a source of bewilderment. While it is simplistic to believe that closely controlled listening practice will prepare a student for "the normal uses of listening in life-situations," it is equally simplistic to believe that exposure to the target language alone will produce competency in listening. Listening is a skill that all of us have developed to varying degrees. Native speakers of a language all range somewhere along a spectrum of bad to good listeners. Knowledge of the native language, by itself, is not a passport to complete understanding, as the numerous misunderstandings among native speakers that are a part of daily life illustrate. We can always learn to listen better.

Listening, then, is an active process. One of the chief facilitators of listening, what helps one "get the message." is *redundancy*. Basically, redundancy is the repetition of a message feature. In other words, redundancy yields more information than is necessary to make sense out of communication. We can have syntactic redundancy. *He* eats flies — where the idea of third person singular is given by "he" and repeated by the "s" of "eats." We can have phonetic redundancy, an excess of phonetic features, or else how can /did ju: it/ readily become [dzit] and still be interpretable as "Did you eat?" We can have simple repetition of lexis: "I uh... I uh... I uh... think I'll go." All the factors that go into the active process of listening offer some redundancy. Redundancy is a necessary part of the communication process. There are many factors working against real communication such as outside noises, wide variation in people's speech, physical state of the listener, knowledge of the language and the situation that listener and speaker share. Redundant information gives us a second chance, allows us to lapse in our attentiveness, enables us to figure out what was said when we've only heard a part of the whole message. Students of foreign languages commonly have great difficulty communicating over the telephone because the redundancy that the visual field affords is not present in a phone conversation. We cannot hear a man chop his hand down to emphasize or listen to him make great circular motions to illustrate some vivid experience.

The concept of listening as an active process, and the idea that language has redundancy built into it have direct bearing on listening activities in the language classroom. For the most part, listening comprehension, when treated separately at all, has been a controlled exercise in edited, artificially delivered language. Typically a passage is read, repeated, and questions are asked; from simple yes/no-answer type questions to *wh-* or information-type questions. The listening exercise might end with student summaries of the passage. The problem with using mainly edited language passages followed by a standard questioning order is that it does not prepare the student for listening to unedited, natural speech. To this one could add that classroom language exercises eliminate much of the redundancy necessary for understanding. To see that this is so, one needs only examine the two passages below.

I	II
You realize	You really
how hard it is	you realize
for them to come into a new	uh you know how hard it is.
country.	for them to come into a country uh
One lady I worked for had missed	where they're come from you know I
worked for	
out on the gas chambers four times.	one lady and
	um
	four times she'd missed out on the gas chambers
	four times

The first passage is edited speech, the kind of speech one finds used for listening comprehension exercises. The second passage is the actual language that occurred in conversation. The false starts, repetitions, and hesitations of the second passage allow the listener to process the information more easily than in the first passage because there is more time and there are more clues to the message in the natural, unedited passage. Very often a teacher reading a listening passage will slow down the rate of speech to the point of disrupting the natural flow of the language as indicated by its syntax. To deliver a passage to students who do not have a great deal of fluency in the target language, the teacher should read the passage at normal speed, but pause longer at natural pause points. For example:

> Once upon a starless midnight/ there was an owl/ who sat on the branch of an oak tree/ Two ground moles tried to slip quietly by/ unnoticed/ "You!" said the owl/ "Who?" they quavered/ in fear and astonishment/ for they could not believe/ it was possible/ for anyone to see them/ in that thick darkness/ "You two!" said the owl. (p. 45. Fables For Our Time, James Thurber, Harper and Row, Perennial Library, 1974)

When practicing listening, we are also practicing what Gattegno calls, "stressing and ignoring," that is, we listen for certain things at the expense of disregarding others. Luria cites (as related by Rivers and Melvin, 1977: 162-3) the case of a person who was unable to forget the information he was taking in. He remembered all things equally well and consequently remembered nothing unless he made special effort. Now, the student faced with a series of questions after a listening comprehension passage is like this man with the uncontrollable memory, since before the student listens to the passage he doesn't know what he is listening for. All information is equally salient. It is no wonder a student might have trouble giving precise answers to questions put to him after listening. The native speaker/listener on hearing speech distills the essential message without trying to recall it word for word. The learner of a second or foreign language cannot do this because he does not know very well what to stress and what to ignore. Therefore, it helps to give the questions before the listening passage. Rivers and Temperley call the type of exercise which tells students what to look for before the passage is given an "Information Search." Here is an example (Rivers and Temperley, 1978: 79).

Questions supplied beforehand

1. What day is it?
2. What time is it?
3. Where is Elizabeth?
4. Where is she sitting?
5. Where is Julia?
6. Has the class begun?
7. What does Elizabeth take out of her pocket?
8. Where does she put it?

PASSAGE

It's the first of April. It's nearly one o'clock. Elizabeth is in school. She's sitting in her usual place in the third row. Her friend, Julia, is sitting in front of her. The afternoon class is about to begin. Elizabeth takes out of her pocket a little piece of paper on which she has written, "Kiss me." Very gently, she pins it to the back of Julia's dress.

This type of exercise allows the students to concentrate on discrete points of information while dealing with large chunks of language.

To summarize the discussion thus far, listening has been "the forgotten skill" (Chastain, 1976: 278) which has been practiced in a narrow, unnatural manner as far as macrolanguage, "the ability to use language holistically for normal life-purposes" (Rivers and Temperley, 1978: 92) is concerned. If as Chastain says, "The goal in listening comprehension is to be able to understand native speech at normal speed in unstructured situations," (1976: 283), then one way to achieve this is with natural listening passages containing redundancy. These passages are best read at normal speed with lengthened pauses. Information search type exercises where students have prior knowledge of which questions they must answer before they listen to a passage, are worthwhile activities for listening practice. In this way, students will listen to long chunks of language, secure in the knowledge that they need only to find out certain things and consequently can pay less attention to the rest of the passage. This sort of practice can lead to confidence in facing a native speaker.

The following exercises are meant to add to the teacher's repertoire of listening practice technique using macrolanguage.

1. Picture Communication

Level: lower intermediate and above

Students are paired up. One student has a simple line drawing which he then describes to his partner. His partner must duplicate the drawing without looking at it. The pair may not look at each other's drawings. Both may ask for and give information.

The teacher should make it clear to the students that they are to try to effect as perfect a duplicate drawing as possible. Artistic rendering is unimportant, but scale is important. In this way, expressing dimension, location, approximation, and comparison through the foreign language, students take turns listening for the information which will bring them to their goal.

2. Listening For Word Order

Level: elementary to advanced

The teacher presents the students with a list of words in alphabetical order and instructs them to number them in the order they hear them in the passage. Then the passage is read at normal speed, varying pause length according to student level. The teacher may read the passage (or play the tape) as much as the students request.

The exercise ends when students agree on the order of the words. Here is an example. (level: intermediate)

The Fairly Intelligent Fly

A large spider in an old house built a beautiful web in which to catch flies. Every time a fly landed on the web and was entangled in it the spider devoured him, so that when another fly came along he would think the web was a safe and quiet place in which to rest. One day a fairly intelligent fly buzzed around above the web so long without lighting that the spider appeared and said, "Come on down." But the fly was too clever for him and said, "I never light where I don't see other flies and I don't see any other flies in your house." So he flew away until he came to a place where there were a great many other flies. He was about to settle down among them when a bee buzzed up and said, "Hold it, stupid, that's flypaper. All those flies are trapped." "Don't be silly," said the fly, "They're dancing." So he settled down and became stuck to the flypaper with all the other flies.

WORD LIST FOR THE PASSAGE

appeared
buzzed
came along
came to
devoured
entangled
flew away
landed
said
settled down

3. Reflecting Language

Level: upper intermediate to advanced

Students are grouped in 5's or 6's and a discussion topic is given or students start a discussion themselves. Before a person can take the floor in the group discussion, that person must summarize the basic ideas of the person who has just spoken, to the satisfaction of that individual. Other group members act as judges. The discussion continues with each student summarizing the thought and feeling of the previous one. This exercise is not as easy and simple as it seems and students may experience frustration. It should continue for about 15 minutes or so. Here is an example.

Juan: We're talking about giving animals some rights. I don't think we should assume that humans can do anything they wish to animals just because they're dumb.
Ilsa: Yeah, there are a lot of dumb people around.
Juan: I didn't say that.
Ilsa: Oh, you mean to say people shouldn't think that whatever they do to animals is okay.
Juan: That's right.
Ilsa: Well, I agree to a certain extent, but. . .

From Spaventa, L. J. *Listening: listening comprehension*, Selected from a continuing monograph series for the overseas teacher of English as a foreign language which were made in a lecture at Indiana Univ., Bloomington in 1977.

17. ENGLISH BY DRAWING: MAKING THE LANGUAGE LAB A CENTER OF ACTIVE LEARNING

On hot, humid summer days in our school in rural Japan, I noticed that my students would often nod off while listening to conversational English language tapes in the language lab. Noting how much my students liked to draw in their free time, I decided that offering them listening tasks in which they had to draw responses to the language tapes they were hearing might keep them more alert. I call this approach to listening English by Drawing. Besides keeping students awake, the approach has several pedagogical advantages.

First, pictures are an obvious component of educational materials, evidenced in our field by increasingly attractive illustrated ESL texts. Romiszowski (1988) and Travers (1967) have shown that pictures aid comprehension and recall of texts. Moreover, learners react positively to such tests (Hill, 1990; Romiszowski, 1988). One researcher (Hoosain, 1986) recognizes that learners from particular language groups, such as those whose native language contains pictographic morphemes, "are better in tasks that utilize specific memory codes or involve visual spatial discrimination" (p. 521). Some of our ESL and EFL students come from such language groups and may be encouraged by the presence of visuals with target language text.

Still, why have students draw the pictures rather than using the more prevalent tool of prepared pictures? First, as Romiszowski (1988) points out, preprinted pictures may not work for all viewers: "one must control the content of a picture to ensure that the viewer focuses on those aspects of the lesson which are of significance for progress in the lesson" (p. 106). This may be particularly true when individuals from different cultures evaluate the same visual aid. For instance, Romiszowski (1988) found that African learners interpreted perspective in drawings differently from Europeans. Young learners or those from a culture different from the one that produced the visual may misinterpret illustrations in other ways as well. Coching and McHale (1981) found that the shading of graphics was sometimes interpreted by students to be dirt. Hewings (1991) found that his Vietnamese students in Britain interpreted pictures, maps, charts, and graphs in EFL texts in ways different from those intended by the text authors: "For those learners with a limited exposure to 'Western' conventions of illustration [perception of illustrations] may present a barrier to learning" (p. 237).

Drawing, then, lets the students create their own visuals, thus alleviating misinterpretation.

ESL materials makers like Brinkman and Walker (1991) show their belief in the importance of drawing to student understanding and expression of subjective concepts in their activities for literacy when they ask students to, "Color the boots dirty" and "Color the socks your favorite color."

Of equal importance is that many students enjoy drawing, or at least the opportunity to feel active while "receiving" information from the teacher, a tape, or a text. Even students who don't draw well or don't like to draw can diagram simply or work with a partner to complete the drawings. Like Total Physical Response, English by Drawing is an active approach that allows students to move (if only hands and eyes) while they listen, thus making for more active and memorable learning experiences.

The pedagogical advantages of drawing to facilitate students' interpretation of texts (Wright, 1989) or oral descriptions (Christison & Bassano, 1981; Hill, 1990; Ehrlich, Avery, & Yorio, 1988; Morgan & Rinvolucri, 1983; Mrowicki & Furnborough, 1982) may explain why it is found scattered throughout ESL materials. English by Drawing is not limited to beginning students. I have used it successfully with various levels, from preschoolers to adults.

DESIGNING LESSONS FOR ENGLISH BY DRAWING

The basic methodology requires a few simple steps.

1. Prepare a tapescript and tape (or read or have one student read the tapescript) that includes the target grammar point(s), functions(s), or other linguistic structure(s) that will be the focus of the activity.
2. Prepare any forms or writing materials needed for the activity. Often, only blank paper is needed.
3. Introduce the topic of the lesson and explain the drawing task students will need to do.
4. Play the tape or read the tapescript one or more times while students draw on prepared paper.
5. Have students paraphrase what they heard on the tape by looking at their own drawings and describing what they have drawn. Their paraphrases may need to be in response to your specific prompts or questions. This follow-up activity allows you to check whether the passively heard structures can be actively produced by students.
6. (Optional) Have students perfect their drawings with color or other artistic touches. These can later be displayed in the classroom or language lab as reminders of the lessons and their target pedagogical goals.

SAMPLE ACTIVITIES DESCRIBING PEOPLE

This is one of my favorite activities for upper level students.

Skill area: Describing people, adjectives.

Materials and methods: Give students a piece of 8 1/2 by 11 paper, divided into eight equal boxes. Students listen to a tape containing descriptions of people, which you've prepared to incorporate the vocabulary you want to review. For instance, "George is tall. He has long brown hair and blue eyes. He always wears his glasses." Students draw "George" on their paper and get involved by creating this person. Later, after all pictures have been drawn, ask students to orally describe "George" and the other characters by looking at their self-made visuals.

SAMPLE TAPESCRIPT

1. Who's that?
It's Martin.
He has long brown hair.
He has brown eyes.
Look... his feet are really big!
2. Here's a picture of my best friend.
He is short and stocky.
He's a teenager. His eyes are big and dark.
Can you see — he wears contact lenses.
3. My sister is 27 years old.
Let me tell you what she looks like.
She's fat.
She wears glasses.
Her eyes are hazel.
She has wavy, shoulder-length hair.
4. Look at that girl!
She's about 10 years old.
She's a brunette.
Her hair is really thin.
She has big blue eyes.
5. This is my father when he was a boy.
He was skinny and had long arms.
He had big hands.
His ears were pretty big.
6. The owner of that store is very old.
He has short gray hair and a moustache.
He has green eyes.
He wears glasses.
He always wears a hat.

DRAWING EMOTIONS

A related activity is one in which students draw pictures to represent human emotions.

Skill area: Understanding the words describing feelings in English.

Rationale: Though picture dictionaries and other such books show students what these emotions look like, emotions and their expression are subjective across cultures and individuals. One way to have students remember this vocabulary is by drawing their own representations.

Materials and method: Students need a blank sheet of paper, pencils, and markers. Provide a tape or read a script describing simple situations and an emotion, such as "Fernando had a low grade on his English test. He was disappointed." or "Mayumi climbed Fiji! She was proud." Students draw their own response. Later, they can make up their own sentences, like those on the tape, to fit the emotions drawn.

Variations: Other people-related activities can revolve around drawings related to age, sex, family members, occupations, and tools used in them, personality traits.

DRAWING TO INTERPRET SIZE AND QUANTITY

Skill area: Learning the meaning of size and quantity in English.

Rationale: These expressions can be interpreted quite differently among cultures and individuals (even by individuals from the same culture), so it is useful for students to draw what they perceive the words to mean. Then, they can compare their drawings with those of other students to check for differences. This activity can be followed up by some commentary and explanation by the teacher.

Materials and methods: It consists of phrases involving quantities, such as "I had *enough* for breakfast this morning," or "There are a *few* apartment buildings on my street."

DRAWING TO INTERPRET EXPRESSIONS OF TIME

Skill area: understanding and using expressions of time during the day, and expressions of time used with various verb forms.

Rationale: This activity is especially good for subjective interpretation of time expressions. For instance, an expression such as "I'll turn in my homework soon" might be interpreted differently by a student from Venezuela than one from Taiwan. Although differences in interpreting time might be hard to explain in words (requiring vocabulary more difficult than that which is focused upon in the lesson), students can express complex interpretations of time with simple pictures.

Materials and methods: Prepare a worksheet showing a series of blank clock faces or time lines. Students can shade or fill in a clock face or time line diagram to show how they interpret these time phrases. For example, if the student hears, "I went shopping for the afternoon," he or she will shade in the correct set of hours on the clockface and write *p.m.* next to the clock. A time line can be used to interpret ambiguous expressions such as next weekend and last week. The middle of the timeline would be the current date; students would draw a mark on the days before or after the current date on the timeline to indicate next weekend and last week. Interpretation of these expressions might change depending on whether the current date is Monday or Friday. In small groups, students from different cultures can compare their drawings to look for differences. You can later give further instruction in linguistic structures that seem confusing and open to different interpretations by students.

DRAWING THE STUDENTS' LEARNING ENVIRONMENT

In this activity, students create a decorative drawing from a description provided by the instructor or a prerecorded tape.

Skill area: Learning prepositions and the names of objects

Materials and methods: Students need only a blank sheet of paper and drawing implements such as crayons or pencils. Describe (or prepare a tape describing) a room filled with objects in varying locations, such as: "The bookcase is next to the desk. The lamp is on top of the desk. A trash can is under the desk." Students draw a picture modifying (by erasing) the position of objects in the picture as more information is heard. It's helpful if you draw a model beforehand so that single objects can be described by more than one correct description. Multiple descriptions of object location can help reinforce the meaning of prepositions being taught. Students should be encouraged to erase and make as many changes as they want. They can color in or finish off the drawing later.

After students have completed their drawings, they give their own oral descriptions of object location by consulting their own pictures. This is a check on their productive ability with the target structures.

Variations: This activity can be adapted for drawings and descriptions of things such as classroom objects; maps — such as a map of your school building, campus, or town; things in a purse or school backpack; equipment for a specific task (useful for ESP teaching), and so on.

For lower levels: Students who are able to make drawings can pair off with students for whom drawing is too complex. When the illustrator describes the objects, the listener must point to the objects(s) described.

DRAWING COMPARISONS AND CONTRASTS

Skill area: Understanding comparatives and superlatives.

Rationale: In this activity, drawing is an asset because students can change the physical attributes of what they draw as they hear new information. When two objects are described relative to one another, such as "My history book is thicker than my math book," the relationship can be drawn clearly. If, then, a third book is added, as in: "My English book is my thinnest book," students might have to re-draw, depending on how they drew the math book. In this way, you can illustrate the relative nature of size and the various forms with which English speakers express comparatives.

Materials and methods: Again, a teacher script or tapescript is needed. Students get a handout, divided into the same number of sections as number of descriptions. The tapescript might start simply, with descriptions involving only two objects; later it can build to longer descriptions.

After the pictures are drawn, you can check student comprehension and production by having them describe their work using comparatives and superlatives. Differing descriptions of the same group of objects will illustrate to students that comparison can be made from more than one perspective.

DRAWING IN RESPONSE TO WEATHER INFORMATION

Skill area: Understanding weather information.

Materials and methods: Give students a handout of repeated weather symbols. Students listen to a tape-script that includes either simple one-sentence descriptions of daily weather, or for higher level students, short weather reports in a style similar to that used on television or radio. Students circle, shade in, cross out, or use another means to indicate the weather description heard. The strip format of the handout allows for easy numbering and reference to individual weather descriptions. Students follow up with their own oral descriptions of the weather they have portrayed in each strip.

DRAWING IN ENGLISH FOR SPECIAL PURPOSES (ESP)

Skill area: ESP, in particular, hotel English.

Rationale: This activity can be used to clarify the teaching of real-life phrases. Also, it gets students realistically and communicatively involved by having them and their teacher adopt real-life roles.

Materials and methods: You or a student play the role of a hotel manager. Students are hotel staff. Make a tapescript consisting of various prospective guests calling to make hotel reservations. Before the tapescript is played, the "hotel manager" gives each of the staff members a page of the hotel reservation book. Then play the tapescript, caller by caller. For instance, one caller might call and say, "I'd like a double room, with a minibar, for the night of October 16th." Next to the date, students must draw a picture that diagrams what the caller has said. After all the calls are played and drawn, the "manager" tells the staff that they must now review the reservations for the coming month. The "staff" then describe day by day the room reservations and special needs of their guests, using their own pictures as cues.

Variation: Some restaurants use a table diagram on which they draw or mark to indicate customer dinner reservations. You could use a similar diagram and tapescript for prospective diners so that students can practice numbers, times, dates, and associated restaurant vocabulary.

There are many other activities you can devise that use drawing to enhance the learning experiences of your students. In addition, the attractive finished products from these activities, hung on your classroom walls, will make interesting and instructive decorations for your ESL or EFL class. Among the benefits of English by Drawing are that it allows students to be active, to clarify culturally based misinterpretations of expressions such as time and quantity, and to generate their own simplified representations of target language structures. And, perhaps as I did, you'll see formerly lethargic students begin to stretch their limbs and sharpen their pencils as they wake up to English by drawing.

■ References

Brinkman, K., & Walker, J. (1991). *Start right: A positive approach to literacy*. Englewood Cliffs, NJ: Prentice Hall.

Christison, M. A., & Bassano, S. (1981). Drawing out: using art experience in ESL. *TESOL Talk*, 13, pp. 35-40.

Coching, R. R., & McHale, S. (1981). A comparative study of the use of picture and objects in assessing children's receptive and productive language. *Journal of Child Language*, 8, pp. 1-13.

Enrlich, S., Avery, P., & Yorio, C. (1988). Discourse structure and negotiation of comprehensible input. *Studies in Second Language Acquisition,* 11, pp. 397-414.

Hewings, M. (1991). The interpretation if illustrations in ELT materials. *ELT Journal*, 45, pp. 237-244.

Hill, D. A. (1990). *Visual impact. Creative learning through pictures.* Essex, England: Longman.

Hinkel, E. (1992). L2 tense and time reference. *TESOL Quarterly*, 26, pp. 557-572.

Hoosain, R. (1986). Language, orthography, and cognitive processes: Chinese perspectives for the Sapir-Whorf hypothesis. *International Journal of Behavioral Development*, 9, pp. 507-525.

Morgan, J., & Rinvolucri, M. (1983). *Once upon a time: Using stories in the classroom.* Cambridge: Cambridge University Press.

Mrowicki, L., & Furnborough, P. (1982). *A new start: A functional course in basic spoken English and survival literacy. Literacy workbook 2.* Exeter, NH: Heinemann.

Romiszowski, A. J. (1988). *The selection and use of instructional media.* London: Kogan Page.

Travers, R. M. W. (1967). *Research and theory related to audiovisual information transmission.* (U.S. Department of Health, Education, and Welfare Contract No. 3-20-003).

Wright, A. (1989). *Pictures for language learning.* Cambridge: Cambridge University Press.

From Rathet, I. (1994). English by drawing: Making the language lab a center of active learning, *TESOL Journal*, 3, pp. 22-25.

PART FIVE

TEACHING READING

우리는 자주 '대부분의 한국사람은 문법과 읽기는 상당한 수준에 와 있지만 쉬운 말이나 영작은 못한다.'는 말을 한다. 그렇다면 과연 우리는 우리가 필요로 할 때 영어로 쓰여진 원서를 읽고 이해할 수 있다는 말인가? 이는 우리의 읽기 능력의 정도를 가늠하게 한다. 왜냐하면 이 질문에 대한 대답은 분명히 부정적이기 때문이다.

읽기 교육의 목적은 두 가지로 축약할 수 있다. 하나는 정보를 얻기 위해서, 그리고 다른 하나는 즐기기 위해서이다. 즉 'We read for information and pleasure.'이다. 그러므로 초보단계에서는 문어에서 사용되는 어휘, 구문에 초점을 맞추면서 점차 다양한 종류의 읽기 자료를 접해야 한다.

이해 기능에 속하는 듣기와 마찬가지로 읽기 역시 능동적인 기술이라는 견해가 지배적인 이유는 글을 이해하기 위해서는 자신이 그 동안 터득한 배경지식(background information) 또는 선험지식(schema)을 이용하여 추론하는 부분이 많기 때문이다. 그러면서도 모국어에서의 읽기 실력이 제 2언어나 외국어의 읽기에 전이되지 않는다는 주장은 읽기에서 필요로 되는 어휘, 문법, 유추 기술 등이 가르쳐져야 한다는 것을 말해 준다.

이 장은 우선 우리가 글을 읽을 때 잘못된 습관을 지적하면서 읽기의 정의를 내린 후 그러한 습관에 빠져들지 않고 올바른 읽기를 할 수 있도록 지도하는 방법을 기술한 Kalnitz & Judd의 글로 시작한다.

읽기에는 정독(intensive reading)과 다독(extensive reading)이 있다. 현재 중등학교에서 정규 영어시간에 교과서를 단원별로 지도할 때 핵심이 되는 읽기 부분은 정독을 하도록 구성되어 있다. Paulston & Bruder는 이를 지도하는 순서에 따라 각각의 구체적인 절차를 충분한 예와 함께 제시한다. 한편 Carroll & Mordaunt는 단어 card의 양면을 사용하여 어휘를 효과적으로 지도하는 방법을 소개하는 데 실제 적용이 용이할 것이다.

다음으로 Melendes & Pritchard는 정독이건 다독이건 읽기에서 반드시 이용해야 하는 선험지식이 어떻게 읽기 교수의 각 단계에서 적용될 수 있는가를 보여주고 마지막으로 문학 작품을 가르칠 때의 이점과 실제로 가르치는 방법이 McKay에 의해 소개된다.

18. AN APPROACH TO TEACHING E.S.L. READING TO LITERATE ADULTS

We have found that despite the fact that our students may be fluent readers in their native languages, they often cannot transfer these skills to reading in English. They are focused on the word rather than on the entire text, are tied to their dictionaries, read slowly word by word, and have unreasonable expectations about how much they should be able to understand. We have to help our students learn how to relax with reading. We have to teach them how to guess meanings by using signal words and context clues. Our students need to be aware of the rhetorical patterns of English so that they can identify main ideas, distinguish generalizations from specifics, and read critically. We have to be aware of the underlying cultural assumptions in readings we assign and we need to promote cultural awareness in the classroom. Most importantly, our students need to be able to choose appropriate strategies to achieve their goals.

By asking our students, we learned that they need to read a variety of different things in English: textbooks, newspapers, business reports and letters, menus, signs, etc. As we examined the skills of successful reading, we found that there is a lot of overlap between the skills needed to read the various materials that our students confront. For example, students may skim a newspaper as well as the phone book. Context clues can be used to determine the meaning of an unfamiliar word in a textbook as well as in a novel. This paper will explain approaches to teaching reading skills which we believe can help our students to improve.

We begin with some assumptions about reading based on Kenneth Goodman and other readings. Goodman says that reading is a "psycholinguistic guessing game" (1972), involving the reader actively in the process of receiving the message that the writer has put on the page. Another way to say this is that reading consists of an interaction between the knowledge the reader has and the message (information) the writer has communicated. Reading is not just putting sounds together; native speakers decode directly from the text to the meaning without recourse to sound. The goal for second-language readers, of course, is to approximate as closely as possible the skills of native speakers. Reading is not just word recognition. For example: *saw this is one I the* — is a collection of words, but it has no meaning at all. Rearranged, "This is the one I saw," it still has very little meaning without a context. Is *one* a movie, a dog, a person, a house? Reading is ideas, and anything less than that is not really reading but word-calling. There must be interaction between the reader and the writer (via the message). The reader must be an active participant in the communicative process, bringing ideas and expectations to the text and integrating the author's ideas into what s/he knows of the world. In summary, reading is getting meaning, always in context.

Given here are skills approaches to reading, because we want students to apply what they learn in our reading classes to whatever reading they do outside of class.

How do our students approach reading in English, and how does their approach inhibit them from becoming fluent readers? Perhaps one of the misconceptions about reading is that adults who are fluent readers in their native language will automatically be able to transfer these reading skills to a second language once they have learned enough of the language to be able to read it. Our own experience reading in the languages we studied in college shows us that such is not the case. We found ourselves frustrated and unsuccessful despite the fact that we are fluent readers in English. We all have also had numerous students who were well-educated in their native countries who are, nevertheless, extremely handicapped when attempting to read in English.

Why is this the case? Our students, because they are reading in a language that is not their own, tend to focus on the word as the unit of meaning instead of looking beyond the word to the sentence, paragraph and the entire text. As a result, they find themselves immensely frustrated since they may encounter several words in a single sentence whose meaning they are unsure of. They stop at each unfamiliar word, afraid to go on for fear of missing something. They are tied to their dictionaries, relying on translation to understand word meanings. They end up spending more time looking up words than they do reading the text.

Other strategies also inhibit our students when they read in English. For one, our students tend to have unrealistic expectations of how much they should be able to understand. They feel frustrated and dissatisfied if they have less than 100% comprehension. In addition, our students generally read everything the same way, regardless of the type of text; they read newspapers, stories and textbooks in the same manner. Finally, many of our students read aloud or subvocalize which slows them down and may inhibit comprehension.

HOW CAN WE HELP STUDENTS TO CHANGE THEIR STRATEGIES?

First of all, we need to help our students relax with reading and to reconsider the strategies they use. We like to begin our reading classes each semester by discussing with our students how they read in English, what they think is the best way to read, and the problems they have in reading. This is usually a lively and thought-provoking discussion for our students because it gets to the heart of their frustrations with reading in a language not their own. Although this is only the first step in our campaign to help our students change their reading strategies, some of our students exhibit a visible sense of relief as they are introduced to the idea that they are not expected to understand 100% of what they read, that they don't have to look up every word, and that they can and should read faster.

Of course, we have not won over our students to our side with this initial discussion. Some may concede that our approach has validity, while others may remain unconvinced. Therefore, we like to spend the first week or two of the semester doing classroom exercises that focus on what our students know rather than what they don't know. They are only too aware of what they don't know. Our goal is to convince them that in many cases, they already possess the tools to understand what they are reading.

We can use exercises that help students realize that they don't need to understand every word in order to understand the general idea of what they are reading — and that understanding the general idea is all they can expect from themselves until they are fluent in English. One way to do this is by having the students read a passage with words missing. Students discover that they are still able to understand the meaning of the passage. Another kind of exercise that can accomplish this same purpose is a recall exercise. Students read a passage without the help of a dictionary, then close their books and either recall orally or write down everything they remember. We have done this exercise, first asking students what percent of the passage they understand, and have gotten low estimates like 40-50%. However, when asked to recall, students covered all the main ideas of the passsage. They were surprised when it was pointed out to them that they had understood everything that was important, and that they had only missed some of the details. Students tend to base their percentages on the number of words they don't recognize rather than on whether or not they got the idea. These kinds of exercises help to change their concept of what is important in reading.

In addition, we can also present exercises that convince them that when they need to know words, they can often figure out the meanings by themselves. We can do this by presenting exercises where the contexts are so obvious that students can't fail to understand the meaning of a new word. For example: It was *hazy* outside, so I could not see clearly.

Once we have gotten our students to think differently about their approach to reading, we can begin to teach additional skills in the reading class. For the sake of convenience, we have divided these skills into two areas — language-related skills and text-related skills, though this is an artificial division, and they overlap one another.

Language Skills

After we have proven to the students that they don't have to depend on the dictionary each time they come across an unfamiliar word, we have to teach them skills that will help them to guess the general meaning of the word. Guessing cannot be exact, nor is the exact meaning necessary. This needs to be pointed out to our students. The skills we have to teach fall into three categories:

1. determining the part of speech of the unknown word
2. using context clues to guess the meaning of the word
3. using morphological clues to guess meaning.

Our students need to be aware of clues that will help them to determine the part of speech of the unknown word as this will help them to limit the range of their guessing. If the word could be any part of speech, the student has nowhere to start from in trying to guess. We have found this to be a problem with our ESL students, who need to be taught a sensitivity to the clues that are present. However, these clues are not infallible. Students must also be taught to look not only at the word itself, not only at the surrounding words, but at the entire sentence, paragraph and text for clues.

There are two types of clues that can help students determine the part of speech of an unknown word. These are grammatical markers and syntactic clues. The parts of speech identified by these clues are nouns, verbs, adjectives and adverbs.

Students can be sensitized to these clues by using worksheets that focus on the clues. For example, a sample worksheet focusing on syntactic clues would contain sentences with words missing, but with the signal word present. Students would be asked to determine the part of speech of the missing word and to identify the signal they used. The exercise is good to help students use more than one signal, and to show them that no signal works 100% of the time. For example:

> In order to be eligible for financial aid at Truman College a _____ must be a citizen or permanent resident of the U.S.

Students should be able to identify *a* as a signal for a noun. However, an article can also be followed by an adjective or an adverb, so students must look beyond to see that a modal follows the blank and therefore, the missing word is a noun. The exercise can be carried one step further by asking students to supply any noun that fits the meaning of the sentence.

A similar worksheet can be devised for grammatical markers. Students can be given sentences where one word is unknown, and they should be able to use grammatical markers and any other clues present to determine the part of speech. For example:

> The school *determines* who is eligible for the work-study program, how much they will earn, and where they will work.

The students should be able to identify the *s* as a grammatical marker. The *s* by itself isn't enough, however, to signal a verb, as it is also the plural marker for nouns. Students must also use syntactic clues here.

After doing exercises with isolated sentences, students can then be asked to do the same thing when reading an entire text. This kind of skill can be reinforced throughout the semester.

After students know how to determine the part of speech of the unknown word, they can also be taught to use the clues within the text, both before and after the unknown word, to narrow the meaning of the word. Again, students should not be aiming for an exact definition.

The third element in word attack skills is the morphological analysis of words. We can teach them the most common prefixes, suffixes and stems and show them how these combine and how this can aid in understanding words within a context. In class, we can give students worksheets in which they have to match meanings once they know the meaning of a particular prefix, suffix, or stem. We can also have them create words with a particular meaning. Again, context is a must as some prefixes and suffixes have more than one meaning. For example, *-en* can mean *made of* as in *wooden, cause to be* as in *sharpen*, and *put into* as in *encircle*. Or, there may be different stems with similar meanings where only context will help. For example, *-dis* and *-un* both can mean *not* or *opposite of*, so that only context will help our students understand the difference in meaning between *dislike* and *unlike* or *discover* and *uncover*.

The other language area that interferes with our students' understanding of a text is substitutions and deletions. A breakdown in understanding a text, particularly a complex one, may occur when words are substituted or deleted and students are unaware of what the substitutions stand for or what the deleted words are. We used *A Concise Grammar of Contemporary English* by Quirk and Greenbaum (1975) to aid us in our compilation of the kinds of substitutions and deletions that occur in English. We have eliminated some of them, and recombined and reorganized others with pedagogical considerations in mind. We have listed two kinds of substitutions and three kinds of deletions that should be taught in the ESL reading class.

In the classroom, one effective way to sensitize students to substitutions is to take a text, such as an article in a student newspaper, circle all the pro forms, and have students identify what they refer to. Students can also be asked to do substitution exercises themselves, where they actually supply the pro forms.

To sensitize students to deletions, students can work with the same text, and can be asked to supply what has been deleted. They can also be asked to create deletions themselves.

Text-related Skills

One important rhetorical device of English is the use of generalizations supported by examples in expository prose. Like everything else that seems clear and straightforward to native speakers, this concept is one which ESL students need to be made aware of. They need to know how to recognize and identify generalizations and distinguish them from examples. We introduce the concepts of generalization and example and teach the vocabulary peculiar to each (*in general, on the whole, always/never vs. for example, for instance*). First, we ask students to identify the generalization in a paragraph, noting its location, and then we ask them to identify the examples, noting the proportion of examples to generalizations. We provide other paragraphs or longer writings for students to examine as well. A more sophisticated skill is determining whether or not the examples given actually suppport the generalization. These are skills of critical reading. After teaching generalizations and examples early in the semester, we continue identifying them throughout the semester, making sure that students know what to look for and how to spot them. Students can then make use of the concept as a means of identifying the main idea, in skimming, and in locating topic sentences. They need to be able to distinguish examples in scanning for specific information and evaluating arguments.

Not all cultures and languages organize information in the same way; as a result the rhetorical conventions of expository prose differ from one language to another. Kaplan (1966) points out the circular pattern of exposition in Oriental writing vs. linearity in English vs. the greater latitude of digression permitted in Semitic writing. Our students need to be exposed to the styles of English rhetoric so that they can make use of them in understanding what they read in English. If successful reading depends upon accurate prediction of what is to follow, as in Goodman's guessing game, then knowing the rhetorical structures and how they function will enhance fluent reading by increasing the likelihood of successful prediction.

In English, the concept of generalization and example leads to the structure of main idea and details. Many reading texts ask questions about the main idea of a reading selection, but usually there are far more questions about the details. Since the main idea is the most important one, it seems logical that more attention in reading class should be devoted to finding it, being sure all students understand it, and clarifying how the details are subordinate.

The ratio of detail to main idea questions in most reading texts, however, is just the opposite of this, leading students to focus on minute details while running the risk of missing the main point.

Just as students should be exposed to the vocabulary of generalizations and examples, they should be taught the clues that English rhetoric provides for identifying the main idea, such as topic sentences, conclusions, and phrases *(most important*, etc.). Ideas that support the main idea are generally identified by *for example, in addition, more over*, etc. Students also need to know how to identify and evaluate ideas which are in opposition to the main idea. These may be introduced by phrases like *on the other hand, some say, however*, and others. In a text, we expect to find fewer of these than supporting ideas.

If the reader understands the main idea of a piece, this is often sufficient. Many of our students believe that they must understand every small detail of what they read. ESL reading texts may give far more comprehension questions than a passage warrants. The questions often focus on minute, nonessential details. If that's what texts do, teachers may follow, even though it goes against their common sense. We do our students a disservice, however, if we insist they read everything that we give them to find all the little insignificant details. This practice only reinforces their (fallacious) idea that every word on the page is equally important and deserving of attention.

Two of the tools students need for maximally efficient reading are skimming and scanning. Skimming is quick reading for the general idea(s) of a passage. Preview skimming is used to decide whether or not to read something more thoroughly, while overview skimming is used when there is no time for a more complete reading. Scanning is looking quickly for specific information using textual clues plus graphic information. We scan to find information in a dictionary or telephone book as well as to find the answer to a specific question in prose.

If preview skimming and other reading exercises are to be meaningful, there must be time for reading of student-selected materials in class. Only by having students spend time in class reading can the instructor ensure 1) that they read the assignment and 2) that they read quickly, without their bilingual dictionaries. A reading lab with a large selection of materials at different levels and on different subjects is best suited for this; another possibility is to collect articles from newspapers and magazines (choosing those which will not be out of date next week) and to provide a file of these for students to choose from for in-class reading. The follow-up exercises can include explaining the article's idea or story's plot to another student who has not read it, answering questions the teacher has prepared, or —nothing. Sometimes just reading is enough. In real life, we often read either for pleasure or to pass the time. Students sometimes need to read things for which they are not held accountable.

An essential idea in all of this is the concept of determining purpose for reading and then suiting reading strategy to meet that purpose. Students need to be flexible both in speed of reading and in choice of strategy; as teachers, our goal is to teach students to determine their own purpose and to adopt the needed strategies (Clarke & Silberstein, 1979: 50). We find that our students tend to approach everything to be read in English as if it had to be studied, but we try to teach them a variety of techniques and show them how different ones are appropriate in different situations. Among the various techniques students should be able to employ are skimming and scanning, as mentioned above, as well as study techniques such as SQ3R (Survey, Questioon, Read, Recite, Review). ESL students need to increase their reading rate, but they must also know when to slow down for specific tasks.

In prereading activities, ESL teachers are familiar with the technique of previewing unfamiliar vocabulary or syntax likely to present problems in comprehension for students. Selekman and Kleinmann (1978) argue that we should not neglect previewing unfamiliar socio-cultural concepts as part of prereading. Based on their examples, we have used previewing of cultural concepts in our classes with good results.

Selekman and Kleinmann maintain that students' active involvement in a simulation focusing on the cultural concept is the best way to ensure students' understanding of, as well as involvement in, the reading. We have found that identifying the underlying cultural assumptions is in itself a worthwhile project for the instructor, who is forced to examine American culture somewhat from the viewpoint of the non-native student. The result of this can be increased awareness on the part of the instructor that there are indeed assumptions which are not shared — or even recognized — by students from other cultures.

CONCLUSION

The approaches to reading instruction described here can be incorporated into reading classes for literate adults at various levels of ESL study. Beginning with the deliberate modifications of their reading strategies and continuing throughout the course to add flexibility by means of increasing the repertoire of skills students have to draw upon, we hope to produce independent second-language readers who can set their own reasonable goals and then accomplish them with success and confidence.

■ References

Goodman, K. S. (1972). Reading: A psycholinguistic guessing game, In Larry A. Harris and Carl B. Smith (eds.) *Individualizing reading instruction: A reader*. New York: Holt, Rinehart, and Winston.

Kaplan, R. B. (1966). Cultural thought patterns in inter-cultural education. *Language Learning,* 16. pp. 1-20.

Quirk, R. and Sidney G. (1975). *A concise grammar of contemporary English*. New York: Harcourt Brace Jovanovich.

Selekman, H. R. and Howard H. K. (1978). Aiding second language reading comprehension. In Charles H. Blatchford and Jacqueline Schacter (eds.) *On TESOL '78 EFL Policies, Programs, Practices*. Washington, D.C.: TESOL. pp. 165-175.

From Kalnitz, J. & Judd, R. K. (1981). An approach to teaching E.S.L. reading to literate adults, *TESOL Newsletter*, 15, pp. 15-19.

19. INTENSIVE READING

CHECKING COMPREHENSION QUESTIONS

Comprehension questions are in West's terms either *after*-questions or *before*-questions. After-questions are just that, questions which are asked or read after the actual reading and whose purpose is to check that the students did the reading assignment and that they understood it. More importantly, before-questions serve to focus the student's attention on the important points of the passage during the reading and are a teaching rather than testing device. They are asked or read, and occasionally discussed, before the students do the reading. Both after-and before-questions can be any of the five types of questions Norris outlines:

> Five types of questions for comprehension can be described and graded according to (a) the linguistic form of the required response, and (b) the relation between the information that is needed to answer correctly and the information provided in the reading selection. I list the five types here in order of increasing difficulty for the student.
>
> Type 1: Information from the reading sufficient for the answer is contained in the question itself.
>
> a. Answerable simply Yes/No or True/False
> Before Frank left for town, did his wife hand him an umbrella? (Yes or No)
> Before Frank left for town, his wife handed him an umbrella. (True or False)
>
> b. Multiple choice of answers is given with the question.
> What did Frank's wife hand him before he left?
> _____ an umbrella, _____ a piece of cloth, _____ a letter
>
> Type 2: Answerable with information quoted directly from the reading selection. (WH questions—who, when, where, what—usually not why or how questions.)
>
> What did Frank's wife hand him before he left for town?
> Answer: (She handed him) a piece of cloth (before he left for town).
>
> Type 3: Answerable with information acquired from the reading selection, but not by direct quotation from a single sentence (Usually why or how questions).
>
> How did Frank explain his difficulties to his wife?
> Answer: First, Frank tole her. . . Then he said. . .

Type 4: Answerable from inference or implication from the reading; the information is not stated explicitly in the selection.

How do you suppose Frank's wife felt about his explanation?
Answer: Well, since she looked cross, I suppose that she. . .

Type 5: The answer requires evaluation or judgment relating the reading selection to additional information or experience of the reader.
What would you have done in Frank's place?[1)]

Type 4 and 5 questions are rarely included in textbooks and do not lend themselves easily to written answers. It is important that the teacher remember to add such questions to the oral discussion of the reading. Students can also be assigned to prepare some type 4 and 5 questions for their classmates. They can be very simple: "Was Snow White's stepmother a nice person?" "Why didn't you like her?" and should be included in the curriculum as early as possible.

As little time as possible should be spent on going through the answers to the written comprehension questions. There is no sense at all to have each student first read the entire question aloud and then add true, false or whatever is the correct answer. The students have all read the questions, they have them in front of them, and it is quite sufficient for the teacher to say: "What is the answer to Question 1, Mary?" and for Mary to answer simply "False." Only where there is divergent opinion should the question be discussed. Class time is much better spent on inference and opinion questions, interspersed by the teacher among the factual questions. Teachers tend to waste a lot of time on comprehension exercises, and it is unproductive: the students have already achieved what they stood to profit from the exercise and all they need is a rapid verification of their work. This is not to say that questions the students had difficulty with should not be discussed, but rather not to spend time on what the students already know.

The teacher should check that each student really does prepare comprehension questions before coming to class. Simply walking through the classroom while checking the exercises and glancing at each student's paper will usually achieve this. The students should be told to correct their papers in a different color pencil or ink and to tally up their number of correct answers. The exercises should be collected and checked, if not each time at least occasionally, so the teacher can see how each student is doing. Depending on the situation, the exercises may be graded.

The reasons for these procedures are obvious. First of all, it ensures that the students

1) W. Norris. (1970). "Teaching second language reading at the advanced level: goals, techniques, and procedures," *TESOL Quarterly,* 4, pp. 28-29.

do the reading, a serious worry for most teachers of reading. Second, it gives the students an indication of how they are doing. Third, it gives teachers an indication of how both they and the students are doing. Fourth, and most importantly, it provides a mechanism for the teacher to react to individual student's behavior. There is nothing more discouraging to students, even with teachers they dislike, than the teacher's ignoring or ignorance of the individual's efforts and performance. Especially with reading, where achievements are rather intangible, as many records as possible should be kept.

For a very beginning class, the teacher may want to add a lot of *after*-questions of the WH kind (*who, what, where, when, how* kind of questions): "Whom did he meet?" "What did he say to the girl?" This gives the class opportunity to talk in a controlled situation where the answers are simply lifted from the reading — they must speak the answers rather than just read them — but it is an exercise in improving short-term memory rather than in reading. On intermediate and advanced levels there need not be a close discussion of the text unless the teacher wants to use the reading as a springboard for class discussion, a perfectly valuable activity but it is not teaching reading.

INTRODUCTION OF THE NEXT READING ASSIGNMENT

Meaning and Pronunciation of New Words

The study of vocabulary is the most neglected area of all in language teaching, yet there is increasing evidence both from first and second language acquisition studies that the semantic relationship is more important than the syntactic for receiving messages. The one thing that most interferes with our students' reading is poor vocabulary and we have recently come to accept the fact that our students have been right all these years when they have complained about not knowing and not being taught enough words.

Vocabulary study is just that, the learning of words, item by item. We distinguish between vocabulary taught for productive and receptive use. In the grammar class all words are taught for productive use, for the ability to recall and use these words for communicative purposes. We teach the more common content words, those words which have semantic rather than grammatical meaning, like *dog* and *run* and *fast*. But in grammar the primary emphasis is on the functors or function words, those words which primarily carry grammatical meaning, like the auxiliaries, articles, conjunctions and the like. The students must learn most of the functors for productive use if they are to speak grammatically.

In reading the emphasis conversely is on content words, but for receptive use, for the ability to recognize the meaning of a word in context, which is after all what reading is all about. But it is not possible to make any absolute statements about teaching vocabulary for productive or receptive use in reading because some students will *use* words they have learned through reading while others will not. Reading does lend itself to the enrichment of productive vocabulary, and the teacher can indicate to the students the words they should learn for their own usage.

The two major concerns in teaching vocabulary are what to teach and how to teach it. The criteria for selection of vocabulary differ depending on whether the vocabulary is taught for productive or receptive use. For productive use the two most cited criteria are frequency of occurrence and degree of difficulty.

Frequency of occurrence can be established by reference to word lists such as Thorndike and Lorge's[2] and West's[3]. Although there are many problems with word lists, they can serve as a guideline for the selection of vocabulary if used with some common sense. The word lists are also useful as check lists; at the intermediate level, students should be familiar with most of the words in the West list.

The other criterion which is often discussed is degree of difficulty (difficulty is defined as the time it takes to learn an item), usually with the recommendation that one should proceed from easy to difficult. There are, however, serious problems with "difficulty" as a criterion for selecting vocabulary. There is no "absolute" difficulty, and although one may identify causes of difficulty as due to phonology, morphology, codability, distribution, etc., that identification still does not allow any accurate ranking of words by difficulty. With heterogeneous classes, the task becomes hopeless since mother tongue interference is an important factor of difficulty. But more important, many words which are difficult (we can observe the difficulty by the errors made on them) are of extremely high frequency and must be taught in the very beginning lessons. *Do* and *make* are a good example of a very difficult pair, especially for speakers who have one word for the two of them. Degree of difficulty, therefore, should not be considered as a criterion for the selection of vocabulary, but rather it should be taken into account for methods of teaching vocabulary.

In our view, the most important criterion for selecting vocabulary should be semantic saliency, the marked need for a word in order to make or understand a statement that is of importance to the speaker. The higher the semantic saliency of a word, the easier it is learned. Taboo words are a good example; our students learn them with no teaching at all. The needs and interests of the students then should be the major guideline in selecting vocabulary to be taught for active production.

The criteria for selecting productive vocabulary should also be kept in mind when choosing

2) E. L. Thorndike and I. Lorge. (1944). *The teacher's word book of 30,000 words* (New York: Teachers College, Columbia University).

3) M. West. (1953). *A general service list of English words* (New York: Longmans, and Green, and Company).

a reading text. But once the selection of a reading passage is made, it becomes in fact the criterion for selecting vocabulary items for recognition in order to facilitate the reading. The main consideration simply should be to select the key words necessary to grasp the main plot or main theme, whatever the frequency of the words in English. It should be admitted that this is an intuitive and nonobjective process, but we know of no other. At advanced levels it is difficult to know with a given class which are new vocabulary items. The teacher can simply ask a good student to read the passage ahead of time and to underline the words he doesn't know. We have found this to be a very helpful guide.

Once the selection of vocabulary is made, the words will have to be taught. It is probably more true of vocabulary than any other aspect of language learning that words are learned rather than taught. So it would be more accurate to say that the words will have to be presented to the students so that they can learn them. On the very beginning level the teacher reads the whole passage aloud while the students follow silently in their books. At this level so many of the words are new that we don't attempt any written glosses, and the teacher explains the meaning of the new words. Furey has listed a number of different ways of giving explanations:

1. If the word is one which the teacher feels is known by the other students and could be clearly explained by them, he might refer the individual's question regarding meaning to another member of the class. This method is particularly useful for fairly common, concrete items which can be easily explained in simple terms.

Ex: S1: What are trousers?
S2: A kind of clothing. Pants. (S2 points to the pants of one of the male students in the class.)

2. Especially at the beginning level, gesture and pointing out of referents in the real world is a succinct and efficient way of illustrating meaning.
What does *put on* mean in the sentence, I put on a sweater if it is a cold day.

T: Making the appropriate "putting on" or dressing gestures, the teacher says "I put on my hat," "I put on my sweater.")

3. The listing of synonyms (or antonyms), as long as they are terms the student already knows, can be an effective way of illustrating meaning. This technique seems to be particularly useful in explaining common adjectives.

Ex: S: What is a kind person?
T: A person who is nice, pleasant, helpful, good.

4. When a questioned item refers to a class or group of items or activities, the citing of specific examples of these objects or activities may be an appropriate way of directing the student toward comprehension.

Ex: S: What does the word *continent* mean?
T: Asia, Africa and Europe are all continents.

5. Sometimes an abstract term may be best explained by means of illustrative sentences.

The teacher must be certain to use examples which clearly delimit the meaning of the item under consideration.

Ex: S: What does the word *respect* mean in the sentence, I respect that man more than anyone I've ever met.
T: We respect a person who is very brave. We admire and respect someone who does good things for other people. We don't like and respect people who are mean and selfish.

6. In many cases, it is possible to give a fairly lucid dictionary-type definition of a word.
Ex: S: What does lighting mean?
T: Lighting is the very bright light we see during a rainstorm.

7. If the student has been exposed to the appropriate word study materials, the teacher might direct him toward inferring the meaning from both structural clues and context.
Ex: S: What does the word *governor* mean in the sentence, the governor of Pennsylvania met with the president last week to try and get more money.
T: What kind of word is governor? Tell me what kind of word it is by looking at its position in the sentence and its suffix. What does the-or ending on words mean? etc.[4)]

To this should be added the use of translation. If the teacher knows the students' native language, the glossing of individual words in the mother tongue is by far the most efficient way of explaining a word at this level. We realize that such a procedure sounds like heresy to many, but there is considerable psycholinguistic evidence to support such a viewpoint, and our own experience both in teaching and learning foreign languages bears this out. We are firmly in favor of translation of individual words as a technique for teaching vocabulary at the beginning level. But this technique only works when the student knows the lexical equivalent in his mother tongue. At more advanced levels, the students learn words for new concepts for which they have no equivalent in their mother tongue, and these words have to be taught in English, in context. Translation of an isolated word should not lead to a general discussion in the native language; the translation is simply intended to forestall any discussion of words.

Beyond the very beginning level, the teacher does not read the entire reading selection aloud but only pronounces the new words, with the class repeating them. In many texts, the new words are identified and glossed by the textbook writer; if not, the teacher will have to identify and gloss them. Words to be mastered for productive use may be identified by an asterisk.

Here are some vocabulary items and glosses which we have had to prepare for Asimov's *Nine Tomorrows,* which we use with the advanced beginners. They are on dittoes and handed

---

4) P. Furey. (1974). *Some notes on the teaching of vocabulary,* manuscript (Department of General Linguistics, University of Pittsburgh).

out in class. The words are to be learned for recognition.

1. *warrant* — justify; defend by giving a good reason for
 The good quality of the cloth warrants the high price of the dress.
2. *fee* — a sum of money paid for a service
 Doctors and lawyers get fees for their services.
3. *drive* (n) — energy; a force that makes one work harder
 That young man with drive will rise fast in the company and may become president some day.

In writing glosses, one attempts to use simple and familiar words in the explanations, but with languages closely related to English, words we feel to be esoteric and difficult in English are often cognates and as such easily recognized by the students. They find the inclusion of such cognates in the explanations to be very helpful. With homogeneous classes, a gloss in the mother tongue is also helpful. There is no need to spend class time on the explanations and glosses; they can safely be left to the students' perusal at home.

A key question concerns the number of words per lesson a student can be expected to learn for recognition. In an experiment with our Spanish speaking students at the intermediate level, Levenson showed that they could easily handle 25 words and probably more.[5] These students' major deterrent to facile reading lies in poor vocabulary, and we are putting increasing emphasis on lexical acquisition. These students are highly motivated, but it seems likely that any adult student should be able to handle 20-30 new words for each lesson. Whether he would want to is another question.

Comprehension Questions on the Next Assignment

As we said above, as far as possible the comprehension questions given before the reading should serve to focus the students' attention on the important points of the reading rather than being just trivial polite questions. They lend themselves very well to dealing with cultural information, such as American attitudes toward competition, winning and home towns, topics which are likely to be unfamiliar to the students and which might conceivably interfere with their interpretation of the reading. Only those questions which are meant to focus on cultural phenomena need to be discussed in class; the rest can be left for the students to decipher at home.

The format of the questions one chooses will depend partially on the kind of testing

---

5) C. Levenson. (1973). *Presentation of vocaburary of a foreign language: optimum number of new items per lesson and effect of context,* manuscript (Department of General Linguistics, University of Pittsburgh).

situation the students will eventually face. Our students will have to take objective standardized tests, such as the Michigan or TOEFL, and they do many true-false and multiple choice type questions, such as these on a selection from the *Nine Tomorrows:*

1. Before the competition started, what were George's feelings about Trev?
   a. He hoped that Trev would win, and he felt no resentment against Trev.
   b. He did not want Trev to win.
   c. He hoped Trev would win, but he also felt resentment against Trev.
2. The gray-haired man said he was cheering for Trevelyan because
   a. he was from the same hometown.
   b. there was no one from the man's town competing, so he cheered for the town George was from.
   c. he was George's friend and would cheer for anyone George cheered for.

   Write true or false

_________7. Trevelyan always wanted to work on Novia.

_________8. Most people want to stay on Earth rather than go to Novia.

In addition to such objective questions, the teacher might add some inference or opinion questions for the students to reflect on as they read the passage. An opinion question on the reading serves very well as the topic of brief essays for the writing class.

On the intermediate and advanced levels, when the students are beyond simple narrative, they may also be asked to do outlines, summaries, paraphrase, or brief analyses of the main points. The discussion of this work should be as closely correlated as possible with the writing part of the curriculum.

Preparing for the next reading assignment demands much of the teacher's time outside of class, but in class ten minutes is ample time for this activity. But it is a crucial activity and should not be overlooked.

Intensive Study of Grammar Patterns for Recognition

The proficient reader draws on syntactic information as well as lexical in order to decode the message of the passage. Native speakers already know the grammar of their language and they use this knowledge for clues in their reading. Foreign students must be taught to do so. As Wilson points out, structural clues are especially important for foreign students because they have a limited vocabulary and can therefore not afford to ignore structural cues as native speakers often do. Another reason, she points out, for stressing the importance of structural clues is that they can help the student increase his content vocabulary.

On the elementary level we teach recognition, i. e., *decoding only* of (1) those structural patterns which occur late in the curriculum for production but are needed early in reading (such as relative clauses) and (2) those patterns which occur mainly only in writing (such as certain types of nominalizations). The teacher "briefly presents the pattern to the class and helps them understand the significance of the word, order and important function words," in other words a linguistic explanation of the grammatical rule. Our assumption is clearly that reading is a problem-solving activity where an explanation of general principles helps students in their reading. This exercise from Wilson will clarify the procedures[6]:

Teaching point: One Type of Relative Clause

Step 1. Review of familiar patterns

The teacher writes the following sentences on the blackboard, he reads them aloud and the students repeat.

Food at Webster Hall Hotel is expensive.

Some students have a lot of money.

These students eat lunch at Webster Hall Hotel.

He then asks simple comprehension questions such as "Who has a lot of money?" and "Where do these students eat?"

Step 2. Presentation of new pattern

The teacher combines the second and third sentences.

Students (students have a lot of money) eat lunch at Webster Hall Hotel.

He then replaces the word "students" inside the parentheses with "who" and erases the parentheses. Finally, he repeats the comprehension questions.

Step 3. Generalization

The teacher asks the class what "who" means in this sentence. He also asks them what the two sentences are in this sentence.

Since this pattern is a difficult one the teacher should present one or two additional examples using "which" and "that." At least one of these examples should have the relative clause at the end of the sentence. Possible sentences are:

The only apartments which are vacant are too expensive.

There are several organizations that help people with emotional problems.

After these examples the teacher can tell the students that the included sentence beginning with "who" or "which" or "that" is called a relative

6) L, I. Wilson. (1973). Reading in the ESOL classroom, *TESOL Quarterly 7,* no. 3. pp. 264-265.

clause and relative clauses always follow nouns.

The students are then given a set of sentences with questions to complete for homework:

1. The cafeteria which is in the Student Union serves lunch and dinner.
   Where is the cafeteria?
2. The men who were appointed by the chairman will go to Washington.
   Who will go to Washington?

It is important to remember that at this stage the students are never asked to produce the pattern, only to recognize the structural cues for accurate decoding.

Allen points out that the recognition of synonymous sentences has often been left to chance, and that students need practice in recognizing which two sentences in a set of three have approximately the same meaning in exercises like this:

a. Ed had to stop running long enough to catch his breath.
b. Although Ed longed to stop and catch his breath, he had to keep running.
c. Ed longed to stop and catch his breath, but he had to keep running.[7)]

She also points out the value of writing as training for reading. Here is another exercise called sentence synthesis, formerly popular in British textbooks, which can be used for recognition of synonymous sentences. The class is divided into groups, and each group handed a set of sentences like this:

1. Someone asked Larry Smith a question.
2. The question was about his reading habits.
3. He answered.
4. The answer was that he read detective stories.
5. Detective stories take the mind off pressing concerns.

They are told to rewrite them in one sentence.[8)] When finished, each group writes their sentence on the blackboard. The sentences are invariably different and usually synonymous. The class then decides with the teacher's guidance which is the more elegant version. This

7) V. F. Allen. (1973). "Trends in the teaching of reading," *TESL Reporter 6,* no. 4. p. 17.

8) The sentence will be something like: *Asked about his reading habits, Larry Smith answered that he read detective stories in order to take his mind off pressing concerns or When someone asked Larry Smith about his reading habits, he answered that detective stories take the mind off pressing concerns and that is what he read or Someone asked Larry Smith a question about his reading habits and he answered that he read detective stories because they took his mind off pressing concerns.* The first version was the original sentence, adapted from *Time Magazine.*

exercise can be done in five or ten minutes; the competitive aspect (the class makes it competitive whether the teacher wants it or not) gives it the quality of a game and is a pleasant change of classroom activity, but above all it provides intensive practice in examining synonymous sentences and their syntactical devices. The easiest way to construct such exercises to begin with the long embedded sentence and then to rewrite it in shorter sentences, leaving out as many of the syntactical devices as possible. Teachers can either write the sentence themselves or else select a suitable sentence from the reading passage.

From Paulston, C. B. & Bruder, M. N. (1976). *Teaching English as a second language.* Cambridge, MA: Winthrop Publishers, Inc., pp. 165-178.

20. THE FRONTIER METHOD OF VOCABULARY PRACTICE

English as a second language (ESL) students studying in the United States at an intensive language center or at a college or university face the task of acquiring vocabulary that will serve both their social and academic needs. They must also advance to a point where their pronunciation and syntactic ability meet the minimum competency requirements to operate in the second language environment. By the time they enter a program in higher education, however, most have demonstrated a basic grammatical competency through some formal credential (a diploma from a U. S. high school, completion of requisite coursework in an intensive English program, a minimum score on one of the standardized ESL tests, such as the TOEFL [Test of English as a Foreign Language] or the Michigan Test of English Language Proficiency). Students are also liable to get a lesson in pronunciation or dialect leveling every time they turn on the radio or TV or try to make a business phone call.

Certainly, the ESL community has done much to strengthen the teaching of grammar and pronunciation, but as ESL professionals we can serve our students better by providing them with a systematic and self-conscious approach to vocabulary acquisition rather than the perfunctory or artificial treatments this skill sometimes receives in ESL classrooms when teachers rely on indirect learning alone. An adaptation of the Frontier Method of vocabulary learning (first devised by Johnson O'Connor and popularized by Pauk) helps the ESL student to become better acquainted with the use of a monolingual English dictionary and to practice informal phonological, morphological, and contextualizing activities. This article considers the usefulness and effectiveness of the method.

The major learning burden that ESL students face as they enter a program in higher education is to enlarge and refine their vocabularies beyond the minimum 5,000-7,500 recognition items and 1,500-2,000 productive items that should constitute the lexical range of intermediate ESL students. Students will want to master words and expressions that they encounter in other courses, both ongoing and upcoming, especially in the major area of study. Furthermore, students will want to know the English words that will enable them to describe and experience more fully the English-speaking culture they have entered.

What problems do these students face as they approach the task of acquiring this vocabulary? We know that a native speaker will leave college with a receptive vocabulary of approximately 60,000-100,000 words learned and acquired. Yet the task challenges even the native speaker. Mina Shaughnessy, commenting on the native speaker, also frames the problem of the basic writer of English:

> Little has been done as yet to help the student grapple with the college vocabulary. What has been done tends to help him more as a reader than as a writer. Yet vocabulary looms as perhaps the most formidable and discouraging obstacle he faces in his struggle for advanced literacy.

Lacking the native idiom, typical ESL learners are beset with even greater impediments to full communication. For example, the gap between the number of words in receptive vocabulary (words decoded when listening or reading) and productive vocabulary (words encoded when speaking or writing) is wider for ESL learners than for native speakers. Naturally, the more words students can promote into the productive vocabulary, the greater their general facility with English.

The ability to manipulate academic vocabulary may be our students' best chance for success. Shaughnessy does not exaggerate when she identifies academic vocabulary as "the medium of instruction in all classes." Yet, although such word mastery underlies our students' success in every class, few instructors, even in language arts areas, find the time to teach the vocabulary of their courses, writing-across-the-curriculum intentions notwithstanding. Thus the skill must be presented formally in the ESL classroom, if it is to be consciously presented. Fortunately, in our experience a well-designed classroom vocabulary program can help the ESL learner increase both general and discipline- or course-specific word knowledge.

TECHNIQUES OF VOCABULARY INSTRUCTION

Although a passive method in and of itself, the rather random method of vocabulary acquisition through natural growth or indirect learning will generally increase the ESL learner's stock of words and provides the best situation for the contextual guessing needed to learn any language, first or second. For the intermediate ESL student, however, the target language is more self-consciously *acquired* in the manner of a skill than gradually and developmentally *learned*, as would have been the case with the language of nurture.

A more formal approach to vocabulary enhancement is reliance upon controlled word lists of 5,000 or fewer high frequency words (see Michael West's [1953] list of 2,000 highest frequency words; also, Barnard's list of 3,000 words [Richards, 1976, p. 432]. These lists can be helpful diagnostically or in the preparation of a basic text or text lesson, but simply handing a word list to students ignores both the importance off context in vocabulary learning and the unmotivating nature of lengthy lists, as well as questions of multiple meanings and word frequency. To illustrate, a vocabulary lesson in a current college ESL text includes *aqueduct* (never a high frequency term here on the Great Plains) as a significant lexical item.

Monotony may also attend the study of lists of prefixes, suffixes, and stems that students are sometimes asked to master. Certainly some discussion of affixation can be helpful to the student. Yet such work encourages students' receptive abilities (decoding) rather than their productive skills. And even though prefixes often provide constructive clues for contextual guesswork, they regularly lack a fixed, discernible meaning (e. g., *un*lock, *un*wise) or they may confuse the student as a simulated prefix (e. g., *un*tie vs. *un*ite). Suffixes commonly do provide the learner with a more reliable signal of a word's part of speech (e. g., *-tion, -ly*). This basic degree of morphemic skill, however, should already be a part of the competence of students whose language arts abilities can be diagnosed as intermediate.

More effective, less random lists are those developed for indirect presentation in a situational lesson. Such a lesson would gather — with a widely variant degree of glossing — words and phrases relevant to specific people, places, tasks, or social situations, such as going to the movies, visiting a sick friend in the hospital, applying for a job, and the like.

Another method, the cloze text, is useful as a diagnostic tool but can also be effective for presenting and discussing vocabulary.

Taken together, many of these vocabulary acquisition methods will at one point or another find the ESL student grappling with uncertainty and finally reaching for a dictionary. The students must acquire English much more self-consciously.

Although ESL students will want to rely on the dictionary, their vocabulary will also grow through contextual guessing — inferring a word's meaning from its morphemic structure and syntactic and semantic surroundings. Not all researchers are convinced that contextual learning is more productive than studying words in isolation. Still, students must be persuaded to use this most common and most valuable method of approximating the encoder's intended meaning by guessing contextually at a word's meaning rather than halting a train of thought in mid-sentence to seek complete knowledge of the word in the dictionary. Students are best advised to accept temporarily the vague familiarity of the lexical item that context provides and only later to move closer to a more complete mastery of the word's use.

THE FRONTIER METHOD

A problem, then, is how to encourage ESL students to add to this crucial language-learning step of contextualized guessing a dictionary look-up procedure that can move them toward mastery. One solution we have found is to encourage students to note semifamiliar words that they can imagine themselves writing or speaking in the near future. These words or phrases are on their frontier or verge of mastery. We tell our students to check or somehow flag such a frontier word but to continue decoding the message until a logical stopping place (perhaps at the end of a paragraph; ideally at the end of a longer block of text). The frontier words can be selected from a variety of sources: texts, other classes, newspapers and magazines, conversations with friends and associates, and so on.

For each lexical item selected over the semester, the student creates a 3x5 or 4x6 file card with information about the word that has been culled from the dictionary entry, along with the source sentence containing the word and an original sentence of the student's own composition (see Figures 1 and 2).

One important function of the skeletal system is to augment the muscle system during movement activities.

aug · ment, v.t. (og-ment)
aug · men · ta · tion, n.
(og-men-ta-shan)

Source: Dental Admissions Test preparation text

Figure 1

[Latin augere, to increase]
1. To make greater as in size, extent, or quantity; to enlarge, increase
2. To assist by an increase of resources

Varied reading will help me augment my vocabulary.

SYN: To add to
ANT: To diminish, subtract from

Figure 2

We ask students to submit a few of their cards for feedback each week. Whether we use these submissions as the basis for a classroom exercise or not, we return the cards promptly, marked for their conformity to the prescribed format. We note the word's frequency and its register, best gauged by looking at the sample and original sentences written on the card. At the end of the semester, we ask students to compose an original essay that uses several of the words they have found on their frontier and submitted over the term. This method has helped improve the students' judgments about the words' appropriateness to the registers they choose for their original sentences as well as their sense of the words' frequency of occurrence in their milieu.

ADVANTAGES OF THE FRONTIER METHOD

The format of the cards requires students to examine several facets of the word and perform several operations on it as they promote it from their receptive toward their active vocabulary. On the card's front, the example sentence and the specific source give the word from the student's chosen context. Below the source sentence, the student writes the word, broken into syllables to help with the spelling, followed by an indication of the word's part of speech as used in the student's source sentence. Because students are encouraged to show what they guess to be common derivative forms of the word along with the word itself, they are more likely to associate certain suffixes with parts of speech that they indicate. To the right of the word's spelling, the student copies the phonetic spelling, attempting to pronounce the word as the dictionary's pronunciation key indicates.

On the back of the card, the word's etymology and synonym and antonym entries (optional but encouraged) offer exposure to the word's derivational morphology. As an example, one student recently expressed pleasure at coming up with another high frequency word (i. e., *impractical*) in his search for an antonym for *practical*. Additionally, the student is asked to list on the card two or three of the definitions presented in the dictionary, marking with an asterisk the definition that most closely fits the use of the word in the source sentence given on the card's front. Finally, writing the original sentence on the card is the student's first step toward advancing the selected word from its frontier status as part of the receptive language modes — listening and reading — to at least one of the productive modes — writing. The original sentence may also reveal telling but addressable gaps in the student's idiomatic competence, and students take pleasure in finally composing an effective message. In general, we have found that the source and original sentences from the cards uninvasively provide the ESL instructor with some better understanding of the students' curiosities and interests.

This textless method can be adapted efficiently to meet the pedagogical complexities of most ESL classrooms in the limited time available. In fact, the method could be easily integrated into most other classroom activities and protocols as well as all four language arts modalities.

Adult ESL students appreciate the opportunity to address their own vocabulary needs. The Frontier Method provides for content-based ESL learning that is learner generated or inductive rather than prescribed or dictated. Consequently, the approach is in keeping with notions of functional language learning; that is, it focuses on context and referential meaning instead of rote memorization. Also, it offers cognitive enrichment: Asking for a variety of sources for the frontier words ensures a certain degree of meaningful contextualization, as well as the acquisition of ancillary language arts skills, such as using the dictionary as a resource.

SUMMARY AND DISCUSSION

Most intermediate ESL students in our ESL courses over the past 4 years have considered the Frontier Method extremely useful, though some, especially the lower intermediate students, prefer not to bother with the word's etymology. These same students often prefer to use advanced learners' dictionaries instead of college-level dictionaries. The more advanced and dedicated students, however, see this exercise as both a challenge and an opportunity to investigate further the sometimes familiar affixes and stems of English.

In general, students respond positively to Frontier card assignments. They regard the preparing of cards as very useful and see the method as a basis for further vocabulary development. Many carry the cards as flashcards with which to test themselves in a simplified form of programmed instruction. Also, students enjoy the fact that the words are student generated rather than given to them as an assignment, making the process personal and therefore more meaningful. Although students often need the assistance of a native speaker with a word's pronunciation, they find the phonetic spelling helpful.

We believe that the Frontier Method provides a direct vocabulary technique that complements indirect learning through contextual guessing. The method adapts well to a variety of classroom materials and techniques. It has given our students a conscious method of using much of the material they encounter in a typical dictionary entry. At the same time, it encourages students to promote receptive vocabulary into productive usage.

From Carroll, C. M. & Mordaunt, G. O. (1991). The frontier method of vocabulary practice. *TESOL Journal*, Autumn, pp. 23-25.

21. APPLYING SCHEMA THEORY TO FOREIGN LANGUAGE READING

At a time when innovative methodologies for oral language instruction are gaining recognition in the classroom as well as in the research literature (Wolfe and Jones, 11; Lafayette and Strasheim, 4), most materials developers and classroom teachers still continue to disregard the newer body of theory and application that has developed in reading (Schulz, 8). As a result, reading materials and instruction for foreign language students remain dominated by the practices of the past which view reading as deriving meaning from print, without recognizing the full importance of the reader's background knowledge. The alternatives presented in this article are based on an interactive model of reading, which maintains that background knowledge readers bring to the reading act is as important as the information residing in the text.

SCHEMA THEORY AND READING COMPREHENSION

The following paragraph offers the readers of this article personal experience with the implications of schema theory. The paragraph contains four nonsense words: doogledorph, gleep, klem, and sleechy. Even though these words all follow the conventions of English spelling, and readers can undoubtably pronounce each one, it is impossible to assign them meaning out of context. However, as one reads the paragraph, the English equivalent meanings will become apparent.

> He kept on climbing until he reached the top of the doogledorph. He was suddenly engulfed by a dense sleechy. As the wind carried it away, he found himself gazing out over a breathtaking panorama. White peaks surrounded him, some with fluffy sleechies seeming to be skewered on their points. The klem was a deep blue, and everything seemed to sparkle as the bright sun beamed down. As he looked down into a valley, he saw a two-humped gleep ambling along the river bank. It was the most unusual one he had ever seen, but he was sure it was a gleep. He wondered what a gleep was doing in doogledorph area. They usually inhabited only desert areas.

As most readers go through the paragraph, they recognize that the English equivalents for the nonsense words listed above are mountain, camel, sky, and cloud, respectively. Of course, these are the terms that make sense as one tries to fit real words into the spaces filled by nonsense. But, why are readers able to do this?

For several years theorists in the field of reading have recognized readers' knowledge of the general topic area for a given piece of printed information as one of the major contributors to successful comprehension (Adams and Bruce, 1; Spiro, 9). The psychologist Piaget supplies us with a hypothetical process which portrays the role of an individual's existing knowledge in constant adaptive responses to environmental input.

Piaget hypothesizes mental structures that guide humans in making sense of the world. At the time of birth these schemata are extremely rudimentary, producing only reflexive behavior, but they grow and develop in response to environmental input during the maturation process, adults usually being able to process highly abstract information. Piaget uses the term assimilation to refer to the process of fitting new information into what one already knows about the world. In other words, a particular schema is activated and simply absorbs the new bit of information, growing in the act, but not changing significantly in nature. However, people sometimes come up against environmental information so novel as to be anomalous to their existing schemata and have no adequate knowledge structures to absorb the input. This throws a person into a state of intellectual unbalance or, in Piaget's words, disequilibrium. It is at this point that the process of schema accommodation begins, and a person restructures his or her conceptual organization of the general topic at hand in order to be able to adequately absorb the new information and restore intellectual balance or equilibrium in relation to the surrounding environment.

If this article's readers were to take the four nonsense words and the paragraph they read above seriously, they might say that they had "assimilated" new vocabulary items into their existing schema for mountain scenes. However, in reference to the camel-like animal, they would have "accommodated" their existing schema for camels' habitats, expanding it from including only desert areas to include mountainous areas. Of course, people without adequate knowledge of mountain scenes such as the one described, and with no knowledge of camels and their usual habitats, would not have been able to assign English meanings to the nonsense words.

Essentially, schema theory of comprehension is the idea that, when people encounter new information, they attempt to understand it by fitting it into what they already know about the world, schemata being the mental structures that store people's knowledge in memory. When they come up against something so novel that it does not fit comfortably into an existing schema, they go through an adjustment process in which the view of the environment shifts in order to deal with the new input. Students often lack well-developed schemata so important to a comprehensive understanding of their academic reading materials. Even having the appropriate schema, students sometimes fail to utilize what they already know in their efforts to understand the new information they are reading. This is especially so when attempting to read something written in a foreign language representing a foreign culture.

CULTURAL SCHEMATA

Just as the existence of a schema related to a topic can enhance one's understanding of it, the lack of a relevant schema will inhibit, if not preclude, comprehension. The likelihood of this occurring is directly related to one's cultural background. If a reader's background differs significantly from that of the author, it is likely that schema needed to understand a particular concept will be lacking or ignored. Current research findings indicate that, in either case, comprehension will suffer.

In one of the most significant attempts thus far to examine this process, Steffenson, Joag-Dev, and Anderson had twenty college-level students from the United States and twenty college-level students from India read and recall a passage describing a traditional wedding in each culture. In this experiment, a wide range of variables was assessed, including reading time, the amount of the text recalled, and the amount of elaborations and distortions. After analyzing the results, the researchers found that when reading the passage about their native culture, the subjects read faster, recalled and elaborated more, and distorted less than when they read the foreign one.

Other researchers (Johnson, 3; Reynolds, et al., 7), studying subjects from a variety of cultural and linguistic backgrounds, have come up with similar findings. Thus, evidence exists to support the view that cultural schemata influence reading comprehension. The relevance of this finding for foreign language teachers becomes evident when one considers that foreign language students usually find themselves in situations in which their primary —and perhaps only—exposure to the target language is in the classroom. As a result, they may lack not only relevant schemata for understanding their texts, but also the type of cultural environment which would facilitate the development and reinforcement of those schemata. Faced with this dilemma, what can foreign language teachers do? In order to help answer that question, one must now turn to a consideration of specific ways in which teachers can apply the principles of schema theory to their teaching in an effort to increase their students' reading proficiency.

PREREADING ACTIVITIES

Students need a general knowledge of the norms, values, and behaviors found in the cultures where their target language is typically spoken. In other words, they need a feel for the culture, an at-homeness with it. To help them gain this familiarity, teachers can show modern movies and taped television programs from target language countries, having the students discuss the differences they notice. During the discussion the teacher may attempt to fill in cultural information that the students do not come with on their own. It is important that the materials be current; the cultures should be portrayed as they are today.

Teachers can also help their students to become familiar with target language countries and their respective cultures through slides, picture books, travelogues, and visiting speakers. Using these nonprint materials will help students to develop a framework they can use in approaching their target language readings. They will be able to image situations and understand the content of the materials they are reading more easily through this general cultural familiarity with the target culture. People often enjoy reading a book when they have already seen the movie. This familiarity makes it easy to follow the plot and supplies ready-made images which enhance comprehension.

In addition to developing a general cultural framework for reading comprehension, there are reading activities based directly on the text to be read. To activate appropriate schemata, students should form expectations for the content they are to read. They skim the text, looking for any helpful clues such as titles, headings, subheadings, pictures, captions, and introductory statements. They should be alert for anything that can give them clues to content. After they have surveyed the reading, they predict the content of the text, telling a partner what they think it will deal with. This gets them ready to read and test their hypotheses. Sometimes, during the prediction phase, students learn cultural information from each other or from the teacher. It is fine if they have predicted inappropiately, because the prediction will still get them actively reading for meaning, causing them to alter what they had predicted as they understand the new information. If they have founded their predictions purely on their native culture, there will be a basis for comparison as they read, gather the new information, and adjust their topical schema to include patterns from the new culture.

Another method of activating cultural schemata is to give the students pre-reading suggestions or questions that orient them to watch for certain cultural factors different from their own culture. The teacher can also supply an overview of the reading, or one of its major aspects, in the form of a diagram similar to the one in figure 1.

Figure 1

Cultural Use of Time

Patterns of Punctuality

Home Culture		Target Culture	
formal	informal	formal	informal

This overview deals with time use in different cultures, and is designed to activate existing knowledge about the topic of an upcoming reading in which one of the major potentially confusing factors is the cultural use of time. To get class discussion started and stimulate students' thinking about the topic, the teacher can ask some leading questions such as, "Can you think of differences in punctuality patterns that might come up in a reading from your target culture?" Or, the teacher might alert students by having a class discussion about conventions in the United States, and asking them to watch for differences that could fit into the other cultural framework as they read.

Langer's PREP method for native speakers helps students activate their existing knowledge about a given topic, as well as exchange pre-reading ideas about the topic. The writers of this article have adapted Langer's small-group activity for larger language classes by developing a set of three questions that students can use in pairs or triads.

1. What do you think when you see (title, phrase, or word the teacher has chosen)? What does it mean to you?
2. What made you think of your answer to the first question?
3. Talk about your reaction with the other member(s) of your pair or group. What does this title (phrase or word) make you expect from the reading?

To do this activity with their students, teachers usually choose three phrases or words that represent key ideas from the reading. One might want to use just the title, or one or two phrases, if time is limited. Students are given the three questions for each title, key phrase, or key word with which they are to work. They write the target item in the blank space. They are then to write down what comes to mind when they think of the word or phrase, or what the phrase means to them. They then try to identify what made them come up with their reaction. In pairs or triads, they compare their reactions and discuss how these reactions affect their expectations for the content of the reading. The teacher moves around among the groups, monitoring progress and lending a hand when necessary. Sometimes discussion of these predictions with the entire class is beneficial before reading. In this group exercise, a great deal of idea sharing and development goes on in a relatively short time.

The purpose of these pre-reading activities is to form a mindset of readiness in the students for what they are about to read. Some of the activities simply stimulate them to bring to mind what they already know about the upcoming reading topic, while others help them develop topic appropriate schemata. Thus, the thrust of the activities is to have students approach reading tasks with conscious expectations for the information they are about to process, and to have them build schemata that will assure cultural appropriateness of those expectations.

DURING READING ACTIVITIES

Effective reading requires the active participation of the reader. When reading is viewed, as it often is, as a passive activity, the reader is less likely to engage the active processes which appear to enhance comprehension (Baker and Brown, 2). In order to encourage this type of processing, teachers may utilize activities during the reading act.

One such strategy is the use of adjunct questions which require students to interact with the text and thereby become active readers. These teacher-generated questions are usually embedded in the text or located adjacent to it. If embedded, they appear at the point(s) where the teacher wants the students to stop and reflect on what they have read. If adjacent to the text, they also encourage reflection but at the discretion of the readers. In either case, the type of questions asked should vary. From a schema-theoretic perspective, the strength of this activity is that it encourages the use of relevant background which the readers already have but may not activate on their own.

Mid-reading predictions are an especially effective way to have students maintain deep involvement with narratives. Working in pairs, students read up to a stipulated point in a story. At that point they stop reading and each writes a prediction as to what will happen next in the story. Each student reads another student's prediction, exchanging reasons for making the predictions. They then continue reading to compare what does happen in the story with their predictions. This procedure can be done more than once within any given story of sufficient length. The students are usually fascinated by comparing their predictions with those of other students and with the story itself. They often realize that, as they gather more information, their predictions become closer to the events of the story.

POST-READING ACTIVITIES

Post-reading activities have too often been little more than a literal level rehashing of the reading passage. In order to promote the development of higher level thinking skills in students, effective questioning strategies must incorporate an awareness of all levels of comprehension. This can be accomplished by including open-ended questions which require students to infer, evaluate, and/or justify their conclusions. This is an especially important consideration for foreign language students who are too often faced with questions that require nothing more than searching a reading passage for a literal level fact to fill in a blank.

The following is an example of a post-reading activity incorporating these principles and designed for use with a passage dealing with a cheating scandal at West Point.

Directions: Listed below are several statements.
In the first column, check those statements that you believe are true or right. In the second column, check those statements that General Berry of West Point would check. Be prepared to defend your answers.

_____ _____ 1. It's not whether you win or lose that counts, but how you play the game.
_____ _____ 2. You could escape from a difficult situation by turning against your friends who trusted you.
_____ _____ 3. A "white lie" never hurt anyone.
_____ _____ 4. Truth is relative.

After reading the passage, students are asked to respond to statements such as these. The process of thinking through their answers and then defending them with other students helps them to synthesize the information and thereby create or expand schemata which can be used in the future. This is often a very effective activity when done in three stages: first, students answer individually; next, they discuss their individual answers in small groups; and finally, they discuss the group results with the whole class.

Mapping is a postreading activity that helps students gain an overall understanding of what they have just read. The procedure enhances comprehension by obliging the reader to engage in an intense involvement with the meaning that has been encoded in the text. In this case, mapping refers to the process of selecting key words or phrases from a printed text and organizing them in a visual display that portrays the mapper's understanding of the content. Maps may take the forms of hierarchies, flowcharts, timelines, pictorial displays, or any other visual device by which a reader may graphically demonstrate comprehension. The procedure requires the reader to think in depth about what has just been read; it is a translation or recoding process through which the reader discovers the holistic meaning off a printed text, then produces that meaning in an alternative representation.

For a highly structured form of mapping, students might be asked to fill in a very general pre-reading overview, such as the one represented in figure 1, after they have finished reading. This can be done individually or in small groups and then judged for appropriateness by the teacher or other students. Finished maps supply excellent focal points for class discussion.

Finally, it is also improtant to recognize the significance of the reading-writing relationship and to utilize it as a tool for facilitating comprehension. The use of written summaries and retellings is one way to do this. If students have the requisite skills, these can be done in the target language. If not, doing them in the native language will also enhance students' foreign language learning. Regardless of the language used, the focus must always be on content, not form. The teacher should be looking for indications of global comprehension rather than concentrating on spelling and punctuation.

CONCLUSION

This article has offered some alternatives to traditional methods of teaching reading in foreign languages. Drawing on current theory and research, these activities can improve learning environments, processes, and outcomes in foreign language classrooms. When used in a way which supplements what is currently being done, the result will be a more balanced view of the reading process which recognizes the importance of the written word without overlooking the full importance of reader input.

■ References

Adams, Marilyn, and Betram Bruce. (1982). Background Knowlege and Reading Comprehension, In Judith A. Langer and M. Trika Smith-Burke (eds.) *Reader Meets Author: Bridging the Gap*. Newark, Delaware: International Reading Association, pp. 2-25.

Baker, Linda, and Ann L. Brown. (1984). Metacognitive Skills and Reading, In P. David Pearson (ed.) *Handbook of Reading Research*. New York: Longman, pp. 353-394.

Johnson, Patricia. (1981). Effects on Reading Comprehension of Language Complexity and Cultural Background of a Text, *TESOL Quarterly, 15,* pp. 169-181.

Lafayette, Robert C., and Lorrain A. Strasheim. (1984). The Standard Sequence and the Non-Traditional Methodologies, *Foreign Language Annals, 17,* pp. 567-574.

Langer, Judith A. (1982). Facilitating Text Processing: The Elaboration of Knowledge, In Judith A. Langer and M. Trika Smith-Burke (eds.) *Reader Meets Author: Briding the Gap*. Newark, Delaware: International Reading Association, pp. 149-162.

Piaget, Jean. (1963). *The Origins of the Intelligence in Children, New York*: W. W. Norton and Company, Inc.

Reynolds, Ralph E., Marsha A. Taylor, Margaret S. Steffensen, Larry L. Shirey, and Richard C. Anderson. (1982). Cultural Schemata and Reading Comprehension, *Reading Research Quarterly, 17,* pp. 353-366.

Schlz, Renatte A. (1983). From Word to Meaning: Foreign Language Reading Instruction after the Elementary Course, *The Modern Language Journal, 67,* pp. 127-134.

Spiro, Rand J. (1980). Constructive Processes in Prose Comprehension and Recall, In Rand J. Spiro, Bertram C. Bruce, and William F. Brewer (eds.) *Theoretical Issues in Reading Comprehension.* Hillsdale, N. J.: Erilbaum.

Steffensen, Margaret S., Chitra Joag-Dev, and Richard C. Anderson. (1979). A Cross-Cultural Perspective on Reading Comprehension, *Reading Research Quarterly, 15,* pp. 10-29.

Wolfe, David and Gwendolyn Jones. (1982). Integrating Total Physical Response strategy in a Level 1 Spanish Class, *Foreign Language Annals, 14,* pp. 273-280.

From Melendes, J. E. and Pritchard, H. R. (1985). Applying schema theory to foreign language reading, *Foreign Language Annals*, 17, pp. 399-403.

22. LITERATURE IN THE ESL CLASSROOM

Should literature to be part of an ESL curriculum? Today with the current focus in ESL on meeting the particular academic and occupational needs of the students, it is easy to view any attention to literature as unnecessary. Is there a rationale for including literature in the curriculum?

Let's first examine the common arguments *against* using literature. The most common ones are the following. First, since one of our main goals as ESL teachers is to teach the grammar of the language, literature, due to its structural complexity and its unique use of language, does little to contribute to this goal. Second, the study of literature will contribute nothing to helping our students meet their academic and/or occupational goals. Finally, literature often reflects a particular cultural perspective; thus, on a conceptual level, it may be quite difficult for students. These arguments certainly need to be addressed if we are to reach a decision as to whether or not to use literature.

Clearly, we all share the objective of promoting our students' awareness of the structure of the language. However, there are as Widdowson (1978:3) points out two levels of linguistic knowledge: the level of *usage* and the level of *use*. According to his definition, usage involves a knowledge of linguistic rules, whereas *use* entails knowing how to use these rules for effective communication. Can a literary text contribute to a knowledge of either one?

Most present day literary texts assume that literature can provide a basis for extending language usage. Many of these texts focus on the particular grammatical points that are salient in the text (see, for example, Fassler and Lay, 1979). Furthermore, vocabulary expansion is dealt with by attention to word forms and common expressions. Povey (1972:187), in summarizing the aims of using literature in ESL classes, argues that "literature will increase all language skills because literature will extend linguistic knowledge by giving evidence of extensive and subtle vocabulary usage, and complex and exact syntax." Later I will examine the wisdom of using literature as a basis for teaching usage.

Whereas literature has traditionally been used to teach language usage, rarely has it been used to develop language use. Yet the advantage of using literature for this purpose is that literature presents language in discourse in which the parameters of the setting and role relationship are defined. Language that illustrates a particular register or dialect is embedded within a social context, and thus, there is a basis for determining why a particular form is used. As such, literature is ideal for developing an awareness of language use.

A second common argument against using literature is that it will do nothing toward promoting the students' academic and/or occupational goals. First of all, it is important to remember that one need not assume that literature be studied to the exclusion of other types of texts. Hence, it need not be a question of either literature or prose. Rather, the question is one of whether or not the study of literature can in any way contribute to academic and/or occupational goals. Certainly, in so far as literature can foster an overall increase in reading proficiency, it will contribute to these goals. An evaluation of reading proficiency rests on an understanding of what is involved in the reading process. Widdowson (1979:74) and others regard reading "not as a reaction to a text but as *interaction* between writer and reader mediated through the text." This interaction, it seems to me, occurs on two levels: linguistic and conceptual. In other words, reading necessitates the ability to interact with a text by decoding the language and comprehending the concepts presented. Furthermore, these two levels often interact. Johnson (1981), in examining the effects of the linguistic complexity and the cultural background of a text on the reading comprehension of Iranian ESL students, found that the relationship between these variables is complex; in some instances familiarity with the text in interpreting it. What is critical in selecting a text is to examine it for both its linguistic and conceptual difficulty. Whereas readability formulas provide some index of the former, unfortunately we have little to aid us in dealing with the latter.

The perspective of reading as *interaction* presupposes, of course, that a reader is willing to interact with a particular text. It is here that the motivational factors involved in reading become critical. As Gaies (1979:48) points out, "since the reading process . . . is the interaction of a reader and a text, we stand in equal need of more research on the affective, attitudinal and experiential variables which would differentiate individual or groups of learners in terms of their willingness and ability to decode written input in a second language." For some students, literature may provide the affective, attitudinal and experiential factors which will motivate them to read. As such, literary texts can aid in the development of reading proficiency and in this way contribute to a students' academic and occupational objectives.

Finally, critics of the use of literature maintain that to the extent that literary texts reflect a particular cultural perspective, they may be difficult for ESL students to read. Clearly, this can be a problem. The question is whether or not any benefits can arise from examining the cultural assumptions of a piece of literature. Marshall (1979:333), in using English literature with Puerto Rican students, found that as she worked to help students overcome the difficulties of the text, her own appreciation of the text was clarified and her respect for the students' own cultural framework enhanced. Thus, literature may work to promote a greater tolerance for cultural differences for both the teacher and the students. Northrop Frye (1964:77) summarizes this benefit of literature in the following manner: "So you may ask what is the use of studying the world of imagination where anything is possible and anything can be assumed, where there are no rights or wrongs and all arguments are equally good. One of the most obvious uses, I think, is its encouragement of tolerance."

A second benefit of struggling with the potential cultural problem of literature is that it may promote our students' own creativity. Again as Frye puts it (1964:129), "It is clear that the end of literary teaching is not simply the admiration of literature; it's something more like the transfer of imaginative energy from literature to the students." Thus, whereas students may indeed be unfamiliar with some of the cultural assumptions in literature, the advantages of confronting these assumptions may be well worth the struggle.

In summary, literature offers several benefits to ESL classes. It can be useful in developing linguistic knowledge both on a usage and use level. Secondly, to the extent that students enjoy reading literature, it may increase their motivation to interact with a text and thus, ultimately increase their reading proficiency. Finally, an examination of a foreign culture through literature may increase their understanding of that culture and perhaps spur their own creation of imaginative works.

SELECTING LITERATURE

The key to success in using literature in the ESL class seems to me to rest in the literary works that are selected. A text which is extremely difficult on either a linguistic or cultural level will have few benefits. One common method of solving the potential problem of linguistic difficulty is the simplification of the text. There are, however, serious disadvantages to using this approach. As Honeyfield (1977:434-35) points out, simplification tends to produce a homogenized product in which the information becomes diluted. The additional words in the text tend to spread the information out rather than to localize the information. Furthermore, the simplification of syntax may reduce cohesion and readability. Since proficient readers rely heavily on localized information and cohesive devices, deleting these elements will contribute little to the development of reading skills.

Are there any alternatives to using simplified versions? One obvious solution is to select texts which are relatively easy according to readability counts. However, such counts typically are based on some measure of vocabulary difficulty and some indice of syntactic complexity, such as sentence length. In dealing with literature, these counts, of course, give no indication of the complexity of the text in terms of plot, character, or cultural difficulty.

A second solution is to select texts from literature written for young adults. Such literature, according to Donelson and Nilsen (1980:14-15), tends to have the following characteristics. Frequently, the theme of such literature deals with the problem of personal growth and development. Furthermore, most literature for young adults tends to be relatively short, and the characters usually limited to a small cast of characters with a young adult as the central character. Most importantly, from an ESL perspective, many of the books tend to be stylistically less complex.

In addition to selecting literary texts that are stylistically uncomplicated, it is important to select themes with which the students can identify. Certainly, one common experience of most ESL students is their struggle with a language and culture with which they are unfamiliar. Thus, literature which deals with either of these themes should be highly relevant to them.

USING LITERATURE IN THE CLASSROOM

Selecting the text is only the first step. An equally important issue is how to deal with such texts in the classroom. Here, I think Rosenblatt's (1978:24) distinction between efferent and aesthetic reading is critical. She defines efferent reading (from the Latin "to carry away") as reading in which the reader is concerned with what she will carry away. In aesthetic reading, on the other hand, "the reader's primary concern is with what happens during the actual reading." In both cases the text is merely the stimulus; the reader creates her own poem as she interacts with the text bringing her own experience to bear. For Rosenblatt, this interaction is an event in time involving a specific reader, and a specific text at a specific time and place; if any of these are changed, there is a different event. Hence, while a text may not be involving for an individual at a certain time, later the same person, by bringing additional experience to the text, may find it involving. Because of this, Rosenblatt suggests that a student typically be allowed to put aside a particular piece of literature, an option which we rarely allow our students. Widdowson makes a similar point when he states (1978:80), "to present someone with a set of extracts and to require him to read them not in order to learn something interesting and relevant about the world but in order to learn something about the language being used is to misrepresent language use to some degree."

In short, the classroom approach to efferent and aesthetic reading must of necessity be very different. Exploring the usage of a text which is being approached efferently is in keeping with the aim of using a text to gain information. On the other hand, since in aesthetic reading the experience is primary, this is where a classroom approach should begin and language usage should be explored only to the extent that it is relevant to that experience. The fact is that literary experiences outside of a classroom proceed in this manner. What is most important to a reader in aesthetic reading is the enjoyment attained by interacting with the text. Usage comes into play only when it impedes or highlights that experience. To do other than this in the classroom results in what Widdowson (1979:80) terms a lack of authenticity i. e. an inappropriate relationship between the text and the reader.

APPLICATION

Let us examine how a particular literary passage might be approached aesthetically rather than efferently. The following selection is taken from *Sweet Promised Land* by Robert Laxalt (1957:62-63). The book is a biography of Laxalt' father, a Basque sheepherder who came to America when he was sixteen. As Laxalt puts it, "My father was a sheepherder, and his home was the hills. So it began when he was a boy in the misted Pyrenees of France, and so it was to be for most of his life in the lonely Sierra of Nevada." The following passage describes his father at the age of sixty-three in an exclusive New York restaurant on the way back to his homeland for the first time since he came to America.

> We made it through the soup and the salad without incident. It began when the waiter came to take away our salad plates and put on others for the main course. He collected John's and mine, and then reached for my father's. But he could not lift it, because my father was holding it to the table with both hands.
> "I'm sorry," said the waiter. "I thought you were finished."
> "I am finished," said my father.
> "Oh," said the waiter, and again reached for the salad plate. My father held on.
> "May I take your plate, sir?" said the waiter.
> "No," said my father mildly.
> The waiter stood in confused silence for a moment. "But I have to put another plate there, sir."
> My father shook his head. "It's all right," he said. "Don't go to any bother."
> The waiter blinked and then smiled weakly. "Oh, it's no bother at all," he said, and again reached for the plate.
> This time, my father put his hands over the plate to protect it. The waiter stopped short and straightened up. He looked at us in something akin to frenzy, and John gestured with his head. The waiter retreated to the back of the room and stood there watching us from long distance. He was pale and he still had a plate in his hands.
> "Pop," said John, "Why don't you give him your plate?"
> My father shrugged. "It's clean enough," he said.
> This time John blinked. "I don't understand what you mean."
> "They shouldn't waste a plate," said my father. "This one's fine."
> John regarded my father for a long moment. "It's really no bother," he said. "They've got a washer back there that does all the work."
> "Well, they might run short, my father said."
> "I'm telling you, Pop," said John. "There's no danger." He took a deep drag of his cigarette and leaned forward again. "Pop," he said. "You're going to get that waiter in trouble."
> "What?" said my father concernedly.
> "It's this way," said John. "They're supposed to put a new plate on for each course. That's the way the management wants it. If the waiter doesn't do it and one of the

> managers sees him, he gets fired on the spot."
> "I never heard of such a thing," my father said.
> "It's true," said John. "That waiter's probably worried plenty by now."
> "Well, hell," said my father. "Tell him to take it then."

> One follow up activity that is often used in ESL texts is to begin with comprehension questions like the following.
> Was this the first incident the father had with the waiter?
> What did the waiter say when the father refused to give him his plate?
> How many times did the waiter attempt to take the plate?

The problem with such questions is that they seek to determine, in an efferent mode, the information that the student is carrying away from the text. Whereas this knowledge may be very important in reading scientific or business texts, this passage was obviously not written to relay the information that is questioned above.

A second common activity is to use the text to promote language skills on the level of usage. Thus, the use of the present and past tense might be explored. Students could be asked to circle all the verbs in the past tense, to list the irregular past tense verbs, and to explain why the present tense is used in sentences such as the following: "They're supposed to put a new plate on for each course. That's the way the management wants it." However, since the text was not written to exemplify a contrast between the use of the present and past tense in English, such activities create what Widdowson terms an inappropriate relationship between the reader and the text.

Another alternative, which unfortunately is less frequently used, would be to explore the language of the text in terms of language use. In this case, students could write down all of the comments made by the waiter, resulting in the following list.

> "I'm sorry. I thought you were finished."
> "May I take your plate, sir?"
> "But I have to put another plate here, sir."
> "Oh, it's no bother at all."

Then the class could discuss why the waiter used "sir" and "may I." They might also be asked to suggest the tone of voice used by the waiter in making these comments. Such activities would naturally result in an exploration of the role relationship of a central concern of the passage; namely, the father's refusal to let the waiter take his plate and even more importantly the question of why he refuses to do so. Since any reader interacting with the text aesthetically cannot overlook this question, this is where an examination of the passage should begin. This discussion may lead back to a closer reading of the text, as readers point to what the father says about his refusal.

In aesthetic reading, a reader often relates his world of experience to the text. After reading the passage, students might be asked if anything similar has ever happened to them. The following response by one student to *Sweet Promised Land* was based on such a shared experience.

> The essay which I enjoyed reading the most is Sweet Promised Land because it is closely related to my family. The story of *Sweet Promised Land* talks about a father who came to the United States, but he is not fully adjusted in this new culture. He doesn't let the waiter take his plate, and he also wound his wallet with a black inner-tube band. As I remember, my mother needed to do that too when we just came over to the United States. She still puts a big band around her wallet.

Since in aesthetic reading, readers often make judgements about the characters, another follow up activity might involve having the students comment on their opinion of the father, the son, or the waiter. Furthermore, in aesthetic reading a reader often fantasizes as to what he would do in a similar situation. Hence, students could be asked what they would have done if they had been the father, the son or the waiter. Such discussion, it seems to me, goes much further toward promoting an interaction between the reader and the text than an exploration of the usage in the passage.

An interaction with a literary text depends on a reader's familiarity with the cultural assumptions in it. The excerpt from *Sweet Promised Land* contains several specific cultural assumptions. It is important that students understand these for as Allen (1975:111) puts it, "Literature is a facet of a culture. Its significance can be best understood in terms of its culture, and its purpose is meaningful only when the assumptions it is based on are understood and accepted." In this passage it is assumed that the reader understands that in a high class restaurant a waiter must at all costs be polite, that the number of dishes and the amount of work needed to keep these dishes clean is inconsequential, and that loud confrontations are generally avoided. The son is aware of these assumptions, whereas the father obviously is not. Furthermore, since the son is aware of the problem, he tries as unobtrusively as possible to resolve the conflict.

In order to prepare students to deal with these assumptions, they might be asked to indicate if the following items are typical (T) or unusual (U) in exclusive American restaurants.

_______ 1. The number of dishes is kept to a minimum so as to reduce costs.
_______ 2. Each course is brought on a separate plate.
_______ 3. It is appropriate for a waiter to insist that he do his job even if the customer is unhappy.

_______ 4. It is appropriate for a customer to insist that a restaurant alter its standard procedures to meet his wishes.

_______ 5. Any conflict between waiter and customer is resolved in as quiet a manner as possible.

If a student is unaware of any of these assumptions, the context of the passage will help to illustrate what is appropriate and what is not appropriate. In this way the passage can serve to clarify the cultural expectations of a particular social context.

CONCLUSION

Literature does indeed have a place in the ESL curriculum. For many students, literature can provide a key to motivating them to read in English. For all students, literature is an ideal vehicle for illustrating language use and for introducing cultural assumptions. Our success in using literature, of course, greatly depends upon a selection of texts which will not be overly difficult on either linguistic or conceptual level. Ultimately, however, if we wish to promote truly aesthetic reading, it is essential that literature be approached not efferently, but in a manner which establishes a personal and aesthetic interaction of a reader and a text.

■ References

Allen, P. (1975). The sacred hoop: A contemporary Indian perspective on American Indian Literature. In A. Chapman (ed.) *Literature of the American Indians: Views and interpretations.* New York, Meridian.

Donelson, K. and A. Nilsen. (1980). *Literature for today's young adults.* Glenview, Illinois: Scott, Foresman and Company.

Fassler, D. and N. Lay. (1979). *Encounters with a new world.* Englewood Cliffs, New Jersey: Prentice-Hall, Inc.

Frye, Northrop. (1964). *The educated imagination.* Indiana: Indiana University Press.

Gaies, S. (1979). Linguistic input in formal second language learning: The issue of syntactic gradation and readability in ESL materials. *TESOL Quarterly, 13,* 1, pp. 41-50.

Honeyfield, J. (1977). Simplification. *TESOL Quarterly, 11,* 4, pp. 431-440.

Johnson, P. (1981), Effects on reading comprehension of language complexity and cultural background of a text. *TESOL Quarterly, 15,* 2, pp. 169-181.

Lexalt, R. (1957). *Sweet Promised Land.* New York: Harper and Brothers Publishers.

Marshall, Madleine. (1979). Love and death in Eden: Teaching English literature to ESL students, *TESOL Quarterly, 13,* 3, pp. 331-340.

Povey, J. (1972). Literature in TESL programs: The language and the culture. In H. Allen and R. Campbell

(ed.) *Teaching English as a second language.* New York: McGraw-Hill.
Rosenblatt, L. (1978). *The reader, the text, the poem.* Carbondale, Illinois: Southern Illinois University Press.
Widdowson, H. G. (1978). *Teaching language as a communication.* England: Oxford University Press.
Widdowson, H. G. (1979). *Explorations in applied linguistics.* England: Oxford University Press.

From Mckay, S. (1982). Literature in ESL classroom, *TESOL Quarterly*, *16,* pp. 529-536.

PART SIX

TEACHING WRITING

언어의 네 기능 중에서 가장 소홀해지기 쉬운 기능이 쓰기이다. 표현기능이라는 의미에서 쓰기는 말하기와 유사한 점이 많지만 말할 때는 대체로 청자와 함께 있어서 표정, 몸짓 등이 의사전달을 훨씬 용이하게 하는 반면 쓸 때는 인쇄물로 독자에게 전달되기 때문에 정확한 의미로 표현되어야 하는 점이 큰 차이이다. 따라서 정확성이 많이 요구된다고 말할 수 있다. 그러나 말하기 지도에서와 마찬가지로 쓰기에서도 자신의 의사를 정확하게, 분명하게, 그리고 적절하게 글로서 표현할 수 있도록 지도하는 것이 궁극적인 목표이다.

쓰기 연습 활동으로는 통제작문(controlled writing), 반 통제작문(semi-controlled writing 또는 guided writing), 그리고 자유작문(free writing, composition)이 있다. 그렇지만 우리의 교과서에는 통제작문이 전부를 차지한다고 해도 과언이 아니다. 그러나 말하기를 지도할 때 단순한 문형연습에서 끝나지 않고 자유롭게 개인의 의사를 표현하는 기회를 부여해야 하듯이 쓰기 지도에서 역시 자유작문으로 진행되어야 한다.

이 장에서 Rivers는 외국어지도에서 쓰기의 중요성을 언급하고 쓰기 지도에서 위의 여러 단계별 학습활동들을 구체적으로 적고 있다. Paulston & Bruder는 통제작문을 좀 더 의미 있게 할 수 있는 세 종류의 전환(conversion) 연습과 반 통제작문의 실례를, Thiede- Gonzo는 학생들에게 많이 익숙한 문장결합(integrating 또는 sentence combining)이 수준에 따라 어떻게 다양하게 변형되어 사용될 수 있는가를 보여주면서 이들의 이점을 기술한다. 특히 쓰기 지도에서는 오류의 수정이 중요하게 인식된다. 그러므로 이와 관련하여 Hendrickson은 여러 가지 전통적인 방법을 정리하고 있다.

마지막으로 최근에 등장한 이론으로 쓰기에 대해 새로운 해석을 하는 Zamel의 글을 소개한다. 한마디로 쓰기는 여러 단계의 과정을 거쳐서 발전해 가는 기술이기 때문에 지도에 있어서도 이들 과정을 따라야 좋은 결과를 낳게 된다는 것이다. 미국 학교에서 작문 시간에 널리 활용되고 있고 앞으로 우리의 상황에 맞게 널리 적용할 가치가 있는 이론이다.

23. THE WRITING SKILL

To be literate in the native language implies the ability to read and write. It is these skills that students, for centuries, have practiced in class. This approach to native-language learning has transferred to the foreign-language classroom, without much consideration of its appropriateness or inappropriateness for students who do not already have the spoken form of the language at their command. Writing exercises keep students busy and out of mischief. Conventional written exercises are easy to construct. The inexperienced or poorly qualified teacher may take them directly from the textbook, with which an answer booklet is usually provided. They may often be corrected as a group procedure in the classroom, and they yield a wide spread of evaluative grades for the teacher's records.

With so much writing in foreign language classes over so many years, one would expect to find highly effective methods for teaching this skill and marked success in learning it. Unfortunately, examination papers in composition the world over are, with few exceptions, disappointing. Many college and university students with four, five, even six or more years of study of another language behind them are still unable to express themselves in a clear, correct, and comprehensible manner in writing. We would do well to examine critically the role of writing in foreign- and second-language learning, to analyze what is involved in the process of writing another language, and to trace out the steps by which this skill can be progressively mastered.

At this stage it may be well to recall two facts often ignored by language teachers, who traditionally have expected students to write something as a demonstration of learning: first, that many highly articulate persons express themselves very inadequately in writing in their native language, and, second, that only a minority of the speakers of any language acquire the skill of writing it with any degree of finesse, and then only after years of training in school and practice out of school.

We must realize that writing a language comprehensibly is much more difficult than speaking it. When we write, we are, as it were, "communicating into space." When we communicate a message orally, we know who is receiving the message. We know the situation, including the mood and tone it requires of us, even if it is as impersonal as "someone in the office" taking a phone message. We receive feedback from the interlocutor or audience (oral, emotional, or kinesthetic) which makes clear how the messages is being received and if it is being comprehended. With spoken messages, many things are visible, or are part of shared knowledge, which cannot be taken for granted in writing. The novice writer has to learn how to make such things explicit and unambiguous, once and for all, through syntactic arrangement and lexical choice, whereas in speech the omissions, ambiguities, and misconceptions can be clarified by action, restatement, or expansion on the part of the speaker or even of the interlocutor. It must not surprise us, then, that many students are hesitant to begin to write on some ill-defined subject which seems to have little purpose but its own existence, with no clearly indicated recipient for the message. For expressive writing they need preparation and specialized instruction.

After they have left school, the vast majority of students will never be required to write in a non-native language for anything but the most straightforward of purposes: an occasional letter or short note at most. Those few who will later write the language for career purposes will be expected to write correctly in a specific form, as, for instance, in the writing of business letters dealing with precise operations (much of which is now done by computers), or in the preparing of reports on clearly defined proposals or projects. For this they need specialized training. Only at undergraduate or graduate level will students attempt to write essays in the new language, and then only some students for whom it is clearly important. Even for these, their instructors will bless them if they can write accurately and idiomatically, without attempting flights of fancy or a literary style which is beyond their capacity. It is in listening comprehension and reading that students need to be able to handle the language at the most sophisticated level, because in these areas they will have no control over the complexity of the material they encounter. These are the skills also through which they can improve their knowledge of the language independently at a later stage. In speaking and writing, the non-native speaker rarely achieves the same degree of mastery as the native speaker, even after living in a country where the language is spoken. What students most need in these production areas is to be able to use what they know flexibly, making the most of the resources at their command to meet the occasion.

This does not mean that writing has little to contribute to language learning. Apart from its intrinsic interest or value, it is an essential classroom activity. As we shall see, it is of considerable importance for consolidating learning in the other skill areas; it provides a welcome change of activity; and it will always remain useful as part of a program of testing. Except for students who intend to continue their studies in their second language, writing should be considered the handmaid of the other skill, not the major skill to be developed.

Traditionally, writing activities in language classes have taken the form of the writing out of paradigms and grammatical exercises, dictation, translation from native language to target language and from target language to native language, and imitative and free composition. These activities have at times been the major forms of testing, acquiring, as a result, an undue importance in the eyes of both students and teachers. This has had the unfortunate consequence of reducing the amount of time spent on activities more generally useful to the majority of students, such as listening, speaking, and reading.

It will be readily admitted that the taking of dictation and the writing of grammatical exercises and paradigms, useful as they may be, are means rather than ends, and that skill in these intermediate activities does not necessarily ensure ability to comprehend and communicate in natural settings. Nor can the ubiquitous translation exercises be considered ends in themselves. Few of our students become professional translators, and for those who wish to do so we should provide, at the advanced level, specialized courses in the art of translation. For the rest of our students, continual emphasis on translation from the earliest stages inculcates the naive belief that languages have a basic one-to-one equivalence which must be identified, with the dictionary as an indispensable tool. This attitude hinders the forging of direct links between meaning and foreign-language expression, a process which is essential for rapid comprehension of oral and written communication, for fluent speaking, and for idiomatic writing. Some translation exercises do have a place in foreign-language teaching, but the value of each type of translation exercise and the degree of emphasis it will receive must be considered carefully in relation to the whole program for developing ability to use language for real-life purposes.

WRITING ACTIVITIES IN THE CLASSROOM

Up to this point in our discussion the term "writing" has been used, without definition, to refer to several activities which are obviously quite distinct in the demands they make upon the student. These may be classified as writing down or notation, writing in the language, production, expressive writing or composition, and translation.

In its simplest form, writing may be just *notation*: copying in its conventional graphic form something already written, or reproducing in written form something which has been read or heard. This act may involve nothing more than the ability to use the writing system of the language (already an important skill where a different script must be learned). It may require ability to associate with well-known graphic symbols unexpected sound sequences which for the student have no clear meaning and no significant interrelationships. An activity like this is sometimes used to sensitize students to a new phonological system and to important sound discriminations they must be able to make. Where the spelling system of the new language does not correspond in a one-to-one relationship with the sound output, reproduction in writing from spoken output can be a necessary long-term activity. For effective spelling practice of this type, students must, of course, be presented at all times with meaningful units in context.

Writing in the language becomes more complicated when it involves writing meaningful segments of language which might be used in specific circumstances by native speakers. This is the type of writing which is involved in grammatical exercises, the construction of simple dialogues, uncomplicated translation exercises, dictation, and the cloze procedure. This activity we may call *writing practice*. Writing practice moves from the more guided types of exercises, where elements of structure and vocabulary are manipulated, expanded, transformed, and restated in various ways, to more flexible production in writing, where students begin from the material provided and develop it out in an individual way. These flexible production activities may be related to what has been read or heard. They may also be preparatory to oral production in the form of short talks, oral reports, or dramatizations using material being currently studied.

In its most highly developed form, writing refers to the conveying of information or the expression of original ideas in a consecutive way in the new language. This we will call *expressive writing* or *composition*. Composition may be for practical purposes (the writing of instructions, reports, resumes, concrete descriptions, or essential correspondence connected with everyday affairs), or it may be more creative. The ultimate goal in creative expression will be to express oneself in a polished form which requires a nuanced vocabulary and certain refinements of structure. Finally, as a different form of written expression, we have fine *translation*, which is to some extent a meticulously controlled activity and to some extent creative, depending on the type of translation and its purpose.

In our language classes, all of these stages of writing have some place, although many students will only approach expressive writing at a relatively unsophisticated and unpretentious level, preferring to remain with the practical. With the time at our disposal at the elementary level, we will concentrate on giving our students training and practice in writing down what they would say in various circumstances, with some attention to the differences between the conventions for spoken and written style. At the more advanced level, we will encourage them to express themselves with some finesse in oral discussion of more significant subjects, and then to write their ideas, with careful attention to lexical and structural choice.

Skill in writing in an elegant fashion in a foreign language, according to the canons of an educated elite, is an aim impossible of realization at the high school stage and demands a mastery of the foreign language which many high school teachers themselves do not possess. For undergraduate or graduate students it will be necessary to decide, after due consideration of their objectives in learning the language, to what level of felicitous expression the students need to be trained. For most students, ability to express their meaning clearly and accurately will be sufficient; specialized composition classes will meet the needs of the few who require more than this.

These distinctions among types of writing activities reflect the major areas of learning involved in the writing process. Students must learn the graphic system and be able to spell according to the conventions of the language, if what they write is to be comprehensible and acceptable to a native speaker. They must learn to control the structure according to the canons of good writing. They must learn to select from among possible combinations of words phrases those which will convey the meanings they have in mind, and, ultimately, they must be able to do this so that nuances in the appropriate linguistic register are expressed through their writing. To reach this stage, students must have such a control of the mechanics of good writing that they are able to concentrate all their efforts on the process of selection among possible combinations.

At each stage, emphasis will be placed on writing something that will be read by someone, preferably not just by the teacher. Material may be copied or reproduced for display on a bulletin board (if individuals are copying different passages, this becomes more interesting). Dialogues written as recombinations will be acted by other students. Students will write instructions for activities or information as part of a game, competition, or out-of-class activity, in each case supplying something which other students will need to read in order to proceed. Even at an elementary level, they will write items of news which may be posted on a bulletin board, passed around in multiple copies, or gathered together for a weekly class news sheet. To give students a sense of purpose in their writing, the teacher must think out ways of making the exercises themselves purposeful.

INTEGRATION OF THE SKILLS

Writing is not, then, a skill which can be learned in isolation. In the apprentice stage of writing, what the student must learn, apart from the peculiar difficulties of spelling or script, is a counterpart of what has to be learned for the mastery of listening comprehension, speaking, and reading — a nucleus of linguistic knowledge. The activity of writing helps to consolidate the learning to render it available for use in these other areas. Writing gives the student practice in manipulating structural variants and in selecting and combining lexical elements, adding the reinforcement of the kinesthetic image to the auditory and visual. Where a new script is involved, writing helps the student distinguish one form from another. It is impossible to reproduce forms correctly if one cannot visually detect the differences among them. As one becomes familiar with forms and shapes, rapid recognition for reading purposes is facilitated. Written questions based on a reading passage encourage the student to read the text more attentively and discover areas which were misinterpreted on the first reading.

In its more advanced form of composition, writing is dependent on progress in the other skills. Accurate, idiomatic writing is quite different from the mere piecing together of language elements in some artificial patchwork which would never be encountered outside the classroom. Only by hearing and reading a great deal of the language as it is spoken and written by native speakers can language learners acquire that feeling for the appropriate use of language forms and combinations which is basic to expressive writing. What they are unable to say over to themselves, they will be unlikely to write with ease, and until they have read a great deal they will not be familiar with the way native speakers express themselves, for various purposes, in writing.

It is obvious, then that the most effective writing practice, and the most generally useful, will have a close connection with what is being practiced in relation to other skills. Writing practice will at first be a service activity, consolidating work in the other areas. While the students are using it to reinforce other learning, they will be mastering the technical details of the art of writing. The higher levels of composition will be possible only when the student has attained some degree of mastery of the other skills. It will be well for the teacher to keep in mind that some will never reach a high standard in composition in another language. These students should not be driven into a stage of frustration by examinations heavily weighted in favor of the writing skill, when it is evident that they have achieved a satisfactory mastery of the skills of listening comprehension, speaking, and reading.

Many writing weaknesses in advanced classes can be traced back to lack of systematic practice during the earlier stages of the language course. Often students in elementary classes are encouraged to try their hand at creative writing in the foreign language for fun, while the teacher turns a blind eye to the monstrosities they create. Students are soon in over their heads, and develop the habit of attempting to express themselves in strange words, often sought out in an inept way in a dictionary, before they have any adequate control of language structure. Believing that they are writing acceptably, they contrive expressions on the pattern of native-language forms, happily constructing hybrid phrases without realizing that these are quite incomprehensible in the context of the new language. To be sure, attempts at writing creatively can and should be encouraged from an early stage, so long as students have a clear realization of the limitations of knowledge within which they are composing. They then try to use in original combinations structures and expressions they have already learned in oral practice and reading, often creating interesting and amusing pieces of expressive writing. In so doing, they use and reuse in novel combinations much language material which otherwise would gradually be slipping from their active memory. Meanwhile, they continue systematic study through the various types of activities we have outlined, which will now be discussed in detail.

WRITING DOWN: NOTATION

Copying

Copying (sometimes called transcription) is often despised by teachers as an unworthy and unchallenging occupation for language learners. This attitude is unfortunate, since it ignores the fact that there are many aspects of another language which are very strange to learners, and with which they need to familiarize themselves thoroughly if they are to write the language confidently. Where there is a new script to be learned, a disdainful attitude is less likely to arise, because accurate copying is obviously needed for purposes of recognition and reproduction. Where the script is the same as in the native language, and where there are many similarities between the two languages, careful copying focuses the student's attention on the differences between the native and target languages. The work to be copied should consist of sections of work already learned orally and read with the teacher. As students are copying, they should repeat to themselves what they are writing. In this way they deepen the impression they have acquired of the sounds the symbols represent, and they have further practice in producing fluent sentences. Particular attention should be paid to diacritical and punctuation marks which are distinctive elements of the written language.

In languages where sound-symbol correspondences are particularly complicated, copying activities may be continued side by side with more advanced writing practice. Students who have made lists of short sentences containing words with different spellings for the same sounds may copy these lists several times, concentrating on the variations in spelling. If they are assigned lists of words to be learned because of their peculiarities of orthography, they may be asked to copy the words several times as they are learning them, thus imprinting the graphic outlines more firmly in their minds. In the early stages, credit should be given for accuracy in copying, in order to encourage students in careful observation of details.

Reproduction

At the reproduction stage, students will attempt to write, without originality, what they have learned orally and read in their textbooks. This they will be able to do all the more successfully if they have been trained in habits of accuracy during the copying stage. If sound writing habits are to be firmly established, the learning situation should be structured so that the students will write correctly, not incorrectly, particularly since it becomes impossible for the teacher to check every item that is written down. Students will initially be asked to reproduce from memory only sentences and phrases which they have learned to copy. As a first step they will be asked to rewrite immediately each sentence they have copied without reference to their copy or to the original. They will then compare this version with the original for correction. Next they will be asked to write down sentences they have both learned and copied, as they are dictated to them.

When dictation procedures are employed for reproduction, it is well for the teacher to realize that two skills are being exercised at once: listening and writing. Since all the skills are finally integrated in language knowledge, this is not necessarily a disadvantage, but the teacher must be aware of the fact that what is being required of the student is more than a simple exercise in writing. Where particular difficulties of spelling are being emphasized, the spot-dictation procedure may be adopted: a complete sentence will be read, but only the word or words which are repeated will be written. To avoid confusion in this exercise, some teachers supply an outline with blanks to fill in.

At a further stage, the teacher will call for the writing of a learned phrase as a response to a question, or as a description of a picture. Here students will be demonstrating understanding of meaning and memory for learned response, as well as ability to distinguish aurally and write accurately. Where the direct method is being used, the students will be asked to reproduce in writing, at a cue from the teacher, sentences which have been practiced orally in classroom activity and read in the textbook. At the reproduction stage, the students' writing activity does not require variation of learned phrases, since the emphasis is entirely on accuracy of reproduction.

WRITING PRACTICE

Recombination

At the recombination stage, students are required to reproduce practiced sentences with adaptations. This parallels in conception the recombination stage in oral work and reading. The work for recombination in writing, however, will always be what is being spoken and read. The writing of recombinations of practiced sentences requires not only the ability to manipulate grammatical structures to express meaning (which is also basic to the speaking skill), but also a sound knowledge of the intricacies of representing graphically what the student is required only to recognize in reading. More effective results will be achieved in writing exercises if there is a continual integration of practice in all the skills. At first, the students will have already heard, produced orally, and read in their textbook recombinations of the type they will write. When the students have demonstrated that they can say over to themselves correctly what they are to write, they will be asked to construct recombinations themselves. In this way, the beginning students is much more likely to write correctly.

At this stage, writing practice may take a number of forms. Students will write out grammatical exercises of different kinds: making substitutions of words and phrases, transforming sentences, combining them in various ways, expanding them to include further information within the limits of what they have learned, contracting them by substituting pronouns for nouns or single words for groups of words. The writing of grammatical exercises not only gives valuable practice in accurate and correct construction of sentences but consolidates what has been learned orally. It is a useful home study exercise, ensuring that the student gives careful thought to work studied and practiced in class during the day.

Although fill-in-the-blank and multiple-choice exercises have their uses as a rapid check of how accurately certain grammatical features have been learned, they provide little or no practice in writing the language. To learn to write, one must write — and write full sentences, not isolated words. For the teacher, this naturally means more work to correct. If students are trained from the beginning, however, in disciplined rereading and checking of what they have written, this burden can be reduced. They may occasionally check each other's work, but only for class exercises, to ensure immediate confirmation of the correctness of the response and to save some teacher time. Where a grade is involved, the teacher must also check the work to make sure that the grading is equitable.

When students have acquired some confidence in writing simple substitutions and transformations, they may be asked to make novel recombinations around a theme presented to the class in a picture or a series of pictures. These pictures will represent situations in connection with which the students have learned phrases orally or in their reading. The recombinations may take the form of variations of dialogues, which, after correction, may be acted out in the classroom. At first these recombinations will not involve much new vocabulary. Later they may provide the occasion for some expansion of vocabulary into new areas. This vocabulary will be introduced orally and then learned in some group exercise or game before being used in writing. The teacher will see that students are not required to make a recombination which involves a structural change and new vocabulary at the same point in the sentence. The simple rule of one problem at a time will decrease the possibility of error and make for more effective learning. Correctness in writing may be further ensured if recombinations are first constructed orally in class. Students will not be asked to write such recombinations unsupervised until they have had sufficient practice to ensure success.

Recombination Dictation

Recombination dictation — a mixture of recombination and reproduction — consists of rearrangements of dialogue sentences, or narratives constructed from the conversational material or from pattern sentences used in classroom oral practice. Since dictation involves ability to recognize these recombinations aurally and retain them, as well as reproduce them graphically, such dictations must be constructed carefully so that problems of aural recognition do not coincide with problems of graphic representation. At this stage, work to be written from dictation should not contain distinctly new elements. Elements recombined should be ones which have already been practiced and learned thoroughly, studied in graphic form, and used in some kind of writing practice, with, at most, the addition of some simple analogic variants of these. The dictation will then serve as a form of review, the possibility of error will be reduced, and the students will be encouraged by their progress.

The teacher should dictate at a normal speed of utterance, not distorting the phrases and the flow of speech in any way. Segments dictated should consist of meaningful word groups. Each phrase should be repeated clearly only once before students are expected to write it. Since some students become flustered when expected to retain what they have comprehended aurally long enough to write it accurately, students should be encouraged to repeat aloud to themselves what they have heard before attempting to write it from dictation, and then to repeat it again as they write it. This oral repetition helps them to retain what they have heard long enough for them to write the complete phrase. After they have had time to write the whole phrase, the same segment should be repeated to allow students an opportunity to check what they have written and correct any inaccuracies. At the end of the dictation of the whole passage, time should be allowed for rechecking of accuracy of writing before the passage is reread a final time, with normal intonation and fluency. This period for checking forces students to do some thinking for themselves before the final reading, and makes them more alert to the sections of the final reading which they most need to hear again.

If the procedure outlined is adopted from the early stages of learning the language, students will be trained to retain whole phrases in their immediate memory. The dictation practice will then be reinforcing practice in listening comprehension as well as providing practice in accurate writing. As students advance in language learning, phrases dictated will gradually be lengthened, until the students are eventually able to retain complete sentences in their immediate memory and write them down correctly.

PRODUCTION: GUIDED WRITING

At the guided writing stage, students will be given more freedom in the selection of lexical items and structural patterns for their written exercises. This will, however, be within a framework which restrains them from attempting to compose at a level beyond their state of knowledge. They will begin with outlines which allow for some individuality, but which also help them to keep to what they have learned. They will gradually move on to composition which is so closely associated with what they have read or heard that, without feeling unduly restricted, they will still be using and reusing what they know. As their control of writing techniques increases, they will be ready to move into the composition stage, where they will be attempting to express their personal meaning in the new language.

Early in the production stage the student may attempt completion exercises, where parts of sentences are given and the structural pattern for the completion is thus established. Each student will, nevertheless, be expected to construct an individual answer in the choice of a completion. Some types of drills provide useful guides for writing. Replacement exercises may be devised in which a section of the sentence can be replaced by a number of different phrases, giving the student the opportunity to express new meanings. Expansion of a simple sentence by the addition of modifying words and phrases, or the inclusion of further information, can give practice in developing meanings within a framework. Along the lines of a substitution drill, the student may take a given sentence and see how many different meanings can be expressed by lexical changes, within the limits of the structure provided. Another form of outline supplies lexical items in their unmarked form[1)] in a fixed order which forces the student to use certain grammatical structures. This restricts the semantic area within which the students may express themselves but leaves them free to vary such elements as person, tense, and number.

As students advance in skill, they may be allowed more freedom in their choice of expression. The framework will now come from stories and articles they have been reading. At this stage they will be learning something about the differences between the conventions for spoken and written style. They may answer questions on a text read or heard, the questions requiring more and more individuality of response as their skill in writing increases. They may write summaries of stories they have studied in class, heard in the laboratory, or enjoyed for extensive reading. They may rewrite a story, or a part of a story, from a different angle. (This exercise may be designed so as to require a different tense; the story may be rewritten in the first person as told by one of the characters; or one of the characters may give explanations or explain the reactions of others, thus forcing the student into using indirect discourse.) A story may be rewritten in dialogue form or a dialogue rewritten as a narrative. The setting or main personalities of a story or dialogue may be changed in such a way as to require certain changes in the description, in the action, or in the tone of the conversational exchange. The skeleton of a story or dialogue may be supplied for development by the student, or an outline given for a description or narration based on a picture or

1) "Unmarked form" is a linguistic term. It refers to the base form to which morphological variations are made (bat: bats).

a succession of pictures. As a variation of this procedure, a series of questions may be so constructed that in answering them the students write a continuous narrative. If pictures are used, the writing activity may be associated with intensive work in vocabulary building. With some imagination, the teacher will not be at a loss for finding ways of guiding students in elementary composition.

Writing at this stage is still under supervision. The teacher should see that the students do not lapse into the habit of writing native-language versions which they then translate inexpertely into the target language. As at all stages in developing the writing skill, problems which may arise in the exercise are anticipated in oral group work so that students know what is expected of them. Most of their difficulties are thus overcome before they are left to their own resources. Students work without bilingual dictionaries, endeavoring to use what they know or what they can learn from the model on which their guided writing is based. In this way, they are likely to adapt and paraphrase in order to reuse language material from previous lessons, rather than rush to a dictionary every time they need an expression which does not come readily to mind.

Until students have acquired the technique of relying on variations of what they have learned for the expression of their own ideas, and have begun to appreciate the role of the outline or basic text in stimulating ideas (while serving as their guide to authentic expression), they should continue to do their initial writing with the teacher available for assistance. In an unsupervised situation they will be required at first only to rewrite or improve work which has been prepared in class. These restrictions are essential if students are to be trained in good writing habits. Left to their own devices too soon, they will hasten to the dictionary and attempt a standard of expression beyond their state of knowledge. As a result, their developing skill in this area will soon deteriorate.

EXPRESSIVE WRITING: COMPOSITION

The final stage of composition involves individual selection of vocabulary and structure for the expression of personal meaning. In a second or foreign language, students are still not able to use as wide a range of expression as a native speaker. Their knowledge of the second language is still very inferior to their knowledge and control of the native language. If asked to write on subjects which are too general, too philosophical, or too literary, they will be frustrated by their desire to write at the standard they have reached in native-language composition, at a stage when their resources of expression in the new language are still comparatively limited. If they have been carefully prepared, however, through the preceding stages, they will have developed an attitude of mind which will prevent them from committing the worst excesses of clothing native-language expressions and structures in foreign words.

The key word for students in this dilemma is "simplify." They must clothe their thoughts in simple, lucid language which is well within their command. Encouraged to use a monolingual rather than a bilingual dictionary and to think before they write, they will be more likely to use what they know, checking on its accuracy and examining the possibilities of suggested alternatives, rather than seeking inexact and misleading equivalents for notions they have not yet encountered in their experience with this new language.

At this stage they will be increasing their understanding of the differences between spoken and written in the language. Apart from observing the conventional differences between spoken and written language, they will be trying to express themselves more concisely, more descriptively, less casually. This will severely test their control of structure and their precise understanding of lexical meaning. The composition stage provides teacher and student with the opportunity to identify persisting areas of misunderstanding on an individual basis, so that remedial practice may be undertaken where necessary.

When students have reached what is considered to be an advanced language class, the teacher will need to exercise great care to see that they are not plunged abruptly from guided writing into the limitless sea of free expression. The transition has to be gradual. Exercises in composition will at first be closely linked with material being read and discussed. Students will be asked merely to describe, narrate, explain, or summarize. As they become more accustomed to expressing themselves within voluntarily accepted restrictions, they will be asked to comment on or develop ideas beyond those in the material read. Only when their skill in writing lucidly, comprehensibly, and accurately is established may they be expected to imitate the style of great writers, write literary criticism, or discuss ideas at a philosophical or sociological level. For these types of exercises, they need a specialized vocabulary and training in concepts which go beyond what the language teacher is aiming to supply. Time taken out for these things reduces the time available for developing overall proficiency in handling the new language.

It is as well to remember that not all students have a ready flow of ideas when asked to write, even in their native language. Composition exercises which are not closely related to intensive reading assignments should be so designed that they do not become tests of originality and invention (although imaginative students with a good grasp of the language should never be discouraged from going beyond what is required from the less inspired). Precise descriptions of persons, places, and things provide excellent training in exact expression, as do instructions and arrangements. The writing of an original dialogue, using the vocabulary area of some recent reading, keeps the student practiced in the style of spoken language. Further practice in a more casual style of writing may be provided by the keeping of a personal diary or by international correspondence on an individual basis. (In the latter case, students are appropriately instructed in the accepted formulas for letter writing.) Students may have read to them, or be asked to read, parts of stories, which they are then required to complete for themselves; in this way, they have already been initiated into the appropriate vocabulary area and level of language before they attempt to write on their own.

Composition exercises may profitably be linked with assignments for extensive reading. As each book, story, or play is completed, the student is asked to submit, for correction and evaluation, a short composition based on it. This composition may consist of a summary of the contents with a personal commentary, or the narration of some aspect of the story assigned previously by the teacher. Students with imagination and a flair for invention will be encouraged to use their originality in selecting their own approach, and in this way they will be able to demonstrate the level of expression of which they are capable.

Extensive reading assignments may direct students to articles of current interest in foreign-language magazines or newspapers. To ensure that students do not become bogged down in reading which is too complicated or esoteric, the teacher will be well advised to discuss the selection of articles to be read, with due regard to the special interests of the readers. Otherwise, discouraged students will take little pleasure in what had promised to be an interesting activity. Where newspapers in the language being learned are freely available, students may be asked to submit at regular intervals short written accounts of items of news they have read. These reports may also be given orally, without consulting the written text, thus providing subject matter for class discussion and further exercise in the speaking skill.

In classes where students have been encouraged to undertake group or individual projects to deepen their understanding of the culture of the people who speak the language, they will have valuable practice in composition as they draw up reports of their research in such areas as geography, history, sociology, art, music, education, political institutions, conditions of work, lives of famous men and women, and so on. For such projects the students should be required to draw their information from sources in the target language so that they may use authentic forms of expression in their written and oral reports. They should be asked to submit short reports on sections of their research for correction at regular intervals, rather than one long report at the end. The teacher can then guide them in the progressive improvement of their writing efforts. These reports, like those on extensive reading, should also be given orally to the class at some stage and used as a basis for further discussion.

From Rivers, W. M. (1981). *Teaching foreign-language skills.* (2nd ed.), Chicago, IL: The University of Chicago Press. pp. 291-306.

24. SAMPLE WRITING EXERCISES

Model passages lend themselves to two kinds of writing activity: conversions and what might be called semicontrolled composition, where the model passage serves to suggest content and ideas but with little structural control. The latter is an important step in going from controlled to free composition.

There are three types of conversions: substitutions, transformations, and modifications. In a substitution conversion the structural patterns of the sentence remain the same as in the model while slots are filled by a specific class of fillers. In a transformation conversion the structural patterns differ from the model although the output remains controlled by the original sentence structures. Modification exercises involve primarily expanding the patterns in the model and are the result of the student's choice.

SUBSTITUTION CONVERSIONS

As with substitution tables, there are single, correlative, and multiple substitution conversions. They lend themselves primarily to exercises in the grammatical categories of gender, number, and tense, and in replacing synonyms and transition words. Here's a correlative substitution conversion on gender changes.

Model: from Clarence Day, *Life with Father*

Father had the same character as a boy, I suppose, that he had as a man, and he was too independent to care if people thought his name fancy. He paid no attention to the prejudices of others, except to disapprove of them. He had plenty of prejudices himself, of course, but they were his own. He was humorous and confident and level-headed, and I imagine that if any boy had tried to make fun of him for being named Clarence, Father would simply have laughed and told him he didn't know what he was talking about.

Assignment:

Rewrite the entire passage, changing the word *Father to Mother* each time it appears. Remember to change the pronouns, nouns and names wherever it becomes necessary.

Student's Composition:

Mother had the same character as a girl, I suppose, that *she* had as a *woman*, and *she* was too independent to care if people thought *her* name fancy. *She* paid no attention to the prejudices of others, except to disapprove of them. *She* had plenty of prejudices *herself*, of course, but they were *her* own. *She* was humorous and confident and level-headed, and I imagine that if any boy had tried to make fun of *her* for being named Clarissa, *Mother* would simply have laughed and told him *she* didn't know what he was talking about.

TRANSFORMATION CONVERSIONS

The usual transformation conversions are exercises on changing the imperative to various tenses, passive to active and active to passive, statements to questions and questions to answers, negative to positive and positive to negative, adjectives and adverbs to clauses and phrases and phrases to clauses, direct to indirect and indirect to direct speech.

Change the following sentences from passive to active voice.
Note: If there is no agent you must supply one as the subject in the active voice.

1. First I was directed to my seat by the stewardess.
2. We were told to fasten our seatbelts.
3. A few minutes after take-off, magazines and newspapers were distributed.
4. I was given some gum to chew because my ears hurt.
5. We were given instructions on what to do in case of an emergency.

The student's composition will be something like this:

First the stewardess directed me to my seat. Then she told us to fasten our seatbelts. A few minutes after takeoff, the stewardesses distributed magazines and newspapers. One of them gave me some gum to chew because my ears hurt. The captain gave us instructions on what to do in case of an emergency.

MODIFICATION CONVERSIONS

Modification exercises are primarily compositions to which the student has added or completed some patterns of the model. They are similar to expansion drills in pattern practice.

They lend themselves primarily to the adding of adjectives and adverbs, articles and noun modifiers, phrases and clauses, and transition words. Completing a sentence which has been partially begun can also be considered a modification exercise.

The following are some typical exercises on the sentence level:

Complete the following sentences using adjective clauses.

a. This is the house where ______________________________.

b. The lawyer whom _________________ lives in San Diego.

c. The class which _________________ starts at 9:00 A. M.

Complete the following sentences using noun clauses.

a. I believe ______________________________.

b. I asked the policeman ______________________________.

c. I don't know ______________________________.

Directions:

Complete the following paragraph of partial statements with time clauses in the simple present tense, underlining the time clauses.

Hing will go to the college cafeteria in a few minutes for another meal. He will take off his cap as soon as... He will not take off his coat until after... He will continue to carry his briefcase while...

Here is a last example of a modification conversion in sentence connectives:

Factual Account:

American higher education has a rural tradition. America began as a civilized but rural nation. Its first colleges and universities quite naturally began in the country. Land was cheap in rural areas. It was less expensive to build schools there. Country people thought city life would have a bad influence on their children. They wanted them to go to rural schools.

Unified Report:

American higher education has a rural tradition for three reasons. First, America began as a civilized but rural nation. Therefore, its first colleges and universities quite naturally began in the country. Also, land was cheap in rural areas, so it was less expensive to build schools there. In addition, country people thought city life would have a bad influence on their children; thus they wanted them to go to rural schools.

SEMICONTROLLED COMPOSITION

As Maryruth Bracy has pointed out, there "exists a broad gap between the least-controlled writing and entirely free compositions."[1] Left to his own devices the student will still make a great number of errors, but his proficiency is such that he needs to move beyond carefully controlled manipulation of structures and vocabulary. Bracy comments on an experiment where her students wrote fewer errors when the content was controlled:

> The problem is not to structure the content so that specific sentence structures will result; otherwise, the students are back to controlled writing. The suggestion is to explore ways of re-structuring topics so as to graduate the control.... The result would be a range of "freeness" in composition similar to the already well-defined range of control in writing.[2]

In the absence of such an established range, we can merely list some established techniques of semicontrol. The one principle that they all share is that the model supplies the content or the ideas for the composition, while there is little structural control.

Directions:

Add three more sentences that develop the topic sentence:

1. Once I visited a village which was located . . . .

____

____

____

____

2. The people of the village had their own distinct customs.

____

____

____

____

Instructions: Write a biographical sketch of the imaginary Russian novelist Ivan Ivonovich. You may describe him as you like, but the following questions and information may help you. Most of the action will, of course, be in the past tense.

Parentage

Born 1812. Father dies when Ivan is three — How? from tuberculosis? by political

1) Maryruth Bracy, "The Move from Controlled Writing to Free Composition, or, Write 300 Words on Being a Foreign Student at UCLA" *Workpapers in English as a Second Language,* Vol. Ⅳ. Department of English, University of California at Los Angeles, (Los Angeles: June 1970), p. 22.

2) Ibid, p. 22.

assassination? of grief over his wife's infidelity? from being thrown from a horse? Mother — rich or poor? beautiful or homely? aristocratic or commoner? strong(domineering, self-willed) or weak? selfish or generous? like or unlike her husband?

J. A. Bright has some good exercises for letter writing:

SUDAN LIGHT AND POWER COMPANY, LTD.

(Incorporated in England)

Khartoum	Branches:
P. O. Box 86	Omdurman. Tel. No. 5623
Tel. No. 2217 (Accounts)	Khartoum N. Tel. No. 2723
Tel. No. 2479 (Repairs)	

KHARTOUM ELECTRICITY AND WATER SUPPLY

(a) Write to the above company saying that you have been sent the bill for somebody else's house.
(b) Write to the above company asking whether it is not possible for them to run later buses between Omdurman and Khartoum, and whether the bus service could not be extended to cover Khartoum North.
(c) Reply to (b), agreeing to the first suggestion, but rejecting the second. Give reasons.
(d) Write to the above company asking about the terms upon which special buses may be hired. Answer your own letter.

From Paulston, C. B & Bruder, M. N. (1976). *Teaching English as a second language,* Cambridge, Mass.: Winthrop Publisher, Inc. pp. 214-227.

25. SENTENCE COMBINING: AN APPROACH TO TEACHING WRITING THAT WORKS

In the past fifteen years, there has been a great deal of research on the effects of sentence-combining practice on students' writing ability. This has led to the creation of a number of textbooks designed to teach writing through sentence combining. While most of these studies have focused on native speakers of English, teachers of English as a foreign language would do well to ask what practical applications this approach might have for the teaching of writing to nonnative speakers. This article proposes to explore the following questions: (1) What is the sentence-combining approach? (2) How is it assumed to be beneficial in teaching writing to native speakers of English? (3) How can this approach be applicable to the teaching of English as a foreign language? (4) What benefits might we expect to derive from sentence combining in an EFL grammar and writing program?

THE SENTENCE-COMBINING APPROACH

Sentence-combining practice ranges from syntactic exercises performed on individual sentences apart from any rhetorical context to composition practice featuring the construction of whole discourses and requiring attention to matters such as transition, cohesion, tone, style, and mechanics. The difficulty of the exercises is determined by the number of sentences to be combined, the nature of the instructions for combining the sentences, and the number of possible solutions.

The simplest and most basic type of exercise is one in which the student is given two sentences with specific directions on how to combine them into one sentence. An example of this type of exercise, called a "signaled" or "cued" exercise, is given below:

Directions: Combine the sentences in each group into only one sentence, using the word in parentheses ( ) to join them.

1) a. John went to the library. (AND)
   b. Mary went home.
2) a. The students were happy. (BECAUSE)
   b. The students passed the test.
3) a. The woman bought a new camera. (WHO)
   b. The woman took a vacation.

For each of the examples above, there are only two correct answers, depending on the order in which the student uses the two sentences. Thus, the following are possible correct answers:

1) John went to the library and Mary went home.
OR
Mary went home and John went to the library.
2) The students were happy because they passed the test.
OR
Because they passed the test, the students were happy.
3) The woman who took a vacation bought a new camera.
OR
The woman who bought a new camera took a vacation.

At the most advanced level, students may be given a group of sentences which can be combined in any way they choose to create an effective paragraph. An example of this type of "open" exercise is given below.

Directions: Combine the following sentences into an effective paragraph.

1. Anteaters are mammals.
2. Anteaters are found in tropical America and Africa.
3. Anteaters have long snouts.
4. Anteaters feed on white ants.
5. White ants are also called termites.
6. The ant bear, the three-toed anteater, and the silky anteater are common types of anteaters.
7. These common types have mouths.
8. The mouths are small.
9. These common anteaters have tongues.
10. These tongues are long.
11. The tongues can be extended to catch insects.
12. Anteaters have claws.
13. The claws are long.
14. The claws are hooked.
15. The hooking is for digging insect nests.
16. The claws are strong.
17. The claws are sharp.
18. The strength and sharpness are for self-defense.
19. The anteater generally sleeps during the day.
20. The anteater is a nocturnal animal.

21. The anteater's tail is curled around him.
22. The tail protects him from the enemies.

It should be obvious that an exercise such as this one has a number of possible solutions, one of which is given below.

Anteaters, found in tropical America and Africa, are mammals which have long snouts with which they feed on white ants, also called termites. The ant bear, the three-toed anteater, and the silky anteater are common types of anteaters which have small mouths and long tongues which can be extended to catch insects. Anteaters have long, hooked claws for digging insect nests. For self-defense, the claws are long and sharp. The anteater is a nocturnal animal which generally sleeps during the day with his tail curled around him to protect him from his enemies.

THE BENEFITS OF SENTENCE COMBINING FOR NATIVE SPEAKERS

Among the first claims for the beneficial effects of sentence combining were increased syntactic growth and improvement in overall quality of writing. Syntactic growth, now commonly referred to in the literature as "syntactic fluency," refers to the complexity of the sentence in terms of the number of sentence embeddings (structures such as nominalizations, adjective or relative clauses, adverbial clauses, etc.). Studies by O'Hare (1973), Vitale et al. (1971), Morenberg (1978), and Stewart (1978), to name only a few, have demonstrated that practice with sentence combining produces significant growth in syntactic fluency. Claims for improvement in overall quality (sentence length, complexity, and variety) in the writing of students who have practiced sentence combining have been made by a number of researchers including O'Hare (1973), Daiker et al. (1978), and Combs (1976).

Recent studies have suggested that additional benefits may be derived from sentence-combining practice. In their evaluation of the overall quality of student writing, Daiker et al. (1978) found students who had practiced sentence combining to be superior in five of the six criteria commonly used in composition evaluation: ideas, supporting details, organization, voice, sentence structure, and diction. The relationship of sentence-combining practice and reading comprehension has also been looked at in a number of studies which suggest that there is an indirect positive influence on reading habits.

SENTENCE COMBINING AND TEACHING ENGLISH AS A FOREIGN LANGUAGE

Since the linguistic skills of an EFL student are not the same as those of a native speaker of English, how can sentence-combining exercises be used in the EFL classroom? Proponents of sentence combining for native speakers have claimed that these exercises provide the students with the opportunity to write that which they already have the linguistic ability to say. Zamel (1980) suggests that the basic assumption that student already possess the requisite linguistic abilities makes the applicability of sentence-combining practice to non-native speakers of English questionable. In short, she feels that "sentence-combining practice, thus, cannot and should not be expected to improve the syntactic writing skills of students if the linguistic ability does not already exist." It seems to me, however, that we need not concern ourselves with this criticism of sentence-combining practice as applied to non-native speakers of English if we use it to help the students develop the necessary linguistic ability.

As was pointed out above, sentence-combining exercises range from very easy to very difficult, depending on the structures being taught, the nature of the instructions for combining the sentences (signaled or open), the number of sentences to be combined, and the number of possible solutions. The exercises used to teach a given structure could range from easy to difficult, depending on the level of the students being taught. For example, students who have just been introduced to relative clauses would first be given highly controlled sentence-combining exercises with only one possible solution, as in the example below. Exercises of this type can also be used for students of more advanced proficiency in order to familiarize them with the methods and goals of sentence-combining exercises as well as to review structures they have already been taught. As Kameen (1978) has pointed out, these exercises correspond to the mechanical exercises of Paulston and Bruder's (1976) classification. Since mechanical exercises require little thought (and can actually be done without understanding the meaning of the sentence), they are not as useful in building the skills that students need in actual writing as are meaningful and communicative exercises.

Directions: Combine each pair of sentences into a single sentence. Make the second sentence into a relative clause using the word in parentheses ( ).

1) a. The man is my father. (WHO)
   b. The man is standing near the door.
   (Answer: The man who is standing near the door is my father.)
2) a. The necklace belonged to my mother. (WHICH)
   b. I am wearing the necklace.
   (Answer: The necklace which I am wearing belonged to my mother.)

Once the students have mastered the highly controlled exercises, they can move on to some less controlled exercises that practice the same grammatical structures, as in the example below. The students are now allowed to choose from a wider range of stylistic variants in arriving at a correct solution. Exercises of this type could be classified as "meaningful" (cf. Paulston and Bruder 1976; Kameen 1978) because they come much closer to real communication.

> Directions: Combine each sequence of sentences into a single sentence with at least one relative clause.
>
> 1) a. The woman speaks English fluently.
>   b. The woman got a job as a translator.
>   (Answer: The woman who speaks English fluently got a job as a translator.
>   OR
>   The woman who got a job as a translator speaks English fluently.)
> 2) a. The Basques live in the mountains.
>   b. The mountains separate Spain from France.
>   c. The Basques were never conquered by the Romans.
>   (Answer: The Basques, who live in the mountains which separate Spain from France, were never conquered by the Romans.
>   OR
>   The Basques, who were never conquered by the Romans, live in the mountains which separate Spain from France.)

At the most advanced level, students would be given a longer set of sentences, such as the example provided at the beginning of this paper, and told to combine the sentences into an effective paragraph, perhaps with the additional instruction that they include several relative clauses. This last type of exercise obviously has the least control and the largest number of possible correct responses, and (as Kameen 1978 suggests) corresponds to the communicative exercises in Paulston and Bruder's sequence. Because these exercises are controlled by the information in them, they must still be considered exercises in controlled rather than free composition.

Since the level of difficulty of sentence-combining exercises can vary greatly, this approach can be adapted to suit students of varying degrees of English proficiency, ranging from basic intermediate (TOEFL 250-350) to advanced (TOEFL 480+). The obvious prerequisite to sentence-combining exercises is that the students be ready to go beyond the most basic sentence patterns to sentences that include structures such as modifying phrases and clauses, nominalizations, and other embedded sentences. Using controlled or signaled sentence-combining exercises, students with lower English proficiency can be taught basic structures such as relative clauses and adverbial clauses. More advanced students can gain facility with these same structures by using less controlled exercises. For the advanced students, more difficult structures, such as nominalizations, can be introduced using controlled exercises. Grammatical explanations can be kept brief, since learning takes place primarily through doing rather than listening. Sentence-combining practice then becomes the core of the grammar and writing program.

Sentence combining can be an especially useful adjunct to an ESP (English for special purposes) program. Researchers and teachers of English have long been aware that there are great differences between the vocabulary and grammatical structures used in one field of study, for example, engineering, and those of another, for example, economics or sociology. An ESP program designed for students with a particular vocational goal could base its sentence-combining exercises on the syntactic structures and vocabulary the student needs to know in that field. In the absence of a formal program, an individual teacher could look at some of the textbooks that the students are expected to read and "decompose" sentences into the simple sentences from which they are made, thus creating an appropriate set of sentence-combining exercises.

THE BENEFITS OF SENTENCE COMBINING FOR EFL STUDENTS

Research on the benefits of sentence-combining practice for EFL students has not been nearly as extensive as that dealing with native speakers of English. The studies which have dealt with EFL students have all shown positive results. In an early study (Crymes 1971), EFL students who practiced sentence-combining exercises involving nominalizations wrote compositions containing more nominalizations than did the EFL control group. Klassen (1977) found that a program of sentence combining led to a growth in syntactic fluency for EFL students in an intensive course. Buckingham and Gonzo (1977) reported an increase in both syntactic fluency and grammatical correctness in the compositions of EFL students as a result of sentence-combining practice. In addition to favorable reports from research, sentence-combining practice has received enthusiastic endorsement from teachers. Bulter (1980: 26) states that as a result of using a new textbook based on sentence combining, "ten percent more students were evaluated at the end of their courses as being prepared for freshman English than the year before." He goes on to point out that a high percentage of repeaters, who had previously failed the course, passed, and concludes that " this meant that several students understood concepts and gained skills which they had once given up being able to learn." The sentence-combining approach has proven very successful in the intermediate-to-advanced-level EFL grammar and writing courses in which I have used it for the last four years. Objective evaluations of the change in the students' writing after ten weeks of sentence-combining practice have shown an improvement in overall quality, grammatical correctness, and syntactic fluency.

What is it that makes sentence combining so successful? For one thing, students of all levels of proficiency seem to enjoy doing the exercises. The easiest exercises — the mechanical ones — virtually guarantee success. Thus, the students gain self-confidence. The less controlled exercises are more challenging, and are perceived by many students as language puzzles or games. Students seem eager to make suggestions and to discuss the merits of various solutions, probably because they do not feel that they are discussing their own writing or that of their classmates. In this way, the entire class becomes involved in a discussion of the grammatical correctness and relative effectiveness of different solutions. This is not normally a very productive subject for discussion in a class setting where all the students have written their own compositions independently. Class discussion is also facilitated by the fact that most of text in the exercise is "given," so the students' attention can be focused on one variable at a time. Thus, they don't feel overwhelmed and confused. This brings me to another advantage of sentence combining — the students are forced to use structures which they might otherwise avoid in their writing. The highly controlled, signaled exercises are especially good for forcing the students to use specific structures, and for this reason their use should never be abandoned altogether, even with the more proficient students. The longer, less controlled exercises provide the students with the opportunity to develop the skills needed in producing whole units of discourse, such as the paragraph — including transitional devices, mechanics, cohesion, and emphasis.

CONCLUSIONS

Sentence combining is an approach to the teaching of writing which has been very successful with native speakers of English, and I believe that it will prove to be equally useful in teaching grammar and writing to EFL students of varying levels of proficiency. Its emphasis on constructions (phrases, clauses, and sentences) makes it one of the best approaches for teaching students how a sentence works and taking them from mere recognition of syntactic units to the combining of these units into complex sentences. Sentence-combining practice not only gives students practice in using a range of syntactic structures, but also leads to overall improvement in terms of such things as grammatical correctness, sentence variety, and even organization and cohesion. A program in sentence combining can be flexible, with exercises ranging from highly controlled to relatively free, from purely mechanical to relatively creative, from combining two sentences to combining groups of three to six into sentences which then make up a coherent paragraph. Students like sentence combining. They like to talk about the process and the merits of different solutions to an exercise. Sentence combining is not the answer to all of our problems in teaching grammar and writing to EFL students, but it is an approach that shows great promise. In my classroom, it is an approach that really works.

■ References

Butler, Jeffrey. (1980). Review of writing and combining standard English sentences, by Alice Pack and Lynn Henrichsen. *TESOL Newsletter, 14,* pp. 25-26.

Buckingham, T. and S. Gonzo. (1977). *The effects of transformational sentence combining practice on the writing ability of non-native speakers of English.* Paper presented at 11th Annual TESOL Convention, Miami, April 1977.

Combs, Warren. (1976). Further effects of sentence-combining practice on writing ability. *Research in the Teaching of English, 10,* pp. 137-149.

Crymes, Ruth. (1971). The relation of study about language to language performance: with special reference to nominalization. *TESOL Quarterly, 5,* 3, pp. 217-230.

Daiker, D., A. Kerek, and M. Morenberg. (1979). *The writer's options.* New York: Harper and Row.

Kameen, Patrick T. (1978). A mechanical, meaningful, and communicative framework for ESL sentence combining exercises. *TESOL Quarterly, 12,* 4, pp. 395-401.

Klassen, Bernard. (1977). *Sentence combining exercises as an aid to expediting syntactic fluency in learning English as a second language.* Ph. D. dissertation, University of Minnesota.

Mellon, John C. (1967). *Transformational sentence combining: a method for enhancing the development of syntactic fluency in English composition.* Harvard University, Cambridge, Mass.

______. (1979). Issues in the theory and practice of sentence combining: a twenty year perspective. In *Sentence combining and the teaching of writing*, eds. D. Daiker, A Kerek, and M. Morenberg. Conway, Arkansas: The Department of English, the University of Akron, and the Department of English, the University of Central Arkansas, pp. 1-38.

Morenberg, M., D. Daiker, and A. Kerek. (1978). Sentence combining at the college level: an experimental study. *Research in the teaching of English, 12,* pp. 245-256.

O'Hare, Frank. (1973). Sentence combining: improving student writing without formal grammar instruction. In *National Council of Teachers of English, Research Report*, No. 15. Urbana, Illinois.

Pack, Alice and Lynn Henrichsen. (1980). *Sentence construction: writing and combining standard English sentences, Book Ⅰ.* Rowley, Mass.: Newbury House.

____. (1981). *Sentence combination: writing and combining standard English sentences, Book Ⅱ.* Rowley, Mass.: Newbury House.

Paulston, Christna Bratt and Mary Newton Bruder. (1976). *Teaching English as a second language: techniques and procedures.* Cambridge, Mass.: Winthrop.

Stewart, Murray F. (1978). Freshman sentence combining: Canadian project. *Research in the Teaching of English, 12,* pp. 257-268.

Strong, William. (1973). *Sentence combining: a composing book.* New York: Random House.

Vitale, M. R., R. J. King, D. W. Shontz, and G. W. Huntley. (1971). Effects of sentence-combining exercises on several restricted written composition tasks. *Journal of educational psychology, 62,* pp. 521-525.

Zamel, Vivian. (1980). Re-evaluating sentence-combining practice. *TESOL Quarterly, 14,* 1, 81-90.

From Thiede-Gonzo, S. (1983). Sentence combining: An approach to teaching writing that works, *English Teaching Forum*, pp. 14-17.

26. THE TREATMENT OF ERROR IN WRITTEN WORK

INTRODUCTION

Recent research in second language acquisition suggests that language learning is a creative process whereby learners produce oral and written utterances based upon the rules of a language system which they have internalized.[1] If a learner understands and uses the rules correctly, he or she will produce utterances that are meaningful, grammatical, and appropriate. If a learner's hypotheses of the language rules are occasionally incorrect, however, some of his or her utterances will contain errors of varying types and frequencies. It is virtually impossible to avoid errors when learning any new skill, particularly when learning a foreign language. It is logical, therefore, to ask a rather critical question: Can error correction benefit language learners?

According to Krashen,[2] children learn their native language as well as foreign languages in a "natural" or subconscious way. Normally, children are more interested in communicating meaningful information than concerned with producing linguistically correct sentences. Krashen believes, therefore, that error correction will not significantly influence the linguistic performance of children. By contrast, adults who learn a foreign language in formal situations such as in classrooms and in self-study courses, are often quite conscious of their errors. For these adults, whom Krashen calls "monitor-users," error correction helps to discover the functions and limitations of the grammatical structures and the lexical forms of the language they are studying. Put another way, error correction in the adult foreign language classroom helps many learners become aware of the exact environment for applying grammatical rules and for discovering the precise semantic range of lexical items.[3]

---

1) I wish to thank Gerard L. Ervin (Ohio State Univ.) for his many helpful suggestions and comments concerning this paper. For any errors in its content or form, I assume full responsibility.

2) Stephen D. Krashen, "The Monitor Model for Adult Second Language Performance." *Viewpoints on English as a Second Language*, ed. Marina Burt, Heidi Dulay, & Mary Finocchiaro (New York: Regents. 1977), pp. 151-56.

3) Stephen D. Krashen & Herbert W. Seliger, "The Essential Contributions of Formal Instruction in Adult Second Language Learning." *TESOL Quarterly,* 9 (1975), pp. 173-83.

GUIDELINES FOR CORRECTING COMPOSITION ERRORS

Discovery Learning and Error Correction. Experienced teachers are quite familiar with the various kinds of errors their students produce when speaking spontaneously or writing creatively in a foreign language. Unfortunately, few teacher training programs (in the United States, at least) provide adequate instruction, if any, on how to deal with student errors. The current status of error correction in foreign language teaching remains ambiguous. Research on the subject is both scant and speculative.[4] Indeed, no standards exist on whether, when, which, or how student errors should be corrected or who should correct them.[5] Moreover, little empirical research has been conducted to test the effectiveness of various approaches and techniques that teachers use for correcting students' oral and written errors.

One common technique for correcting composition errors produced by native and foreign language learners is simply to provide the correct forms and structures in students' faulty sentences. Teachers often supplement these corrections with marginal notes that explain why particular errors are incorrect, such as errors in spelling, lack of subject-verb agreement, and inappropriate style. (One might call this procedure "editing" rather than "correcting.") One thing is certain: providing all the correct forms in students' imperfect sentences is a time-consuming ordeal that can also be frustrating to teachers, especially when they see that identical types of errors appear repeatedly on compositions written over a period of time by the same student. Certainly, from the learner's perspective, it is disconcerting to receive a "corrected" composition with many words crossed out, new words added, and an array of marginal comments — all usually written in bloodred ink. Small wonder, indeed, that some students are embarrassed and lose confidence when they receive their written work corrected in this way. Supplying all the correct forms on adult students' written work may actually hinder rather than facilitate the process of second language acquisition in formal learning situations.

Recently, Dulay and Burt,[6] and Krashen[7] proposed that a selective approach to error correction, tailored to the learner's internal level of linguistic development, might be beneficial to students in both cognitive and affective terms. According to Corder,[8] Gorbet,[9] and

4) James M. Hendrickson, "Error Correction in Foreign Language Teaching: Recent Theory, Research; and Practice," *Modern Language Journal,* 62 (1978), pp. 387-98.

5) Marina K. Burt, "Error Analysis in the Adult EFL Classroom," *TESOL Quarterly,* 9 (1975), pp. 53-63.

6) Heidi Dulay & Marina Burt, "Remarks on Creativity in Language Acquisition," *Viewpoints on Englishas a Second Language* (see note 2 above), pp. 95-126.

7) Krashen (note 2 above).

8) S. Pit Corder, "The Significance of Learners' Errors," *International Review of Applied Linguistics,* 5 (1967), pp. 161-70.

9) Frances Gorbet, "Error Analysis: What the Teacher Can Do: A New Perspective." Ottawa: Research Division, Public Service Commission of Canada. November 1974 (EDRS: ED 100 193).

Valdman,[10] a discovery approach might also be worthwhile. These three researchers suggest that a discovery approach would help students make inferences and formulate concepts about the target language, and would help them to fix this information in their long-term memories.

Considerations in Error Correction. When deciding which errors to correct and how to correct them, one should consider at least four critical learner factors. First, one needs to be aware of a student's purpose and goals for communicating in writing. For example, does the student need to develop his or her writing skills in the foreign language well enough to compose a class term paper, or to write a master's thesis? Or does the student simply want to be able to write a letter of invitation or a thank-you note to a friend? We might suppose that many readers would be more tolerant of a thank-you note replete with errors than they would be of a master's thesis that contains proportionately fewer errors.

Second, one must take into account students' written proficiency in the target language at any given time. I have found that as students' level of proficiency increases, they become better equipped to correct their own errors. Because beginning and intermediate students have presumably internalized the foreign language system to a lesser degree than have advanced learners, their limited linguistic repertoire is often insufficient to allow them to locate and find solutions to their errors. Consequently, less advanced students need specific clues about their errors. Advanced students, however, are better able to correct their own errors if their teacher indicates where the errors are.

A third critical factor in error correction is the teacher's awareness of error types and frequencies as well as an understanding of how these two aspects relate to students' writing goals. Certainly, errors that impair the intelligibility of sentences merit a higher priority for correction than errors that do not. Similarly, errors that stigmatize the writer from the perspective of native speakers should be among the first corrected. Also, mistakes that occur frequently in students' compositions probably deserve more immediate attention than those that are less frequent.

The fourth and possibly most critical factor in correcting written errors is the students' attitudes about their nature and correction. According to Carroll,[11] willingness to use a foreign language — and to make errors — is one characteristic of a successful language learner. Carroll states that a student's attitude toward learning involves "a kind of self-control and confidence whereby the learner can attempt self-expression without feeling self-conscious or threatened by making errors and being corrected" (p. 6). One implication of the statement is the need for teachers to create a healthy learning environment in which students recognize

---

10) Albert Valdman, "Learner Systems and Error Analysis," *Perspective: A New Freedom,* ed. Gilbert A. Jarvis (Skokie, IL: National Textbook Co., 1975), pp. 219-58.

11) John B. Carroll, "Characteristics of Successful Second Language Learners," *Viewpoints on English as a Second Language* (see note 2 above), pp. 1-7.

that making errors is a natural, indeed, a *necessary* phenomenon in language learning. Excessive embarrassment caused by one's errors can be an obstacle to learning from them. A more positive attitude would be to seek information actively on the correctness and appropriateness of one's efforts to communicate. Such an open attitude toward learning from errors can and should be cultivated by the language teacher. Generally speaking, students who manifest low self-confidence in their ability to express themselves in a foreign language need a greater amount of supportive feedback on their errors than do their more confident peers. Teachers can help build student self-confidence by focusing on high priority errors while tolerating less important ones, particularly when students are not required to rewrite their compositions. Moreover, it may be wiser to give low-confidence students more credit for the *content* of their ideas rather than for the *form* in which they are expressed. As these students gain greater control in using the foreign language, the teacher can shift to other error correction strategies

Indirect and Direct Correction Treatments. Recently, I have been experimenting with various combinations of indirect and direct treatments for correcting compositions written by students of intermediate Spanish.[12] I require my students to write five picture-story compositions as homework assignments. As they write, the students are encouraged to use self-help resources such as their textbook, dictionaries, and grammar books. The students have several days to complete and turn in a first draft of their picture-story composition.

Indirect correction treatments may indicate either the presence or the specific location of errors. I use such treatments whenever I assume that students will be able to discover an acceptable solution for a given error by reconsidering the error itself or by using the appropriate self-help references mentioned above. Some suggestions for making errors are as follows:

1. Underlining incorrect orthographic and morphological forms.
   Example:[13] The woman wont to kook the fich.
2. Circling an inappropriate word.
   Example: They are very happy with their plays. ("games")
3. Inserting an arrow (∧) to indicate a missing word.
   Examples: The man∧saying good-bye to his wife.
4. Placing a question mark alongside a confusing phrase or structure.
   Example: Two girls are going that brought other tree.?

12) These students complete three 11-week Spanish courses prior to enrolling in this "intermediate" class. This class stresses reading vocabulary improvement, review of grammatical structures, small group conversation, and the development of basic writing skill.

13) The example sentences are based on common errors produced by intermediate adult learners of English as a Second Language, French, Spanish, and German.

Direct correction treatments not only indicate the presence or location of errors in a sentence, but also provide clues or tips on how students can correct their own errors. I use direct treatments whenever I assume that students will not be able to correct certain errors if I merely identified them; I have found that providing this additional, more specific feedback often leads students to provide solutions to their errors. Here are several suggestions that vary in their degree of directness, beginning with the *least* direct correction treatment:

1. Underlining a word and providing a written tip.
   Example: She finds her watch inside the drawer.
   use past tense
2. Bracketing a misplaced word or phrase and indicating its proper place in a sentence.
   Example: "Well, nothing is forever," told them [their mother].
3. Crossing out a superfluous word.
   Example: When the boy was riding his bicycle, a car hit to him.
4. Providing a correct form or structure of an incorrect word or phrase.
   Example: They digged around a small tree.
   dug

I have found that indirect and direct correction treatments can be more effective if they are used together in hybrid fashion. The combined treatments that a teacher uses will vary not only from one learner to the next, but also from one composition to the next. As stated previously, when correcting an individual's written work, the teacher needs to be aware of the learner's writing goals, level of writing proficiency, types and frequencies of errors, and motivation to learn from those errors. The composition in Figure 1 was corrected using a combination of indirect and direct treatments. It was written by an intermediate adult student of English as a second language in a community college, and who intends to transfer later to a four-year institution. The types and frequencies of errors in the composition are those that this highly-motivated student typically produced.

FIGURE 1

A SAMPLE COMPOSITION[14)]

This story is about a man who gott up late everyday and he often arrived late to his office. So one day he dicided to but an alarm o'clock ^ that ^ can gett early by it and can arrive to his office on time. After he bought it he wanted ^ try it, so when he wanted

14) This composition was elicited by Picture Story 23 in L.A. Hill's *Picture Composition Book* (London: Longman, 1960).

to go ∧ bed he stringed ↑ up [it]. Than he slept. In the morning when the alarm o'clock
wrong verb

began to ring, he wake up nervousness and suddenly shoot out his pillow over the alarm
wrong tense tense

o'clock. Than the table with alarm o'clock and pillow fell down on the ground. So the
wrong word

o'clock stooped to ring_ and Mr. Lazy slept again Because he usued to gett up late. So that was very difficult for him ∧ get up early.

When I return my students' first drafts, I ask them to rewrite the compositions at home and turn them in at the next class meeting. At that time I collect both their first and second drafts, then supply the correct forms and structures of any errors remaining on the second draft. I assume that the students were unable to correct these remaining errors by themselve s.[15] A student's grade is based on a ratio of the number of words in a composition to the number of errors remaining on the second draft.[16]

It is important to emphasize at this point that the treatments presented and illustrated above are merely suggestions. Teachers will want to modify and add to them according to their own teaching style and their students' communicative and linguistic needs. Nevertheless, students need to be given as many opportunities as possible to discover solutions to their written errors. This discovery approach to correction allows students to assume a greater responsibility for their own learning. Also, the approach may well develop students' abilities to write more clearly and accurately in a foreign language than would be the case if teachers supplied all the correct forms and structures of students' errors.

Certainly, many research questions on error correction still remain. For example, how do students react to different correction treatments? Which correction techniques are most effective for particular cognitive styles and personality types? To what extent does error correction actually benefit (or hinder) language learning? Undoubtedly the answers to these queries will raise additional questions, but they can also lead to the development of more efficient and humane ways to correct student errors.

Final Suggestions. It has been stated that using combined indirect and direct treatments

---

15) Because approximately 15 students are enrolled per quarter and because their compositions seldom exceed more than 200 words, it is not overly time-consuming to correct the second drafts. For teachers who have many students who write lengthy compositions, however, a modified approach would be advisable. For example teachers could draw the student's attention only to serious communication errors, highly stigmatized errors, and to mistakes that occur very frequently in their compositions. This procedure focuses on linguistic problems that need greater and more immediate attention than do less important errors.

16) By dividing the number of words in a composition by the number of errors it contains, one can determine such a ratio. The teacher can then develop a *word: error ratio* scale for evaluation purposes. For example, one could assign number or letter grades to particular ranges of *word: error ratios,* thereby making it possible to compare writing accuracy from one composition to another for any individual or, if desired, between two or more students' compositions.

to correct compositions is probably more beneficial to students than providing all the correct or appropriate solutions to their written errors. Nevertheless, teachers need to reinforce any correction approach or treatment with monitoring and learning activities designed to improve the writing skills of their students. Here are seven such activities, some of which have recently been mentioned elsewhere in the professional literature.

1. Chart and tally written errors in order to diagnose students' individual communicative and linguistic problem areas, and to measure their writing proficiency. In addition, make a master error chart to help you decide which errors should receive high, medium, or low priority for correction.[17)]
2. Identify mistakes that occur frequently on individual students' compositions. Ask students to search out and correct their own high-frequency errors before turning in the first draft of each subsequent composition.
3. Discuss the kinds of errors that students produce most often on their compositions. Distribute sentences or short paragraphs containing these common error types, then ask students to locate and correct them. This exercise can be assigned as homework, then discussed at the next class meeting.
4. Try to discover the cause of students' errors by discussing their compositions with them on an individual basis. Understanding why particular errors occurred on one composition is an initial step in helping students to avoid similar errors on future compositions.
5. Record comments concerning written errors on cassette tapes that students supply along with their compositions. This technique provides a highly personalized approach to error correction whenever it is difficult to meet with students individually.[18)]
6. Develop and implement communicative drills based on grammatical structures and vocabulary items that are most troublesome for students. These kinds of drills provide valuable practice in using language meaningfully.[19)]
7. Instruct students to work in pairs and to correct each other's compositions before submitting them. This procedure allows students to work in a non-threatening educational setting that helps build their self-confidence and fosters learning by discovery and sharing.[20)]

---

17) James M. Hendrickson, "Evaluating Spontaneous Communication Through Systematic Error Analysis," *Foreign Language Annals,* 12 (1979), pp. 357-64.

18) Maryruth B. Farnsworth, "The Cassette Recorder: A Bonus or a Bother in ESL Composition Correction?" *TESOL Quarterly,* 8 (1974), pp. 285-91.

19) Christina Bratt Paulston, "Structural Pattern Drills: A Classification," *Foreign Language Annals,* 4 (1970), pp. 187-93.

20) Michael C. Witbeck, "Peer Correction Procedures for Intermediate and Advanced ESL Composition Lessons,"

CONCLUSION

While waiting for basic and applied research on second language learning to provide more information on the issues surrounding error correction in foreign language teaching, teachers will need to continue experimenting with different feedback strategies in their classrooms. In this paper, I have discussed some general guidelines as well as specific treatments for dealing with written errors in the adult foreign language classroom. Teachers and researchers should regard these guidelines and treatments as suggestions. Experience suggests that what works effectively for one teacher may not necessarily be equally effective for another. Nevertheless, based on current language learning theory and research as well as on observation and practical experience, one can indicate a logical direction for error correction to take. The suggestions presented herein were built upon that premise — one that awaits the necessary rigor of empirical experimentation and further refinement.

From Hendrickson, M. J. (1980), The treatment of error in written work, *The Modern Language Journal*, 64, 216-220.

TESOL Quarterly, 10 (1976), pp. 321-26.

27. WRITING: THE PROCESS OF DISCOVERING MEANING

Research on composition has traditionally been concerned with the written product. The studies reported by Braddock et al. (1963) reflect this concern since, by and large, researchers investigated the effects that certain teaching methodologies had on writing. In many cases these studies sought to prove the efficacy of one grammar over another, thus perpetuating the belief that a better pedagogical approach, particularly one that focused on usage, structure, or correct form, would improve writing.

Since this line of research depended upon the evaluation of compositions that students wrote after having received certain types of instruction, little attention was paid to other, more important considerations such as purpose, audience, and the process of composing itself. Questions dealing with why or for whom students were writing were not taken into account. The whole notion of how writers write — where ideas come from, how they are formulated and developed, what the various stages of composing entail — was ignored. And this state of the art was both influenced by and, in turn, influenced classroom practices and the textbooks that were written (Young, 1978: 31-2). Given the emphasis on the composed product, teachers adopted methods and materials they assumed would positively influence their students' writing.

Recently, however, the focus of research on composition has shifted. Rather than investigating what students write, teachers and researchers are beginning to study the composing process itself. They are now working under the assumption that before we know how to teach writing, we must first understand how we write. And what they are finding out about this process seriously challenges the ways in which composition has been taught in the past. The composing process seems to be an extremely complex undertaking, the nature of which "militate[s] against prescriptive approaches to the teaching of writing" (Witte and Faigley, 1981: 202); it involves much more than studying a particular grammar, analyzing and imitating rhetorical models, or outlining what it is one plans to say. The process involves not only the act of writing itself, but prewriting and rewriting, all of which are interdependent.

ESL teachers concerned with language acquisition and error analysis emphasize, even more than other writing teachers, correctness and form. Widdowson(1978) is particularly critical of ESL teaching practices because they focus upon usage rather than real communication. A cursory look at ESL composition texts indicates that, for the most part, writing assignments are made for the sole purpose of testing the mastery of specific grammatical structures and that few involve invention techniques or prewriting strategies. Furthermore, research on ESL composition is almost negligible. Those few studies that do exist are directed towards investigating the effects of certain types of writing practice on composition, thereby still indicating a concern with product (see, for example, Konneker and Perkins, 1981). It is therefore important that ESL teachers of writing take into account the current findings in research on composition. While this point has been made before (Zamel, 1976), it is especially appropriate now, given the absence of our own research and our continuing emphasis on the surface features of writing.

RESEARCH ON THE COMPOSING PROCESS

Janet Emig's(1971) classic study represented one of the first attempts to investigate what writers do when they compose. Adopting a case-study approach, which in and of itself was a break from the more traditional experimental designs, she discovered how naive our past assumptions about composing had been. While composing, students seemed to exhibit a variety of behaviors, all of which indicated the nonlinear nature of writing. Emig therefore concluded that teachers of composition tend to "underconceptualize and oversimplify the process of composing" (1971: 98).

Perhaps one of Emig's most important findings was that writing involved a continuing attempt to discover what it is one wanted to say. It is this act of discovery that Murray (1978, 1980) has identified as the main feature of the writing process. While this process entails several stages, such as "rehearsing," "drafting," and "revising" (Murray, 1980: 4-5), these stages interact together and repeatedly in order to discover meaning. Writing viewed from this perspective is the process of exploring one's thoughts and learning from the act of writing itself what these thoughts are. Rather than being the development of some preconceived and well-formed idea, writing is "the record of an idea developing. [It] is a process whereby an initial idea gets extended and refined" (Shaughnessy, 1977: 234). As one writes and rewrites, thereby approximating more closely and more accurately one's intended meaning, the form with which to express this meaning suggests itself. Given this definition of composing, the short-comings of traditional approaches to teaching composition become obvious. Requiring students to formulate their ideas beforehand, to elaborate upon them by using some prescribed rhetorical framework and to submit these written products for grading purposes seems to ignore everything we have learned about the process.

Sondra Perl (1980a), again using the case-study approach of the current research paradigm, found that even unskilled writers employ consistent and stable composing strategies which represent their attempts to discover meaning. "Through the act of seeing their ideas on paper, students are enabled to reflect upon them and develop them further" (Perl, 1980a: 24). In this way, these unskilled writers, reexamining what they had already written in order to discover the direction of their thoughts, were using behaviors identified by other researchers:

> We [shape] the utterances as we write; and when the seam is 'played out' or we are interrupted, we get started again by reading what we have written. (Britton, 1978: 24)

Perl also found that writing was affected by the mode of discourse specified. Students wrote more and with greater fluency and satisfaction when their writing involved them personally, while they wrote with less facility when the writing was more objectified (1980a: 30-1). This is certainly an important finding, given that the purpose of most assigned writing seems to be the transmission of objectively described information for the teacher (Britton, 1978: 15).

Perl went on to study the writing strategies of more proficient writers and again observed the recursive nature of the writing process, that is, that writers go back in order to move forward. She reiterates the notion of writing as discovery:

> When we are successful at this process, we end up with a product that teaches us something, that clarifies what we know (or what we know at one point only implicitly), and that lifts out or explicates or enlarges our experience. (Perl, 1980b: 368)

While Perl indicates that all writers, both skilled and unskilled, use what she calls retrospective structuring in order to discover, less skilled writers who view composing as more mechanical and formulaic are so inhibited by their concerns with correctness and form that they cannot get beyond the surface in order to anticipate the needs and expectations of their readers (1980b: 368). This ability to project oneself into the role of another reader, what she calls projective structuring, is a skill that most beginning writers lack and another important aspect of the composing process (see, for example, Barritt and Kroll, 1978; Brostoff and Beyer, 1980; Emig, 1978; Flower, 1979; Judy, 1980).

Sommers (1980), like Perl, studied the writing strategies of less experienced and more experienced writers. While she focused on revision, one should bear in mind that revision and writing were being viewed, as most researchers now view them, as interchangeable terms. She found that less skilled writers revised in the most-limited way; they were basically concerned with lexicon and teachers-generated rules and rarely modified ideas that had already been written down. While the unskilled writers in Perl's study(1980a) seemed to understand that writing is a process that involves constant revision, it should be pointed out that they too were concerned almost constantly with form, usage, and grammar. Unlike these writers, the more experienced writers observed by Sommers viewed their writing from a more global perspective. In the process of discovering meaning, these experienced writers changed whole chunks of discourse, and each of these changes represented a reordering of the whole. Sommers concluded that "it is a sense of writing as discovery — a repeated process of beginning over again, starting out new — that the less experienced students failed to have"(1980: 387).

Perl and Sommers both suggest that inexperienced writers pay so much undue attention to form that the ongoing process of discovery is constantly interrupted. As Perl put it, "premature and rigid attempts to correct and edit their work truncate the flow of composing" (1980a: 22). Rose (1980) arrives at the same conclusion after investigating why certain writers experience writer's block. Like Perl's unskilled basic writers and Sommers' less experienced writers, Rose's "blockers" felt restricted by "writing rules or planning strategies that impeded rather than enhanced the composing process" (19890: 390). The "non-blockers," on the other hand, while operating according to certain rules and plans, were also aware that these rules and plans are subject to modification. It is this flexibility that allowed these writers to review what they had written and shift directions when necessary. Thus, when writing is experienced as the mechanical act of transcribing one's ideas, when the language itself rather than "the purpose for which the language is used" becomes the focus (Britton, 1978: 24), when production becomes more important than meaning (Barritt and Kroll, 1978: 52), when attention to form becomes the "dominant and absorbing activity" (Emig, 1978: 62), the act of writing as discovery cannot be explored. Halsted (1975: 882) comments, "The obsession with the final product . . . is what ultimately leads to serious writing block. More importantly, it is a sure way to close off avenues to discovering what it is you have to say."

THE COMPOSING PROCESS OF PROFICIENT ESL WRITERS

While the research thus far reported has taught us a great deal about the composing processes of both less proficient and more proficient writers, it became important to investigate to what extent the findings apply to ESL writers. Are ESL students experiencing writing as a creative act of discovery, or are they attending so much to language and correct form that writing is reduced to a mechanical exercise? How do these students generate their ideas? What happens after these ideas are written down? What does a record of their writing, (from the initial notes to the final draft), indicate about their writing experiences?

These are some of the questions I tried to answer. As in the other process studies, a case-study approach was adopted. Eight ESL students (one Japanese, one Hispanic, two Arabic, two Italian, and two Greek) were interviewed individually about their writing experiences and behaviors. Different stages of their writing were also studied to determine whether their actual writing reflected the experiences that were reported. These ESL students were proficient to the extent that they were no longer enrolled in ESL writing courses and were successfully completing the writing assigned in university-level content area courses. While their writing still indicated some linguistic idiosyncrasies, it was basically free of the kind of language-related errors that can obfuscate meaning and demonstrated almost total control of organizational skills. Proficient writers were used for this study not only in order to find out whether their writing experiences resemble those of other writers, but also because it is by studying the composing processes of skilled ESL writers that we can begin to evaluate whether our teaching methods and approaches promote and reinforce these processes or inhibit and undermine them.

An important dimension of the writing process involves the period before the actual writing begins, that is, how writers get and form ideas before putting pen to paper. All of the students talked about the importance of classroom discussion specifically related to a particular topic and how these discussions helped them delineate their ideas. Several mentioned the frustrations they felt, as beginning writers, when they were assigned a paper that was totally unrelated to what had been discussed in class or one that they had no interest in writing about. This raised another important issue, whether or not they had preferences for specific types of discourse. While they indicated that writing about what they knew was important when they first were learning to compose, they by and large now preferred more objective, informationally based assignments. One student, recalling some of his first ESL writing assignments, thought that personal matters were "none of my teacher's business," while another exclaimed, "My teacher is not a confessor, preacher, or psychologist!"

Since these students are now taking courses which require papers that may only be peripherally related to the lectures and discussions, they talked about the strategies they now use to generate their ideas. While at first they may just read and reread course materials until they experience what Perl (1980b) calls a "felt sense," what may happen at this point is quite intriguing. Several students reported having some sort of internal dialogue, "a conversation with an invisible person," as one student put it, in order to figure out how to proceed.

Once the actual writing begins, it may take the form of some sketchy notes or fully articulated sentences and paragraphs. Only one student reported using a formal outline and depending upon it in order to write. This student indicated a still-felt insecurity with English and didn't feel confident enough to compose without resorting to a fairly complex outline. While the use of this outline gave him a sense of control, he did admit that once the outline was completed, he found the actual writing both boring and mechanical. One can not help but speculate, since his writing was fairly accomplished, as to whether he really needed the outline or whether he had learned his English teacher's lessons too well. One other student reported writing an outline, but not necessarily using it: "Very often the paper I wind up with is different from the outline. I don't see the missing pieces when I write the outline. I can't anticipate what's going to go wrong in my logic when I do the outline." The other students never wrote outlines, although two recalled courses in which they wrote outlines after they wrote the papers in order to comply with their teachers' assignments. One student asked, "How can I write an outline when my ideas are flying back and forth?," while another indicated that only "when the material falls together, I discover my outline."

These students talked about writing down ideas, rethinking them, and then writing some more, not exactly sure of what would next appear on the paper. They discussed the thinking they do about their writing even as they are involved in the most mundane activities, for example, washing the dishes or getting ready for bed. They mentioned needing a great deal of time not only to actually write, but also to leave their writing and come back to it again and again and reread it in order to go on. As one student put it, "The more days go by, the more ideas come. It's like fruit; it needs time to ripen." For some students the inner dialogue that began prior to the actual writing continues as they reread their papers. As one student indicated, "It's through the conversation with myself that I learn what I'm going to say." This dialogue also allows them to "hear" and thereby evaluate the clarity of their writing. One student resorts to using her hands while she reads her writing aloud, as if she were talking to somebody else. As they reread what they have written, they may experience a sense of dissatisfaction, at which point they may have to make partial changes or start anew. If, however, what they have written expresses what they intended to say, they continue writing, finding out in the process what they will say next. These activities do not take place in a series of stages, but rather are transactional and overlapping. Thus, new insights can occur at almost any time during the process, thereby creating the need for more time for the incubation of these ideas (Britton, 1978: 23). While the students talked about the pain involved in the act of writing, they also discussed the feeling of accomplishment they experience when they are satisfied with what they have written. This satisfaction derives not only from the accomplishment itself, but from the knowledge that another reader will be able to appreciate the product of all these efforts. As one student indicated: "When I write, I keep in mind the reader. The professor is not the reader because he has heard it a million times before. My reader is an imaginary person who may not know something about which I write. You have to think that you are informing somebody even though this person never sees it."

An interesting discovery was made when the most proficient writer, a graduate student of English, admitted to writing first in her own native language and then translating into English. None of the other students used translation except when they were stuck, couldn't think of a particular word in English and, in order not to lose their thread of thought, put down the word or expression in their own language. Otherwise, they reacted negatively to the idea of translation. As one student hypothesized, "It would be like being pulled by two brains." This student in resorting to translation, however, did not in fact contradict any of the experiences reported by the other students; rather, it corroborated the fact that writing and creating seem to be simultaneous and reciprocal. She explained that for her writing had to be continuous. If she had to stop because she lacked a particular vocabulary word, she lost the flow of thought and this made her anxious. "When I write in my own language, I feel great because I can express my writing as part of myself. It's like painting. It materializes on a piece of paper, and other people can share what I feel." Many of the students comments reflected the same idea, that writing provides a means for discovering, creating, and giving form to one's thoughts and ideas. The students themselves articulated it best: "I have in my mind some general ideas. I don't know where I'm going to end. By rereading, the direction, although shapeless, comes to my mind..." And, "Writing helps me assess the clarity of my ideas. When I have a new idea, I try to write it as soon as possible because this is a way of checking if my ideas are clear or confused." Again, "When I go back to my writing, I often find that the order of ideas that I planned get reversed. As soon as you are writing and your ideas are coming, you realize that secondary arguments become primary. I don't know why this happens."

IMPLICATIONS FOR TEACHING

It is quite clear that ESL writers who are ready to compose and express their ideas use strategies similar to those used by native speakers of English. Their writing behaviors suggest approaches to the teaching of composition that ESL teachers may have felt were only appropriate for native speakers but which, in fact, may be effective for teaching all levels of writing, including ESL composition.

Students first of all need ideas to explore and write about. While more skilled writers have established certain methods that allow them to proceed with this exploration, less proficient writers need to be taught how to make use of prewriting strategies or invention techniques. As Shaughnessy points out, "Instruction in writing must begin with the more fundamental processes whereby writers get their thoughts in the first place and then get them underway" (1977: 245). An instructional method based on the traditional read-analyze-write model of teaching composition ignores this crucial aspect of the composing process. It fails to take into account that students need the opportunity to "talk about, to expand and even to relearn or reexamine their experiences... prior to writing" (Judy, 1980:

39). Since students may lack systematic strategies necessary for finding a focus and beginning (Brostoff and Beyer, 1980: 39-40), they need to be taught how to explore topics, develop ideas, and discover relationships by making use of the kinds of invention techniques described by Koch and Brazil (1978: 25-63), Lauer (1980: 57-59), Maimon et al. (1981: 23-45), Wiener (1980: 90-92), and Young (1978: 35-39). While the ESL field is beginning to recognize the importance of these activities (see, for example Daubney-Davis, 1981; McKay, 1981; and Taylor, 1981), it still seems dominated by a concern with product, thus supporting the finding that school-sponsored writing provides little time for prewriting (Emig, 1971: 92).

Another important aspect of the composing process concerns the way writers feel about the topics they are asked to write about. Raimes is critical of the narrow range of topics ESL students are typically assigned (1979: 17-19), and Taylor claims that "Rarely is a writing assignment compelling enough to give students an opportunity to immerse themselves totally in the topic to the extent that they have something important to say" (1981: 9). Writing instruction that focuses on rhetorical forms and requires students to compose papers on artificial topics in order to demonstrate mastery of these forms fails to recognize that writers write both quantitatively more and qualitatively better when they are composing papers about topics that engage them (Perl, 1980a: 30-31). Students' writing thus should be motivated by their feelings about the responses to a topic with which they have had some experience (Judy, 1980: 39; Lauer, 1980: 56). This does not mean, however, that writing assignments need be entirely student generated or that they involve only personal accounts, but rather that even academic writing should allow students to become involved in a subject (Weiss, 1980: 146-146) or provide them with a way into the topic (Perl, 1980a: 31).

As far as writing about truly personal topics is concerned, it should be kept in mind that the ESL students that were interviewed expressed dissatisfaction with more personally oriented assigned writing, a finding that has been reported before (Kroll, 1979). Perhaps this dissatisfaction stems from the fact they are in the habit of using their own native language when writing about more private matters and therefore feel that the academic setting is inappropriate for this type of discourse. Or, perhaps because these assignments were collected, evaluated for error, and graded, these students were never given to understand the purpose of this type of writing, that it was meant to get them in touch with and value their felt thoughts and responses. Once students and their teachers recognize the function of expressive or reflective writing (Britton, 1978: 16; Emig, 1971: 91), they may begin to appreciate its importance. By keeping personal journals, for example, students may come to realize that writing is indeed a way to explore one's feelings and thoughts.

While students are rarely provided with pre-writing practice and may have little idea as to the reasons why they are asked to write particular types of discourse, it is the actual process of composing of which they may have the least understanding and with which they are probably given the least experience. Not knowing how writers behave and what the process involves, students "tend to think that the point of writing is to get everything right the first time and that the need to change things is the work of the amateur" (Shaughnessy, 1977: 79). They may have the misconception that, because of our attention to form, "writers know the form before they know the content" (Murray, 1980: 13). They may have the impression that writers "know exactly what they are going to say before they say it" (Murray, 1978: 100). But we know from the research findings that this is not the case, and this knowledge needs to be imparted to our students. We must allow them to experience the process of discovering what they want to say through writing. We must provide them with ample time to write and rewrite, to learn that several drafts may be needed before intention and expression become one. We need to show them our own attempts to write and the different transformations that this writing undergoes, for "one of the most important facts about the composing process that seems to get hidden from students is that the process that creates precision is itself messy" (Shaughnessy, 1977: 222). In this way they may come to appreciate that revising may mean deleting and adding paragraphs or even pages, not the deleting or proofreading that revising has traditionally been synonymous with. They also need to be taught that since writers do not produce perfect essays in one sitting certain features of composing are focused upon before others. This helps reinforce the idea that content and organization are of primary importance and that editing, though to some extent inevitable throughout, is really the province of the last stage of composing. Furthermore this may keep students from experiencing a cognitive overload, a situation which results when too many factors, concerns, or problems are being attended to simultaneously (Maimon et al., 1981: 10; Hirsch, 1980: 159).

Rather than require students to prepare comprehensive outlines (Britton, 1978; Halsted, 1975; Taylor, 1981), we should encourage them to take more informal notes or jot down ideas and reassure them that they need not know from the outset what it is they are going to say. Otherwise, rather than struggling to make sense of their ideas, they may be struggling because "we have put writing in a framework that inhibits communication and/or expression" (Petty, 1978: 83). We may also need to reexamine our use of the prose models which we ask our students to imitate, a practice that seems to be pervasive in ESL, perhaps because of Kaplan's (1967) study of culture-specific rhetorical thought patterns. But this methodology can be misleading because it may give students the impression that the linear, straightforward writing they are supposed to imitate is the result of a process that was itself linear. It fails to show students that the thinking and writing that preceded these models may have been chaotic and disorganized and that their own attempts to write may involve this same disorder. The study of such models puts undue emphasis on the final and correct product and by doing so threatens students with the idea that they are expected to achieve the same level of competency and may render them incapable of even beginning (Eschholz, 1980: 23). Instead of asking students to match their writing to a particular model, we need to teach them that "form grows from content and is inseparable from it" (Judy, 1980: 41), that structuring and organizing one's ideas and thoughts only make sense with reference to the nature of those ideas and thoughts. Finally, because ESL students may still be in the process of acquiring language skills, it needs to be emphasized that grammar-based approaches to teaching writing serve neither as substitutes nor prerequisites for instruction in the process of composing (Lauer, 1980: 54). Extensive research has shown that grammar study may have little to do with composing (Zamel, 1976: 72-74), and it has been pointed out that even low-level students should be given the opportunity to explore this process (Taylor, 1976: 310-311; Raimes, 1979: 3).

Writing taught as a process of discovery implies that revision becomes the main focus of the course and that the teacher, who traditionally provides feedback after the fact, intervenes to guide students through the process. Teacher-student conferences need to be regularly held between drafts so that students learn, while they are creating, what areas need to be worked on. Some educators feel that individual conferences are so effective that they should take the place of all in-class instruction (Carnicelli, 1980). This, however, would deny the students the opportunity to share their writing with other students, an activity that forms the basis of much process-centered instruction (see, for example, Dowst, 1980; Judy, 1980; Lauer, 1980; Maimon, 1980; Murray, 1980; Wiener, 1980). This shared experience reinforces the fact that the teacher is truly not the only reader, a claim which we repeatedly make but fail to convince our students of, and that audience considerations therefore need to be taken into account. Moreover, this type of experience helps develop in students the crucial ability of reviewing their writing with the eyes of another. Most beginning students who are unable to adopt another's frame of reference, compose essays that are ego-centric (Brostoff and Beyer, 1980: 44; Odell et al, 1978: 5). They may not be aware that their prose is writer-based rather than reader-based (Flower, 1979) and that as we write "our needs as readers become paramount" (Emig, 1978: 66). Peers who serve as a real and immediate audience can help establish these needs.

It should not be concluded from the foregoing discussion that engaging students in the process of composing eliminates our obligation to upgrade their linguistic competencies. Raimes (1979) talks about the numerous language skills that ESL composition teachers need to attend to. But what needs to be emphasized is that this obligation should not form the basis of our writing instruction. Syntax, vocabulary, and rhetorical form are important features of writing, but they need to be taught not as ends in and of themselves, but as the means with which to better express one's meaning. Otherwise, students may never understand why these features are important.

■ References

Barritt, Loren S., and Barry M. Kroll. (1978). Some implications of cognitive-developmental psychology for research in composing. In C. Cooper and L. Odell (eds.), *Research on Composing.* Urbana, IL: National Council of Teachers of English.

Braddock, Richard et al. (1963). *Research in written composition.* Champaign, IL: National Council of Teachers of English.

Bitton, James. (1978). The composing process and the functions of writing. In C. Cooper and L. Odell (eds.), *Research on Composing.* Urbana, IL: National Council of Teachers of English.

Brostoff, Anita, and Barry K. Beyer. (1980). An approach to integrating writing into a history course. *Journal of Basic Writing 2*, 4: 36-52.

Carnicelli, Thomas A. (1980). The writing conference: A one-to-one conversation. In T. R. Donovan and B. W. McClelland (eds.), *Eight Approaches to Teaching Composition.* Urbana, IL: National Council of Teachers of English.

Daubney-Davis, Ann E. (1981). Invention techniques: What we can learn from freshman composition. Paper presented at the Fifteenth Annual TESOL Convention, Detroit, Michigan, March 1981.

Dowst, Kenneth. (1980). The epistemic approach: Writing, knowing, and learning. In T. R. Donovan and B. W. McClelland (eds.), *Eight Approaches to Teaching Composition.* Urbana, IL: National Council of Teachers of English.

Emig, Janet. (1971). *The composing processes of twelfth graders.* Urbana, IL: National Council of Teachers of English.

Emig, Janet. (1978). Hand, eye, brain: Some "basics" in the writing process. In C. Cooper and L. Odell (eds.), *Research on Composing.* Urbana, IL: National Council of Teachers of English.

Eschholz, Paul E. (1980). The prose models approach: Using products in the process. In T. R. Donovan and B. W. McClelland (eds.), *Eight Approaches to Teaching Composition.* Urbana, IL: National Council of Teachers of English.

Flower, Linda. (1979). Writer-based prose: A cognitive basis for problems in writing. *College English 41*: 19-37.

Halsted, Isabella. (1975). Putting error in its place. *Journal of Basic Writing 1*, 1:72-86.

Hirsch, Donald E. (1980). Research in writing: The issues. In L. N. Kasden and D. R. Hoeber (eds.), *Basic Writing.* Urbana, IL: National Council of Teachers of English.

Judy, Stephen. (1980). The experiential approach: Inner world to outer worlds. In T. R. Donovan and B. W. McClelland (eds.), *Eight Approaches to Teaching Composition.* Urbana, IL: National Council of Teachers of English.

Kaplan, Robert B. (1967). Contrastive rhetoric and the teaching of composition. *TESOL Quarterly 1*, 3: 10-16.

Koch, Carl and James M. Brazil. (1978). *Strategies for Teaching the Composition Process.* Urbana, IL: National Council of Teachers of English.

Konneker, Beverly H., and Kyle Perkins. (1981). Testing the effectiveness of sentence-combining for ESL composition. Paper presented at the Fifteenth Annual TESOL Convention, Detroit, Michigan, March 1981.

Kroll, Barbara. (1979). A survey of writing needs of foreign and American college freshmen. *English Language Teaching Journal 33*, 3: 219-226.

Lauer, Janice M. (1980). The rhetorical approach: Stages of writing and strategies for writers. In T.

R. Donovan and B. W. McClelland (eds.), *Eight Approaches to Teaching Composition.* Urbana, IL: National Council of Teachers of English.

Maimon, Elaine P. (1980). Demythologizing writing across the curriculum. *Journal of Basic Writing 2*, 4: 3-11.

Maimon, Elaine P. et al. (1981). *Writing in the Arts and Sciences.* Cambridge, MA: Winthrop Publishers.

McKay, Sandra L. (1981). Pre-writing activities. *TECFORS Newsletter 4*, 3: 1-2.

Murray, Donald M. (1978). Internal revision: A process of discovery. In C. Cooper and L. Odell (eds.), *Research on Composing*. Urbana, IL: National Council of Teachers of English.

Murray, Donald M. (1980). Writing as process: How writing finds its own meaning. In T. R. Donovan and B. W. McClelland (eds.), *Eight Approaches to Teaching Composition*. Urbana, IL: National Council of Teachers of English.

Odell, Lee et al. (1978). Discourse theory: implications for research on composing. In C. Cooper and L. Odell (eds.), *Research on Composing*. Urbana, IL: National Council of Teachers of English.

Perl, Sondra. (1980a). A look at basic writers in the process of composing. In L. N. Kasden and D. R. Hoeber (eds.), *Basic Writing*. Urbana, IL: National Council of Teachers of English.

Perl, Sondra. (1980b). Understanding composing. *College Composition and Communication 31*, 4:363-369.

Petty, Walter T. (1978). The writing of young children. In C. Cooper and L. Odell (eds.), *Research on Composing*. Urbana, IL: National Council of Teachers of English.

Raimes, Ann. (1979). Problems and teaching strategies in ESL composition. *Language in Education: Theory and Practice 14*. Arlington, VA: Center for Applied Linguistics.

Rose, Mike. (1980). Rigid rules, inflexible plans, and the stifling of language: A cognitivist analysis of writer's block. *College Composition and Communication 31*, 4: 389-401.

Shaughnessy, Mina P. (1977). *Errors and Expectations*. New York: Oxford University Press.

Sommers, Nancy. (1980). Revision strategies of student writers and experienced adult writers. *College Composition and Communication 31*, 4: 378-388.

Taylor, Barry P. (1976). Teaching composition to low-level ESL students. *TESOL Quarterly 10,* 3: 309-319.

Taylor, Barry P. (1981). Content and written form: A two-way street. *TESOL Quarterly 15*, 1: 5-13.

Weiss, Robert H. (1980). Writing in the total curriculum: A program for cross-disciplinary cooperation. In T. R. Donovan and B. W. McClelland (eds.), *Eight Approaches to Teaching Composition.* Urbana, IL: National Council of Teachers of English.

Widdowson, H. G. (1978). *Teaching Language as Communication*. New York: Oxford University Press.

Wiener, Harvey S. (1980). First days' thoughts on process and detail. In T. R. Donovan and B. W. McClelland (eds.), *Eight Approaches to Teaching Composition*. Urbana, IL: National Council of Teachers of English.

Witte, Stephen P., and Lester Faigley. (1981). Coherence, cohesion and writing quality. *College Composition and Communication 32*, 2: 189-204.

Young, Richard E. (1978). Paradigms and problems: Needed research in rhetorical invention. In C. Cooper and L. Odell (eds.), *Research on Composing*. Urbana, IL: National Council of Teachers of English.

Zamel, Vivian. (1976). Teaching composition in the ESL classroom: What we can learn from research in the teaching of English. *TESOL Quarterly 10*, 1: 67-76.

From Zamel, V. (1982). Writing: The process of discovering meaning, *TESOL Quarterly 16,* pp. 195-209.

PART SEVEN

TEACHING CULTURE

의사소통 능력은 언어 능력과 사회문화 능력을 통합한 능력이라고 이미 지적하였다. 유창성 속에 포함되며 적합성(appropriateness)을 의미하는 부분이 사회문화 능력이라고 할 수 있다. 이는 'Are you married?'와 같은 개인적인 신상에 관한 질문은 일반적으로 하지 말아야 한다는 등의 구두언어 사용규칙뿐 아니라 대화를 수반하는 손짓, 몸짓, 눈 위치, 미소, 침묵, 소리의 크기 등의 규칙까지 두루 망라하는 의사소통의 총체적인 부분이라 할 수 있다.

Applegate의 논문에서 우리는 미국인들의 일반적인 말하기 규칙과 다른 나라 사람들의 그것과의 차이를 발견할 수 있을 것이다. 언어능력 못지않게 이와 같은 언어사용 규칙의 중요성을 인식하고 그들을 익혀 실제로 올바르게 적용하도록 노력해야 할 것이다.

두 번째 논문에서 박상옥은 영어를 배우는 학생들의 사회문화 능력과 관련하여 이를 문화라는 테두리에서 미국인들의 일상생활 양식에 관한 부분으로 보았다. 특히 영어교사가 알고 있어야 하는 우리와 미국인들의 차이를 논하고 지도와 평가방법을 간단히 소개하고 있다.

마지막으로 Mckay는 영어를 국제어로 가르치는 상황이 많은 지금 종래의 영어권 문화와 영어를 함께 다루어야 한다고 주장해 왔던 생각은 바뀌어야 한다면서 새로운 문화교육의 목표와 내용에 대해 말하고 있다.

28. THE LANGUAGE TEACHER AND THE RULES OF SPEAKING

The ways people use language to communicate can differ radically from society to society. A knowledge of some of these cultural differences in the use of language will enable the language teacher to help his students avoid many potential misunderstandings. The student is quite conscious of certain kinds of problems in learning a second language: new sounds, new vocabulary, and new grammatical patterns. But even if the student can pronounce his second language correctly and put words together in the proper order, he still has to *use* the language like a native. He must know when to talk and when to keep silent, how loud to talk and with what intonation, what constitutes a polite request and what a refusal, how to initiate a conversation and how to end one, when to interpret an utterance literally and when to take it as a formulaic convention, and so on. Knowledge of this sort constitutes what the sociolinguist calls "the rules of speaking."

Our knowledge of the rules of speaking is only partly conscious even in our native language. We learned some of these rules explicitly as children when our parents told us to say "please" when we ask for something or not to interrupt when adults are speaking. But most of the rules of speaking are much harder for us to verbalize: they are unconscious habits we acquired in imitation of the adults around us. Our natural tendency is to regard our own rules of speaking not as culture-specific but as part of human nature. We question them only when we encounter another culture and a way of speaking which might be radically different from our own.

My intention here is to show some of the ways in which rules of speaking can vary from culture to culture. I take middle-class American English as a background many of us are familiar with, but I won't try to deal with every aspect of American rules of speaking. For remarks addressed to an audience of ESL teachers, it would be handiest if I dwelt on the kinds of *faux pas* likely to be made by foreign students learning American English. But it is equally useful to show what blunders Americans would make in another cultural setting. We are much in need of this kind of sensitivity.

SILENCE

In discussing rules of speaking, a good starting point would be the rules governing silence: when to speak and when not to speak, and how silence is interpreted. One of the most explicit treatments of silence is Keith Basso's "To Give Up on Words" (1970), on the role of silence among the Western Apache. Basso concludes that the Apache tend to keep silent in situations in which the status of key parties is ambiguous, situations for which there are no clear-cut rules governing expected behavior.

As one example, the Apache prefer to keep silent in the presence of strangers. They are suspicious of a talkative stranger — especially an Anglo stranger — and they do not feel compelled to introduce two strangers to put them at ease with one another. Apache silence here is likely to be interpreted by the Anglo as sullen or distrustful; our rules of speaking in this situation call for an introduction. A graceful introduction is more than just an exchange of names; in making an introduction we feel more comfortable if we can also mention some subject of mutual interest to the people we introduce, so that they immediately have something in common to talk about.

The American tends to interpret silence nagatively. Karl Reisman compares American and Scandinavian attitudes toward silence in a conversation:

> Many Americans (and many English people) have a rule that in social conversations silences must be filled. A silence maintained too long is a sign of some kind of failure of rapport (unless it is defined as somehow seeking the solution to a problem, etc.). In Denmark by contrast there is a tendency to treat silences as valuable signs – perhaps of the well being of those present, at least a kind of affirmation that people speak only when moved to do so, that their feelings are genuine, etc. Some Danes appear to "nourish" a silence as one might appreciate a cozy fire. (1971: 6)

Discussing the relation of silence and privacy, Edward T. Hall points out that

> When the American wants to be alone he goes into a room and shuts the door.... For an American to refuse to talk to someone else present in the same room, to give them the "silent treatment," is the ultimate form of rejection and a sure sign of great displeasure. (1966: 131)

In contrast, the Arab and the Englishman may achieve privacy through silence:

> Their way to be alone is to stop talking. Like the English, an Arab who shuts himself off in this way is not indicating that anything is wrong or that he is withdrawing, only that he wants to be alone with his own thoughts or does not want to be intruded upon. (1966: 148)

Citing another instance of our negative evaluation of silence, Edmund Glenn says:

> If you express an opinion and there is a little silence and then the subject is changed, you know you have said something with which the person you are talking to does not agree. In many other cultures, in contrast, silence is a sign of agreement. When the Russians, French, Portuguese, Spanish, or Italians express an opinion and you do not

> reject it explicitly, they assume you have accepted it. Later, when they find you haven't they feel you are hypocritical. (1973: 278)

This is true of Moroccans and Persians, too. But the Egyptian, like the American, interprets silence here as disagreement.

In the Orient there is a tradition of respectful silence before elders, and especially before teachers. An American teacher might well be disconcerted by the silence of Oriental students in an otherwise talkative class in the United States. Much the same is true of Latin American students. By this strategy of silence, the student does not show his ignorance by asking questions; he does not lose face by volunteering possibly wrong information, and he does not imply that the teacher's original explanations are unclear by asking for restatements. But he is not necessarily inattentive or uninterested.

VOLUME AND INTONATION

Suppose you do presume to speak. Then you must consider volume and intonation. The normal conversational volume in many Mediterranean societies often strikes Americans as loud. The same is true of many African and West Indies peoples, and it shows up in a dialectal difference in American English, too. Certain Black English speech styles call for greater volume than normal in more "standard" varieties of English. This difference in some key rules of speaking has given rise to a stereotype of Blacks as being loud. On the other hand, the volume most Americans regard as normal for conversation may sound far too boisterous in the Far East. Hall points out that the American reputation for loudness in England and in northern Europe stems not so much from Americans' louder talking as from the fact that in public Americans don't mind being overheard by others, unless they are having a confidential talk. The English take more care to pitch their voices so as not to intrude on those around them; this may look conspiratorial to Americans (Hall 1966: 133-34).

Differences in intonation are harder to learn. An American teacher of Portuguese reported that his students have trouble with yes-no questions, since the proper Portuguese intonation here is like a challenge in English: "You speak Portuguese!?" John Lamendella (San Jose State University) told me that, as an example of cross-cultural differences, he once mentioned in a class that even a polite request in Germany may have an imperious intonation to American ears. A German student in the class said "Give me perhaps an example!," thereby proving Lamendella's point. Even though he understood intellectually that the German intended no offense, Lamendella found his ire roused at the wording and the intonation.

Studying life in an Egyptian village, John Boman Adams made an explicit statement of a few of these dangerous differences in intonation:

> The speech melody and rhythm that connote "sincerity" in Egypt usually seems to an American to sound "cross" or "belligerent." Conversely, the melody and rhythm that connote "righteous indignation" to an American is often interpreted by Egyptians as "hostile," "vengeful," and "nervous (uncontrolled)." (1957: 273, in Hymes (ed.) 1964)

Intonation is crucial. A compliment with the wrong intonation is no compliment, and a polite request with the wrong intonation is not polite. We probably tend to play down the importance of intonation because we are not used to writing it (except for such crude devices as question marks and underlining). Certainly in cross-cultural studies, intonation is generally neglected in favor of more tangible language differences.

CONVENTIONAL LANGUAGE

Much of the language we use is formulaic, much more than we realize. In every culture, certain social situations call for conventionalized utterances: greetings, leave-takings, apologies, consolations, congratulations, and the like. The use of formulas may be quite predictable when the alternatives are limited. In much of the Arab world, among people who are not acquainted, A invariably greets B with *salaam 'alaikum* 'peace be with you,' and B replies *'alaikum salaam*. In American English, depending on the formality of the situation and the age and mood of two unacquainted parties, there is a wide range of possible greeting formulas, including "hi," "hello," "good morning," "how are you?," "what's happenin'?" and "how's it goin'?" Generally, the more tradition-oriented a society is, the richer its repertoire of situational formulas is likely to be. Karl Zimmer (UC Berkeley) points out that in those situations which require a set formulaic response, the omission of the response is somehow felt to be wrong — either impolite, thoughtless, or the result of an imperfect knowledge of the language.

Different cultures may not agree in having a formula for a particular situation. Zimmer (unpublished ms.) presents a number of Turkish formulas with no set English equivalents, such as *afiyet olsun* 'may health be' said to someone who is eating or about to eat; it is used like French *bon appetit* or German *Guten Apetit*. As an expression of condolence to someone who has just lost a friend or relative, the speaker of Turkish uses the formula *basiniza saglik* 'health on your head.' The options in Egyptian Arabic are wider: "God took pity on him," if the deceased had been suffering much, "the rest is up to you [to carry on]," if he died young, and "it comes to all of us," if he was ripe in years. In English we must patch together something awkward like "I'm awfully sorry to hear about your Uncle Jonah."

Formulas may be required in unexpected situations. Compliments in much of the

Mediterranean world are associated with the evil eye. A compliment may invite the evil eye by arousing envy in others, or as an expression of envy it may be the actual vehicle of the evil eye. In Egypt, compliments are followed with the disclaimer "I didn't really mean it." In Morocco one follows up a compliment, on the good looks of a child, for example, with the formula "May the blessing of Allah be upon him." These formulas negate the possibility of conveying the evil eye via the compliment. If one fails to use the formula, then the recipient of the compliment may utter the counter-formula "five in the eyes of the covetous" to ward off evil. In Yiddish, the formula *keyn ayn-hore* 'no evil eye' can be used not only with compliments but with any expression of well-being or good fortune: "But for me things are going — *keyn ayn-hore* — very well." (Matisoff 1972: 52) Had the speaker failed to use the formula here, then the hearer might use it as a rejoinder.

When two cultures agree in having a formula for a particular situation, it is safe to assume that translating literally won't produce exactly the effect you hoped for. A student of mine who worked as an overseas operator used to be taken aback by the Korean equivalent of "good morning" when he would hear "Have you slept well? I have a call from Korea."

When equivalent formulas *do* occur, it is dangerous to think that you can use them in exactly parallel situations. There is a formulaic equivalent to "thanks" or "thank you" as an expression of gratitude in most languages. But in France or Germany, if you accept the offer of a cup of coffee with *merci* or *danke*, just as you would say "thanks" in American English, you won't get the coffee. "Thanks" here means refusal; to accept you must say something like "please" or "I would like some." In Japanese and Korean, a question is more polite when phrased negatively: "Wouldn't you like more tea?" In accepting this offer, an American would say "Yes [I would like more tea]." But the Japanese and Korean, and the Filipino too, would respond with "no," logically for "No [it is not the case that I would not like more tea]."

For the student whose grasp of the formulaic conventions in a second language is still weak, there are the twin dangers of taking a formula literally and of reading a purely conventional meaning into an utterance intended literally. In response to the greeting "How are you?." the American expects to hear "fine" or "OK" rather than a complete catalogue of woes. In fact, he may respond with this automatic "fine" when asked seriously "How are you today?" by a doctor or nurse during an office call.

When a host says to his departing guest "We'll have to get together again sometime," the guest knows not to take this too literally unless the host sounds particularly earnest or specifies a time: "Let's get together again next week." A Punjabi told me how he had once received a similar send-off; when he came back the next day, he couldn't understand the host's look of consternation.

NORMS OF INTERACTION

A discussion of conventional formulas soon leads into what Hymes (1972: 63-64) calls "norms of interaction," those rules governing how people relate to one another verbally in various situations. Suppose a language has a particular formula, such as "thanks" for expressing gratitude; just when is it appropriate to say "thanks?" In Morocco, "thanks" is used sparingly, only when someone has gone far out of his way to do you some favor. Americans use "thanks" in more trivial situations, such as when a bus driver has waited for you, or someone tells you what time it is, or holds a door open for you. The Moroccan response in these situations would be silence. "After all," a Moroccan explained, "the other person would expect you to do the same for him." On the other hand, the Japanese use the expressions *domo* and *arigato*, both usually translated "thank you," much more often than would Americans in similar situations. Japanese politeness often calls for thanking a person not just at the time he does you a favor but also the next time you see him.

Given a particular situation, such as an exchange of greetings, norms of interaction may vary on who utters the first greeting or when or how. In the West Indies, you are expected to call out a greeting to any acquaintance who passes by within shouting distance (Reisman 1971: 10-11). Here, the stationary person greets anyone approaching him. But the story is told of a British agent in Crete during World War II — he spoke fluent Greek and dressed like a Greek — who was once sitting beside a road as an old woman approached. *Cherete* 'hello' he called out, but she walked on toward him with no reply. Passing him, she said in a low voice "God bless you, my son, and take you safe back to your native land." At length he figured out how she had penetrated his disguise: he had violated an unspoken rule that the moving person utters the first greeting.

After greetings, what then? When getting acquainted with a stranger, Americans usually expect relatively trivial or impersonal questions. In India or the Middle East, an American may be taken aback by a barrage of questions which seem quite personal. "How old are you?" "Are you married?" "How many children do you have?" Personal in a different way is "How much money do you make?" While the American interprets such questions as rude, the intent behind them is not to pry but to show a personal interest in a stranger. This is politeness working through different rules (see Lakoff 1973). On the other hand, a question which we regard as perfectly innocent might be offensive; it may be out of order to ask a Navajo what his name is (Hall 1959: 34).

Once a conversation is underway, an American does not like to be interrupted during his turn speaking. Children are taught this very explicitly. But of course, Americans *do* interrupt one another. We are more tolerant of interruptions by peers than by juniors or subordinates, and an interruption is less irksome as we trail off or grope for words than when we are just warming up to a subject. In Japan and northern Europe, interruptions are considered ruder and they are correspondingly less frequent. A Swedish student told me that it used to annoy her to be interrupted by Americans. Gradually she adopted the habit; she found during a visit back to Sweden that people criticized this newly acquired lapse in her manners.

But in the West Indies interruptions are considered normal. Failing to call out a greeting to a passer-by, for example, is a worse offense than interrupting the conversation you might already be involved in, and an interruption does not require an apology (Reisman 1971: 8-10). In the Mediterranean area, in the Philippines, and in India, interruptions are more common than in the United States. A Hindi speaker said that one of the hardest things for her to learn in the United States was not to interrupt; Americans would often react to her interruptions with an impatient "Let me finish what I was saying!"

Norms of interaction may differ on points like the expected pattern of offer and acceptance. There is a general Mediterranean and Middle Eastern rule that an offer is never accepted the first time. In Greece, politeness may require at least four offers. In the exchange below, notice how firm both parties sound.

> Host: Why don't you have a piece of baklava?
> Guest: Thanks, I just ate.
> Host: Have a piece of baklava!
> Guest: I couldn't possibly.
> Host: I insist, just one piece!
> Guest: I can't.
> Host: Come on! I've got all this baklava: what am I going to do with it?
> Guest: Well, I'll have a little then.

If you don't want what is being offered, then you refuse each time, maybe five or six times, until there is no further offer. Of course, certain offers can't be refused; in Greece, a guest must accept at least one glass of *ouzo* or serving of preserves, and everyone understands this. Where such a pattern prevails, it is considered quite ill-mannered to accept immediately. A Greek friend of mine who came to this country as a child recalls how a friend's mother might offer her a snack after school: she would refuse, of course, and there would be no second offer. On the other hand, in Greece an American unused to this pattern of repeated offers will succumb to the insistence of the offers and find himself accepting food and drink that he either doesn't want or has no room left for.

And when an offer is being refused, the ways of refusing vary. As mentioned earlier, where an American would say "no" or "no, thanks," the French and Germans simply say "thanks." In Paraguay, the pattern is never to refuse anything overtly. Just as in French or German, *gracias* means "no, thanks" here. Another way of refusing an offer or request is to offer to comply sometime in the future. If you are on an errand when someone calls out "Come and sit with us a while," you say *si, para la vuelta* 'yes, on the way back.' An alternative reply might be something like "Yes, yes, but my cousin just arrived in town, so I'll come tomorrow." In the Philippines, too, an outright "no" is insulting, and the Filipino in refusing says "well," "maybe," "I'll see," or "I'll try."

HANDLING INFORMATION

As a potential obstacle to communication, one of the most pervasive ways in which norms of interaction differ is in the informational content of speech. I you have a topic in mind, how do you bring it up? How openly do you talk about it?

Americans are concerned — even obsessed — with getting exact information about such matters as times, places, routes, directions, prices, conditions, reasons, and so on. We often come to the point immediately in asking and in being asked about such details.

When an American is asked for specific information, he generally shares this information if he knows it. If not, he may admit uncertainty or even outright ignorance, but then venture a guess. Information may not be handled so freely in other cultures. The person you ask may not always share what he knows. In Vietnam, the usual pleasant response to a question by someone more than a few steps higher socially is *do phai* 'that's OK' or 'that must be.' When you ask "Is this the way to the station?," the invariable answer is *da phai*, no matter how far from the station the route indicated might lead. Here, agreement is intended to avoid contradicting the superior party or making him look ignorant. Given this pattern, a superior does not ask a question of anyone much lower socially: he seeks an intermediary. Hall points out another form of strategic evasion in which information is not forthcoming:

> In the Middle East..., refusal of one party to come to the point and discuss the topic of a meeting often means he cannot agree to your terms but doesn't want to turn you down, or simply that he cannot discuss the matters under consideration because the time is not yet ripe. He will not, moreover, feel it improper to meet without ever touching on the topic of meeting. (1959: 182)

On the other hand, when you ask someone for information which he doesn't know, he may still try to oblige you by offering some other information. He might even make something up and tell you what he thinks you want to hear. A friend of mine recalls wandering through the streets of Mombasa for hours one night, looking for a particular hotel. No Europeans were out; every African he met assured him that the hotel was just a few blocks away.

The American and northern European, accustomed to a more direct handling of information, may interpret such responses as evasive, irresponsible, or even deceitful. But the native of the culture has little trouble in discerning which of these responses are factual and which merely tell him what he wants to hear.

In many parts of the world, the normal pattern is to ease gently into talk about a particular subject through exchanges of greeting formulas, polite inquiries about the health of the other person's family and friends, and sage observations on weather, crops, politics, or life. You bring up the central topic at last as something quite incidental. It is considered ill-mannered to plunge precipitously into shop-talk. Hall cites the instance of a meeting between Greek and American officials ending in a stalemate over just such a difference in approaching the topic:

> ... Americans pride themselves on being outspoken and forthright. These qualities are regarded as a liability by the Greeks. They are taken to indicate a lack of finesse which the Greeks deplore. The American directness immediately prejudiced the Greeks. (1959: 15)

This reluctance to come to the point immediately may well be a liability for the foreign student here. Students from the Middle East, and particularly from Japan, often have difficulty with expository prose in English. Even if the student's grammatical command of the language is adequate, if he indulges in too long a preamble or approaches the topic too circuitously, the result will not be judged good writing. This is especially important on examinations: there simply isn't time to lead gradually into a subject and then develop it fully too. Robert Kaplan discusses this approach in relation to teaching the mechanics of paragraph structure in English:

> Some Oriental writing... is marked by what may be called an approach by indirection. In this kind of writing, the development of the paragraphs may be said to be "turning and turning in a widening gyre." The circles or gyres turn around the subject and show it from a variety of tangential views, but the subject is never looked at directly. (1972: 252-53)

Even when the conversation has turned at last to a particular topic, speakers have much latitude in how openly they discuss it. Oriental indirection is a well-known bit of linguistic folklore to Americans, who may well find themselves baffled by allusions and oblique references. The preference for indirect reference is not just Oriental; many Middle Eastern, Indian, African, and American Indian societies show the same predilection. In her article on signifying, Claudia Mitchell-Kernan (1972) discusses indirection as a verbal art in Black English. Indirection is a recurrent theme in Ethel Albert's ethnography of speech in Burundi in central Africa (1964), where strategies like allusion, embellishment, discrete avoidance, and even falsehood are all prized over strict adherence to the naked truth.

The American doesn't always say just what he means, and he may take a while in approaching a topic — such as asking a favor — but generally we are less tolerant of indirection than many other peoples. Why else would we have so many expressions like "Get to the point," "Out with it," "Don't beat around the bush," or "Let's get down to brass tacks."

CONCLUSION

The examples of differing rules of speaking sketched above can be multiplied indefinitely. Patterns slowly begin to emerge. In some respects, American English stands about midway on some continuum, as in the light to heavy use of "thank you" in Morocco and Japan. Sometimes American English seems to stand more by itself, as in the negative evaluation of silence as a conversational response, where silence means agreement or affirmation in many other cultures.

What is crucial here is not the mere multiplication of examples, but the realization that cultural differences in the use of language can be subtle and far-reaching. It is important for all of us to recognize the relativity of these rules of speaking and to recognize differences for what they are. All too easily, we form stereotypes on the basis of a few observations. As a blanket statement, for example, someone might claim that "Greeks are pushy," where a more objective report of the situation would be to say "Greek politeness requires that offers be made with firm insistence."

For the ESL teacher, awareness of these cultural differences is especially important. They may account for much that others will find strange and even aggravating in the behavior of the foreign student. The teacher can help the student by pointing out and discussing with him those speech habits which are likely to baffle or annoy English speakers. It might be helpful in turn to have the student talk or write about what is strange and aggravating in American speech behavior. Certainly the ESL teacher is in the best position to pass on this awareness and tolerance of other people's ways of speaking. As the representative not only of a new language but also a new society, the ESL teacher ought to sensitize the student to the social implications of language use.

■ References

Adams, John Boman. (1957). Culture and conflict in an Egyptian village. *American Anthropologist 59*, pp. 225-235. In Hymes (ed.), *Language in culture and society,* 1964, Harper and Row.

Albert, Ethel. (1964). 'Rhetoric,' 'Logic,' and 'Poetics' in Burundi: cultural patterning of speech behavior. *American Anthropologist* 66, 6, pp. 35-54. In Gumperz and Hymes (eds.), *The ethnography of communication*, 1972, Holt, Rinehart, and Winston.

Basso, Keith. (1970). To give up on words: Silence in Western Apache culture. *South-western Journal of Anthropology* 26, 3, pp. 213-230. In Giglioli (ed.), *Language and social context*, 1972, Penguin.

Glenn, Edmund. (1973). On communicating across cultural lines. In Liedlich (ed.), *Coming to terms with language*, 1973, Wiley.

Hall, Edward T. (1959). *The silent language*. Doubleday, NY: Anchor Books.

____. (1966). *The hidden dimension*. Doubleday, NY: Anchor Books.

Hymes, Dell. (1972). Models of the interaction of language and social life. In Gumperz and Hymes (eds.), *The ethnography of communication*, Holt, Rinehart, and Winston.

Kaplan, Robert B. (1972). Cultural thought patterns in inter-cultural education. In Croft (ed.), *Readings on English as a second language*, Winthrop.

Lado, Robert. (1957). *Linguistics across cultures: applied linguistics for language teachers.* University of Michigan Press.

Lakoff, Robin. (1973). The logic of politeness, or, minding your P's and Q's. In Corum, Smith-Stark, and Weiser (eds.), *Papers from the Ninth Regional Meeting of the Chicago Linguistic Society*, Chicago Linguistic Society.

Matisoff, James. (1972). *Psycho-ostensive expressions in Yiddish.* Unpublished manuscript, revised version, UC Berkeley.

Mitchell-Kernan, Claudia. (1972). Signifying and marking: Two Afro-American speech acts. In Gumperez and Hymes (eds.), *The ethnography of communication*, Holt, Rinehart, and Winston.

Reisman, Karl. (1971). *Contrapuntal conversations in an antiguan village.* Penn-Texas Working Papers in Sociolinguistics, No. 3.

Zimmer, Karl. (1958). *Situational formulas.* Unpublished manuscript, UC Berkeley.

From Applegate, R. B. (1975). The language teacher and the rules of speaking, *TESOL Quarterly*, 9, pp. 271-181.

29. 영어교육에 있어서 문화지도(Teaching Culture in the English Education)

Ⅰ. 서 론

외국어 교육의 목표에 대하여 외국어 교사에게 질문을 던지면 우선 순위에 있어서 물론 차이가 있기는 하겠지만 대략 듣기, 말하기, 읽기, 쓰기의 4기능과 문화이해와 관련된 부분을 반드시 포함할 것이다. 우리나라에서도 영어가 제2외국어로 채택되어 각급 학교에서 가르쳐지기 시작한 과거 1세기 이상동안 영어사용 국민들의 문화를 이해함으로써 우리 문화발전에 이바지하게 한다는 의미에서의 문화교육이 상당히 큰 비중을 차지하는 목표로 나타나 있어왔던 것 같다.

그러나 영어교육이 과연 명시된 문화지도의 목표를 어느 정도 달성해 왔는가를 평가해 볼 때 반성하지 않을 수 없게 된다. 왜냐하면 대부분의 영어교사들은 아직도 그 목표를 위하여 무엇을 어떻게 해야 하는지도 모르고 교육을 기계적으로 습관적으로 해오고 있기 때문이다.

그런 의미에서 본 논문에서는 문화란 무엇이고 문화교육의 목표는 무엇이며 우리나라 영어교육에서 그 부분의 구체적인 내용은 어떤 것이어야 하고 교육의 방법에는 어떤 것이 있고, 그리고 평가는 어떻게 할 수 있을까 하는 문제를 논의해 보고자 한다.

Ⅱ. 본 론

1. 문화의 의미

문화의 정의를 내리기는 매우 어렵고, 특히 외국어 교육의 목표를 달성하기 위하여 관련 학자나 일선교사들이 반드시 정확하게 이해하여 교육에 직접 적용해야 하는 측면에서의 문화의 의미는 지금까지 많은 논란의 대상이 되어 왔으나 이제는 어느 정도 윤곽이 잡혀가고 있다고 볼 수 있겠다.

Brooks(1968)에 의하면 언어교육에 있어서 문화의 역할에 대하여 관심을 가지게 되었던 것은 1953년 이후였다고 하는데, 그가 문화의 개념을 분명히 하려고 시도했던 1968년에도 그는 그 개념의 모호성을 매우 안타깝게 여기면서 조심스럽게 문화의 의미와 혼동하기 쉬운 그것과는 다른 것부터 이유를 들어가며 나열해 갔다. 즉 문화는 지리, 역사, 민속, 문명, 문학과 사회학을 모두 포함하지만 이들 중 어느 하나와도 일치하지 않는데 그 이유는, 문화는 인간 개개인의 존재를 전제로 하고 있으나 그것들은 그렇지 않기 때문이라는 것이다. 계속해서 그는 언어교육의 초기단계에서 가장 중요한 문화의 국면은 생활양식이라면서 다음과 같이 그것의 의미를 설명한다(1968: 210):

> ... refers to the individuals' role in the unending kaleidoscope of life situations of every kind and the rules and models for attitude and conduct in them. By reference to these modes, every human being, from infancy onward, justifies the world to himself as best as he can, associates with those around him, and relates to the social order to which he is attached.

그에 의하면 지리, 역사, 문학 등은 구성원의 생활양식을 결정하는 배경이 되는 것이고 초기의 언어교육에서 중요한 것은 그들 구성원에게 기대되는 생각, 믿음, 말, 행동, 음식, 옷, 인내, 분노, 명예 등을 가르치는 일인데, 왜냐하면 의사소통을 원만하게 하려면 무엇보다도 중요한 영역이 바로 이것들이기 때문임을 덧붙인다. 이 단계의 학습이 어느 정도에 다다르면 문학과 예술 등을 포함하도록 하는 문화교육을 이상적인 것으로 제안한다.

그 후에 외국어 교육학자들이 문화의 개념을 논할 때 당연한 것으로 사용해 온 인류학적인 의미에서의 문화의 구분은 "C" (large C culture)와 "c" (small c culture)이다. 전자는 그 언어를 사용하는 국가의 정치 · 경제 · 사회적 상황, 위대한 정치가, 영웅, 작가, 예술가 등을 가리키는 것이고 후자는 거기에 소속된 국민들이 생활하는 방식을 나타내는 것으로 되어 있다. 학자들은 한결같이 "c"가 외국어 교육의 기초이면서도 가장 중요한 부분이 되어야 한다는 점을 강조한다 (Chastain, 1976; Lafayette, 1978; Hendon, 1980; Rivers, 1981).

결론적으로 영어교육에 있어서 문화의 의미는 미국인들의 생활방식과 행동양식에서 출발하여 단계적으로 이들의 배경이 되는 그들의 지리, 역사, 인물, 문학, 예술을 동시에 포함하여 나타내는 것이 가장 바람직하다고 생각된다.

2. 문화교육의 목표

순수 언어학자들이 정의를 내린 언어능력(linguistic competence)은 언어의 발음, 문법, 의미를 정확히 아는 능력이었으나, 사회 언어학자들이 사용하기 시작한 의사소통능력(communicative competence)은 여기에 사회에서 받아들여질 수 있도록 언어를 사용한다는 의미에서의 적합성(appropriateness)이 추가된다.

Ide(1982)는 의사소통이 언어의 가장 중요한 역할이라고 하면서 우리나라의 영어교사들이 지니고 있는 일반적인 문제점을 다음과 같이 지적한다(1982: 61):

> ... the social and cultural aspects of the English language have been neglected by the teachers of English in Korea, and that greater efforts are needed on the part of the teachers to provide the students of English with better instruction in the area of culturally appropriate English language use.

어느 외국인 교수는 다방이나 지하철에서 혼자 앉아 있으면 거의 틀림없이 영어에 관심 있는 학생이 다가와 말을 시작하는데 다음과 같은 당혹스런 질문들이 계속된다고 털어놓았다:

> "Where are you from?", "How long have you been in Korea?", "What do you do for a living?", "Are you married?", "How old are you?", "What's your hobby?", "Where do you live?"... .

그 열성적인 학생은 그와 같은 영어표현법을 학원에서 혹은 학교에서 기계처럼 반복하여 학습한 후 그 때를 가장 적합한 실력발휘의 기회로 삼고 당돌하게 질문공세를 폈을 것이 분명하며, 그러한 질문내용들이 상대방의 감정을 얼마나 상하게 할는지에 대해서는 아무런 지식도 없었을 것이다.

또 하나의 실례를 들어보자. 우리는 대부분 영어를 배우는 초기단계에서 인사법을 배운다. 그리고는 영어시간이 시작될 때마다 사용하게 되는데 다음과 같은 순서로 진행된다:

Student (S): Good morning.
Teacher (T): Good morning
S: How are you?
T: Fine, thank you. And you?
S: Fine, thank you.

그 학생이 미국으로 유학을 가게 되었다. 정해진 지도교수와 진지한 면담을 한 다음날 우연히 그 교수를 복도에서 만났을 때 학생은 미소를 머금고 "Good morning, Dr. ________. How are you?"라고 물었다. 그런데 그 교수는 "Fine."하고는 지나가 버렸다. 학생은 무안하고 무시당한 듯하여 한동안 어쩔 줄 몰랐다. 왜냐하면 "And you?"라고 반문하지 않았기 때문이다. 결국 학생의 영어교사는 인사법은 경우에 따라 매우 형식적이어서 어떤 응답을 진지하게 기대해서도 안되고 응답을 반드시 할 필요도 없다는 문화적인 지도를 하지 않았다는 말이 된다.

이러한 종류의 오류가 얼마나 심각한가를 Kim(1979: 109)은 잘 묘사해 준다:

> In fact linugistic errors by foreigners are pardoned and even enjoyed without causing any hard feelings, but cultural mistakes are quite often inexcusable.

이때 외국인은 충격을 받게 되는데 이것은 문화충격(culture shock)이라고 불리워진다.

그렇다면 외국어 교육에서 앞에서 다루어진 문화의 정의에 입각한 문화교육의 목적은 무엇보다도 문화권이 다른 사람들간의 의사소통(intercultural communication)을 할 수 있는 능력을 개발시키는 것이라고 하겠다.

이때 언어적인 요소와 함께 비언어적인 요소는 당연히 가르쳐져야 한다. 몸의 동작(머리, 눈, 입술, 손 등의 움직임), 상대방과의 거리유지 그리고 언어를 사용할 때의 음의 높이, 길이, 침묵 등을 의미하는데, 그들이 얼마나 의사소통에서 중요한 역할을 하는가는 Stevick(1982: 163)과 Abercrombie(1968: 55)가 잘 표현해 주고 있다:

> If verbal communication is the pen which spells out details, nonverbal communication provides the surface on which the words are written and against which they must be interpreted. (Stevick)
>
> We speak with our vocal organ, but we converse with our whole body. (Abercrombie)

좀더 정확하게 Birdwhistell(1970: 158)이 말을 통해서는 사회적 의미의 30~35%만이 전달되고 비언어적 요소가 나머지 65~70%의 의미를 전달한다고 한 주장은 비교적 많은 지지를 얻어왔다.

최근에 미국에서의 한 연구는 감정의 상호전달에서는 비언어적 요소가 93%를 차지하여 결정적 역할을 한다고 보고하기도 했다(Levine & Adelman, 1982: 43). Levine & Adelman(1982: 179~190)은 한가지 대표적인 예를 들고 있다:

> A young woman from one culture is looking at out of the window and sees a male aquaintance from another culture. He signals to her by puckering his lips. She quickly looks away from the window. Later she ignores him. He is confused and she is angry.

상대방의 비언어적 신호를 잘못 이해하여 발생한 문화적 마찰인데 그 여성은 남성이 성적(性的) 접근을 시도한 것으로 판단하여 그렇게 행동한 것이다. 그러나 남성은 단지 "어머나, 여기서 만났군요"하는 단순한 반가움을 나타내는 시선을 보냈던 것이다. 아마도 그 여성은 한국인이었을는지 모른다.

박명석(1979: 53)은 본인이 겪은 우스운 경험담을 소개하는데 지도교수의 손짓을 잘못 이해한 데서 생긴 것이었다. 즉 공항에서 헤어지면서 지도교수가 잘가라는 신호를 잠깐 오라는 신호로 보고 성급히 달려갔을 때의 당혹감이었다.

이러한 일상생활에서의 사소한 오해는 때로는 국제적인 정치문제로까지 비화되기도 하는가 보다. 박남식(1972: 89~91)은 1971년 미국과 일본의 경제 무역 회담에서 닉슨대통령과 사또수상 사이에 비밀회담시 발생했던 사건을 소개했다. 그 당시에 닉슨 대통령은 미국측이 일본으로부터 틀림없이 언질(commitment)을 받았다고 결론지었으나 사또수상은 결코 어떤 언질을 주지 않았던 것이다. 구체적으로, 사또수상은 고개를 끄덕이며 "잘 알겠습니다." 또는 "저도 당신과 같은 의견을 가지고 있기는 합니다." 또는 아무 말 없이 미소를 머금고 고개를 끄덕였으나 닉슨대통령은 그들을 모두 긍정의 표시로 받아들였던 것이다.

문화권이 다른 사람들 사이의 원활한 의사소통이 문화교육의 가장 중요한 목적이 되므로, 이를 위한 언어적이고 비언어적인 내용을 영어시간에 충분히 다루어야 한다는 것은 분명해졌을 것이다.

다음으로 서로 다른 문화에 대한 이해를 하고 아울러 학습자 자신의 문화를 더 잘 이해하게 한다는 목적에서의 문화교육이 되어야 하겠다. 이러한 목적을 달성하는 과정에서 위험한 부작용이 따를 수 있다. 그것은 외국의 문화가 자기 나라의 그것보다 우월하다거나 또는 반대로 자기 나라의 문화가 우월하다거나 하는 편견을 가질 수 있다는 것이다. 지나치게 문화적인 차이점만 강조할 것이 아니라 어떠한 배경이 그와 같은 차이나는 행동양식이나 생활습관을 심어주게 되었는지에 대한 것도 단계적으로 교육의 중요한 내용으로 정해야 할 것이다. Tinsley(1972: 5)는 이것을 그대로 지적한다:

> ... emphasis on differences should in no way engender feelings of superiority and inferiority. It is only through recognition and understanding of cultural differences that we become aware of the fact that cultures are not based on absolute values but upon learned behavior passed from generation to generation.

예를 들면 남의 집을 방문할 때 우리나라는 아무 때나 예고 없이 찾아가는 것이 예사인데 미국의 경우는 미리 전화를 하여 사정을 확인하고 방문하는 것이 예의에 벗어나지 않는다는 두 나라 사이의 문화적인 차이점만 지적을 해주고, 미국 사람들은 모든 것을 희생하고 오로지 야심을 가지고 스스로 운명을 개척해 온 역사적 배경으로 인하여 사적인 생활을 매우 중요시하는 전통을 가지고 있지만 우리는 유교적 생활습관과 사고방식이 개인보다는 친지, 친구들을 중시하는 풍토를 낳아 그러한 문화적인 차이가 난다는 것을 설명하지 않는다면, 학습자는 나름대로 판단을 하여 자신에게 편리한 쪽을 우월하다고 생각하고 따르는지도 모른다.

또한 우리는 오래 전부터 미국사람은 모두 부자이고 거지가 없다는 말을 주위에서 들었었다. 이러한 결론은 매우 단편적인 어떤 상황을 보거나 듣고는 잘못된 판단을 하게 되는 단적인 예가 될 수 있다. 그러므로 문화교육의 중요한 목표인 서로 다른 문화에 대한 올바른 이해는 충분한 자료의 단계적인 제시와 함께 필요한 부분에 대한 교사의 보충설명 및 토론을 통하여 가능하다고 여겨진다. 특히 우리나라의 경우는 오래 전부터 지속되어 온 미국과의 정치적 · 경제적 · 군사적 관계 때문에 사회 깊숙이 파고든 그들의 영향으로 인하여 많은 경우에 학습 대상자들이 이미 미국의 문화를 우월하게 평가하는 경향이 있는 것 같다. 이러한 상황에서 대부분의 교사들은 오로지 언어면의 지도에 치중하기도 하고 때로는 억지로 우리 문화의 우월성을 주장하려고 애쓰기도 하는가 보다. 전자의 무책임한 태도나 후자의 비교육자적인 교육방법은 개선되어야 하겠다. 그리하여 장기적으로는 학습자의 의사소통 능력의 발달과 함께 스스로 외국문화 지식을 객관적으로 평가할 수 있고 필요와 관심에 따라 여러 가지 내용을 조사하여 분석할 수 있는 능력까지 개발하게 될 것이다.

문화교육의 목표로 또 한 가지 지적할 것은 학습자의 동기를 자극하여 언어교육의 효과를 가져오게 된다는 것이다. 이 부분에 대하여 Hendon (1980: 192～193)은 다음과 같이 언급하고 있다:

> ... such activity stimulates interest in foreign language study. Cultural materials provide many topics of personal interest to a student, thereby increasing motivation. The inclusion of culture in the foreign language classroom could well provide an important bridge for the language student in his search for relevance.

동기가 언어학습에 있어서 대단히 중요하다는 것은 이미 많은 연구결과 충분히 증명되었음을 Park(1981: 55)은 지적하고 있다:

> Research studies in second-or foreign language learning clearly indicate that motivation, attitude, and interest of the learner are factors of crucial importance in determining his achievement.

특히 영어에 대한 흥미가 학습자의 내부에서 오는 진정한 것일 때 외부적인 압력 (진학이나 취직)때문에 할 수 없이 영어를 공부해야 하는 것과 성과면에서 차이가 있을 것이다. 전자를 내적동기(internal motivation), 그리고 후자를 외적동기(external motivation)라 하는데 두 가지가 적절하게 조화된 상태에서 좋은 결실을 얻게 될 것이다. 그러나 불행하게도 우리나라 학생들은 중학생의 90% 이상이 영어 학습이 필요하다고 느끼고 있으면서도 학년이 올라갈수록 흥미도가 점점 낮아지는 현상을 보여주고 있었다. 구체적으로 중학교 1학년에는 20% 정도가 2학년에는 11%, 그리고 3학년에는 1%만이 영어 과목을 매우 재미있다라고 대답한 것으로도 그것을 추측할 수 있었다(박상옥, 1985: 333). 그들에게 문화교육을 병행하는 것은 내적인 동기를 자극하는 촉진제가 되리라 기대된다.

지금까지 문화교육의 목표를 크게 문화권이 다른 사람들과의 의사소통 능력개발, 그 사람들의 문화이해와 이를 통한 우리 문화의 이해, 그리고 동기자극의 세 가지 측면에서 논의해 보았다.

마지막으로 Seelye(1976)가 제시한 문화교육의 7가지 목적을 소개해보겠다. 특별히 그는 문화교육은 의도적이어야 한다는 점을 강조하면서 행동목표(behavioral objectives)로 기술하였다.

1. The student should demonstrate an understanding that people act the way they do because they are using options the society allows for satisfying basic physical and psychological needs.
2. The student should demonstrate an understanding that such social variables as age, sex, social class, and place of residence affect the way people speak and behave.
3. The student should indicate an ability to demonstrate how people conventionally act in the most common mundane and crisis situations in the target culture.
4. The student should indicate an awareness that culturally conditioned images are associated with even the most common target words and phrases.
5. The student should demonstrate an ability to evaluate the relative strength of a generality concerning the target culture in terms of the amount of evidence substantiating the statement.
6. The student should show that he has developed the skills needed to locate and organize information about the target culture from the library, the mass media, and personal observation.
7. The student should demonstrate intellectual curiosity about the target culture and empathy toward its people.

3. 문화교육의 내용

A. 한국문화와 미국문화의 심층적 차이

문화교육의 목표를 달성하기 위해서는 영어교육자는 필요한 지식을 가지고 또한 방법을 알고 있어야 한다. 그런 의미에서 이 장에서는 우선 심층적인 미국문화의 특징을 (물론 절대적인 의미를 지니는 것은 아니다) 우리의 것과 비교하며 부분적으로 정리해 보겠다.

첫째, 미국 사회의 성격은 수평적이라고 말해진다. 즉 미국사회에서는 모든 인간은 평등하고 그렇기 때문에 자립심이 높이 평가를 받고 "나"의 존재가 매우 중요하게 인식된다. Okabe(1983: 26)는 Takao Suzuki의 말을 인용한다:

> The American value of individualism encourages self-assertion and frank expression of opinions and shows up in the American propensity to argue back when challenged.

자기 주장을 중요시하는 의사소통 양식을 박명석(1976: 92)은 "instrumental communication style"이라고 표현했다. 따라서 자기를 직접적으로 나타내는 성향이 강하고 가계나 혈통보다는 개인의 능력에 의해 평가를 받게 된다.

이와 같은 강력하고 직접적인 개인의 의사전달 방법은 미국 사람들로 하여금 "absolutely", "certainly", "positively" 그리고 최상급의 사용을 빈번하게 하고 절대적인 주어 "I"를 문장의 앞에 많이 쓰게 하는 것 같다고 Okabe(1983: 34)는 지적한다. 덧붙여서 질문에 대하여 명백한 대답을 해주는 것도 특징이다. 그러므로 침묵은 긍정적으로 받아들여지지 않는다.

한편 우리사회의 성격은 대부분의 동양에 위치한 국가가 그렇듯이 수직적이라고 말해지는데, 이는 유교적 윤리관에서 나온 것으로 자기의 개인적인 존재보다는 자기가 소속해 있는 가문, 혈연, 지연, 직장 등의 테두리 안에서 그들과의 관계 속에서의 자기를 의식하려고 한다(박형기, 1982: 15). 이 때 나이 역시 매우 중요한 역할을 하게 된다.

일을 처리하는 데 있어서 수동적으로 끌려가기 때문에 행동적이지 못하고 정적이며, 자주성이 부족하다. 단지 소속된 집단에서 조화로운 삶을 영위하고 싶은 욕망이 강하여 솔직하게 자기의 의견을 나타내기보다는 집단의 위 서열에 있는 다른 사람들의 감정을 상하지 않게 하기 위하여 겸손과 자기억제를 미덕으로 여기는 경향이 강하다. 이러한 의사소통 방식을 박명석(1976: 92)은 "situation-oriented"은 "affective style"이라고 표현했다.

이와 같은 우리의 인간관계는 모호하고 암시적인 표현법을 택하게 하여 "maybe", "perhaps", "probably", "somewhat"의 의미를 가진 단어를 많이 사용하게 하고 "I" 대신 "We"를 사용하거나 또는 아예 주어를 생략하는 경우가 많이 있다(Okabe, 1983: 34). 요즈음 비판의 대상이 되는 말로서 젊은이들의 대화에 많이 나오는 "같애"나 "같습니다"도 우리 특유의 표현법이라 생각된다. 그리고 침묵은 흔히 긍정의 표시로 받아들여진다.

둘째, 미국인들의 사고방식은 분석적 · 비판적이며, 객관적이고 과학적이고 논리적인데 이것 또한 개인을 중시하는 그들의 태도에서 나온 것이라고 여겨진다. 왜냐하면 집단 내에서의 동화에 민감한 우리는 대체로 자신의 의견을 감추고 타인의 의견을 따름으로써 마찰을 피하고자 하기 때문이다.

그래서 미국 사람들은 말이나 글에 있어서 우리보다 논리적이고 체계적이다. Okabe(1983: 30) 역시 그 점을 지적하고 있다.

> One of the main features of composition in the English language is the construction of a coherent and unified paragraphy, a series of sentences that develop one central topic in a clear and forceful manner.

끝으로, 미국인들은 인간이 자연을 지배할 능력이 있으므로 끊임없이 도전하여 정복하려고 하는 데 반하여 우리는 불교의 영향을 받아 인간도 자연의 일부이므로 조화롭게 적응하며 살아가야 한다는 생각이다(박형기, 1982: 13).

이제 미국문화와 우리문화의 심층적인 비교를 간단히 마치고 Seelye(1976: 29-32)가 소개한 중국인 Hsu에 의한 미국문화의 9가지 가정(postulate)을 적어보겠다:

Postulate Ⅰ. An individual's most important concern is his self interest: self-expression, self-development, self-gratification, and independence. This takes precedence over all group interests.
Postulate Ⅱ. The privacy of the individual is the individual's inalienable right. Intrusion into it by others is permitted only by his invitation.
Postulate Ⅲ. Because the government exists for the benefit of the individual and not vice versa, all forms of authority, including government, are suspect. But the government and its symbols should be respected. Patriotism is good.
Postulate Ⅳ. An individual's success in life depends upon his acceptance among his peers.
Postulate Ⅴ. An individual should believe or acknowledge God and should belong to an organized church or other religious institution. Religion is good. Any religion is better than no religion.
Postulate Ⅵ. Men and women are equal.
Postulate Ⅶ. All human beings are equal.
Postulate Ⅷ. Progress is good and inevitable. An individual must improve himself.
Postulate Ⅸ. Being American is synonymous with being progressing, and America is the utmost symbol of progress.

B. 한국문화와 미국문화의 표층적 차이

여기서는 한국과 미국의 심층적 문화의 차이에 대한 지식과 함께 영어교사로서 지녀야 할 표층적 미국문화의 특징에 관한 지식 중에서 기초적인 것만을 나열해 보겠다.

먼저 대인관계에 있어서 미국인들은 처음 대하는 사람에게도 매우 상냥하고 따뜻하게 해주므로 그렇지 못한 우리는 오해를 하기 쉽다. 즉 그들은 거리에서 낯선 사람과 눈이 마주치기만 해도 "Hi," "Hello" 등의 인사말을 미소를 지으며 하는데, 경우에 따라 우리는 "이상하다, 언제 저 사람을 만났더라?" 하면서 한참 기억을 더듬어 보기도 하고 이성으로부터 그러한 인사를 받고는 "별일이야, 언제부터 나를 안다고," 하며 이성에 대한 접근을 목적으로 한 행동으로 보고 언짢아 할 수도 있다. 이때 우리는 다만 같은 식으로 미소를 지으며 "Hi," "Hello" 등의 인사말을 하고 지나가면 되는 것이다. 그런 행동에서 미국인은 친구를 쉽게 사귀지만 가까운 친구는 적다고 하는데 이것은 그들이 한 곳에서 오래 머무르지 않고 자주 이사하는 데서 생긴 자연스러운 행동양식이라고 말해지기도 한다(Levine & Adelman, 1982: 67).

우리는 보통 어떤 사람을 공식적인 소개를 통하여 알게 되면 우선 그 사람의 신분, 나이 등을 알아 적절한 대접을 해주기 위하여 서슴지 않고 질문을 하게 되는데 반하여 미국인은 월급, 결혼

여부, 나이와 같은 지나치게 개인적인 질문은 안하는 것이 사회적인 법칙으로 되어 있다.

미국인들은 비판적이고 과학적인 사고를 하고 자기 주장이 강한 성격을 가지고 있으므로 침묵은 부정적으로 받아들여진다고 이미 지적되었다. 이러한 그들의 성격은 대인관계에 있어서 직선적이고 솔직하며 사무적이라는 인상을 주는 표현을 항상 사용하도록 하는데 이는 우리나라 사람들의 간접적인 의사전달 방식과 대조가 된다. 예를 들면 교수에게 용건이 있어 연구실을 방문하게 되었을 때 들어서자마자 “What can I do for you?” “What's the problem?” “Can I help you?”하며 용건을 물으면 우리는 당황하게 된다. Levine & Adelman(1982: 20)은 미국영어 중에서 “Don't beat around the bush”, “Let's get down to business”같은 말은 모두 그들이 직접적인 표현을 좋아한다는 것을 말해 준다고 한다.

또 다른 예로 가정에 초대받아 저녁식사를 할 때 우리는 습관적으로 배가 고파도 일단 조금만 먹고는 숟가락을 놓았다가 상대방이 여러 번 더 먹을 것을 권유하면 못 이기겠다는 듯이 다시 식사를 계속하는 경우가 많은데, 미국인은 한 번 거절하면 보통은 다시 권하지 않기 때문에 이를 모르고는 배가 고픈 상태로 돌아와야 한다. 다음의 미국인 집주인과 손님의 대화는 이를 단적으로 보여준다 (Levine & Adelman, 1982: 21):

Host: Would you like some more dessert?
Guest: No, thank you. It's delicious, but I've really had enough.
Host: Ok, why don't we leave the table and sit in the living room?

여기서 또 한 가지 알아두어야 할 것은 “Thank you.”의 사용이다. 우리는 상대방이 친절을 베풀거나 칭찬을 하면 겸손함을 나타내기 위하여 “뭘요,” “아니예요”와 같은 답변을 하게 되는데 미국인은 “Thank you.”라고 함으로써 친절이나 칭찬을 액면 그대로 받아들인다. 매우 솔직한 표현법으로 우리처럼 용건이 있어도 다른 얘기를 한참 하다가 꺼내고 자식이 부모에게 용돈이 필요하여 편지를 쓸 때도 맨 마지막 추신란에 한 줄 쓰는 태도와는 전혀 다름을 알 수 있다.

직선적인 미국인의 성격은 또한 질문에 답하는 방식에서도 엿볼 수 있다. 우리가 가장 많이 저지르기 쉬운 실수인데 부정의문문에 동조할 때 “예”로 시작되는 습관을 그대로 영어에 적용하기 쉽다는 것이다. 예를 들어 “Aren't you tired?”라는 질문을 받고 피곤하지 않음을 나타내려고 할 때 무의식중에 “Yes”라고 답하기 쉬운데 그들은 자동적으로 “No, I'm not.” 한다는 것이다.

다음으로 미국인은 개인의 사생활을 중요시하기 때문에 지나치게 개인적인 질문은 감정을 상하게 한다고 이미 언급되었고, 그래서 초대를 받았다거나 미리 상대방의 의사를 타진해보지 않고는 남의 집을 방문하는 것이 예의에 벗어난다는 생활규범도 지적되었다. 이제 남의 집을 방문할 때는 선물을 준비해야 하는 우리의 관습은 미국 사회에서는 그대로 적용되지 않는다는 것을 지적하고 싶다. 물론 우리도 그렇듯이 반드시 정해진 법칙이 있는 것은 아니지만 생일, 결혼, 출산, 명절날에는 보통 선물을 준비하고, 저녁초대에는 꽃, 포도주, 과자정도를 가져가도 되지만 안 가져가도 괜찮고 기타 잠깐 방문할 때는 선물이 필요 없다.

손님을 초대할 때도 우리처럼 요리솜씨를 자랑이라도 하는 듯 음식을 많이 장만하지 않고 간소하게 차리는 것이 보통이고 경우에 따라 저녁은 각자 집에서 하고 마실 것만 준비하는 파티,

마실 것까지 각자 가지고 가면 장소만 제공하는 파티 또는 간단히 ice cream이나 차(茶)를 준비하는 파티 등 다양하므로 정확히 이를 알고 준비해가야 한다.

덧붙여서 가정에서의 파티는 우리처럼 남·녀 구분하여 남자들은 노래하며 술을 마시거나 화투를 하고 여자들은 남자들의 시중들며 잡담하는 것이 아니라, 함께 각자 하고 싶은 이야기를 하며 시간을 보낸다. 헤어지는 시간도 각자 편리하다고 생각하는 때를 택하여 다른 사람의 눈치를 보지 않고 자리에서 뜨게 된다. 이러한 그들의 생활습관을 모르고 필자는 유학간 첫해 Christmas 파티에 지도교수 몇 부부를 초대하고는 식사 후 미리 준비한 순서에 따라 게임을 하고 10시 정각에 이제 오늘의 파티는 이것으로 끝마치겠으니 각자 집으로 편히 돌아가시라는 인사를 하여 모두를 당황하게 한 일이 있었다.

우리도 그렇지만 미국인도 초대하는 표현의 진지한 정도에 따라 다양하기 때문에 이들을 잘 해석해야 한다. 가령,

John: Nice talking to you. Let's get together some time.
Kim: I'd love to.
John: Good, I'll give you a call.
Kim: Good.

이들의 대화에서 Kim은 John이 모호한 의미를 지닌 표현을 하므로 진지하게 받아들일 필요가 없다고 판단한 자연스런 응답을 하고 있다. 이때 Kim이 "I'd love to."나 "Good" 대신 "When?"을 사용하면 John은 당황하게 될 것이다. 그러나 John이 "Are you free next Friday to come to dinner?"라고 물으면 분명히 대답을 해주어야 한다.

표층적 미국문화의 특징을 살펴볼 때 또 한 가지 생각나는 것이 있다. 우리는 흔히 말하기를 영어는 사회적 지위나 생리적 나이의 고하를 막론하고 "you," "Mr.," "Ms.," "he," "she" 등을 공통적으로 사용하고 조금만 가까워도 이름을 부르고 우리말보다 훨씬 덜 복잡하다고 하는데, 인간의 평등을 주창하고 나이가 많은 것이 어른 대접을 받을 수 있는 조건이 아니라고 여기며 젊음을 중요시하는 미국인이기는 하지만 대화의 참여자간의 관계에 따라 사용하는 언어가 다르다는 것을 지적하고 싶다. 다음 3가지의 다른 상황을 보면 명확해질 것이다(Levine & Adelman, 1982: 3):

(1) Professor: Mr. Lustig. I would like to introduce you to Dr. Johns, director of the language institute. Dr. Johns, this is Mr. Lustig, the academic adviser from Barnum College.
Mr. Lustig: How do you do, Dr. Johns?
Dr. Johns: It's a pleasure to meet you, Mr. Lustig. I'm glad that we finally have the occasion to meet.

(2) Friend: I'd like you to meet my friend, Nancy Pipkin. Nancy, this is my brother, Jack.
Nancy: Hi, Jack. Nice to meet you
Jack: Hi, Nancy.

(3) Friend: Hi, George, have you met Bill?
George: No, I haven't. Hi, Bill?
Bill: Hi, How ya doing?

다음에는 문화교육에서 반드시 다루어져야 하는 비언어적인 요소를 몇 가지 요약하여 보기로 하자.

우선 대화를 할 때는 상대방과 눈을 마주치도록 해야 하는데 어른과도 마찬가지다. 그렇지 않으면 상대방의 말에 별로 관심이 없다고 느끼게 하기 때문인데, "Never trust a person who can't look you in the eyes"에 잘 나타나 있다.

대화할 때 상대방과의 거리유지(space)도 중요한 비언어적 요소의 하나이다. 물론 대화자간의 관계에 따라 그리고 대화의 내용에 따라 달라져야 하지만 Levine & Adelman(1982: 64)이 Edward Hall이 관찰한 전문직에 종사하는 백인들 사이의 적당한 거리유지를 4가지로 분류한 것을 인용해 보겠다:

For intimate friends: From actual physical contact to 18 inches
For friends and personal conversation: 18 inches to 4 feet
For impersonal conversation: 4 feet to 12 feet
For public speaking: 12 feet or more

Levine & Adelman(1982: 47)은 계속해서 사교적인 대화에서의 상대방과의 거리는 대략 팔의 길이에서 4 feet 정도이고 이보다 가까우면 위협을 느끼게 된다고 말한다. 따라서 가까운 연인관계에 있지 않으면 몸의 어느 부분도 건드려서는 안된다. 그러므로 우리와는 달리 동성끼리 절대로 손을 잡고 다니는 것을 볼 수 없다(동성연애자는 제외). 언젠가 미국에 이민 가서 사는 한국인 할아버지가 이웃 미국 남자아이의 성기를 만졌다가 고소당했던 사건도 미국문화의 그런 점을 몰랐기 때문에 발생했을 것이다.

다음에는 역시 비언어적 행동인 몸짓(gesture)에 대하여 몇 가지 생각해 보아야 하겠다. 먼저 우리가 전통적으로 절을 하거나 머리를 숙여 인사를 하는 데 반하여 (남자들은 물론 친구 사이에는 악수를 하지만) 미국인은 악수를 하게 되는데 이때 강하면서도 짧게 해야 한다. 악수는 남성과 여성 사이에는 여자가 먼저 청할 경우에만 응하고 남자측에서는 청하지 않는 것이 예의였으나 요즈음에는 그렇게 엄격히 지키지 않고 자연스럽게 서로 악수를 하는 것 같다.

손가락의 사용에 따른 의미도 우리와는 다른 점이 많다. 엄지손가락과 집게손가락으로 원을 만들면 우리는 "돈"을 나타내지만 미국에서는 "OK"를 의미하고 엄지손가락을 세우면 우리는 "일등", "최고" 혹은 "우두머리"를 미국에서는 "hitchhiking"이라 하여 지나가는 차를 태워달라는 신호이기도 하고 경우에 따라 "OK"를 의미하기도 한다. 반대로 엄지손가락을 아래로 향하게 하면 반대한다는 뜻이다. 그러나 가운데 손가락으로 상대방을 가리키는 것은 금지되어 있다. 그리고 가운데 손가락을 집게손가락 위에 포개고 나머지 세손가락을 구부리고 손바닥을 밖으로 향하게 하면 "Good luck; I hope it works out"을 나타낸다.

팔과 손 전체를 사용하여 여러 가지 의미를 전달하게도 되는데 우선 양팔을 약간 옆으로 벌리고 손바닥을 자연스럽게 펴서 마주보게 하고는 양어깨를 위로 추켜 올리면 난처해하며 "I don't know"라는 말을 하는 것과 같고, 오른팔을 올려 오른손을 오른쪽 귀 뒤에 대면 "I can't hear you"를, 오른팔을 올리고 이마를 오른 손바닥으로 치면 "Oh, I forgot!"을 오른팔의 팔꿈치까지 오른편 얼굴 옆으로 올려 손바닥을 밖으로 향하게 하면 "Wait a second; Slow down"을 같은 자세로 손을 위 아래로 흔들면 "Good-bye"를 그리고 이번에는 손바닥을 안으로 향하게 하고 가운데, 약, 새끼손가락을 위 아래로 흔들면 "Come here"를 의미한다.

이밖에도 언어대신 미국인이 사용하는 비언어적 행동은 헤아릴 수 없이 많지만 가장 자연스럽게 익히는 방법은 그들의 무의식적인 행동을 실제로 또는 영화 등을 통해 주의 깊게 관찰하는 것이라고 여겨진다.

4. 문화교육의 방법

이제 문화교육은 어떤 방법으로 할 수 있는가를 알아보기 위하여 우리에게는 생소할지 모르지만 그동안 사용되어온 대표적인 방법들을 구체적인 예를 들어가며 소개해 보겠다.

(1) Culture Aside

이것은 가장 많이 사용되는 방법으로서 간단히 문화에 대한 설명을 해주는 것을 말한다. 예를 들어 데이트를 하면서 길을 걸을 때 반드시 남성이 바깥쪽에 서서 여성을 보호해주고 택시를 탈 때 여성이 먼저 타고 남성은 뒤따라 타는 것이 미국 사회의 예절이고, 비용은 전통적으로는 남성이 부담을 했으나 요즈음은 반드시 지킬 필요는 없고, "Dutch treat"를 하거나 여성이 부담하기도 한다는 것을 얘기해주는 것 등이다. 체계적인 지도가 어렵지만 그때그때 상황에 맞는 단계적인 문화지식을 쉽게 전달해 줄 수 있는 장점이 있다. 당분간 우리나라 영어 교사들이 많이 사용해야 할 것이다.

(2) Culture Capsule

최초로 이 방법을 고안한 두 사람은 Darrel Taylor와 John Sorenson이었다. 한 마디로 우리 문화의 한 측면과 외국문화의 그것 사이의 중요한 차이점을 간단히 외국어로 설명하는 것으로서 사진이나 실물체를 동반하는 경우가 대부분이다. 교사는 여기서 끝내지 않고 학습자의 이해를 측정하기 위한 질문을 하고 마지막으로 우리의 문화와 비교할 기회를 줌으로써 이를 통하여 우리 문화의 성격을 측정해 보도록 해야 한다. 미국인의 아침식사에 대한 다음의 Culture Capsule은 한 가지 예이다(Tiersky, 1975: 130-1):

Culture Capsule: American Breakfast

A complete American breakfast begins with fruit or fruit juice (usually orange juice). The main course generally consists of cereal or eggs. The cereal can be either hot or cold. The eggs are accompanied by toast and perhaps bacon, ham, or sausages. For adults, coffee is the usual breakfast drink. Other popular breakfast dishes are waffles, French toast (bread soaked in eggs and milk, then fried), and pancakes – all of which are served with butter and maple syrup. However, many American adults begin the day with just a small breakfast of juice or toast and coffee.

이러한 Culture Capsule을 제시하는 방법은 여러 가지다:
- ◦ 교사나 Tape가 읽고 학습자는 듣는다.
- ◦ 교사나 Tape가 읽고 학습자는 프린트된 용지를 눈으로 따라간다.
- ◦ 한 학생이 대표로 소리내어 읽고 나머지는 프린트된 용지를 눈으로 따라간다.
- ◦ 모든 학생이 프린트된 용지를 조용히 읽는다.

제시한 후에는 Comprehension Question을 통하여 읽기와 쓰기와 연관을 시키도록 하고 학습자의 실력정도에 따라 group 과제로 주어 Culture Capsule을 준비하게 할 수도 있다.

한편 관련된 일련의 Culture Capsule들을 몇 개 종합하여 30-40분 정도의 시간을 배정하여 다루는 자료를 Culture Cluster라 부르는데 일련의 학습내용을 정리하기에 적합하다. 예를 들면 미국인의 아침식사와 관련하여 식탁 차리는 법과 식사하는 법을 각각 소개한 다음 학습자로 하여금 연극을 통하여 이들을 보여주게 한다.

(3) Culture Assimilator

Fiedler, Mitchell, 그리고 Triandis 같은 미국의 사회심리학자들이 문화의 차이에서 오는 오해를 이해시켜 외국문화에 잘 적응하게 할 목적으로 고안해낸 방법이다. 하나의 에피소드가 소개되고 학생은 그것을 읽고 왜 문제가 야기되게 되었는지 생각해본 후 옳다고 판단되는 답을 고르게 되는데, 각각의 그럴듯한 해답에는 설명이 자세히 되어 있어 개별학습이나 분단학습으로 이용하면 효과적이다. 다음에 예를 들어 보겠다:

Culture Assimilator: In the American Restaurant

Chulsoo arrived at a small town of the U. S. from Seoul. He was so hungry that he went to a nearby restaurant. Upon entering, he was shown to a table by a hostess. It was very crowded and many people were having dinner there. Soon a waitress brought him a menu. She was very pretty and kind when she asked him with smile what he wanted to order. Because he was not familiar with American food, he ordered fried shrimp, salad, and a glass of milk. After he finished the meal, the waitress again politely and kindly asked him the kind of dessert he wanted to order. He was so full that he said he did not want any more. In a minute, the waitress put the bill on the table and said, "I hope you enjoyed the dinner." Chulsoo replied, "Yes, I enjoyed it very much. Thank you." He soon paid the amount of money the bill indicated at the front desk and left the restaurant in the good feeling. Next evening, Chulsoo visited the restaurant again for dinner. It was less crowded than yesterday. He waited for the waitress to take his order for a while. At last she came to his table after she served the other two customers who came after Chulsoo. Chulsoo looked at her and smiled. Surprisingly, the waitress did not respond with the same polite attitude as yesterday. She asked him to order bluntly and she did not even say, "I hope you enjoyed the dinner." Chulsoo was very upset when he paid money to the front cashier. Which of the following explains most accurately the waitress' changed attitude?
A. Chulsoo did not order the dessert yesterday.

B. Chulsoo did not leave a tip yesterday.
C. The waitress did not feel good that day.
D. The waitress worried about the decreased number of customers.

You chose A. This is not the right answer. Though Americans generally enjoy dessert after the main dish, they are not necessarily required to have one at every dinner. Moreover, if that had been the problem, she would have changed her attitude right after the incident. Reread the passage and choose another answerr.

You chose B. This is the correct answer. In America, you are generally expected to leave about 15 percent of the bill in small change on the table as a tip for the person who has served you in a restaurant. So Chulsoo should have left the tip to show her thanks for her service.

You chose C. This answer is incorrect. What the waitress has to do is to serve the customers well. The way she feels is not likely to affect her responsibility to the customers, unless the customer really did something wrong to her directly. Reread the passage and make another choice.

You chose D. This answer is incorrect. Worrying about the number of customers is the manager's concern, not the waitress. Her job is to serve the customers in a pleasant manner and to attract them to come back. If she does not give good service, there will be even fewer customers. Reread the passage and choose another answer.

이 방법은 문화교육을 읽기교육과 병행할 수 있어서 좋다. 자료준비에 많은 시간이 소요된다는 단점이 있으나 학습자를 직접 문제 상황에 관련시키고 틀린 답에 대한 이유를 읽으면서 문화의 다양성을 인식하고 이해하게 되는 장점이 있다. 문제지와 답안지를 별도로 작성하여 충분한 사고의 시간을 주는 것이 좋겠다.

(4) Audio-Motor Unit

이 방법은 Theodore B. Kalivods, Genelle Morain 그리고 Robert J. Elkins가 고안한 것으로, 교육하고자 하는 내용을 일련의 명령형으로 만들어 학습자가 명령에 따라 행동하는 동안 문화를 이해하게 된다. 교육의 목적은 다르지만 방법은 James J. Asher의 Total Physical Response와 동일하다. 다음에 소개되는 예를 보기로 하자.

"American Eating Pattern at Dinner Table"

준비재료: 식탁, 의자, napkin, 수저, soup 그릇, 받침접시, fork, salad그릇, 큰 접시, 스테이크, 빵과 빵접시, 칼, 우유

You are in a private home for dinner as a guest.
(1) You are seated at the dinner table.
(2) A prayer is offered by the host. You sit quietly with your head bowed until the prayer

is over.
(3) Pick up your napkin.
(4) Unfold it.
(5) Put it on your lap.
(6) Pick up the spoon on your left in your right hand.
(7) Put a spoonful of soup in your mouth.
(8) Swallow it.
(9) Put down the spoon on the service plate under the soup bowl.
(10) Pick up the fork on your left in your right hand.
(11) Pick up small amount of salad.
(12) Put it in your mouth.
(13) Chew it.
(14) Swallow it.
(15) Put down the fork on the service plate under the salad bowl.
(16) Meat is passed. Put your piece on the large plate.
(17) Bread is passed. Put your piece on the small bread and butter plate at your left.
(18) Pick up your fork on your left hand.
(19) Pick up your knife on your right in your right hand.
(20) Cut two pieces of meat.
(21) Put down your knife on the plate.
(22) Transfer your fork to your right hand.
(23) Put your left hand on your lap.
(24) Eat it.
(25) Put down your fork on the plate.
(26) Take a sip of milk.
(27) Hold bread in your fingers.
(28) Bite off a piece.
(29) Put your napkin on the table and rise.

어떤 문화적인 요소들을 교사의 명령을 듣고 행하면서 배울 수 있었는지를 알아보기 위하여 다음과 같은 질문들이 던져질 수 있을 것이다:

(1) What do many Americans seem to do before meal?
(2) How do many Americans eat meat?
(3) How do many Americans eat bread?
(4) Where do many Americans put their hands when not in use?
(5) What do many Americans drink at the meal time?
(6) What do many Americans have for dinner?

진행하는 방법은 교사가 몇 번 시범을 보여준 후 학생들이 교사를 따라 명령을 듣고 행하는 것인데, 학생들의 수준에 따라 융통성 있게 적용해야 한다. 문화교육과 동시에 듣기 훈련에도 많은 효과가 있을 것이다.

(5) Mini-Drama

Raymond L. Gordon이라는 사회학자가 처음으로 소개했는데, 연극이 3막에서 5막 정도의 길이로 각각은 짧고 의사소통상의 문제점을 포함하면서 점차적으로 원인이 드러나지만 마지막에서 비로소 명확하게 되는데 막이 끝날 때마다 토론을 한다. 생동감이 넘치는 수업을 진행할 수 있는데 다음의 창호와 윤희가 미국에서 겪은 경험담을 어떻게 연극으로 엮어 문화교육을 하는 지를 보면 잘 알게 될 것이다.

"At the American Shoestore"

Act I

Narrator: Changho and Yunhi as a couple came to America to study in a university a few days ago. They are staying at the home of their host family. Today they decided to walk to a nearby shoestore by themselves. They are now outside the shoestore and watch various kinds of shoes through the window.

Changho: (pointing to a pair of shoes) Honey, look at that one over there. I like it.

Yunhi: You mean the blue one?

Changho: Yeh, but it's too expensive. The price tag indicates it's $30, which means 36,000 won in Korean currency.

Yunhi: The price won't mean anything. Let's ask the manager how much we can discount. Let's try from half of that original price.

Narrator: The couple enters the store.

Store woman: Can I help you?

Yunhi: Yes, please. Could you tell us how much we have to pay for this pair of shoes?

Store woman: Well, let's see. It's $30.

Yunhi: I know it. What I mean is that how much I must pay for that.

Store woman: (nervously) I told you it cost $ 30.

Yunhi: (whispers to Changho) I don't understand why she is so upset. (class discussion)

Act II

Narrator: Changho and Yunhi came out of the store and looked around.

Changho: Look, there's a department store. Let's go there and buy one. It'll be the best way, since we don't have to discount.

Narrator: Changho and Yunhi enter the department store and look around.

Yunhi: This is too large to find out the location of shoes. Let's ask the woman over there who wears a uniform.

Changho: Why don't you ask her over there?

Yunhi: Excuse me. Could you tell me where the sports shoes are?

Woman: Sure. Aisle 4 to your left.

Yunhi: Thank you.

Woman: You're welcome.

Yunhi: Let's go to aisle 4.

Changho: Look, there's the same shoes as we saw in the shoestore. Let's see. It's only $27. I'm going to buy this one. (class discussion)

Act Ⅲ

Cashier: (at the checkout counter) Hello.

Changho and Yunhi: Hi.

Cashier: It comes to $28, please.

Yunhi: (looking at Changho) How strange it is! (to cashier) You see this price tag? I think you made a mistake.

Cashier: How do you think this machine made such a stupid mistake?

Changho: (whispers to Yunhi) What a bad day it is! (class discussion)

Act Ⅳ

Narrator: After dinner Changho and Yunhi are in the living room with Mrs. Brown talking about what happened during the day.

Changho: I still don't know why the store woman got mad when Yunhi asked her how much we must pay for the pair of shoes.

Yunhi: There's one more curious thing. I definitely think we paid $1 more than we had to.

Mrs. Brown: Well, it seems to me that today's miscommunication occurred because of some cultural differences between your country and ours. First, I can understand that in your country prices may be discounted at the owner's will in small privately-run stores. On the other hand, in America, prices of products are fairly reasonably tagged by the employer and they cannot be discounted. Besides, the price of a product varies depending on where it is placed. Second, the extra money, $1.00 was a tax. While in your country it seems that tax is imposed only on total personal income, in America we have to pay tax for almost everything in our daily life, things we buy in the store(there is no tax for grocery items in some states), foods we eat in the restaurant, and so on. Therefore we must expect extra 4 to 10 percent of the tagged price as tax depending on which state you live in.

한편 Gordon은 토론을 하는 동안 비판적인 분위기를 조성하기 않고 학습자 스스로 문제점을 발견해 가도록 하기 위하여 교사에게 다음과 같이 질문내용과 방법에 유의해야 할 것을 충고한다:

- "어떤 인상을 받았는가?" "무엇이 일어나고 있는가?" "어떻게 생각하는가?" "주인공의 감정을 어떻게 표현하겠는가?" "만약 그 상황에 있다면 어떻게 하겠는가?" 등과 같이 일반적이고 광범위한 질문을 한다.
- "음", "그래서", "흥미 있는데", "계속 하시오." 등의 말을 함으로써 중립적인 자세를 취하고 자유로운 분위기를 조성하여 유도해 간다.
- 토론이 끝날 때마다 간략하게 요약한다.

(6) Revised Mini-Drama

Gordon의 Mini-drama와는 달리 외국인이 직접 어려운 상황에서 곤란을 겪는 것이 아니고 미국인의 행동을 가까이에서 지켜보며 의아해 하는 고민을 함께 토의해 보는 것이다. 흔히 지나쳐 버리기 쉬운 중요한 문화적인 면을 깊이 생각해 보고 우리의 것과 비교하는 기회가 될 것이다.

Levine & Adelman (1982: 102-103)은 다음의 예를 회화 연습용으로 소개하고 있는데 좋은 문화교육의 자료도 될 수 있다고 본다.

> Media, a foreign student, has been invited to the Turner's home for dinner. She is sitting at the table and enjoying dinner and conversation with the rest of the family. During dinner the phone rings and Carol's younger brother answers it.
>
> Carol's brother: Carol. It's Bill.
>
> Mrs. Turner: (surprised) Bill? I thought you weren't seeing him any more, Carol.
>
> Without replying, Carol leaves the room to answer the phone. When she returns, she silently continues her dinner.
>
> Dr. Turner: Carol, was it Bill?
>
> Carol: Yes.
>
> Dr. Turner: Are you still seeing him even though we told you we didn't approve?
>
> Carol: (angrily) Do I have to tell you everything? Listen, Dad, I know Bill doesn't have a college education but he is working for his brother in a construction company. He's trying to earn enough money to return to school. You always say that you respect hard-working people. Why shouldn't I see him any more?
>
> Dr. Turner: (softly but seriously) I hope you're not serious about Bill, Carol. He promised to stay in college but he dropped out two times. Do you want to marry someone whose personality you'll have to change?
>
> Mrs. Turrner: Carol, Bill is different from us. We're only saying this because we love you. Bill just isn't your kind.
>
> Carol: (furious) What do you mean, "my kind?" He's a human being! Just because he comes from a family that has less money than we do? What kind of democracy do you believe in? Everyone is supposed to be equal. He and his family are just as good as we are (By now, Carol is shouting loudly). Media is feeling embarrassed and stares at her plate.
>
> Carol's brother: Come on, Mom and Dad. Bill's a nice guy.
>
> Carol: Just because his parents are farmers who work with their hands and you are professors who work with your head. What difference does that make?
>
> Mrs. Turner: Carol, we're very disappointed in you. After all, you know what is best for you. Suddenly Carol gets up, takes Media's arm, and pulls her to the door.
>
> Carol: Come on, Media. Let's go to my room and study.

Carol과 부모와의 문제는 무엇이고 궁극적으로 Carol과 Bill의 사이는 어떻게 예상되고 우리의 상황에서와 비교를 할 수 있는지 등의 주제에 관하여 토론을 하게 될 것이다. 이때 교사는 미국에서의 결혼 결정은 당사자들 간의 상호 합의하에 되는 것이 보통이며 18세가 넘으면 부모의 승인이 큰 의미를 지니지는 않는다는 문화지식을 지니고 있어야 하겠다.

(7) 신문과 잡지 (Newspapers and Magagines)

비교적 쉽게 구할 수 있고 값도 저렴하고 무엇보다도 신빙성이 있으며 가장 최근의 문화정보를 제공하는 자료로서 효과적으로 이용된다면 대단한 가치를 가질 것이다. 물론 지방 신문들은 구하기가 어려워 아쉽지만 Time, Newsweek, Korea Herald 혹은 Korea Times에 실려 있는 관련기사를 학습자의 실력 정도에 따라 그대로 또는 부분적인 수정을 하여 Culture Capsule이나 Culture Aside의 자료로 사용할 수 있을 것이다. 다음은 잡지에서 발췌한 내용이다:

> **Bye-Bye, American Pie**
> Next to Mom, there was nothing as American as apple pie. Alas, that most national of desserts is in decline. According to a survey by "Restaurants and Institutions" magazine, apple pie now appears on the menu at 64% of the nation's restaurants, hotels, school and other food-serving institutions, down from 88% in 1971. Among those chefs who still dish it out, apple pie is called a "good seller" by only 57%, vs. 84% a decade ago. It is still the nation's most popular dessert, but as Editor in chief Jane Young Walace points out, "There is a trend toward healthy, low-cal foods. People seem to prefer fruit these days." Next time, make it apple pie, but hold the pie.

(8) 노래 (Songs)

학습자의 어학실력의 향상을 위해서 뿐만 아니라 문화이해 증진을 위하여 노래를 이용할 것을 추천한 Taylor(1980: 466)는 특히 초급과정을 지난 단계에서 자주 할 것을 제안하는데 이유는 첫째, 그들의 단어나 문법실력이 노래가사를 이해할 수 있게 할 것이고 둘째, 듣기교육에 도움이 되며 셋째, 지루한 문형연습에 변화를 주고 넷째, 문화이해를 도와주기 때문이다.

사실 음악과 노래는 그 나라 그 시대의 여러 면을 반영하는 거울이 된다. 이제 1880년대 미국의 개척시대를 배경으로 하는 노래가사 하나를 소개하겠다:

1.
There's a low green vally on the old Kentucky shore.
There I've whiled many happy hours away,
A sitting and a singing by the little cottage door,
Where lived my daring Nelly Gray.
Oh, my poor Nelly Gray, they have taken you away.
And I'll never see my daring any more.
I'm sitting by the river and I'm weeping all the day.
For you've gone from the old Kentucky shore.

2.
One night I went to see her but "she's gone," the neighbors say.
The white man bound her with his chain.
They have taken her to Georgia to wear her life away.
As she toils in the cotton, and the cane. Chorus.

그 당시 백인과 흑인의 관계가 잘 나타나 있으며 동사의 시제 (과거, 현재, 미래, 현재완료)를 정리해 볼 수 있을 것이다.

이 밖에 영화, 외국인 초대손님, 민속담, 학습자 과제, 게시판, 속담 등을 이용하는 방법이 있을 수 있는데, 효과면에서 어떤 것이 우월하다고 할 수는 없고 영어교사 각자가 상황에 따라

택하여 지도하는 것이 가장 바람직한 것이겠다.

마지막으로 문화교육을 위하여 시급한 것은 각 학교마다 필요한 만큼의 영어교실을 만들어 모든 영어수업을 거기에서 받도록 해야 할 것이다. 그 교실은 영어교육의 목적을 달성하는 데 기여하도록 미화시켜야 한다.

또 한 가지 언급할 것은 문화교육을 염두에 두고 수업을 진행할 때 영어와 우리말의 사용비율을 정하는 사람은 교사 자신이어야 하는데, 이때 교사가 반드시 알아야 할 사항은 학습목표이다. 이것은 극단적으로 문화지도가 우선일 때 언어요소를 희생할 각오가 되어야 한다는 의미이다. 그러나 학습자의 언어능력의 향상에 따라 점차 목표어의 사용을 증가시켜야 할 것이다.

5. 문화의 평가

교육의 단계는 먼저 학습자가 무엇을 필요로 하는가를 알아내어 목표를 정하고 방법을 적용한 후 평가를 하고 평가결과에 의해 목표나 방법을 수정하여 다시 적용하는 순서를 따르게 된다. 문화교육에서도 설정한 목표를 어느 정도 달성했는지를 판단하는 평가가 반드시 되어져야 하는데 우리나라에서는 거의 무시되어온 영역이다. 그러나 문화교육의 목표가 매우 중요하다는 것을 알게 된 이상 잘 가르쳐야 하고, 또한 평가되어야 한다. 그런 의미에서 이 장에서는 문화의 평가방법을 간단히 논의해 보고자 한다.

먼저 사지선다형의 문제를 다음과 같은 식으로 출제할 수 있다:

· When introduced to an old American professor, what would you say?
 a. "Hi! Glad to know ya."
 b. "Hello," and bow.
 c. "Hello, it's nice to meet you." and then shake hands.
 d. "How do you do?"

· When you are being introduced to an American, what would you do in addition to speaking?
 a. Shake hands lightly.
 b. Shake hands firmly for a few seconds.
 c. Shake hands until the introduction is completely finished.
 d. Shake hands and then bow.

· When an American compliments the watch you are wearing, you would
 a. say, "Oh, this cheap thing? It's not worth much."
 b. give it to him.
 c. say, "Thanks" and smile.
 d. say, "Oh, no. Yours is better."

· If a student does not understand a point that an American teacher makes in class, it is best to
 a. raise a hand and ask for clarification.
 b. look confused.

c. remain silent and ask the teacher after class.
d. leave the class.

다음에 True-False 질문형식으로 평가할 수 있다.

· It is common for an American to invite guests into the kitchen while she is preparing a meal. ( )
· Punctuality is not important in America. ( )
· Silence in America indicates acceptance. ( )
· Young Americans usually offer their seats to elderly people. ( )

객관적인 평가가 곤란하고 시간이 소요되지만 가장 이상적인 평가방법은 직접 말과 행동으로 보여주도록 하는 것이다. 개별적으로 할 수도 있고 Role play로 할 수도 있다.

· Congratulate the bride on the occasion of her marriage.
· Welcome someone to your home.
· Thank someone for his hospitality to you.
· Extend condoleness to a person on the death of a partner.
· You accidently step on B's toe. You apologize to B and B politely accepts your apology.
· You request B's permission to do something. But B expresses reluctance to permit you to do it with a reason.

이 평가방법은 물론 교육방법으로도 효과적으로 이용될 수 있다.
이상의 세 가지 평가방법은 미국인의 생활방식을 가르치고 이해도를 측정하기 위한 것인데 그들의 역사, 지리, 교육, 문학, 예술 등 Large "C"에 속하는 문화교육과 평가도 또한 단계적으로 포함시켜야 할 것이다.

II. 결 론

본 논문은 외국어로서의 영어교육에 있어서 문화지도의 필요성을 강조하고 이와 관련된 문제들을 토의하려는 목적으로 우선 영어교육이라는 측면에서 문화의 의미를 미국인의 생활방식이나 행동양식에서 출발하여 생각해야 한다고 보았다. 따라서 목표에 있어서는 미국인들과의 원활한 의사소통, 그들의 문화이해와 함께 우리문화의 가치인식, 그리고 강제로 끌고 가는 교육이 아니라 자발적으로 흥미를 가지고 참여하는 교육이어야 함을 지적했다.
이어서 위와 같은 목표를 달성하기 위하여 특히 일선 영어교사들이 알고 있어야 할 미국문화의 내용을 심층적인 것과 표면적인 것으로 구분하여 나열하였고 문화교육의 방법을 구체적인 예를 삽입하며 소개하였으며 마지막으로 문화의 평가방법을 간단히 살펴보았다.
아직도 유아기에 있다고 할 수 있는 문화교육의 각 부분에 관한 깊은 연구가 뒤따라야 하고 문화교육을 할 수 있는 새로운 교과서의 개발이 절실히 요구된다.

참고문헌

박명석. (1969). 문화적 차이에 기인한 의사소통의 차이 — 한국과 미국의 경우를 중심으로. 영어영문학, 59, pp. 91-107.

박상옥. (1985). 효율적인 조기 영어교육방안에 관한 연구. 영어교육, 29 & 30, pp. 321-346.

박형기. (1982). 영어교육의 입장에서 비교한 한국문화와 미국문화의 특성. 영어교육, 23, pp. 9-30.

신용진. (1985). 영어교육공학 Ⅰ. 서울: 예지각.

Abercrombie, Dovid. (1968). Paralanguage. *British J. of Disorders of Communication*, 3, pp. 55-59.

Birdwhistill, Ray L. (1970). *Kinesics and Context*, Philadelphia: University of Pennsylvania Press.

Brooks, Nelson. (1964). *Language and Language Learning*, N. Y.: Harcourt, Brace, and World, Inc.

______. (1968). Teaching Culture in the Foreign Language Classroom. *Foreign Language Annals*, 1, pp. 204-217.

Brown, Roger W. et al. (1953). Developing Cultural Understanding: Through Foreign Language Study: A Report of the MLA Interdisciplinary Seminar in Language and Culture. *PMLA*, *68,* pp. 1203.

Bruder, Mary Newton. (1973). *MMC-Developing Communicative Competive in English as a Second Language.* Pittsburgh: University of Pittsburgh, Center for International Studies.

Chastain, Kenneth. (1976). *Developing Second-Language Skills: Theory to Practice.* Chicago: Rand McNally College Publishing Company.

Hendon, Ursula. (1980). Introducing Culture in the High School Foreign Language Class. *Foreign Language Annals*, *13,* pp. 191-199.

Henderson, Ingeborg. (1983). Cultural Strategies in Elementary College Language Courses. *The Modern Language Journal, 67*, pp. 191-196.

Ide, John H. (1982). Teaching Culturally Appropriate English. *영어교육, 23,* pp. 61-76.

Kim, Duk Ki. (1979). Some Postulates for Establishing EFL Goals. *영어교육, 18,* pp. 103-115.

Lafayette, Robert C. (1978). *Teaching Culture*: *Strategies and Techniques.* Center for Applied Linguistics.

Levine, Deena R. & Mara B. Adelman. (1982). *Beyond Language.* Englewood Cliffs, N. J.: Prentice Hall, Regent.

Okabe, Roichi. (1983). Cultural Assumptions of East and West. ed. by William B. Gudykunst, *Intercultural Communication Theory.* Sage Publications, pp. 21-44.

Rivers, Wilga M. (1981). *Teaching Foreign Language Skills.* Chicago and London: The University of Chicago Press.

Park, Won. (1981). Reorientation for English Teaching in Korea. *영어교육, 21,* pp. 45-772.

Seelye, H. Ned. (1976). *Teaching Culture, Strategies for Foreign Language Educators.* Skokie, Ill: National Textbook Company.

Stevick, Earl W. (1982). *Teaching and Learning Language.* Cambridge: Cambridge University Press.

Taylor, Marisa Gatt. (1980). Songs as a Linguistic and Cultural Resource in the Intermediate Italian Class. *Foreign Language Annals*, *6,* pp. 465-469.

Tiersky, Ethel & Martin Tiersky. (1975). *USA, Customs and Institutions.* Regents Publishing Company, Inc.

Tinsley, Royal L. Jr. (1972). A Culture is a Culture is a . . . ? *The Arizona Foreign Language Teachers FORUM, 19,* pp. 2-6.

Vallette, Rebecca M. (1977). *Modern Language Testing.* Harcount Brace Jovanovich, Inc.

From Park, S. O. (1985). 영어교육에 있어서 문화지도, *홍익대학교 논총(인문, 사회과학편)*, 17, pp. 487-511.

30. TEACHING ENGLISH AS AN INTERNATIONAL LANGUAGE : IMPLICATIONS FOR CULTURAL MATERIALS IN THE CLASSROOM

Many teachers use cultural content in their classroom, believing that such a focus will motivate their students. However, as English assumes the role of an international language, the question of which culture to teach and how to teach it raises several important issues. To explore the link between culture and an international language, this article begins with an examination of what is meant by an international language. This is followed by a consideration of the role of culture in language learning and a description of the various levels of culture that can be included in teaching materials. The article concludes by considering whose culture to include in language materials, suggesting that there are many benefits to including a variety of cultures, not just Western cultures, in classroom materials.

English as an International Language

Crystal (1997) argues that English is rapidly assuming the role of a world language. He maintains that in inner-circle countries, where English is spoken as a native language, there are approximately 320-380 million native speakers of English. In outer-circle countries, Where English has an official role, as in India and Singapore, for example, there are roughly 150-300 million second language (L2) speakers of English. And in expanding-circle countries, where English is used as a foreign language, there are perhaps as many as 100 to 1,000 million learners of English. Hence, as a conservative estimate, there are approximately 570 million people in the world today who have a native or nativelike command of English. As Crystal points out, no other language has spread around the globe so extensively, making English a truly international language.

What exactly is an international language? Smith (1976) was perhaps one of the first to define the term, noting that an "international language is one which is used by people of different nations to communicate with one another"(p. 17). Elaborating on this definition, Smith makes several assertions regarding the relationship between an international language and culture, namely, that

- learners of an international language do not need to internalize the culture norms of

native speakers of that language
- the ownership of an international language becomes de-nationalized
- the educational goal of learning an international language is to enable learners to communicate their ideas and culture to others

More recently, Widdowson (1994) discussed the question of the ownership of an international language. As he put it,

> The very fact that English is an international language means that no nation can have custody over it. To grant such custody of the language, is necessarily to arrest its development and so undermine its international status. It is a matter of considerable pride and satisfaction for native speakers of English that their language is an international means of communication. But the point is that it is only international to the extent that it is not their language. It is not a possession which they lease out to others, while still retaining the freehold. Other people actually own it. (p. 385)

If an international language, by definition, means that such a language belongs to no single culture, then it would seem that it is not necessary for language learners to acquire knowledge about the culture of those who speak it as a native language. There are some, however, who argue that a language cannot be taught without knowledge of a target culture. Whether or not target culture content should be included in language classrooms is highly dependent on what one sees as the role of culture in language learning.

Culture in Language Learning 27

In her discussion of language teaching and culture, Kramsch (1993) emphasizes the notion that culture is "a social construct, the product of self and others' perceptions" (p. 205). Informed by a view of culture as a social construct, she outlines several new lines of thought regarding the teaching of language and culture.

- Establishing a sphere of interculturality—This line of thought promotes the idea that the learning of culture is more than just the transfer of information between cultures. Rather, learning about a culture requires that one consider his/her own culture in relation to another. Hence, the process of learning about another culture entails a reflection on one's own culture as well as the target culture.
- Teaching culture as an interpersonal process—This area emphasizes that learning about

a culture does not entail merely a presentation of facts but, rather, a process of trying to understand foreignness or otherness.

- Teaching culture as difference—This notion of culture highlights the fact that national characteristics are not monolithic. Within each culture there exists a variety of national characteristics that are related to age, gender, regional origin, ethnic background, and social class.

As I see it, these areas of emphasis are critical to the teaching of culture, especially in relation to an international language. One of the features that Smith argues is central to the concept of an international language is that one learns the language to be able to communicate aspects of one's own culture to others. Hence, it is important in the teaching of English as an international language (EIL) for learners to be asked to reflect on their own culture in relation to other cultures or, as Kramsch puts it, to establish a sphere of interculturality. This suggests that the teaching of culture should not involve a mere presentation of facts but, rather, a critical and social process of trying to understand other cultures in relation to one's own. Teaching culture as difference is also central to the teaching of EIL. The varieties of English that exist today within many countries are just one indication of the diversity that is present within many national borders.

In relation to the learning of an international language, it is important to emphasize that learning about another culture does not mean that one must accept that culture. Kramsch (1993), for example, argues that knowing about a culture (i.e., gaining cultural competence) does not mean that one has an obligation to behave in accordance with the conventions of that culture. Byram (1998) makes a similar distinction between knowing about another culture and accepting another culture when he distinguishes what he terms *biculturalism* and *interculturalism*. For Byram, biculturalism assumes that an individual identifies with and accepts the beliefs, values, and practices of a particular culture. Interculturalism, on the other hand, assumes a knowledge of, rather than acceptance of, another culture. Clearly, in the EIL classroom, in which the language belongs to its users, interculturalism rather than biculturalism should be the goal.

In reference to the relationship between biculturalism and bilingualism, Paulston (1992) maintains that becoming bicultural differs from becoming bilingual. She argues that "becoming bicultural is not just a cognitive process which can be carried out apart from the members of the culture"(p. 120). She continues that it is "possible to become bilingual without becoming bicultural, while the reverse is not true"(p. 120). Hence, for Paulston, in learning a language, it is possible to become bilingual without identifying with a particular culture. This distinction is important in considering the goals of language learners not only in English as a foreign language (EFL) contexts but also in English as a second language (ESL) contexts such as in the United States. It may well be that for some students. their language learning goal is to acquire EIL in order to explain their culture to others and, hence to become bilingual and not bicultural. Thus, if the role of culture in language teaching, particularly in relation to an international language, is to establish a sphere of interculturality and not to require that learners accept the values of another culture, how might this be done?

Levels of Culture

In examining the issues of culture and language learning, Adaskou, Britten, and Fashi (1990) describe four dimensions of culture:

1. *aesthetic sense,* in which a language is associated with the literature, film, and music of a particular country
2. *sociological sense*, in which a language is linked to the customs and institution of country
3. *semantic sense*, in which a culture's conceptual system is expressed in the language
4. *pragmatic sense,* in which cultural norms influence what language is appropriate for what contexts

In dealing with culture in the aesthetic sense particularly in relation to literature, as well as in the sociological sense, one of the first steps that needs to be taken is to examine what kind of cultural information is in the text and in what ways the content might appear unusual to members of another culture. Let us take. for example, a rather routine lesson on garage sales that is presented in the context of asking for and giving advice(Hynes & Baichman, 1989). The chapter opens with the following instructions:

A garage sale is a sale of items you no longer want or need. People have these sales in their homes, yards, or garages. It is a way for sellers to make money by getting rid of old items. It is also a way for buyers to get secondhand items, or used items, cheaply.

Look at the list below. With a partner decide which items you would want to buy new and which items you wouldn't mind buying secondhand. Write *N or S.* Then discuss your answers with your classmates. (p. 47)

Students are then asked to check the following items: a cassette recorder, shoes, pots and pans, a mattress, children's toys, a rocking chair, sheets, blankets and pillows, a clock radio, babies' clothes, old records, picture with frames, a tablecloth, jewelry, a toaster, a rug, underwear, a winter coat and tools. The chapter then continues with a character named Janina asking Roberto whether or not he thinks she should have the sale on Saturday or Sunday, put an ad in the paper or put signs in the neighborhood, and put signs in the front yard or backyard. The unit ends by asking students to think of some advice they need, ask a partner for this advice, and then decide whether or not they would take this advice.

For those from cultures that have garage sales, the cultural information appears rather innocuous, although it is important to point out that personal reactions to the value of garage sales would vary tremendously among members of cultures that have garage sales. For those from other cultures, however, there may be a good deal that is puzzling. If, for example, this particular text were to be used in Iran, many things would be quite unfamiliar to the students. For instance, when household items are sold in Iran, they are generally sold indoors in the seller's home, and buyers often call and make an appointment to go look at the items for sale. Iranian students would be surprised and perhaps offended by the idea of buying used mattresses, sheets, blankets, and underwear. Also, Iranian students might be puzzled by the selling of pictures because, in Iran, pictures are private items and pictures of family members particularly would never be displayed in a sale. In terms of the exercise on giving advice, this would appear unusual to Iranian students because it is not customary to put signs in Iranian neighborhoods. Finally, Iranian students might be very surprised by the exercise in which they are to ask other students for advice, and then decide whether or not to take the advice. In Iran, one seeks advice from someone who is trusted; hence, it would be extremely unusual not to accept this advice.

How might the cultural elements in the text on garage sales then be dealt with explicitly so as to establish a sphere of interculturality and develop cross-cultural awareness? Obviously, this depends to a large extent on the dynamics of the particular classroom. If the teacher were from a culture that had garage sales, the teacher might explain the meaning that garage sales have for various people in the culture, highlighting the point made earlier that national identities are not monolithic. Hence, for some people, garage sales are a way to save money, for some they are a social activity, for some a diversion, and for others an unpleasant and avoided event. However, since such an event may be largely irrelevant for many Iranian students, what is the value of dealing with the topic? This, again, depends on how the topic is dealt with. One productive approach would be to encourage students to consider their own culture in light of this event. Why do they think garage sales are not common in Iran and that the household sales that do occur differ significantly in what is sold and how the items are sold? Under What circumstances do Iranians seek advice and whom do they consult? In other words, the text could provide a context for students to compare elements of their own culture with another culture, helping them to arrive at a better understanding of their own culture.

The semantic dimension of culture is relevant in the teaching of lexical items. Cultural information on this level is often embedded in common phrases that are introduced in texts with no historical, cultural, or sociological explanation provided. For example, in the United States, readers might come across terms such as the *Big Three Diplomacy, or yellow journalism,* all terms that have developed from the historical and political development of the country. In teaching an international language, teachers are faced with the question of which terms to introduce. Should terms that are highly country specific, such as *yellow journalism,* be introduced, or are there terms that have developed from more general Western traditions, such as *pandora's box, the Midas touch,* or the good Samaritan, that are more applicable to the use of an international language? Clearly, an answer to this question rests largely on the language learning goals of the students. Students who plan to live in the United States may find it useful to know phrases embedded in U. S. culture, whereas students in other contexts may have little need for such vocabulary.

The pragmatic sense of culture is generally introduced in the teaching of speech acts, such as giving and receiving compliments, asking for information, or making and refusing invitations. One danger that can arise in approaching this level of culture is that materials can assume that learners want to acquire rather than learn about how particular speech acts are enacted in specific countries. Hence, in teaching about giving and receiving compliments, many textbooks point out that, in the United State, it is very typical to accept a compliment with phrases such as *thank you.* In this instance, students are essentially presented with information about a particular cultural element. If, however, students are encouraged to receive compliments in this ways of behaving, then the teaching goal becomes one of acquiring rather than learning about culturally bound ways of behaving. Such an approach can present a problem to language learners who, in their own culture, are more likely to scale down or disagree with a compliment. Again, if educators are teaching an international language, then as Smith points out, learners do not need to internalize the cultural norms of another culture.

Cultural Materials in the Classroom

Another important element teachers need to consider with respect to the teaching of an international language is whose culture to teach. Cortazzi and Jin (1999) distinguish three types of cultural information that can be used in language textbooks and materials:

1. target culture materials that use the culture of a country where English is spoken as a first language

2. source culture materials that draw on the learners' own culture as content
3. international target culture materials that use a great variety of cultures in English and non-English-speaking countries around the world

How does the choice of which types of cultural information to use relate to the teaching of EIL? As with all language teaching materials, what to include as content depends on the background and goals of the students and teacher. Let us then examine how the choice of cultural content is affected by the contexts where English is taught.

Today, with the tremendous interest in learning English, one very common classroom context is when the teacher and students come from the same cultural background, but the materials used in the classroom draw heavily on a target culture. This would be the case, for example, in a classroom in Thailand where a Thai teacher is using materials written in the United States or Great Britain. What are some advantages and disadvantages of such an approach to teaching culture? On the plus side. it may be that some students in the class, perhaps due to the popularity of Western films and music, may be interested in learning more about English-speaking culture. Or, it may be that some of the students are preparing to visit or study in English-speaking countries.

On the other hand, it may be that some of the materials are largely irrelevant or uninteresting to some of the students or present cultural conflicts for the students. For example, as was noted above, a discussion of garage sales may be irrelevant to students who do not have such sales in their own country. In a similar situation, a Korean graduate student described his experience using a U.S.-published book with his class in Korea. An exercise in the book instructed students to look at photographs of various scenes depicting different periods of U.S. history and decide in which decade the picture was taken. As one might imagine, students found the task extremely difficult. Furthermore, he as the teacher, had few resources to draw on to help his students. The presentation of such materials may place teachers from the source culture in a troubling position because they may not have the answers to their students' questions about unfamiliar cultural information in the text. This could be especially problematic in a culture where the teacher is considered to be the main source of information. The important question is whether target culture information is useful for teaching an international language in which, as Smith contends, the language becomes de-nationalized and the educational goal is to enable learners to communicate to others their own ideas and culture.

A second situation that can arise in using target culture materials is when the students are from the source culture and the teacher is from target culture, as might happen when a U.S. teacher is working in China. Obviously, many of the advantages and disadvantages mentioned above would apply. However, in this situation, if the teacher were from the target culture dealt with in the text, he or she could explain unknown cultural information. However, this may result in the teacher talking more about his/her culture rather than in allowing the students to use English to tell others about their culture. This is a situation that can also occur in English-speaking countries where the teacher is the provider of cultural information and the students are learning about the target culture. In such a case, there can be a great deal of teacher talk in the classroom, as teachers tell students about their culture. Once again, teachers need to decide the value of such an experience if the students' primary goal is to use EIL to explain their culture to others.

Textbook materials can also use the source culture as cultural content. For example, one Japanese English textbook approved by the Ministry of Education asks students to describe annual Japanese events, such as the Children's Day Festival and the Moon-Viewing Festival, and traditional arts, such as *Haiku* poetry, *Noh* drama, and *Bunraku* puppet shows. These materials could be used with either a Japanese English teacher or a native-English-speaking teacher. What are the implications of such an approach to culture teaching? It is possible that because the students are already familiar with such topics, the textbooks do not motivate them. It may be, however, that students are not well informed about aspects of their own culture and, hence the textbooks could provide them the opportunity to learn more about these topics. Or, if students are familiar with these topics, they may not have the English vocabulary to discuss them. Furthermore, if, as Smith points out, one purpose of an international language is to explain one's own culture to another, then a source culture focus in materials helps students acquire the English needed to do this. Finally, in situations where the teachers are from the source culture, they likely have the background knowledge to provide students with additional information, or at least have access to such information.

It is also possible that source culture texts could be used in contexts where the students come from the source culture but the teacher is from another culture. In such a situation, the teacher, if not familiar with some of the cultural topics, can become an interested listener, creating a real context in which students can tell others about their culture in English. This would seem to be an ideal context for using EIL. What is surprising is that in many non-English-speaking countries where I have worked, teachers and administrators prefer to use a target rather than a source culture in their English textbooks. This, perhaps, is due to the belief that language and culture are inseparable and that English. by definition, still belongs to the countries where English is spoken as a native language.

A final basis for culture materials can be an international target culture in which a great variety of cultural information is presented, representing many English-and non-English -speaking countries. When the students and teachers come from a culture not represented in the text, many of the same problems discussed in reference to the use of a target culture could occur. Students may be uninterested in, or puzzled by, the information in the text, and teachers may not have access to additional information needed to explain some of the cultural information in the materials.

Are there then any benefits that might arise from using content from an international target culture in the teaching of EIL? This, it seems, depends on what cultural information is included and how it is presented. Imagine a text in which L2 speakers of English interact with native and nonnative speakers of English (NNS) in cross-cultural encounters for trade, tourism, and information gathering purposes, including sharing aspects of their culture with others. Such materials could have several benefits. They could illustrate cross-cultural pragmatics in which NNSs, while using English, nevertheless draw on their own rules of appropriateness in interpersonal communication. They could also exemplify the manner in which English is being used effectively by NNSs to communicate with others for international exchange. Finally, they would demonstrate that English today is being used globally by bilingual speakers, who have chosen not to internalize the norms of native-English-speaking countries.

Conclusion

In summary, the teaching of EIL has several important implications for the role of culture in language teaching. First, because individuals who learn an international language do not need to accept the norms of native-English-speaking countries, the teaching of culture needs to focus on giving students knowledge about, rather than suggesting they accept particular cultural values and beliefs. Such an approach need not be limited to EFL teaching; ESL teachers also need to recognize that there are students who would prefer to become bilingual but not necessarily bicultural, even if they plan on living in an English-speaking country. Second, in both ESL and EFL contexts, there is a need to acknowledge the value of including information about the students' own culture. This emphasis on cultural content provides students with the opportunity to learn more about their own culture and to acquire the English to explain their own culture to others, especially to their teacher, if the teacher is from another culture. Ultimately, a recognition that English is an international language highlights the fact that, as more and more individuals learn English, the language belongs to no one culture but, rather, provides the basis for promoting cross-cultural understanding in an increasingly global village.

■ References

Adaskou, K., Britten, D., & Fahsi, B. (1990). Design decisions on the cultural content of a secondary English course for Morocco. *ELT Journal, 44*(1), 3-10.

Byram, M. (1998). Cultural identities in multilingual classroom. In J. Cenoz & F. Genesee(Eds.), *Beyond billingualism* (pp. 96-116). Clevedon, England: Multilingual Matters.

Cortazzi, M., & Jin, L. (1999). Cultural mirrors: Materials and methods in the EFL classroom. In E. Hinkel (Ed.), *Culture in second language teaching* (pp. 196-219). Cambridge: Cambridge University Press.

Crystal, D. (1997). *English as a global language*. Cambridge: Cambridge University Press.

Hynes, M., & Baichman, M. (1989). *Breaking the ice*. New york: Longman.

Kramsch, C. (1993). *Context and culture in language teaching.* Oxford: Oxford University Press.

Paulston, C. B. (1992). *Sociolinguistic perspectives on bilingual education.* Clevedon, England: Multilingual Matters.

Prodromou, L. (1992). What culture? Which culture? Cross-cultural factors in language learning. *ELT Journal*, *46*(2), 39-50.

Smith, L. (1976). English as an international auxiliary language. *RELC Journal*, *7*(2), 38-42.

Widdowson, H. G. (1994). The ownership of English. *TESOL Quarterly*, *28*, 377-388.

From Mckay, S. L, (2000). Teaching English as an international language: Implications for cultural materials in the classroom. *TESOL Journal*, *9*(4), pp. 7-11.

PART EIGHT

TESTING

의사소통 능력을 평가하는 것은 종래의 언어 능력을 평가하는 것과 기본적인 원칙에서 차이가 없다. 다만 정확성만을 평가하는 집필식 방법에서 가능한 한 실제에 가까운 상황을 연출하여 실제 언어사용 능력을 평가하는 식으로 평가방법을 변화시켜야 한다는 평가방식의 차이가 두드러질 뿐이다. 이는 Wesche의 논문을 통해 구체적으로 알아볼 수 있을 것이다.

다음의 두 논문에서는 각각 영어 시험준비 과정과 시험실시 단계에서 교사가 일반적으로 지켜야 할 평가지침과 함께 피해야 할 평가시의 오류를 적고 있다.

마지막으로 비디오 카메라를 사용하여 교실에서 구두 의사소통 능력을 평가하는 구체적인 방법이 소개된다. Haggstrom이 면접, 역할 극 또는 어학실습실을 이용하는 구술평가 방식의 문제점을 인식하고 비디오 카메라로 실험을 하여 효율성을 찾아낸 것이다. 아직도 단순한 듣기평가에 의존하는 우리의 구술평가 방식을 개선하여 진정한 의사소통 능력을 평가하는 방법이 점차 개발되어야 할 것이다.

31. COMMUNICATIVE TESTING IN A SECOND LANGUAGE

In the past decade or so, linguistic science has paid increasing attention to the communicative — or message transmission — aspect of language, as opposed to an earlier almost exclusive emphasis on grammatical forms and the ways in which they could be combined to form grammatical sentences. This shift in our understanding of what it is that native speakers of a language "know" and "can do" has led to widespread rethinking about what the content and organization of second-language courses should be. More recently, attention has increasingly been given to how the communicative ability of second-language speakers can be tested. Some excellent discussions of this question now exist in the literature. This article is an attempt to synthesize for the informed reader some of the main principles as well as some of the unresolved issues which have emerged from these investigations of communicative aspects of language, and to describe several promising approaches to developing "communicative" tests.

WHAT IT IS TO "KNOW" A LANGUAGE: LINGUISTIC AND COMMUNICATIVE COMPETENCE

Chomsky's early hypotheses about the nature of language knowledge were influential in focusing the interests of linguists on formulating the linguistic rules which could describe or "generate" grammatical sentences. "Competence" was viewed as the native speaker's internalized grammar, or regularities underlying his use of the linguistic code (e. g., phonology, lexicon, and syntax). Since competence cannot be directly observed, its imperfect realization in concrete situations, or "performance," although of secondary interest to linguists, was important for the information it could provide about competence. Subsequent work in sociolinguisitcs, pragmatics, and discourse analysis has convincingly demonstrated that the native speaker has, in addition to such a linguistic code grammar, other higher-order internalized rule systems which are also important in determining his or her language behaviour. These include syntactic and semantic constraints and organizational devices at the discourse level which clarify propositional content(reflected in what Widdowson calls the "cohesion" of the discourse). They also include underlying regularities in the ordering of the language functions expressed in discourse which are partially determined by constraints such as speaker intention, the roles and relationships of participants, and other contextual features. These regularities in the illocutionary development of discourse comprise what Widdowson calls its "coherence," and represent one interface between the linguistic code and real-world phenomena. In addition to these discourse phenomena, further extralinguistic constraints on the linguistic forms of verbal behaviour are apparent. For example, sociolinguistic considerations of appropriateness, given the relationship between participants or the formality of a communicative context, may determine the actual choice and ordering of linguistic forms above and beyond considerations of propositional and illocutionary meaning. Non-verbal communicative behaviour is also intimately linked to verbal behaviour, and thus to the particular forms of the linguistic code. Canale and Swain have referred to these regularities in the pragmatic relationships between the linguistic code and the extralinguistic context as "rule-governed, universal and creative aspects of sociolinguistic competence."

Thus there are multiple levels of verbal behaviour at which one may speak of probabilities and constraints, or rule-systems. These include, at least, grammatical, discourse, and sociolinguistic levels. All of these levels of competence are involved in the structuring of communication and contribute to the propositional and social meanings of utterances. Their psychological representation, as an integrated, internalized system for making partial predictions about what will come next in a verbal exchange, has been characterized by Oller as a "grammar of expectancy." The existence of this grammar of expectancy becomes apparent when our expectations about what will happen are violated. We will react with surprise, or may even not understand what is said to us if its form or content is somehow unexpected. On the other hand, we often do not even notice mistakes made by a speaker when we are attending to meaning. Meaning then, does not exist ready-made in the linguistic code, but is rather a function of the relationships between language forms, function, and context, including the intentions of the speaker and the expectations of the hearer.

In this perspective language competence is viewed as a complex system of rule sets which operate simultaneously at many levels to determine the organization of grammatical forms for the fulfillment of communicative and other language functions. Language competence is not "additive," or the sum of discrete sets of syntactic, phonological, morphological, semantic, and discourse-level items and organizational systems. Rather the whole of language knowledge is greater than the sum of the elements and systems which compose it. Communicative competence (which includes linguistic competence), refers, then, to an integrated system of knowledge whose functioning depends at least as much upon the redundancy between the different levels of organization as upon any particular stock of items and patterns.

Language testing which does not take into account propositional and illocutionary development beyond the sentence level, as well as the interaction between language behaviour (verbal and non-verbal) and real-world phenomena, is at best getting at only a part of communicative competence. Small wonder that we often find that a student's success at second-language classroom exercises and tests appears to bear little relationship to his or her ability to use the language effectively in a real-world situation.

Morrow has identified a number of features of language as it is used in communication which have been generally ignored in the teaching and testing of second languages. Language in communication is, for example, *interaction-based* (i. e., occurs between participants in a speech act, each of whom dynamically influences the linguistic behaviour of the other in a multitude of ways). It is to some extent *unpredictable* (although it has norms) so that participants must process new information under time constraints. It is always *purposive* (is intended to fulfill some communicative function such as persuading, conveying information, accepting), is *authentic* (representing a particular dialect, level of formality, etc.), and is *related to the behaviour* of the participants and others. It always occurs in both a verbal (discourse) and an extralinguistic *context.*

The implications of the psycholinguistic model of language competence and of our understanding of the nature of language in use, as described above, are profound. If we aim to evaluate the communicative abilities of second-language learners and speakers, we need to test all levels of competence simultaneously. In other words, we need to engage the examinee's grammar of expectancy. And to do this, the language and the tasks that we use in our tests must have the characteristics of "real" language in use.

CHARACTERISTICS OF LANGUAGE TESTS

Much work is currently in progress in the area of communicative syllabus design. In testing, however, in spite of recognition of the need for communicative tests, recent advances in the development of procedures and guidelines for such tests, and widespread experimentation with communicative tests for specific purposes, the field of testing communicative competence can at best be said to be in an embryonic stage.

Communicative tests share a number of characteristics with other kinds of language tests. They tend to have one of three categories of purpose: evaluation of language *proficiency* (for placement in language courses, admission to programs, certification, etc.), *diagnosis* of particular areas of strength or weakness in language proficiency, and evaluation of *achievement* relevant to a particular instructional unit or program. Tests of all types can also serve to motivate students in their language learning endeavor (or the contrary), and may also be used in the evaluation of instructional programs.

All tests are *samples* of behaviour, intended to reflect whether the examinee possesses certain knowledge, or to predict whether he or she can perform certain acts. Tests generally consist of a number of items, each composed of *stimulus material* and a related *task* which requires a *response* on the part of the examinee. Responses are then scored according to certain *criteria*.

Other important characteristics of a test include its *validity* (does the test measure what it is intended to measure?), *reliability* (will it function in the same way, i. e., will the score gained approach the "true score" of the examinee each time it is given, and in a consistent way with different examinees?), and *feasibility* (is it too expensive and time-consuming with respect to development, administration, or scoring?). (Feasibility is a relative concept based on the time and resources available, and is a consideration which often causes compromises with respect to validity and reliability). Tests should also be interesting, and should not provoke undue anxiety (in the interest of validity and reliability, so that the examinee's best performance will be measured).

Davies has discussed three continua along which tests may be categorized which illuminate several current issues in communicative testing. These are: *discrete point* versus *integrative, indirect* versus *direct*, and *norm* versus *criterion referenced*. The first refers to the degree to which a test emphasizes isolated bits of language knowledge versus more global abilities. "Discrete point" has traditionally referred to tests of grammar in which single sentences are the maximum stimulus unit presented or response required. Such tests also use separate tasks or subtests to assess the "four skills." (Some current writers use the term for all tests in which one element at a time is emphasized, thus including tests of isolated communicative functions. However, such an extension of meaning undermines the usefulness of the distinction between discrete point and integrative tests, since test tasks could conceivably be both at the same time.) The essential point is that discrete point tests select particular levels of language code organization (e. g., phonology, syntax) to test grammatical points (e. g., speech sound discrimination, correct choice of preposition), while generally dealing with only one "skill" reading, writing, listening, or speaking). Test stimuli and/or responses can be discrete point. The higher the level of language organization used in a test, the more "integrative" it is. Tests at the integrative end of the scale present language in discourse (rather than at the sentence, or word, or syllable) level, and activate the expectancy grammar. (Examples include auditory and written cloze, dictation, interviews, reading and listening passages in which questions require global comprehension, and written essays.)

Oller distinguishes that subset of integrative tests which also take into account appropriate extralinguistic context as "pragmatic" tests, and maintains that only with such tests can we validly measure language proficiency (i. e., communicative competence and performance). Some authors argue that discrete point tests (in the old sense) have a place when the purpose of the test is diagnostic, but Oller and others maintain that even for this purpose integrative (or pragmatic) tests are best; that analysis of the examinee's errors on an integrative task can tell more about his or her specific language problems than any highly artificial discrete point task. The implications for communicative competence testing would seem clear; our test tasks should be as high on the integrative scale as possible; the tests should be pragmatic. At the same time, in our analysis of examinee responses we can look at very specific aspects of performance if that fits our objectives (i. e., "discrete point" *scoring* in Morrow's and Howard's sense.)

The indirect versus direct continuum refers to the degree to which a test task approaches the actual criterion performance. A direct test at the extreme end of the scale would involve actually performing the criterion behaviour in a real-life situation (i. e., a university student demonstrating adequate second-language mastery by successfully functioning in a course of study in the host country; a public servant efficiently taking an office telephone message in the second language). Something short of direct testing is needed to predict how the examinee will function in the real-life situation. The tests which we devise for this purpose are always a simulation of some kind, but there is a range of artificiality or authenticity possible in a testing situation. Indirect testing involves using sample of relatively unrelated behaviour to predict the examinee's performance in the eventual target situation. The Test of English as a Foreign Language (TOEFL) is an example of a relatively indirect measure. A written essay or true-false grammar test used to qualify tour guides, or an oral interview used to certify graduate students as being able to do library research in their second language, are at the extreme indirect end of the scale with respect to their objectives. Likewise, a written cloze test used to measure speaking proficiency is an indirect measure. Indirect measures are often favoured for reasons of practicality. There may be some cases where results of indirect tests correlate quite highly with more direct measures of criterion performance. However, in any given case this must be demonstrated. In communicative testing, it would seem that our tests should be as direct as possible, and that any indirect measures must be shown to reliably predict the criterion performance in real-life language use or at least to have concurrent validity with more direct measures.

The issue of norm versus criterion referencing refers to the degree to which an examinee's performance on a test is judged in terms of the performance of others (as in standardized tests which yield percentile rankings), versus the degree to which it is a measure of his or her progress toward a specific objective and level of performance (as in a driving test, where a minimum score must be achieved regardless of the performance of others). Obviously, criterion referencing is only possible where specific objectives exist. The levels required may also be based on norm referencing, as an indication of what degree of proficiency may be reasonably expected. In communicative testing, norm referencing is probably appropriate when the purpose is to determine placement in a multi-level instructional program. But it would seem that achievement tests in instructional programs where learners need to reach a certain level of performance for given objectives, or where different learners are working toward different objectives (as often happens at advanced levels) should give both students and instructors feedback on how far the students have advanced toward each objective. Test tasks should then ideally be designed to give not only a "yes" or "no" answer as to whether the examinee can "do" a task, but should indicate how well he or she can do it relative to how well he or she needs to do it. In some programs it may be appropriate to use both criterion and norm referencing; in others, one or the other may be most appropriate. Because communicative testing presumes adequate definition of objectives, based on learner needs, criterion referencing is a possibility.

CHARACTERISTICS OF COMMUNICATIVE TESTS

How, then, should we test communicative ability in the second language?

1. We want to tap communicative and not only grammatical competence. Therefore our tests, to be *valid,* must activate the internalized rule systems by which discourse is meaningfully processed, including those by which sociolinguistic variables influence language behaviour. Such tests should be *integrative, pragmatic* tests, involving the use of naturalistic language in both a verbal and situational context. Since we wish to test grammatical and discourse-level competence as part of communicative competence, we may wish to look explicitly at the *usage* characteristics of language (the correctness of grammatical forms and their organization) as demonstrated through language in *use*. Such evaluation, however, will center on the way the examinee's responses are scored, rather than on the nature of the tasks presented. The test tasks and scoring criteria should also allow evaluation of the *appropriateness* of the examinee's responses in terms of illocutionary development and the sociolinguistic variables present. At the least, they should require the examinee to recognize appropriate (versus inappropriate) responses.

2. We want to test the examinee's ability to meet specific target language needs in given situations, as defined in the objectives of the test. We want to know whether the learner can "do" something in the second language with an acceptable degree of efficiency (including such considerations as speed of processing and correctness) as well as appropriateness to the situation. Ideally, then, our tests should be as *direct* as possible. Role-playing, listening to or reading authentic second-language material, and carrying out realistic tasks in the language are ways of simulating criterion situations.

3. We wish to test performance in a range of situations which reflect our objectives, thus in most cases we will wish to test the examinee's manipulation of a *variety of language functions.* While oral interview tests of speaking proficiency may admirably evaluate performance of the functions of narration and information-giving in a formal,

stranger/stranger, unequal-status communicative situation, and may also give us information about the quality of the examinee's language usage, they will probably tell us relatively little about his or her ability to "do" other kinds of things in the target language. The range and distribution of situations covered by our test items, then, should — at least until we have a coherent theory of the generalizability of communicative enabling skills — correspond to the range and distribution of our objectives.

4. We want to know how well or how badly the examinee can meet particular objectives. Therefore we will ideally use *criterion referencing* in our tests, so that the performance of each examinee is compared with a definition of adequate performance on the task rather than with the performance of other examinees.

5. We want our tests to be *reliable.* This test characteristic is particularly problematic with respect to scoring criteria and procedures. Communicative tests of global productive skills (e. g., free composition, oral interview) will probably require a scoring method which uses global judgements by native speakers. High levels of inter- and intra-rater reliability can be achieved in such cases, but generally only through the careful training of raters and long experience with a particular test format and scoring grid (i. e., at considerable expense). We must carefully experiment with and analyze the results of our new testing approaches to improve reliability.

6. We want our tests to be *feasible.* Therefore they obviously cannot have all of the above desirable characteristics all of the time. However, by taking into consideration these characteristics we can at least strive to make our tests better measures of communicative competence.

AN EXAMPLE OF COMMUNICATIVE TESTS

This section will present a test which aims to evaluate second language communication skills. Developed in the United States, it is based on van Ek's specifications of threshold second-language objectives for adults.

Function Test For English As A Second Language Students At UCLA

Farhady has recently developed a new approach to communicative test development, based on the van Ek threshold specifications for adults.

Format: A 64-item multiple choice written test based on common university situations involving foreign students. A situation involving several participants is described. Examinees choose the one response of four which is both grammatically correct and socially appropriate.

Purpose: To test "functional competence" (defined by Farhady as consisting of linguistic and socio-cultural competence) in oral communication. Scores are to be used in the placement of incoming foreign students in ESL courses.

Specifications for test items: Two language functions, each with four subfunctions relevant to an academic environment, were selected from van Ek's taxonomy (e. g., "finding out and expressing intellectual attitudes"; "getting things done"). The social relations of friend and stranger and equal or unequal status are reflected in items representing all possible combinations of these variables for each subfunction.

Procedures: Situations were composed based on each subfunction. The test was then tried out in open-ended response form with both native and non-native speakers. Their responses provided the correct multiple-choice responses (the preferred native speaker response) and three distractors for each item (chosen from non-native speaker incorrect responses). In each set of responses, one distractor was linguistically correct but socially inappropriate, one was linguistically incorrect but socially appropriate, and one was both incorrect and inappropriate.

Example

Interlocutors: student and professor (unequal status, friend/friend)

Function: getting things done

Subfunction: requesting others to do something

Setting: academic environment

Stimulus: You were applying to a university and needed a letter of recommendation. You went to a professor, who was also your friend, and said:

Responses

1. "I'd appreciate it if you could write a letter of recommendation for me." (functional response)
2. "I want to ask you to write a letter of recommendation for me." (linguistic response)
3. "I wonder if you could write a letter recommending to me." (social response)
4. "Hey, give me a recommendation letter." (distractor)

Extensive pretesting was done, first to elicit responses, then to verify native-speaker versus non-native-speaker performance on the multiple choice format.

Scoring: For each item the correct *and* appropriate response is worth two points, a response which is either correct or appropriate is worth one point, and the response which is neither appropriate nor correct receives no points.

Comments

This test has certain very strong qualities, notably its testing of both linguistic accuracy and sociolinguistic appropriacy based on an explicit model of communicative competence. It also uses authentic (native speaker) responses among the possible answers, and examinees are required to distinguish these from actually occurring non-native responses. It was constructed in accordance with specific communicative objectives. It presents varied situations requiring a variety of language functions. Statistical properties, including concurrent validity and, particularly, reliability, are high. It is not a direct test, however, of what the speaker would say, but rather an indirect test of his ability to recognize what should be said, based on the choices given. Since only sentence-level responses are required to a situation specified in a brief description, it is doubtful that discourse-level competence is tapped, although the test does have some pragmatic qualities in the sense that contextual constraints on language behaviour are important. The test is only indirectly "interaction based" nor does it require the examinee to deal with unpredictability. Scoring is objective, which makes possible high reliability. The test is very practical in administration and scoring, although the development process was laborious. Where large numbers of students must be tested on a regular basis this represents a feasible approach to evaluating certain aspects of communicative competence.

MAKING TESTS "MORE" COMMUNICATIVE

The preceding discussion and references provide a number of suggestions about how to develop tests which to some extent tap features of communicative competence. These suggestions also have relevance where new tests will not be developed, but where items may be replaced or changed. In situations where for practical reasons one is "hooked into" traditional test formats (e. g., where rapid, mass testing is involved, communicative needs of examinees are heterogeneous or unknown, resources are not available to develop innovative tests, or instruction is grammar-based), so that "ideal" communication tests will not be developed in the foreseeable future, it is at least possible to give some importance to communicative aspects of language. This can be done by including in existing test formats some sub-tests or items clearly based on a communicative view of language competence. One can seek to use authentic, longer (discourse-level), contextualized language texts in stimulus items or multiple-choice responses. (Reading passages, recorded dialogues, and cloze tests all lend themselves to this possibility.) One can ask listening and reading comprehension questions based on a global understanding of the meaning conveyed through language use in context, rather than pinpointing discrete grammatical points. One can ask questions about the appropriateness of contextualized language behaviors, or about situational aspects of an exchange (e. g., the roles, relationships, attitudes, and intended meanings of participants). Scoring of oral and written performance tasks can take into account getting the message across, different ways of expressing ideas, and appropriateness, as well as grammatical aspects. Multiple choice responses and acceptable cloze answers can be based on native speaker responses.

CONCLUSION

An examination of the theoretical constructs, issues, and practical work done so far in communicative testing would appear to have relevance for anyone involved in second-language testing, no matter what the situation. By making our tests more reflective of the kinds of situations, language content and purposes for which second-language speakers will need their skills, we will be able to make more accurate predictions about how well they will be able to function using the target language in "real life." Such testing is likely to have dramatic effects on the format and content of second-language curricula, as well, and to improve student motivation through its increased relevance. The foregoing discussion is an attempt to describe the underlying concepts and current issues in communicative testing, and to illustrate recent application of these ideas for practitioners.

■ References

Bailey, K. M. (1985). If I had known then what I know now: Performance testing of foreign teaching assistants. In P. Hauptman, R. LeBlanc, and M. Wesche (eds.), *Second Language Performance Testing/L'Evaluation de la "performance" en Langue Seconde.* Ottawa: University of Ottawa Press.

Campbell, R., and R. Wales. (1970). The study of language acquisition. In J. Lyons (ed.), *New Horizons.* Harmondsworth: Penguin.

Canale, M., and M. Swain. (1979). *A Domain Description for Core FSL: Communication Skills.* Report for the Ministry of Education, Toronto, Ontario.

_____. (1980). Theoretical bases of communicative approaches to second language teaching and testing. *Applied Linguistics, 1,* 1-47.

_____. and N. Villaroel. (1979). *The Ontario Assessment Instrument Pool: French as a Second Language, Junior and Intermediate Divisions.* Toronto: Ontario Ministry of Education.

Candlin, C. N. (1976). Communicative language teaching and the debt to pragmatics. In C. Rameh (ed.), *Semantics: Theory and Application.* Washington: Georgetown University Press.

Carroll, B. J. (1978a). *Guidelines for the Development of Communicative Tests.* London: Royal Society of Arts.

_____. (1978b). *The Assessment of Communicative Performance.* London: Royal Society of Arts.

_____. (1980). *Testing Communicative Performance.* Oxford: Pergamon.

_____. (1981). Specifications for an English language testing service. In J. C. Alderson and A. Hughes (eds.), *Issues in Language Testing. ELT Documents 111.* London: The British Council.

_____. (1985). Second language performance testing for university and professional contexts. In P. Hauptman, R. LeBlanc, and M. Wesche (eds.), *Second Language Performance Testing/L'Evaluation de la "Performance" en Langue Seconde.* Ottawa: University of Ottawa Press.

Carroll, J. B. (1974). Learning theory for the classroom teacher. In G. Jarvis, *The Challenge of Communication.* Skokie, IL: National Textbook Co.

CITO (Dutch National Institute for Educational Measurement). (1984). *Spreek-toetsen* (Speaking Test

Manual). Arnhem, The Netherlands: CITO.

Clark, J. L. D. (1978). Interview testing research at educational testing service. In J. L. D. Clark (ed.), *Direct Testing of Speaking Proficiency: Theory and Application*. Princeton: Educational Testing Service.

_____. and A. G. Grognet. (1985). Development and validation of a performance-based test of ESL "survival skills." In P. Hauptman, R. LeBlanc and M. Wesche (eds.), *Second Language Performance Testing/L'Evaluation de la "Performance" en Langue Seconde*. Ottawa: University of Ottawa Press.

Commisson Scolaire Régionale de l'Outaouais. (1978). *Program cadre: Programme par objectifs niveau 1, Module 1-4*. Service a l'Enseignement, Départment des Langues Secondes.

Cray, E., and M. Wesche. (1984). The Ontario test of English as a second language (OTESL): A progress report. *TESL Talk*, *15*, 3.

Davies, A. (1979). Continuum categories for language tests. Paper presented at the 13th annual TESOL Convention, Boston.

DesBrisay, M. (1979). A report on the English proficiency test. *Centre for Second Language Learning/Institut de Langues Vivantes Journal, 20*, 99-104.

________. (1982). A feasibility study of large-scale communicative testing. *Journal of Applied Language Study*, *1*, 1, 77-86.

________. M. Wesche, D. Taylor, and W. Feldberg. (1980). Report on the test of English proficiency for graduate students in history. *Centre for Second Language Learning/Institute de Langues Vivantes Journal*, *22*, 52-58.

Educational Testing Service. (1981). *TOEFL Test and Score Manual*. Princeton, NJ: Educational Testing Service.

Emmett, A. (1985). The associated examining board's test in English for educational purposes (TEEP). In P. Hauptman, R. LeBlanc, and M. Wesche (eds.), *Second Language Performance Testing/L'Evaluation de la "performance" en Langue Seconde*. Ottawa: University of Ottawa Press.

Farhady, H. (1979). *New Directions for ESL Proficiency Testing*. Manuscript. TESL Program. University of Southern California, Los Angeles.

Godbout, R. (1980). Un probléme spécifique d'évaluation: La compréhension de l'écrit aux études supérieures en histoire. *Centre for Second Language Learning/Institut de Langues Vivantes Journal, 22*, 46-51.

Green, Dana Z. (1985). Developing measures of communicative proficiency: A test for French immersion students in Grades 9 and 10. In P. Hauptman, R. LeBlanc, and M. Wesche (eds.), *Second Language Performance Testing/L'Evaluation de la "Performance" en Langue Seconde*. Ottawa: University of Ottawa Press.

Hautman, P., R. LeBlanc, and M. Wesche. (eds.). (1985). *Second Language Performance Testing/L'Evaluation de la "Performance" en Langue Seconde*. Ottawa: University of Ottawa Press.

Hinofotis, F. B., K. M. Bailey, and S. L. Stern. (1979). Assessing improvement in oral communication: Raters' perception of change. *UCLA Workpapers in Teaching English as a Second Language*.

Howard, F. (1980). Testing communicative proficiency in French as a second language: A search for procedures. *Canadian Modern Language Review*, *36*, 272-289.

Hymes, D. (1967). Models of the interaction of language and social setting. *Problems of Bilingualism: Journal of Social Issues, 23*, 8-28.

______. (1972). On communicative competence. In J. B. Pride and J. Holmes (eds.), *Sociolinguistics*.

Harmondsworth: Penguin.

Ingram, E. (1978). The psycholinguistic basis. In B. Spolsky (ed.), *Approaches to Language Testing.* Arlington, VA: Center for Applied Linguistics.

Jones, R. L. (1985). Second language performance testing: An overview. In P. Hauptman, R. LeBlanc, and M. Wesche (eds.), *Second Language Performance Testing/L'Evaluation de la "Performance" en Langue Seconde.* Ottawa: University of Ottawa Press.

Krashen, S. D. (1978). Adult second language acquisition and learning: A review of theory and practice. Presentation at the Language Training Branch, Public Service Commission of Canada, Ottawa.

_______. (1981). The "Fundamental Pedagogical Principle" in second language teaching. *Studia Linguistica, 35*, 1-2, 50-70.

_______. (1982). *Principles and Practice in Second Language Acquisition.* Oxford: Pergamon Press.

Krowitz, M. J., and M. Garcia-Zamor. (1978). Towards measuring functional language proficiency. In G. Nickel (ed.), *Applied Linguistics: Language Testing*. Stuttgart: Hochschulverlag.

Krupka, L. (1985). Evaluation de la performance linguistique de professeurs d'université.. In P. Hauptman, R. LeBlanc, and M. Wesche (eds.), *Second Language Performance Testing/L'Evaluation de la "Performance en Langue Seconde.* Ottawa: University of Ottawa Press.

LeBlanc, R. (1985). Le testing de performance en langue second: Perspective canadienne (avec la collaboration de Renée Proulx-Dubé, Mireille Voyer, Diane Pruneau, Pascal- André Charlebois et Marjorie B. Wesche). In P. Hauptman, R. LeBlanc, and M. Wesche (eds.), *Second Language Performance Testing/L'Evaluation de la "Performance" en Langue Seconde.* Ottawa: University of Ottawa Press.

Macnamara, J. (1973). Nurseries, streets and classrooms: Some comparisons and deductions. *Modern Language Journal*, *57*, 250-254.

Morrow, K. R. (1979). Communicative language testing: Revolution or evolution? In C. Brumfit and K. Johnson (eds.), *The Communicative Approach to Language Teaching.* London: Oxford University Press.

Munby, J. (1978). *Communicative Syllabus Design*. Cambridge: Cambridge University Press.

Newmark, L. D. (1971). A minimal language teaching program. In P. Pimsleur and A. Quinn (eds.), *The psychology of Second Language Learning*. Cambridge: Cambridge University Press.

Noyons, J. (1985). The standardized testing of oral proficiency in the Netherlands. In P. Hauptman, R. LeBlanc, and M. Wesche (eds.), *Second Language Performance Testing/L'Evaluation de la "Performance" en Langue Seconde*. Ottawa: University of Ottawa Press.

Oller, J. (1973). Pragmatic language testing. *Language Sciences*, *28*, 7-12.

_____. (1978). Application of pragmatic theory to language teaching and testing. Presentation at the Language Training Branch, Public Service Commission of Canada, Ottawa.

_____. (1979). *Language Tests at School.* London: Longman.

Proulx-Dubé, R. (1985). Ateliers sur divers aspects de l'évaluation de la performance linguistique des candidats inscrits aux programmes de formation linguistique de la fonction publique canadienne. In P. Hauptman, R. LeBlanc, and M. Wesche (eds.), *Second Language Performance Testing/L'Evaluation de la "Performance" en Langue Seconde.* Ottawa: University of Ottawa Press.

Richterich, R. (1975). L'analyse des besoins langagiers: Illusion, prétexte, nécessité. *Education et Culture, 28*, 9-14.

Roos-Wygh, I. (1978). Research and development projects in language proficiency interviewing. In

J. L. D. Clark (ed.), *Direct Testing of Speaking Proficiency: Theory and Application*. Princeton, NJ: Educational Testing Service.

Royal Society of Arts Examinations Board. (1980). *Examinations in the Communicative Use of English as a Foreign Language.* London: Royal Society of Arts.

Savignon, S. J. (1977). Communicative competence: Theory and classroom practice. *Revue de la Société pour la Promotion de l'Anglais au Québec*, 1.

Seaton, I. (1985). Issues in the validation of the English Language Testing Service (ELTS). 1976-1983. In P. Hauptman, R. LeBlanc, and M. Wesche (eds.), *Second Language Performance Testing/ L'Evaluation de la "Performance" en Langue Seconde*. Ottawa: University of Ottawa Press.

Spolsky, B. (1978). What does it mean to know a language? In *Educational Linguistics: an Introduction.* Rowley, MA: Newbury House Publishers.

Stern, H. H. (1975). What can we learn from the good language learner? *Canadian Modern Language Review, 31*, 304-318.

_____. (1978a). Bilingual schooling and foreign language education: Some implications of Canadian experiments in French immersion. In J. E. Alatis (ed.), I*nternational Dimensions of Bilingual Education.* Washington: Georgetown University Press.

_____. (1980). Language learning on the spot, some thoughts on the language aspect of student exchange programs. *Canadian Modern Language Review*, *36*, 659-669.

_____. (1981). Communicative language teaching and learning: Toward a synthesis. In H. B. Altman and P. M. Alatis (eds.), *The Second Language Classroom: Directions for the 1980's.* New York: Oxford University Press.

Stevick, E. (1976). *Memory, Meaning and Method.* Rowley, MA: Newbury House Publishers.

Swain, M. (1982). Large scale communicative language testing: A case study. Paper presented at the International Symposium on Language Testing, University of Hong Kong.

Terrell, T. D. (1977). A natural approach to second language acquisition and learning. *Modern Language Journal, 61*, 325-339.

Tréville, M. C. (1985). Deux tests faits sur mesure. In P. Hauptman, R. LeBlanc, and M. Wesche (eds.), *Second Language Performance Testing/L'Evaluation de la "Performance" en Langue Seconde*, Ottawa: University of Ottawa Press.

van Ek, J. A. (1975). *The Threshold Level in a European Unit/Credit System for Modern Language Learning by Adults*. Strasbourg: Council of Europe.

_______. (1976). *The Threshold Level in Modern Language Learning in Schools*. Strasbourg: Council of Europe.

Wesche, M. B. (1984). Performance testing at the University of Ottawa. *Centre for Sentre for Second Language Learning/Institut de Langues Vivntes Journal*, *29*, 156-166.

_______. (1979). Learning behaviors of successful adult students on intensive language training. *Canadian Modern Language Review*. *35*, 415-430.

_______. (1985). Introduction. In P. Hauptman, R. LeBlanc, and M. Wesche (eds.), *Second Language Performance Testing/L'Evaluation de la "Performance" en Langue Seconde.* Ottawa: University of Ottawa Press.

Widdowson, H. G. (1978). *Teaching Language as Communication*. London: Oxford University Press.

From Wesche, B. M. (1983). Communicative testing in a second language, The *Modern Language Journal, 67*, pp. 41-55.

32. GUIDELINES FOR CLASSROOM TESTING

1. Test objectives

The purpose of a classroom achievement test is to evaluate student attainment of objectives for any given segment of material. Any test, or any portion of a test, that the teacher cannot relate to specific objectives in his lesson plans needs to be carefully scrutinized and probably revamped. Time restrictions may make it impossible to prepare questions for all the objectives, but a representative sample should be covered. The important thing is to remember that any group of items should be thought of as a check on the attainment of goals.

2. Test what has been taught

Just as the test should reflect the objectives, it should also reflect the classroom procedures that were employed to accomplish those objectives. In other words, the test should only include items that are of the same type as the exercises used to teach the structures and vocabulary involved. Words and forms certainly should be recombined, but the types of exercises should be the same. Too often the language teacher is guilty of using certain procedures in class but testing with different techniques. If one were learning to play the piano, for example, the test should include various pieces that have been practiced. It is not uncommon in language classes for the teacher to ask the students to play a different piece, or perhaps even to write a composition, rather than play anything at all.

3. Distinguish between recall and recognition tests

In taking a *recognition test*, the students select the correct answer from a number of alternatives. The alternatives may range from two in true-false questions to more than two in a multiple-choice test (normally three, four, or five) to several grouped items in a matching exercise. The tendency is to have fewer distractors in listening comprehension items and more in reading items. Since listening and reading are receptive skills, recognition-type questions are most suited to the testing of these two skills.

In taking a *recall test,* the students must produce the cued responses rather than select the appropriate one. A recall test measures the students' ability to apply functional understanding in order to produce language. Recall items, then, must be used to test the productive skills, speaking and writing, since the nature of the skill itself involves production rather than recognition. One commonly used type of recall item is to ask students to write answers to personalized questions such as "What's your name?" The principle of testing only one language skill at a time can be modified in this case, since in the normal language situation the receptive skills quite commonly serve as stimuli to the productive skills.

4. Test all four language skills

If the objectives in the course include all four language skills, all four should be tested. The implication here is that each test should include one section to test listening comprehension, one for speaking, one for reading, and one for writing. If the teacher customarily limits herself to pencil-and-paper tests, these types of exercises become, in effect, the practical goals of the students. She can correct this common fault by including some items involving each of the language skills on each examination.

The aforestated guideline also carries another implication — the word *skill*. As well as testing all four skills, the teacher should also be careful to test the material covered as a skill, not as a set of memorized vocabulary words and verb forms. Admittedly, language is made up of sounds, words, and structures. There is a great deal of difference, however, between testing concepts in some communicative context as opposed to regurgitating a word from a memorized list. Testing the students' ability to answer the question, "Are you a student?" by writing, "Yes, I am a student," is entirely different from asking him to write the first-person singular of the verb *to be*. Asking the students to choose a word in the second language that correctly completes a series of statements such as the following does not involve the same skill as asking them how to say "get up" in the second language: *The sun was shining. The alarm was ringing. Slowly I realized that it was time to* _________.

5. Test one thing at a time

There are two considerations related to this statement. First, as far as possible each skill should be tested separately from any other skill. The answers to listening comprehension items, for example, should be given orally. Or the students might possibly choose from pictures or some other visual aid rather than read the answers in the language. There are sufficient visual cues to elicit the desired responses in speaking. Even though visual aids provide excellent stimuli to certain portions of the speaking test, many items on the speaking test will be cued in the language. This type of item does involve listening comprehension as well as speaking, but this practice can be defended on the basis that such a combination is the normal one in everyday conversational situations. The teacher should, however, remember that the primary function of the speaking portion of the test is to test the speaking skill and consequently to limit the oral cues to those that the students are certain to understand. The same relationship also exists between the written receptive skill, reading, and the productive skill, writing.

Second, within each of the language skill tests, the teacher should test only one point at a time. If he is writing an item to test vocabulary, the students should be aware that word or words are to be tested and that syntax is not involved. For example:

For their golden wedding anniversary my grandparents received many gifts and had many ________.

a. weddings b. visitors c. new excuses

If he is testing structural knowledge, all the distractors, i. e., the answers given, should involve forms of words rather than just words. For example:

His sister is ________ the gifts.

a. opening b. received c. looks for

Another case in point is the speaking test. When judging the students' pronunciation, the teacher should grade only one sound per utterance. When evaluating the use of grammatical forms, he should grade only the grammar and not focus upon the pronunciation and vocabulary. Similarly, vocabulary should be graded independently of the pronunciation and structural manipulation. Only in this fashion is objectivity and identification of specific weaknesses possible.

6. Weight exam according to objectives

Since the test is to reflect the classroom objectives, it should be weighted according to the stress placed on each of the language skills. If the teacher wants to emphasie all four language skills equally and has endeavored to do so in his class activities, one fourth of the exam should test listening comprehension, one fourth speaking, one fourth reading, and one fourth writing. This is not to say that each portion of the exam should be equal in length, but that the weights assigned to each should be equal. On an examination graded according to a scale of one hundred points, each portion would be worth twenty-five points. (A test of any length may be converted to a hundred-point scale by multiplying or dividing.) Normally, a test of speaking and writing will include more separate factors to grade. Therefore, each might be worth fewer points even though the total score would be the same as on the listening and reading portions of the test. Conversely, the listening and reading sections will most likely have fewer points to grade, but each will be worth more.

7. Sequence the items from easy to more difficult

Most students enter an examination slightly apprehensive about their ability to answer the questions. Even though most of this anxiety can be extinguished in any given class before it becomes a real problem, the aura of testing remains. Therefore, one of the teacher's tasks in preparing the items is to include a few at the beginning which most students should be able to do fairly easily. This progressive introduction will help to reestablish their confidence and to set them at ease. Thus, the resulting score should be more representative of their true ability.

Another reason for arranging the items in each portion of the test in an order of ascending difficulty is to insure that some items are included that will challenge each student's ability level. There should be some items that each student can get fairly easily and some that challenge each student. In this sense, arranging the items from easier to more difficult is merely another way of acknowledging individual differences on the test. Slower students, for example, should not be expected to complete all the items if they do not feel capable of doing them. Faster students may be given extra-credit items, which will keep them occupied while the others finish the examination.

8. Avoid incorrect language

This guideline is obvious. The students make enough errors in the classroom without the teacher contributing some of her own. Equally obvious is the fact that, with some ingenuity, the teacher can test the common errors without actually committing them herself.

9. Make directions clear

The purpose of a test is to measure achievement, not cleverness in reading the directions. The students should be encouraged to ask questions if they fail to comprehend what is expected, and, if possible, the teacher should circulate through the class during the exam to check whether they did in fact understand. (Many beginning teachers are astounded to learn that asking, "Are there any questions?" is not sufficient. Many students do not know what kind of questions they should be asking. The teacher is always responsible for determining whether there indeed are questions; asking if there are any questions is usually an ineffective procedure.)

10. Prepare items in advance and prepare more than you need

The preparation of test items is a difficult and time-consuming task. Often the teacher is not aware of the weaknesses of his examinations. He can improve this situation by preparing the test in advance and by having more items than are needed. In a few days he can go over all the items again, eliminating the weaker ones. After the test, those questions which appear to be good ones can be placed in an item file for future reference. Categorizing these by structural topic will speed up location later on. The vocabulary associated with each item is easily and quickly changed.

11. Specify the material to be tested

Although the teacher may feel that the students should know what the examination will cover, and although he may have been extremely careful to convey the objectives of each class to them, he still should delineate exactly the material that will be tested. Such a summary motivates the students to study and focuses their attention on the most important concepts in the lessons while they are studying. Much time is wasted by students as they attempt to develop a learning strategy and to organize the basic knowledge to be assimilated. By outlining what should be reviewed, the teacher can assist them in spending their time more efficiently.

12. Acquaint the students with techniques

Normally there should be little difference between the normal classroom activities and test items. However, if the teacher does occasionally consider it necessary to include an innovative type of item distinct from classroom techniques, he should provide the students some practice with this type of item before counting the results as part of a grade. For example, if the teacher decides to ask the students to record their speaking tests in the language laboratory, they must first be well acquainted with the lab. Even then, he may want to consider the first test as a practice run.

13. Test in context

This concept was previously considered in the discussion of testing all four language skills. The teacher who tests vocabulary and structure has a tendency to revert to teaching a problem-solving class, i. e., one in which the teacher and the students focus on the means rather than on the ends, on the building blocks of language rather than on the application of these components to actual communication situations. He should always try to write items as similar as possible to language that would occur in actual usage. Furthermore, testing in context implies that often a contextual situation must be established clarifying for the students exactly what the correct answer would be. In distinguishing between the two past tenses in French and Spanish, for example, the teacher is almost forced to write an entire paragraph in order to establish a definite relationship between the two tenses. Even in testing a vocabulary item, a contextual situation may need to be established. For example:

Did you get the letter?
No, the ____ still has not arrived.
a. card b. code c. male d. mail

14. Avoid sequential items

A sequential item is one that has two or three stages, with the later parts being dependent upon the first. Those students who fail on the first part will automatically be unable to do well on the second or third. An obvious example is giving a dictation and then asking the students to translate the paragraph into English. Those who were not able to write the dictated sentences receive a double penalty. Another example is the test item with a blank in which they are supposed to write the correct form of a verb (given in the first language) in the second language. If they do not know the vocabulary word, it is impossible for them to give the correct form of the verb.

15. Sample fairly the material covered

The teacher should strive on each examination to sample fairly all the objectives and all the various types of activities included in the lesson plans. She may be unable to write specific items testing all the concepts taught, but by randomly sampling those taught in class, she should receive scores that are representative of the students' total learning. This statement also implies two other important concepts in testing: (a) all four language skills should be tested, and (b) items of varying levels of difficulty should be included.

One effective aid for obtaining a random sample is to keep a checklist of all material covered in the view and review in each of the language skills. Using this outline, the teacher should have little difficulty sampling the content in each of the language skills at various levels of difficulty. Attempting to implement the guidelines mentioned in this paragraph, the teacher may tend toward examinations that are too long. Over any given amount of material the possibilities for items are almost unlimited, and the teacher must refrain from attempting to include everything. Testing each selected concept or form once is sufficient. In testing verbs, for example, there is no need to include more than one item testing the ability to use the first-person singular form. In fact, testing all four language skills permits the teacher to test some forms or concepts in one skill and others in another skill, thereby shortening considerably the necessary length of the test.

16. Allow sufficient time to finish

This statement must be qualified in the case of listening and speaking. All students must answer the same listening items given at the same speed. This also applies to speaking tests given in the laboratory, in which all students must respond at approximately the same time. On the written portions of the examination, however, some students will be able to finish much more quickly than others. Since this variety of speeds is common in most classes, and since having to turn in an unfinished test is frustrating to most students, the teacher should take care to allow everyone to finish before collecting the papers. He can accomplish this trick of keeping everyone busy, either by giving the faster students extra-credit questions or by permitting the slower students to omit certain difficult items on the test. The teacher is protecting the students' right to answer all the items, but he cannot permit them to sit and meditate over particular items. Quizzes especially must be completed quickly and collected. Normally, those students in a second-language class who wait for a sudden flash of inspiration continue to remain in the dark. In the case of languages, they either know it or they do not, so little is accomplished by letting the few who are unwilling to accept their fate waste valuable class time.

17. Make the test easy to grade, if possible

Of course, making the test easy to grade is not a primary consideration, but the teacher must arrange her time as efficiently as possible. One way of decreasing her work load is to consider beforehand the amount of time necessary to grade the examination. By choosing types of items that can be graded quickly, she can eliminate some unnecessary work. One simple example is to have the students always place their answers in a column to the left of the number of the item rather than filling in a blank or circling the letter of the correct answer in multiple-choice questions. Their answers then become a list that can be graded almost in a single glance. Another technique that greatly speeds up the grading of examinations is to grade one group of items on all the papers before continuing to the next section. By grading in this fashion, the teacher has the correct answers memorized after the first few papers, and her speed increases tremendously. Grading the entire test of each student before proceeding to the next student's paper is much slower. Writing the number of errors in each section in the margin will speed up the tabulation of the total score at the completion of the last section. Too, preparation of an answer key along with the test is a time-saving device.

Of course, grading tests in which students select answers is easier and quicker than grading tests in which students give their own answers in writing or speaking. In this sense, normally it takes less time to grade tests over the receptive skills than over the productive. This relative ease in grading, however, is counterbalanced by the fact that the preparation of good objective tests in which the students select answers take longer to prepare than short-answer and essay-type questions. Since a test covering all four skills must, by definition, include both selecting and giving answers, the teacher needs to gain expertise in preparing and grading both types of items.

18. Go over the test immediately afterwards, if possible

The students' interest is highest during and immediately after a test. The teacher should take advantage of this peak of interest by giving the correct answers as soon as he collects the papers. Some teachers prefer to have the students exchange papers and grade them in class. At any rate, the point is that an examination is also a learning experience, and as such, it is always preferable to review the correct answers with the students. The best time to clarify difficulties and doubts is at the end of the test. The students should never have to wait more than a day, possibly two, to see the results.

19. Help those students with problems to determine specific areas in need of improvement

Whether or not the test is indeed a learning device depends a great deal upon the teacher. He can return the tests with a lengthy harangue about the lethargy and apathy of the younger generation, or he can praise the students for their fine work, when they deserve it. He can scold them for the poor grades, or he can indicate just what their problems seem to be by means of short notations on the test or in personal interviews. The student in question may need to work with sounds, with vocabulary, or with grammar. The student may need additional practice in listening, speaking, reading, and/or writing. The teacher can provide assistance not only with identifying the problems, but also with suggesting ways and means of improvement. A personal interview may also reveal affective-social problems with which the teacher can help even though they may have little to do with second-language learning per se.

20. Test each concept only once

Testing a single concept more than once not only inflates the true score of those students who know the correct answer; it deflates the true score of those students who do not know the answer. For example, in a group of items testing the students' knowledge of regular verb endings of a single class, one item testing each of the person forms in the singular and the plural covers all the concepts and forms. Additional items not only take additional time and cause extra work but falsify the results as well.

21. Give credit for what a student knows

Although the argument that a response is not correct unless it is entirely correct can be defended strongly, and often is, such a method of grading test papers is not fair to the students. A closer examination of the question often reveals that the students have been asked to make more than one decision in answering the item. It is each decision that should be given credit separately rather than one single grade that is either totally correct or totally incorrect. In working with object pronouns, for example, some students may know the correct form but err in placing them correctly in the sentence or vice versa. In choosing between the indicative and subjunctive, some may choose the right mood of the verb but fail to make it agree with its subject or vice versa. The point is that the teacher should grade from the point of view of what the students do know rather than rejecting all but perfect responses. When testing language skills, the teacher should place primary stress on the ability to communicate. Although students who take rather marked liberties with the grammar of the second language obviously do not deserve as good a grade as those who are able to express themselves with great fluency and with very few errors, they have accomplished the major goal in second-language learning, and they deserve credit for being able to communicate.

22. Distinguish between discrete items and global items

A discrete item consists of a short stimulus followed either by an answer to be chosen (a recognition item) or a space for an answer to be given (a recall item). The important characteristic of a *discrete item* is that it tests only one point. An example of a discrete item is a question followed by four possible replies. An example of a *global item* is a longer passage followed by a series of questions testing comprehension of content. The purpose of such an item is to test one of the language skills in a more sustained sequence.

23. At some point in the learning sequence, the students should have to choose between various grammar structures

Tests, as well as exercises, should foster the assimilation of each component of the language system into a large, meaningful whole. To be discouraged is the memorization of fragmented chunks of information that can be placed in indicated slots on tests, but that the students cannot use in any context involving a choice. After the students have studied the past tense, they should be able to complete an exercise in which they use past tense verb forms. However, if they are going to learn to use the language, they should also be able to choose when to use the present or the past and to use both in the same exercise as the context indicates. Students should be able to complete an exercise on a test labeled *direct object pronouns*. They must also be able to reach the point at which they can use both direct and indirect object pronouns in the same exercise if they are ever to achieve any functional ability to employ these forms for purposes of communication. On each test there should be some items in which the students must make choices that indicate functional control of the components of the language system.

From a handout used in the editor's graduate course in 1976.

33. TWENTY COMMON TESTING MISTAKES FOR EFL TEACHERS TO AVOID

To some extent, good testing procedure, like good language use, can be achieved through avoidance of errors. Almost any language-instruction program requires the preparation and administration of tests, and it is only to the extent that certain common testing mistakes have been avoided that such tests can be said to be worthwhile selection, diagnostic, or evaluation instruments. The list of common testing problems provided here is by no means exhaustive, but it has been drawn from wide experience with tests prepared for classroom and district use, and may therefore be said to be representative. It is intended as a kind of checklist to serve as a guideline for EFL teachers in the preparation of their own examinations.

The common mistakes have been grouped into four categories as follows: *general examination characteristics, item characteristics, test validity concerns, and administrative and scoring issues.* Five specific mistakes have been identified under each of these categories. While some overlap may exist in categories of mistakes and methods of remediation, I believe that each of the following twenty mistakes constitutes a genuine problem which, if resolved, will result in an improved testing program.

GENERAL EXAMINATION CHARACTERISTICS

1. Tests Which Are Too Difficult Or Too Easy

When tests are too difficult or too easy, there is an accumulation of scores at the lower or higher ends of the scoring range. These phenomena are known collectively as "boundary effects." As a result of such effects, there is information loss and reduced capacity of the test to discriminate among students in their ability. The net result is a test which is both unreliable and unsuitable for evaluation purposes. For most purposes, care should be taken to prepare tests and items that have about a fifty percent average rate of student success. Such procedure will maximize test information and reliability. This implies that the test should be tried out on a restricted sample of persons from the target population before it is used for student or program-evaluation purposes.

2. An Insufficient Number Of Items

Test reliability is directly related to the number of items occurring on the test. While tests may be too long and thus needlessly tire the students, a more common mistake is for a test to be too short and thus unreliable. For most paper-and-pencil EFL tests it is difficult to achieve acceptable reliability (say 85 or above) with less than 50 items. This is particularly true with tests of listening comprehension. At the same time, EFL tests with 100 or more items rapidly reach a point where the inclusion of additional items yields little or no increase in reliability.

A similar conclusion is true for tests of written or oral production that do not involve the use of items. For these tests as well, a sample of language usage must be elicited from the students that is both large enough and diverse enough in content to permit reliable measurement.

3. Lack Of Confidence Measures

Most standardized tests come equipped with a user's manual. The manual provides us with information about the reliability and validity of the tests — both what they are and how they were ascertained. This information permits us to estimate the level of confidence that we may place in the test result when it is applied to various situations. When locally developed tests are used for important evaluative decisions, estimates of reliability and validity should be provided for these tests. Appropriate computational formulas may easily be found in measurement-theory texts.

Closely related to this problem is the need to ensure that the persons on whom the test was tried out in its evaluation stage are from the same general population as those with whom the test is ultimately used. It is not uncommon for unwarranted reliance to be placed in some foreign standardized test when the characteristics of the population with reference to which it was developed are vastly different from those of the population with which it is being used. Vast differences of this sort imply a need for reanalysis of the test in the new situation.

4. Negative Washback Through Non-occurrent Forms

Through use of inappropriate structures of the language it is possible to teach errors to the students. Consider the following item:

I __________ here since five o'clock.

a. am being c. will be

b. have been d. am be

Option *d* clearly does not exist in any natural context in the English language. The possibility exists that a learner, particularly at a beginning stage, might learn this form and entertain the thought that *am* may serve as an auxiliary of *be*. While it is necessary that options include incorrect forms as distractors, it is best if these forms, like *a* and *c* above, have some possible appropriate environment in the language.

ITEM CHARACTERISTICS

5. Trick Questions

The use of trick questions must be avoided. As a rule such items impair the motivation of the students, the credibility of the teacher, and the quality of the test. Their use is a distinct sign of poor pedagogy. Consider the following example:

I did not observe him not failing to do his work because he was
  a. always working.
  b. ever conscientious.
  c. consistently lazy.
  d. never irresponsible.

A quick glance at this item reveals that the stem contains a double-negative structure that stretches the bounds of normal English usage. Such items are frequently found to have negative discriminability; i. e., many of the better students who have comparatively greater mastery of the lexicon are fooled, while weaker students manage to pass, perhaps by attending to the fact that option c is different from the other options.

6. Redundant Wording

A common problem in item writing, particularly of multiple-choice type items, is needless repetition. An example would be the following:

He went to school
  a. because he wanted to learn more.
  b. because he wanted to meet new friends.
  c. because he wanted to get a better job.
  d. because he wanted to please his parents.

Such an item is better written as follows:

He went to school because he wanted to
  a. learn more.
  b. meet new friends.
  c. get a better job.
  d. please his parents.

Items with redundant wording greatly reduce the efficiency of a test in that they reduce the amount of information available from a given period of time available for testing.

7. Divergence Cues

In writing options for multiple-choice-type items it is important not to provide cues regarding the choice of the correct option. "Test-wise" students can often answer such items correctly without knowledge of the content these items are said to measure. Typical divergence cues may occur when one option gives greater length or specificity of information. Consider the following example:

In the story we know it was raining because
  a. the sky was dark.
  b. everyone insisted on wearing an overcoat and carrying an umbrella outside.
  c. it was that time of year.
  d. they heard thunder.

Without having read the story, we would imagine that b was the correct answer merely because greater detail is offered. Option divergence of this kind is to be avoided.

8. Convergence Cues

More subtle than divergence cuing is the presence of convergence cuing. Here "test-wise" students can identify the correct option because of content overlap. Look at the following example employing item options without an item stem:

a. crawl　　c. brawl
b. creep　　d. trudge

Even without knowledge of the question or item stem, we may venture an educated guess that *crawl* is the correct option. The rationale behind this selection is that options *a, b,* and *d* refer to motion of a comparatively slow or simple type. Option *c* has as its only obvious commonality with other options the fact that it rhymes with option *a.* Distraction, of both a semantic and a phonological nature, has been employed then, and the point of convergence is option *a*. It is astounding how many items can be correctly answered in this way without any attention to what is being asked of the examinee.

9. Option Number

It is not uncommon to find tests containing items with insufficient or varying numbers of options. Multiple choice or true-false items leave room for possible success due to random guessing. The fewer the options, the higher the probability of measurement error resulting from successful guessing. With a true-false testing format, we should expect the students to score 50 percent by guessing. True ability measurement would only take place in the scoring range from 51 to 100 percent. This implies that, for such tests, a comparatively large number of items would be needed for accurate measurement.

A problem related to that of insufficient options is that of irregularity in the numbers of options. Apart from an esthetic issue, this irregularity also makes it impossible to apply various formulae for the correction of errors due to guessing. In general it is best to be consistent in the numbers of options used for items within a test.

TEST-VALIDITY CONCERNS

10. Mixed Content

A test is valid only to the extent that it accurately measures the content or ability it purports to measure. Sometimes tests have been claimed to measure something different from what many of their items are actually measuring. The following two items are offered by way of example. The first item was said to measure knowledge of verb tenses; the second was said to measure vocabulary recognition:

He ________ the man yesterday.
a. see c. will see
b. saw d. is seeing

The lady ________ to many cities in Europe last year.
a. visited c. visits
b. traveled d. climbed

In the first example, purported to test tense, we find option *a* actually measures knowledge of subject-verb agreement. Similarly, the second item, supposedly measuring vocabulary recognition, includes option *c,* which tests tense. These kinds of inconsistencies make for invalid tests.

11. Wrong Medium

Sometimes one encounters tests that require extensive skill in a response medium other than that which is being tested. Consider reading-comprehension questions that require accurate written responses to show comprehension of the passage. Research has indicated that such tests are invalid in the sense that they measure something other than what they are intended to measure (Henning 1975). Care must be taken that the response medium be representative of the skill being tested.

12. Common Knowledge

Items that require common-knowledge responses should also be avoided. Consider the following reading-comprehension item as an example:

> According to the story, Napoleon was born in
> a. England c. Germany
> b. France d. Italy

Responding correctly to such an item does not entail the ability to comprehend a reading passage, and therefore a high score on tests containing this kind of item may indicate some ability other than reading comprehension.

13. Syllabus Mismatch

Perhaps the most common cause of invalid achievement tests is the failure of a test to measure adequately either instructional objectives or course content. When this happens, we say a test lacks face or content validity. When designing achievement tests, the teacher should have a systematic procedure for sampling course content. The course must fit the instructional objectives, and the test as well should reflect the instructional objectives by reference to vocabulary, structures, and skills actually taught.

14. Content Matching

A word is in order about tests of comprehension (either reading or listening) that require content matching. Mere matching of a word or phrase in a test item with the exact counterpart in a comprehension passage does not necessarily entail comprehension. Memory span or recognition skills are involved, and these are also important. But they are not the same as comprehension. Tests involving such content-matching tasks are usually invalid as measures of comprehension.

ADMINISTRATIVE AND SCORING ISSUES

15. Lack Of Cheating Controls

Obviously, when students obtain higher scores through cheating, tests are neither reliable nor valid. It is the responsibility of the teacher or the test administrator to prevent such activity. In some cultures there is less stigma attached to collaboration on tests. The teacher should take care to separate students, and where possible use alternate forms of the test. These alternate forms may simply consist of exactly the same items arranged in different sequences. Such forms should be distributed in such a way that every other student in a row has a different form. This will effectively minimize cheating behavior.

16. Inadequate Instructions

Instructions must be clear, both to the students and to any test administrators using the test. If the students fail to understand the task, their responses may be invalid, in the sense that the students would have been able to supply the correct answers if they had understood the procedure. There is nothing inherently wrong from a measurement point of view with giving instructions in the native language, unless, of course, it is a test of comprehending instructions in a foreign language.

If the administrators fail to understand the exact procedure, there will be inequities of administration from group to group or administrator to administrator. Procedures should be carefully standardized even if this requires special training sessions for test administrators.

17. Administrative Inequities

Not only can differing instructions to administrators result in administrative inequities, but other factors as well may impair the reliability of the test. Consider the situation when lighting is poor for one class and good for another, or when the test administrator reads instructions or comprehension passage at different rates and volumes for different classes.

This latter problem is sometimes solved by the use of high-quality recording equipment.

Care must be taken to prevent these inequities and others, such as differential noise distractions, length of testing, time of day or week, supportiveness of administrators, etc.

18. Subjectivity Of Scoring

A final, pervasive problem occurs when instructors give subjective, opinionated judgments of student performance. In composition scoring, for example, it has been found that judgments are often influenced by handwriting neatness. Other factors also may distort accurate judgment. Some judges or raters find themselves becoming more strict or more lenient as they proceed through the papers to be marked. In short, if subjective judgment must be relied on, several mitigating procedures should be employed. First, more than one judge should be consulted independently of marks assigned by other judges. The total of all judges' ratings should determine the student's mark. Second, judges should make use of some precise rating schedule. A certain number of marks should be deducted for errors of specified type and number. In this way, judges will be giving equal weight to the same kinds of performance. Finally, sufficient samples of language should be elicited from the students. In writing or speaking tests, students should be given more than one topic, to ensure that a more comprehensive picture is taken of their language use in a variety of situations.

These problems are surprisingly common in the preparation of classroom EFL tests. If they are avoided or resolved, the quality of EFL testing will improve. Other problems may also be cited, but the ones enumerated here are certainly among the more common.

■ References

Henning, G. (1975). Measuring foreign language reading comprehension. *Language Learning, 25*, 1.

Henning, G., S. El Ghawabi, W. Saadalla, M. El Rifai, R. Kamel, S. Matar. (1980). *Comprehensive assessment of language proficiency and achievement among Egyptian learners of English.* Research report of the English Language Testing Unit of the Egyptian Ministry of Education, Cairo.

From Henning, G. (1982). Twenty common testing mistakes for EFL teachers to avoid, *English Teaching Forum, 20*, pp. 33-37.

34. USING A VIDEOCAMERA AND TASK-BASED ACTIVITIES TO MAKE CLASSROOM ORAL TESTING A MORE REALISTIC COMMUNICATIVE EXPERIENCE

A few years ago, as final exam time loomed closer, I was particularly dreading another round of oral exams since I knew I would have to find at least 20 hours outside of class to test the 80 students in my beginning and intermediate French classes. I also knew that, despite my status as a certified ACTFL tester and my considerable experience rating students' performances, my reliability would probably be as low as my morale after the first 15 back-to-back exams. Furthermore, since students typically encounter this type of testing only once or twice a semester, their anxiety level over this part of the final exam was quite high. Oral testing had become an unpleasant and stressful experience for both me and my students. After surviving the semester, I decided to explore various ways to make oral classroom testing less time-consuming, easier to evaluate accurately and, most importantly, a positive learning experience for the students rather than another stress-producing ordeal. What follows are the results of my exploration.

First, I will briefly outline general principles of communicative language teaching and testing. Next, I will provide an overview of the most widely used methods of communicative classroom oral testing, as well as evaluations of their practicality and conformity to the goals of communicative teaching and testing. Finally, I will describe in detail a method of oral testing that I have used successfully in my first- and second-year language classes, as well as in my conversation and composition courses. I have found that this method, which consists of videotaping task-based activities, is one that provides an efficient and accurate means of testing for prochievement and is also an enjoyable experience for students. Moreover, it addresses what Shohamy (1990) has identified as a priority for testing in the 1990s: to use tests "for improvement of teaching and learning..." by shifting "...from tests that are final, summative, and prescriptive, to tests that are more formative in nature and that can be used as part of the instructional process" (389).

COMMUNICATIVE TEACHING AND TESTING

The Communicative Approach has spawned a variety of teaching methodologies, and there is still much debate about issues such as the roles of teacher input and grammar in the communicatively oriented classroom. Nevertheless, those who adopt this approach, whatever their method, accept the notion of language use as "social behavior, purposeful, and always in context" (Savignon 1991, 273) and espouse the view that the primary goal of language teaching is to train students to "perceive and operate within real-world situations, in order to perform real-world tasks" (Swaffar 1989, 33). This new goal has given teachers added responsibilities — not only must we help our students learn the target foreign language and about the cultures in which it is spoken, we must also equip them with the strategic tools necessary to become autonomous learners in the target cultures. This view of language and the purposes of language study, Swaffar (1989) points out, has had considerable impact on recent teaching, testing, and research efforts, one of the most important being its focus on the learner and the learning process, rather than only on language as an end product(34).

If our teaching goal, then, is to develop students' communicative competence and make them autonomous learners, our tests should be designed to evaluate students' language use in real-world communicative tasks. This means, Swain (1984) says, that the assessment tasks we design need to be "capable of generating language that includes grammatical, sociolinguistic, discourse, and strategic performance" (11). Furthermore, Wesche (1983, 42) notes, they must reflect conditions of real-world communication, which Morrow (1979) has identified as including: 1) interaction; 2) unpredictability in language use; 3) a purpose for the communication; 4) language appropriate to the situation; 5) both a linguistic and situational context. From the perspective of the classroom teacher, we are also concerned that our tests allow us to measure students' progress and mastery of specific course material, and in the interest of fairness we want tests that we can score with accuracy and that are also feasible in terms of the amount of time they take to administer and grade.

To date, oral classroom testing has generally taken the form of skits, role-plays, indirect testing in the language lab, or ACTFL-style interviews. Much recent literature and research evaluating these formats in terms of feasibility, reliability, and their fidelity to the goals of communicative teaching and testing, however, point out that there are many drawbacks — and sometimes serious ones — to all of these formats.

ACTFL-STYLE INTERVIEWS

The ACTFL-style interview can give teachers trained in OPI (Oral Proficiency Interview) techniques a great deal of information about the overall oral proficiency level of their students, information that can be very valuable for student placement and in evaluating the global strengths and weaknesses of a foreign language program. To be accurate, however, these interviews must be carried out by trained testers and, in spite of the popularity of the ACTFL workshops, most teachers still have not received this training. Moreover, the OPI was designed to measure global proficiency, not to test mastery of specific course material. In addition, because the various levels of proficiency are quite broad, it is quite common for students to remain within the same level for several semesters, thus making it difficult to use the OPI to measure student progress, particularly during any given one-semester course.

The ACTFL-style student-teacher interview also poses very real problems from a practical standpoint, as any teacher who has tried to administer them to several classes in one semester can testify. First, they are extremely time-consuming to conduct: in order to measure a student's proficiency level with any reliability, the interviewer must go through a warm-up, level checks, probes, and a winddown, which takes between ten and thirty minutes per student. Moreover, it is difficult for teachers to mentally "step back" and arrive at an accurate assessment "on the spot" when they must focus their energies on playing an active role in the interview (van Lier 1989, 501). Taping the interviews and listening to them later, as Omaggio (1986, 345) suggests, only compounds the time problem. Additionally, Mitchell (1985) has demonstrated that it is difficult for teachers to remain impartial when participating in oral conversations and role-plays with their own students. In a study in which she recorded and analyzed an experienced teacher participating in 54 role-play conversations with 13-year-old second-year French students, she found that the teacher tailored her utterances according to her knowledge of each student's ability and self-confidence in the foreign language (171). As a result, only the stronger and more self-confident students were challenged to cope with words and expressions they did not know, allowing them to demonstrate their strategic competence (172).

Another observation about the ACTFL-style interview seems particularly relevant to communicative classroom testing. Newsham (1989) argues convincingly that no matter what role the instructor may pretend to play, it is almost impossible for students to forget that they are talking to their teacher. Consequently, instead of the give and take of natural discourse, the student tends to take a "back seat" and let the teacher initiate and control all exchanges (342). A second criticism is that the ACTFL-style interview places too much emphasis on the more formal question-answer/teacher-student format, and not enough on role-plays that would allow students to demonstrate their communicative proficiency in a variety of sociolinguistic situations (Raffaldini 1988, 200).

ROLE-PLAYS AND MEMORIZED DIALOGUES

Much has been written about using role-plays both for teaching and testing in the classroom. Role-plays have wide appeal in communicative testing because they have the potential of being able to generate grammatical, sociolinguistic, discourse, and strategic performance and meet Morrow's (1979) criteria for characteristics of real life communication (interaction, unpredictability, purpose, authentic language, and context). For classroom testing purposes, students typically act out the role-plays with the teacher assuming one of the roles, or in pairs or small groups with other students. Role-plays can be acted out for the teacher alone, or in front of the other members of the class. Depending on their purposes, instructors can create role-plays that are able to test specific structures, functions, or lexical items ("You are in the post office; buy two aerograms and stamps to send a post card to the U. S."), or open-ended ones to test for more global communicative competence ("You are on a first date with someone you don't know well; make conversation."). While role-plays meet the theoretical criteria of communicative testing, they nevertheless share some of the practical and assessment drawbacks of ACTFL-style testing. First, whether the role-plays have a teacher/student or pair/small groups format, they are still very time-consuming to conduct, especially when the teacher has a large number of students. Second, teacher participation in the role-plays again raises questions of 1) the teacher's ability to assess student performance accurately and impartially; and 2) the impracticality of recording and later listening to perhaps as many as a hundred ten-minute role plays. Third, when the teacher assumes one of the parts in a role-play, students have a tendency to wait for the authority figure/grader to take the lead and direct the course of the dialogue (Valdman 1988, 125; van Lier 1989, 498). Additionally, Newsham (1989) questions whether stronger students are able to display their full competence, and whether they might be penalized when performing with significantly weaker students (342).

Recent research into foreign language anxiety raises another question about the reliability of using role-plays and memorized skits to test communicative competence, especially when performed with other students as an audience. In the area of general classroom anxiety, it has been suggested that while some anxiety can have a positive influence, too high a level of anxiety can be debilitating (MacIntyre and Gardner, 1989), and several studies show that students consider speaking to be the most anxiety-provoking activity in the foreign language classroom (MacIntyre and Gardner 1991; Young 1990; Young 1992; Horwitz,

Horwitz, and Cope 1986). Moreover, this anxiety is compounded when students are singled out and must get up in front of the class and perform in the target language — they fear looking foolish to their classmates and this anxiety can have a detrimental effect on their performance (Price 1991; Young 1990; Horwitz, Horwitz, and Cope 1991, 30). Furthermore, if in communicative testing we want to evaluate how the student is able to perform in real-world situations, having students perform in front of a large group of people is hardly realistic. After all, how often will a student have to ask for a stamp, order a meal, or make hotel reservations or an appointment, with 30 people glued to his every word — and ready to tell him afterward how many mistakes he made?

Evans, Gaudin, and Raveau (1987) found other difficulties when testing students in pairs. They noticed that students were often more concerned with the instructor's reaction to the dialogue — at times even pausing when the teacher would make a notation — than their partner's responses (104). When role-plays were assigned ahead of time, they discovered a second problem: many students had learned what they would say by heart, so that no authentic interaction between students took place. In the worst cases there were "non-dialogues" where, "A talks for two minutes while B listens: B says 'Ah oui,' talks for two minutes and so on... " (105). This same lack of interaction, of real communication during the testing situation, is also the biggest drawback to using memorized skits and dialogues to measure oral competency. It should be pointed out, as several recent articles have shown, that there can be very real communication going on among students in the target language in the preparation of role-plays and skits (Bledsoe 1992; Di Pietro 1987; Haggstrom 1992). Obviously, since it is the collaborative effort, and not necessarily the final recitation that reveals students' ability to communicate in the target language, it should be taken into consideration in the evaluation process. After all, our goal is to test for students' real-world language use, which is generally not rehearsed and memorized. Unfortunately, when the preparation for the skits takes place outside of the classroom, communication among the students most often takes place in the native language, not in the target language.

ORAL TESTING IN THE LANGUAGE LAB

Larson (1984) argues that semidirect testing in the language lab, which elicits speech by means of recorded or written questions, pictures, or the like, is a popular method for oral testing because it has several advantages over direct face-to-face testing: 1) it provides uniformity in testing and in its administration; 2) present-day equipment allows teachers to listen to each station in the lab, thus enabling them to grade a whole class within one class period; 3) lab equipment that permits students to record their answers outside of class and without the teacher present, maximizes efficient use of class time and gives both students and teachers more flexibility in taking or administering oral exams (500-501). In addition, semidirect tests can set tasks that largely conform to the communicative testing principles outlined earlier. There are, however, several important drawbacks to this type of classroom testing. First, while these tests can be communicative, they often take the form of questions or directives that elicit only sentence-level utterances. Second, van Lier (1989) notes that having to speak into a microphone often inhibits student performance and is likely to cause more anxiety than a face-to-face interview (493). Third, Raffaldini (1988) points out that since students never interact directly with another person, the test cannot elicit a sample of interaction-based exchange and the collaborative negotiation of meaning that characterizes it (204). Several recent articles have explored ways to overcome this last limitation by using paired activities that allow students to talk to each other through the language lab audio network (Homstad 1986). This type of testing, however, requires sophisticated language lab equipment not available at many schools and a great deal of practice to learn how to use it successfully. Moreover, the teacher still has the problem of having to come up with a grade for the students "on the spot."

VIDEOTAPING AND TASK-BASED COMMUNICATIVE ACTIVITIES

Although I have experimented widely with a variety of methods of oral classroom testing, including those discussed in the sections above, the method I have found to be most successful in my classes involves the use of a videocamera to record task-based communicative activities similar to those used daily in the classroom. My experience has been that this method appears to overcome most of the disadvantages of skits, role-plays, and ACTFL-style interviews. Importantly, because this testing promotes learning in addition to providing evaluative data, and is not unduly time-consuming to administer or correct, teachers can incorporate it into the classroom much more often than traditional methods. As a result, it both reduces student anxiety and increases accuracy of assessment by providing large and frequent samples of student input. What follows are guidelines and suggestions for implementing this method of oral testing.

Setting And Equipment

Testing takes place in the regular classroom, a procedure students find reassuring since unfamiliar surroundings can be sources of stress in themselves. To videotape the exam, I use the college's fully automatic, battery-operated camcorder that is equipped with a zoom lens, an excellent microphone capable of producing good sound quality even when students are recorded from a distance, and a light sensor that automatically adjusts as I move around the classroom. Since it is not necessary to stand right next to students to videotape them, they are often unaware of when they are on camera. I use no special lighting or props, and am able to do the taping without outside help. As a result, all I need to do is schedule the use of the camcorder, and not call in already overworked technicians or lab assistants.

The Teacher's Role

During the exam, the teacher's function is to move around the room and videotape students as they participate in the task-based activity. Occasionally, it is necessary to remind students to remain in pairs or small groups, since bunching together makes the subsequent evaluation of individual student performances more difficult. To ensure that I have enough samples to be able to evaluate their performance, I videotape each student at three different times during the 50-minute testing period. Since students are frequently changing partners during the activity, it is quite easy to do this.

Preparation

Students regularly engage in interactive activities of the same type as those that will be used in the testing situation, and I frequently videotape them during these activities. This is helpful for two reasons. First, students become accustomed to being videotaped, so that this aspect of the testing process does not inhibit their performance at exam time. Second, the videotapes supply valuable instructional material that can be used as a teaching tool in the classroom and language lab. Several recent articles have described ways in which students' own videotaped actions and speech provide the foundation of classroom activities designed to teach phonetics, vocabulary, and grammar (Orban and McLean 1990: Pelletier 1990). Orban and McLean (1990) stress the value of regular, non-test-mode videotaping as a tool for self-evaluation, and it is in this context that I have found student videotapes particularly useful. Frequent videotaping prepares them for oral testing and real-world communication by increasing their awareness of communicative strategies. When students analyze videos as an in-class activity, I ask questions designed to bring out positive aspects of student communication in order not to embarrass any individual student. For example, in a video taken of students completing a task that gives them practice with greetings and invitations, I might ask students to note the different expressions they heard their classmates use to extend an invitation, the kinds of activities in which students were invited to participate, and the different excuses students gave for refusing an invitation. As a follow-up activity, they might be asked to judge which excuse was the most convincing or the most ingenious. They might also be asked to make a list of the strategies they observed students using to make themselves understood when there was a breakdown in communication.

These exercises are useful for several reasons. First, they help alleviate much of the anxiety about having what they say judged "right" or "wrong" by showing them that there are usually a variety of ways to express the same idea. Second, because strategic behavior to compensate for breakdown in communication is presented as both a natural and a positive trait, students feel less anxious when they are unable to remember specific vocabulary and, from their observations of the videos, they can build a repertoire of compensatory strategies for their own use. Finally, students may not readily recognize the transferability of the skills they are learning (Chamot and Kupper 1989, 13; Thomson 1987, 52; Baker and Brown 1984, 381-2; Brown, Bransford, Ferrara, and Campione 1983, 133-35). To give them practice in seeing how the same skills and vocabulary can be used in a variety of situations, students can be asked to discuss and note down key vocabulary, functions and strategies used in each video. The different lists can then be compared throughout the semester to show how many of them can be used in numerous situations. It is important that the teacher point out explicitly — and often — that what they are acquiring is not just the vocabulary and grammatical structures necessary to deal with a few specific circumstances, but rather general strategies for communicating successfully in a wide range of real-world situations.

When using the videos as individual homework assignments in the language lab, I have students view videos filmed in class and may ask them to identify specific errors they or their classmates have made, including grammar, vocabulary, sociolinguistic, and strategic mistakes. In an activity that includes greeting and leave-taking, they could be asked to notice which individuals remembered to shake hands when extending greetings and saying good-bye, and to avoid "pumping" the other persons' hand in the American fashion. Students are also asked to chart their own progress from week to week, deciding which errors they think are particularly important to correct, and to note down areas where they have improved. Whether used as an in-class activity or in the language lab, student evaluations indicate that they react very favorably to activities and analyses using videotape. Since they themselves are the "stars" of the videos, students find activities based on them to be interesting and worthwhile because they are able to see the relevance of their analyses to their improved oral performance in class and on tests. Furthermore, by increasing student metacognitive and strategic awareness, these analyses help students acquire the tools to become more independent learners. Finally, analyses that use the students' own speech and actions to furnish contexts and spring-boards for classroom and lab activities serve to prepare the students for both the oral exam and real-world communication.

Selecting The Task

To be successful, activities for videotaping need not necessarily be elaborate or original, nor must their preparation be time-consuming for the instructor. There are many excellent sources of activities and tasks currently on the market that can easily be adapted for use in the foreign language classroom in general, and in videotaped testing in particular. By keeping teaching and testing objectives clearly in mind when choosing activities and adapting them to conform to these objectives, I have found that many "tried and true" activities work very well, including the ones that follow.

MODEL 1

This task is a modified version of one described in Penny Ur's (1981) *Discussions that work.* It is one that I have used successfully in both first-and second-year language classes, and is used to test student mastery of the following:

Functions: Introductions; extending, accepting, and refusing invitations politely; expressing hesitation about an invitation; making excuses; trying to convince someone to do something.

Themes: Sports, health, leisure activities (movies, concerts, TV, etc.); school-subject vocabulary.

Grammatical Structures: Telling time; negations; using interrogatives; idiomatic uses of the verb "to do;" the verbs "to want", "to be able to", and "to have to".

Nonverbal Features: Shaking hands when greeting and saying good-bye.

Strategic: Asking for repetition; using circumlocution; using interlocutors' utterances as a source of vocabulary and grammatical structure.

Students are told to imagine that it is their first week in a program for foreigners in America, and that they want to meet their new classmates and stay very busy to keep from feeling homesick. The students are of many different nationalities and English is the only language they have in common. Students are given different partially-completed five-day schedules, and are told to move around the classroom, introduce themselves to their "new" classmates, try to make dates to do something with as many of them as possible, and set a place and time to meet. There are several rules designed to encourage maximum student participation and to make the activity reflect real-world social practices: 1) they must politely refuse any invitation that would involve doing something they would not enjoy doing in real life; 2) they must get the approval of their date before inviting a third person to join them in an activity; 3) they should mark off a realistic amount of time for any activity they schedule (for example, if they make an appointment to go to the movies they must block off at least two hours on their schedule); 4) they may not skip any of the classes or other commitments already on their schedule; 5)they are told that they may describe their own schedule to other students, but are not to show it to them; 6) to keep students from "bunching," they may talk to only one student at a time (or two, if there is an odd number of students in the class).

This activity is successful in stimulating interstudent communication in a number of ways. The fact that students have a time limit and are told that they are to make as many appointments as possible within this time frame produces a sense of urgency and keeps them on task. The situation also creates an information gap, requiring students to interact in order to complete the activity. Moreover, unlike tasks which demand simply a transfer of information, as is often the case in role-plays where students are told, for example, to find out what time a train leaves, how much the ticket costs, and what platform it leaves from, here an exchange of information is necessary to complete the task. As a result, since students do not know each others' schedules, what appointments they have already made, or what their interests are, it is only by sharing information that they are able to make the appointments. Making a date, then, is a collaborative effort since they must find out when they are both free and discuss individual likes and dislikes in order to agree on activities they both enjoy. The initial lack of information about other students' schedules and interests also assures that each interaction will vary, assuring unpredictability in language use — a characteristic of real-life communication. In this situation, it is the students who supply all language input — there is no teacher to supply the initiative — and each student's input in turn determines the other student's response. Furthermore, with no teacher input to "rescue" them when a breakdown in communication occurs, students have the opportunity to demonstrate their strategic competence by asking for or using repetition, circumlocution, gestures, and the like to overcome the difficulty.

After about ten minutes, as dates are made and time blocks are filled, it becomes more and more difficult to schedule appointments and lengthy negotiation is often necessary. At this point, the interaction goes beyond an exchange of factual information (What time are you free on Saturday, Do you want to go to the movies?) and allows students to demonstrate socializing and persuasion functions. For example, if, due to full schedules or a shared interest in a particular type of activity, one student decides to ask another to join in an already scheduled activity, he must use his social and persuasion skills to get his date for a particular activity to agree to have the third student participate. When students must turn down invitations because they do not enjoy an activity, there is often much heated discussion as they try to find some activity they both enjoy, or as one tries to convince the other to reconsider his refusal. In addition, students tend to get involved in the task, often forgetting that it is only an imaginary situation, and in order not to hurt the other person's feelings they go to great lengths to explain why they are not free and to try to find some time when they can meet.

As an important result, they pass from sentence to discourse-level speech.

Ten minutes before the end of the task, students are told that they have just found out that they have an important exam in one of their courses on Friday that will require a great amount of preparation. They will have time to participate in only one nonacademic activity on Thursday and Friday. They must, then, decide which activity they would most enjoy, and politely cancel all their other dates on those days. Since each student can only have one activity during the same two-day period, not only must they cancel appointments with others, but they must also convince the student with whom they have the date to participate in the one activity they want to keep — that he should *not* cancel that appointment.

Assessment And Follow-Up

To ensure ample student samples, the instructor should allot 50 minutes to test a class of approximately 25 students. Even in small classes, where testing could be done in a shorter period of time, I often let the test take up the entire hour — at the student' request.

To grade the oral tests I use a score sheet adapted from the one described in Omaggio's (1986) *Teaching Language in Context* (345-353). As she points out, the advantage of this type of score sheet is that the relative weights of components to be evaluated can be adjusted to reflect teaching priorities and student proficiency levels. For example, if the students are to be tested on a unit that stresses particular vocabulary items or structures, these items can be weighted more heavily to reflect this emphasis. In beginning classes, instructors may want to eliminate the category "fluency," and in an advanced class put more weight on sociolinguistic features (see Appendix).

As mentioned above, I videotape each student at least three different points during the exam, each time speaking with a different classmate. This procedure helps to increase the accuracy of assessment in several ways. First, it largely counters the concern that stronger students may be penalized when paired with students of lesser ability. By choosing tasks that allow students to interact with many others during the testing period, the instructor has the opportunity to evaluate students while they are speaking with partners of various skill levels. Second, it avoids that "one chance to get it right" aspect of many oral testing formats that students find to be particularly anxiety-provoking. Because they are all interacting at the same time, students feel less self-conscious and are better able to concentrate on the task, not on their grade, assuring that they will be able to perform at their best and will provide closer-to-natural speech samples than in most role-play or skit scenarios. Third, in real life it is rare that an individual has only one opportunity to understand others or to make himself understood. Rather, even as native speakers of a language, we must often rephrase or repeat statements several times to make ourselves understood, and, in turn, we must often ask others for clarification of what they are trying to convey. By taping students performing similar tasks at various points during the exam, we are in essence giving them the same opportunities to rephrase, repeat, and ask for clarification that occur in real-world discourse.

The student/student format, in which the teacher is merely an observer, also addresses concerns that educators have raised regarding 1) the teacher's ability to evaluate impartially and accurately oral exams in which they must also actively participate; and 2) teacher-student exams that inhibit student initiative and natural discourse. Furthermore, as a non-participant the teacher cannot tailor questions to fit expectations of individual students, and thus a relatively uncontaminated sample of student communicative competency is obtained.

The videotaped communicative task format for oral exams also offers advantages from a practical standpoint. First, the exam takes only 50 minutes to administer. In addition, the instructor does not have the pressure to formulate a grade immediately since the videotape can be viewed later. Moreover, this video, unlike audiotaped or video recordings of many ten-minute individual or small-group interviews or role-plays, can be replayed in only 50 minutes and allows teacher to observe nonverbal communication as well. Even if the teacher needs to view the video several times to arrive at a grade for each student, the total time needed to both administer and evaluate the oral exam rarely takes over three hours, in fact much less time than teachers often spend correcting written exams. Finally, the video also provides an excellent resource for giving students concrete suggestions about how to improve their oral skills and for providing feedback when students have questions about their grades or performance. Videotaped exams, like the pre-exam videos, are also valuable sources for teaching and learning activities both in class and in the language laboratory.

It should be pointed out that, depending on class size, the total number of minutes each student is filmed is less than in some other testing formats. This drawback, however, is compensated for by the frequency of testing that task-based activities permit. I have found that pair activities work best with beginning students, and since tasks for these students generally require short interchanges, they change partners often. As a result, the instructor can tape a high number of conversations during the testing period. With larger classes and more advanced students, small group activities are more appropriate. Small group tasks, where students are in different areas of the classroom, help ensure sound quality. Furthermore, since there are four or so students per group, the instructor can spend more time with each and film more lengthy interchanges.

Student evaluations of oral testing procedures in my classes indicate that students overwhelmingly find this type of testing to be 1) a fair and accurate means to evaluate oral prochievement; 2) less anxiety-provoking than interview, language lab, role-playing, and skit formats; 3) enjoyable; and 4) a positive learning experience.

CONCLUSIONS

This testing method may not be the definitive answer to all oral testing needs or situations. My experience, however, is that it does away with many of the drawbacks inherent in many classroom testing modes. The nature of the tasks allows teachers to observe both students' global proficiency and their mastery of specific course materials. This testing format is also helpful in improving accuracy of assessment. Because it takes less time to administer and grade, teachers can test frequently, thus ensuring larger samples of student input and fewer assessment errors due to teacher fatigue. Further accuracy is ensured since the teacher is only an observer in the testing process, not a participant, and, as such, is less likely to influence student performance. The videotape of the exam provides the teacher with an accurate basis for evaluating student linguistic and extralinguistic performance. The student pre- and posttesting analyses of videotapes, the nonthreatening format for the videotaped activities, and the open-ended nature of the tasks, encourage students to give their best performances and ensure that even the weakest students will find oral tests to be both an enjoyable experience and an integral part of the learning process. Finally, and perhaps most importantly, by giving students a great deal of independence and regular practice in solving real-world communicative tasks, they acquire the confidence and strategic tools necessary to approach the wide variety of circumstances they may encounter in real-world communication.

■ References

Asher, James J., JoAnne Kusudo, & Rita de la Torre. (1974). Learning a Second Language through Commands: The Second Field Test. *The Modern Language Journal, 58*, pp. 24-32.

Baker, Linda, & Ann L. Brown. (1984). Metacognitive Skills and Reading. *Handbook of Reading Research,* edited by P. D. Pearson, New York: Longman, pp. 353-94.

Bledsoe, Penelope. (1992). Performance and Evaluation of Communicative Tasks: The Video Camera in the L2 Classroom. *Hispania, 75*, 2, pp. 437-440.

Brown, Ann L., J. D. Bransford, R. Ferrara & J. C. Campione. (1983). Learning, Remembering, and Understanding. *Handbook of Child Psychology*, edited by Paul H. Mussen, 4th de, Vol 3, pp. 77-166, New York: John Wiley and Sons .

Capretz, Pierre J. (1987). *French in Action*. New Haven: Yale University Press.

Chamot, Anna Uhl & Lisa Kupper. (1989). Learning Strategies in Foreign Language Instruction. *Foreign Language Annals, 22,* 1, pp. 13-24.

Cicogna, Caterina, Marcel Danesi & Anthony Mollica. (1992). *Problem Solving in Second-Language Teaching.* Lewiston, NY: éditions Soleil.

Curran, Charles. (1976). *Counselling-Learning in Second Languages.* Apple River Press.

Di Pietro, Robert. (1987). *Strategic Interaction: Learning Languages through Scenarios*. Cambridge: Cambridge University Press.

Evans, Colin, Jean-Marie Gaudin & Florence Raveau. (1987). Testing Advanced Communicative Competence through Role-play. *The British Journal of Language Teaching* 25, 2, pp. 104-8.

Haggstrom, Margaret. (1992). A Performance Approach to the Study of Theater. *The French Review, 66,* 1, pp. 7-19.

Hodgson, John, and Ernest Richands. (1966). *Improvisation.* New York: Grove Press.

Homstad, Alice. (1986). El Intérprete: A Pair Activity to Promote Communicative Competence in Spanish. *Foreign Language Annals, 19,* 4, pp. 289-297.

Horwitz, Elaine K., Michael B. Horwitz & Jo Ann Cope. (1986). Foreign Language Classroom Anxiety. *The Modern Language Journal, 70*, 2, pp. 125-132.

_______. (1991). Foreign Language Classroom Anxiety. In *From Theory and Research to Classroom Implications*, edited by Elaine K. Horwitz and Dolly J. Young, Englewood Cliffs, NJ: Prentice Hall. pp. 27-36.

Klippel, Friederike. (1992). *Keep Talking: Communicative Fluency Activities for Language Teaching.* Cambridge: Cambridge University Press.

Krashen, Stephen. (1982). *Principles and Practice in Second Language Acquisition.* New York: Pergamon Press.

Larson, Jerry W. (1984). Testing Speaking Ability in the Classroom: The Semi-direct Alternative. *Foreign Language Annals*, *17*, pp. 499-507.

Maclntyre, Peter D., and R. C. Gardner. (1989). Anxiety and Second-Language Learning: Toward a Theoretical Clarification. *Language Learning, 39*, 2, pp. 251-75.

_________. (1991). Investigating Language Class Anxiety Using the Focused Essay Technique. *The Modern Language Journal, 75*, 3, pp. 296-304.

Maley, Alan & Alan Duff. (1979). *Drama Techniques in Language Learning.* Cambridge: Cambridge University Press.

Mitchell, Rosamond. (1985). The Use of Role Play Tasks in Assessing FL Communicative Performance. *British Journal of Language Teaching, 23*, 3, pp. 169-172.

Morrow, K. E. (1979). Communicative Language Testing: Revolution or Evolution? In the *Communicative Approach to Language Teaching*, edited by C. Brumfit & K. Johnson, London: Oxford Univ. Press.

Newsham, Gwen S. (1989). Communicative Testing and Classroom Teaching. *The Canadian Modern Language Review, 45*, 2, pp. 339-344.

Nunan, David. (1989). *Designing Tasks for the Communicative Classroom.* Cambridge: Cambridge University Press.

Oller, John W., Jr. & Patricia A. Richard-Amato, eds. (1983). *Methods That Work: A Smorgasbord of Ideas for Language Teachers*. Rowley, MA: Newbury House.

Omaggio, Alice C. (1986). *Teaching Language in Context.* Boston: Heinle and Heinle.

Orban, Clara & Alice Musick McLean. (1990). A Working Model for Videocamera Use in the Foreign Language Classroom. *The French Review, 63,* 4, pp. 652-663.

Pelletier, Raymond J. (1990). Prompting Spontaneity by Means of the Video Camera in the Beginning Foreign Language Class. *Foreign Language Annals, 22*, 3, pp. 227-233.

Price, Mary Lou. (1991). The Subjective Experience of Foreign Language Anxiety: Interviews with Highly Anxious Students. In *Language Anxiety: From Theory and Research to Classroom Implications,* edited by Elaine K. Horwitz and Dolly J. Young, pp. 101-108. Englewood Cliffs, NJ: Prentice Hall.

Raffaldini, Tina. (1988). The Use of Situation Tests as Measures of Communicative Ability. *Studies in Second Language Acquisition, 10,* 2, pp. 197-216.

Savignon, Sandra J. (1991). Communicative Language Teaching: State of the Art. *TESOL Quarterly, 25,* 2, pp. 261-277.

Shohamy, Elana. (1990). Language Testing Priorities: A Different Perspective. *Foreign Language Annals, 23,* 5, pp. 385-394.

Spolin, Viola. (1983). *Improvisation for the Theater*. Evanston, IL: Northwestern Up.

Swaffar, Janet. (1989). Curricular Issues and Language Research: The Shifting Interaction. *Profession,* pp. 32-38.

Swain, Merrill. (1984). Teaching and Testing Communicatively. *TESL Talk, 15,* 1-2, pp. 7-18.

Terrell, Tracy D. (1977). A Natural Approach to Second Language Acquisition and Learning. *The Modern Language Journal* 61, pp. 325-37.

______. (1982). The Natural Approach to Language Teaching: An Update. *The Modern Language Journal, 66,* pp. 121-32.

Terry, Robert M. (1986). Testing the Productive Skills: A Creative Focus for Hybrid Achievement Tests. *Foreign Language Annals, 19,* 4, pp. 521-527.

Thomson, Irene. (1987). Memory in Language Learning. In *Learner Strategies*, edited by Anita Wenden and Joan Robin, pp. 43-56. London: Prentice Hall.

Ur, Penny. (1981). *Discussions that Work.* Cambridge: Cambridge University Press.

Valdman, Albert. (1988). Introduction. *Studies in Second Language Acquisition, 10,* pp. 121-128.

Van Lier, Leo. (1989). Reeling, Writhing, Drawling, Stretching, and Fainting in Coils: Oral Proficiency Interviews as Conversation. *TESOL Quarterly, 23,* 3, pp. 489-508.

Ward, Thomas. n. d. Communicating Electronically: Student-Centered Activities for the Language Learning Center. In *The Foreign Language Classroom: Bridging Theory and Practice*, edited by Margaret A. Haggstrom, Leslie Z. Morgan, and Joseph Wieczoreck. New York: Garland Press, Forthcoming.

Wesche, Marjorie Bingham. (1983). Communicative Testing in a Second Language. *The Modern Language Journal, 67,* 1, pp. 41-55.

Young, Dolly. (1990). An Investigation of Student Perspectives on Anxiety and Speaking. *Foreign Language Annals, 23,* 6, pp. 540-553.

______. (1992). Language Anxiety from the Foreign Language Specialist's Perspective: Omaggio Hadley, Terrell, and Rardin. *Foreign Language Annals, 25,* 2, pp. 157-172.

APPENDIX

Sample Testing Score Sheets

First Year

1. STRUCTURES	1	2	3	4	5	x5 =	/25
2. VOCABULARY (Including thematic and functional items)	1	2	3	4	5	x5 =	/25
3. STRATEGIC BEHAVIOR	1	2	3	4	5	x3 =	/15

(For example, circumlocution, asking for repetition, miming, risk taking, etc.)

4. SOCIAL AND INTERPERSONAL (Using appropriate nonverbal gestures, forms of address and register, etc.)	1	2	3	4	5	x3 =	/15
5. ACCOMPLISHING TASK (Ability to communicate and be understood sufficiently to accomplish task)	1	2	3	4	5	x5 =	/20
				TEST SCORE		=	/100

Second Year Advanced

1. STRUCTURES	1	2	3	4	5	x4 =	/20
2. VOCABULARY (Including thematic and functional items)	1	2	3	4	5	x4 =	/20
3. STRATEGIC BEHAVIOR (For example, circumlocution, asking for repetition, miming, risk taking, etc.)	1	2	3	4	5	x4 =	/20
4. SOCIAL AND INTERPERSONAL (Using appropriate nonverbal gestures, forms of address and register, etc.)	1	2	3	4	5	x4 =	/20
5. FLUENCY (Halting speech/natural speech)	1	2	3	4	5	x4 =	/20
				TEST SCORE		=	/100

From Haggstrom, M. (1994). Using a videocamera and task-based activities to make classroom oral testing a more realistic conmmunicative experience, *Foreign Language Annals, 27,* 2, pp. 161-175.

PART NINE

PLANNING LESSONS

학습지도안을 교사가 실제로 수업을 구체적으로 어떻게 할지를 계획하는 내용을 담고 있다. 수업을 잘 하기 위해서는 목표설정을 비롯하여 전체적인 내용이 체계적으로 유기적인 상관관계를 가지며 연결되어 있어야 한다. 따라서 학습지도안은 원칙에 따라 설계될 필요가 있다. 그런 의미에서 이 장은 지도안을 작성할 때의 일반적인 원칙과 지도안에 포함되어야 할 기본적인 내용을 담은 Rivers의 글로 시작한다. 이어서 지도안에서 매우 중요한 부분인 행동목표를 학년목표와 단원목표로 나누어 예로 들은 내용이 소개된다. 행위(performance), 조건(condition), 기준(criterion)이라는 세 가지 요소로 구성되어 있음을 알 수 있다. 그리고 학습지도안의 실례를 세 가지 들고 있다. 교육실습에 나가서 고생스럽게 체험하는 학습지도안 작성요령을 익힐 수 있을 것이다.

35. LESSON PLANNING

GENERAL PRINCIPLES

1. The teacher is *not the slave of the textbook.* Teachers are trained professionals who know the capabilities of various classes and the objectives of their courses. The textbook provides the teacher with material which can be used in innumerable ways. It is essential to know what is in the textbook and to be able to select, omit, recombine, and supplement this material as the class situation indicates. The teacher should know the textbook well enough to be able to prepare students for what is coming, to refer quickly to other parts of the book when this is desirable, and to make up for any deficiencies. Experienced teachers tend to believe that the perfect textbook is the one they themselves have yet to write. While awaiting this great event they should take great care in selecting the one that most nearly meets the needs of the particular class, with due regard to the objectives of the course and the age and maturity of the students.

2. Each lesson must be based on *clearly established aims.* A lesson is not a haphazard collection of more or less interesting items, but a progression of interrelated activities which reinforce each other in establishing and consolidating the learning toward which both teacher and students are directing their efforts. As the lesson proceeds, some of these activities test, in an unobtrusive way, what other activities have been teaching; others reteach what has not been assimilated by the students; while still others refresh the students' memory and enable them to reuse essential material.

3. Each lesson should *move smartly*, the teacher leading the class from one activity to another with assurance, never allowing time to be wasted because of hesitancy or indecision, while always remaining alert to student needs. This brisk tempo will be possible only when the teacher has a sure grasp of the plan.

4. The class should *not* be kept for *too long at one type of activity*, even when the students appear to be enjoying it. The teacher should not wait until the students have ceased to enjoy what they are doing before calling a new tune. Too much drilling, can lead to emotional fatigue, absent-mindedness, and boredom. It can also cause the students to become so fixed in the use of certain patterns that they are incapable of using them flexibly in communication. Too much reading and writing means the neglecting of classroom opportunities for practicing communication skills. Too much unsystematic oral work can deprive students of opportunities for studying new material about which they may talk. A well-designed lesson will contain

a number of different activities, with a return to certain types of exercises at intervals for further consolidation of learning. Frequent, spaced practice is more effective than great blocks of one activity for undue lengths of time.

5. The teacher should plan to *do in class what cannot be done out of class.* This requires careful thought. It means that the student must have plenty of classroom time for practice in communication with the teacher's encouragement and help. This does not mean that *all* reading and writing will be done out of class. The students will do out of class what the teacher knows they can do on their own with reasonable probability of success. Out-of-class work will consolidate learning done in class through some type of creative activity. It will also include preparation for work to be done in subsequent lessons.

6. The lesson should be planned so that the class is on its toes, *never sure of what is coming next.* Nothing is more tedious for the student than lessons which always follow the same pattern. Many class sessions will inevitably contain very similar activities, but the ordering of the elements should be varied: Some may be included today, some left out, a few reintroduced from time to time. Imagination must direct the final form of the plan.

7. The teacher should be ready to *toss aside the plan* or change it as the lesson evolves. The mood of the class, the unexpected difficulty or simplicity of some section of the work, an interesting possibility which did not occur to the teacher when drawing up the plan, student initiative — all of these things, and many others, may lead to a change in the progression. Although ready to change the plan, the teacher should not do it as the result of a whim. The teacher will be conscious of any changes being made and the direction in which they are leading.

INGREDIENTS

1. After the introductory stages, usually aural-oral, when the course is getting under way, each lesson should provide *some practice in each of the four skills,* not necessarily in the same proportion. Not only does one activity consolidate the other, but a change of activity maintains the interest and energy level of the class. This does not mean that there will be practice in listening to, speaking, reading, and writing the same material during the one lesson. What has already been heard or read in a previous lesson may be being used as practice material by the class or as the basis for communicative interaction. What has been discussed or practiced orally may be reappearing in a more developed form in material for reading or writing. There will be a continual interplay among new elements and familiar elements, so that what has already been learned is not allowed to fade from the memory.

2. Each lesson must have *variety and some spice.* Since there are many ways of presenting and practicing material in all the skill areas, the teacher has no excuse for keeping to few well-worn techniques. The spice is provided by surprise items (a language game, an anecdote, some cultural information with a visual accompaniment, a culture quiz, a competitive test of what has been learned, or some pertinent contribution by a student which will interest or amuse the others).

3. The teacher should think up *games and competitions* which provide the same types of activities as exercises. The old game of Twenty Questions gives ample practice in interrogative forms. A chaining game, where each student in turn must change a certain element in the sentence, is very similar to a substitution drill. A game or competition which provides the same kind of practice is more amusing and spontaneous than an exercise, and students who are enjoying the activity will continue doing the same thing for a longer period without boredom.

4. A *repertoire of songs* well learned can always be called upon to bring variety to the lesson. A simple song, with uncomplicated words and some repetition, relaxes and refreshes the class. The period of singing need not be prolonged. Though often more appropriate at the end of the lesson, singing may provide a very welcome interlude in the middle of a period of hard work.

And So,

1. The lesson usually begins with a *warm-up*, where students are encouraged to talk about subjects of interest to them (e. g., what happened during the weekend or a recent startling event in the news). Sometimes this warm-up is built around a picture or an object, selected for its potential for expanding the students' *vocabulary*. In their discussions, students use much material they have already learned and acquire new vocabulary in a meaningful context. With proper planning, the warm-up also provides an opportunity for students to use some of the structures they practiced the previous day, as well as experimenting with material they prepared out of class. Its most useful function is to encourage students to retrieve and reuse much material from previous units in a real exchange of ideas and comments.

2. *New work* is now introduced in an interesting way. In a continuing sequence this will be building on previous work, so that students do not learn aspects of the language in unconnected segments, in a series of jolts and starts. New situations may be acted out with new structures and vocabulary or a dialogue segment learned (depending on the method the teacher is following). It may be the day for some training in direct reading, in which case a passage constructed of known elements with a few novel items — the meaning of which can be ascertained from the context — will be read or played on tape. After discussion of the content, students will read rapidly in silence and be ready to discuss the content,

referring to the text when in doubt.

3. Out of the new work will emerge some structures or syntactic arrangements which must be practiced in *oral exercises* of some form. As these are being practiced, some brief, concise explanations may be necessary. After the main point of the practice exercise appears to be assimilated, some individual response or a competition will show whether the students have thoroughly mastered what they have been learning. If they have not, the teacher will return briefly to practice, or reserve the point at issue for a second practice a little later in the lesson. Some teachers have found that if practice on material which has not been well assimilated is deferred till the next day, student performance shows considerable improvement over the work of the previous day. Once again, teachers will vary their approach on different occasions.

4. There follows a period for the *practical application* of the material of the day. The teacher may engage the students in an interchange of communication using what they have been learning. Later, this work may be combined with elements from earlier lessons to make sure the students recognize the relations between what they have been learning and what they have already learned. The application may involve reading and discussing a passage for which the previous work has prepared the class. It may necessitate some form of written demonstration of understanding and assimilation. It may take the form of a dramatization or some type of role playing in front of the class. The teacher may initiate a game which enables the students to use what they have learned, while concentrating on the progress of the game or on the success of their team. If they are able to use material successfully during such an activity, the teacher has some evidence that they have assimilated it.

5. There will now be some *preparation of the work for home study*. This will not necessarily be overt preparation. The teacher, knowing what the students will be asked to do as preparation for the next class, will see that those aspects of the preparatory work which could cause problems for the students have already been encountered before the end of the lesson. This may involve introducing into some activity new vocabulary which occurs in the study assignment, discussing a cultural aspect of a topic which the students may find puzzling, making sure that any grammatical terminology is well understood, or discussing orally a subject about which students will be asked to write a short composition or read some longer account. The teacher will make very sure that the homework is assigned well before the final bell, so that all students fully understand what is being required of them.

6. The lesson will *end with a relaxing and enjoyable activity* in the target language: some acting out of situations, arousing discussion of a controversial subject, a song, a short illustrated talk on some aspect of the culture, or an oral report from one of the students. No matter what form this activity may take, the teacher should plan the lesson so that the students will have time to relax and enjoy the use of the language before the lesson ends.

The students should always leave the classroom in a cheerful mood, feeling that language lessons are among the best in the day.

7. Another trained teacher will be able to use the plan effectively. For some reason the teacher may not be able to teach his/her students. Still the plan is to be organiged and specific enough for any substitute teacher to follow it.

From Rivers, W. M. (1981). *Teaching foreign language skills,* Chicago, Ill: The University of Chicago Press, pp. 483-488.

36. PERFORMANCE OBJECTIVES

The following objectives are for the intermediate level of Korean secondary school students who are learning English as a foreign language. End-of-Year objectives will appear first followed by unit objectives. Orders for each in terms of four aspects of language skill and culture are as follows: (1) Listening; (2) Speaking; (3) Reading; (4) Writing; and (5) Culture.

A. END-OF-YEAR OBJECTIVES

1. The student will be able to demonstrate comprehension of a simple American film regarding any one of the topics studied, as evidenced by his or her ability of oral summarization in Korean, followed by question-answer practices in English led by the teacher.
2. The student will be able to present a role play in English in a group of four or five, which represents one or combination of the topics learned.
3. The student will be able to prepare a written report in one paragraph about the reading material, which summarizes its salient points in English. The reading material will be selected by the student among several choices that the teacher makes from American magazines or newspapers.
4. The student will be able to submit a written assignment, which is to write a paragraph on a topic which gives the best interest to him or her among those studied during the year. Words, idioms, and structures learned will be maximally utilized. The sentences must be fully understandable to the teacher.
5. The student will be able to express appreciation in his or her own way about several American cultural aspects as a whole which are dealt with during the year, by writing one or two pages of reaction upon it in Korean.

B. UNIT OBJECTIVES

1. When pictures are shown which illustrate the content of the unit and statements about them are made by the teacher one by one, the student will be able to indicate whether they are matched or not by circling 'true' or 'false' on the answer sheet. Criterion: nine out of ten correct.
2. When asked personal questions associated with the unit, the student will be able to

respond to them using the very sentence structures learned. Accurate sounds, intonation, stress, rhythm, and juncture should be accompanied. At least four out of six must be complete without noticeably long pauses.

3. When given one or two paragraphs which is recombination of the vocabulary and structure learned through the unit along with the former units, the student will be able to demonstrate understanding of the reading material, as indicated by answering five true-false and multiple-choice questions about it. Criterion: four out of five correct.
4. When given a passage of familiar vocabulary and structure, the student will be able to rewrite the passage, making necessary grammatical changes according to the direction of "Change present tense of verb into present participle." 90 percent of accuracy will be required.
5. When given an opportunity to make an oral presentation at the last day of the unit, the student will be able to tell the other classmates about the differences and similarities between the American life style and Korean life style concerning the unit studied by using the words he or she has learned. Four students will be selected by the teacher at the middle of the unit so that they may prepare it in advance. They will be evaluated according to the following criteria: Deepness of study as evidenced by following class discussion in Korean and proper use of English language in terms of selection of sentences, pronunciation, stress, intonation, rhythm, and juncture.

From the author's personal assignment note which was done in 1977.

37. SAMPLE COVER SHEET AND LESSON PLAN (1)

COVER SHEET

Student Teacher: Caroline Morris
Regular Teacher: Ms. Bolter
Supervising/Coordinating Teacher: Mr. Evans
School: Lincoln Jr. High
Class: 9th grade
Learning Stage of Class: Intermediate
Age Level of Class: 14-17 years
Size of Class: 29 students
Linguistic/Ethnic Composition of Class: Chicano and Mexican
Other Relevant Factors: Negative attitude toward English, low motivation

LESSON PLAN

Student teacher's name: Caroline Morris
Date of presentation: Oct. 27
Estimated Time of Lesson: 30 minutes
Teaching Point: Vowel length differences before voiced and voiceless final stops
Pre-assessment Activity: Analysis of student pronunciation errors from taped conversations.
Relationship to Current Unit: (None. One general listening-speaking problem is being treated per week.)
Pre-entry Performance: Students have had a lesson on voiced and voiceless stops in initial position with focus on aspiration of voiceless ones.
Performance Objectives:

a. To distinguish aurally and orally between the two members in the following word-level minimal pairs using vowel length as the main factor (i. e., stops not fully released):

rope	*beat*	*wick*
robe	*bead*	*wig*

b. To distinguish aurally and orally between the two members in the following sentence-level minimal pairs using vowel length as the main factor (i. e., stops not fully released):
Where is the cab/cap? Look at my back/bag. I hid/hit the dog.

Criterion Level: 80% of the students will perform as specified at least 80% of the time.
Materials: Blackboard, objects, pictures.

PROCEDURES (Student Activities):

Step 1 - Introduction
(1 minute)

	1	2
on board:	*rope*	*robe*
	beet	*bead*
	wick	*wig*

a. Students listen to teacher read words.
b. Students describe differences between words in (1) and (2): voiced, long vowel —voiceless, short vowel
c. Teacher notes that such words have been a problem and erases words on the board.

Step 2 - Students are shown a rope and a robe.
(3 minutes)

a. Teacher pronounces the words and puts the rope on one side of the blackboard, the robe on the other. Teacher says words at random and the students (class, then individuals) point to the appropriate object.
b. Students listen and repeat each word several times after teacher-emphasis on vowel length.
c. Teacher points to the objects at random and the students (class, then individuals) say the word.
d. A student comes up and points to the object and calls on classmates to respond.

Step 3 - Present a picture of a man with a cap on his head and another one of a taxi on a highway. Attach them to opposite ends of the blackboard.
(6 minutes)

a. Teacher: *Where is the cap?* *On his head.*
Where is the cab? *On the highway.*
(Several times while pointing to appropriate picture.)
b. Students (class, then individuals) respond with either *On his head* or *On the*

highway, depending on teacher's question.

c. Students (class, then individuals) respond with either *the cap* or *the cab,* depending on whether teacher says: *What's on his head*? or *What's on the highway?*

d. One student comes to the front and teacher goes to the back (others look only at student in front). If teacher taps her head, student says: *Where is the cap*? If teacher pretends to drive, student says: *Where is the cab*? Several other students do this.

Step 4 - Show a beet (a picture or a real vegetable) and a large bead (from a necklace) to the class. Repeat procedure used for rope and robe in Step 2.

(3 minutes)

Step 5 - Show class a stuffed toy dog. Hide him behind the desk and then hit him on the nose. Follow procedure of Step 3 using the following phrases and rejoinders:

(6 minutes)

I hit the dog. (on the nose)
I hid the dog. (behind the desk)

Step 6 - Show a candle with a large wick and a wig to the class. Repeat procedure used with *rope* and *robe* in Step 2.

(3 minutes)

Step 7 - Arrange in advance for a student to come up to the front (he has a broad back and a bag full of books, papers, pencils, etc.). Follow procedure of Step 3 using the following phrases and rejoinders:

(6 minutes)

Look at Juan's bag. (It's full.)
Look at Juan's back. (It's broad.)

Step 8 - Students take a short listening quiz utilizing all words practiced to see if they all hear the distinctions. (Skill in production can be judged informally from individual class performances.)

(2 minutes)

Assignment: None

Contingency plans: Let students make up their own question and answer sequences to present to the class using the words or sentences I have prepared.

Comment/Self-evaluation: The lesson took longer than expected. One more pair of words and sentences needed for each contrast. Some students dominated — others got unruly. A fairly good though not brilliant lesson. Contingency plan should have been the final part of the lesson.

From Celce-Murcia, M. & McIntosh, L. (eds). (1979). *Teaching English as a second or foreign language*. Rowley, MA: Newbury House Publishers, Inc. pp. 299-301.

SAMPLE LESSON PLAN (2)

MASTER PLAN

Ⅰ. Instructor:

Ⅱ. Date:

Ⅲ. Grade: 3rd Grade, Middle School

Ⅳ. Text: Middle School English Ⅲ

Ⅴ. Unit: Lesson 10, American and Korean Holidays

Ⅵ. Unit objectives

A. Students will be able to request what their partners have just said using *Beg your pardon.*

B. Students will be able to express hesitation naturally by using *Let me see.*

C. Students will be able to act appropriately when given commands using *just as.*

D. Students will be able to demonstrate understanding of the reading part by answering comprehension question.

E. Students will be able to pronounce /e/ correctly.

F. Students will be able to talk and write about similarities and differences between American and Korean holidays.

Ⅶ. Teaching Points

A. Pronunciation: sound of ‘e’ in such words as American, remember, meter

B. Words: holiday, independence, declare

C. Useful Expressions: Beg your pardon? Let me see

D. Structures:

1. What are the biggest holidays other than Christmas?
2. We eat turkeys just as the pilgrims did.

Ⅷ.

Time Allotment	Materials	Activities	Teaching Aids
1st Period	· Warming-up · Prestudy	· Brainstorming · TPR · Vocabulary study	· PPT · Vocabulary cards
2nd Period	· Listen & Speak · Communication Activity · Pronunciation	· Repetition drill · Substitution drill · Comprehension check-up	· Tape/recorder · Chart · Picture Cards.
3rd Period	· Reading Material	· Spot dictation · Guessing meaning from context · Vocabulary study · Writing example sentences · Comprehension check-up	· Tape/recorder · Chart · PPT
4th Period	· Writing	· Filling in the bland · Outlining · Singing	· Opaque projector · Tape recorder

* SUB-PLAN 2

Ⅰ. Instructor:

Ⅱ. Date:

Ⅲ. Period: 2nd Period

Ⅳ. Unit: Lesson 10, American and Korean Holidays

Ⅴ. Teaching aids: textbook('Listen and Speak' part, 'Communication Activity'), chart, picture cards, tape recorder

Ⅵ. Time: 50 minutes

Ⅶ. Lesson objectives

A. To have the students answer Yes-No, Wh-questions about the materials listened.

B. To have the students have conversation with each other using *Beg your pardon.*

C. To have them pronounce the sound 'e' in the words such as American, remember, meter accurately.

Ⅷ. Teaching Procedure

Procedure	Teacher-Students activities	Time(m)
Introduction	*** Greeting** T: (asks one of the students what he/she did last night.) *** Roll-calling** T: (calls the roll by calling the students' first names.) ***Review and checking assignment** T: (has the class listen to the tape of 'prestudy' part learned last time carefully.) S: (listen.) T: (has one or two students answer the following question concerned with 'prestudy' part.) I think that Seoul is the biggest city in Korea. What is the next biggest city? S: (answers.) T: (pretends that he doesn't understand what S_1 said.) T: pardon? S: (answers again.) T: (shows S_2 the picture below and asks him/her the following question.) Do just as the man in the picture does. S: (acts the man in the picture.)	12
	 *** Presentation of lesson objectives**	
Development	*** Presentation of the new material** T: (has the class listen to the tape of 'Listen and Speak' part carefully.) Ss: (listen twice.) T: (has the students answer the following Yes-No and Wh-questions.) T: Did America declare its independence from England? Ss: (Yes, it did.) T: When did America declare its independence from England? Ss: (It declared it on July 4th in 1776.) T: Do we have our Independence Movement Day on March 1st? Ss: (Yes, we do.)	25

<table>
<tr><td></td><td>
T: When did our Independence Movement start?
S_S: (It started on March 1st in 1919.)
T: When did the Second World War end?
S_S: (It ended in 1945.)
T: (chooses one or two students of the class to have them ask and answer the above questions with the teacher's help, and then has all the class have a conversation with their partner using the above questions and answers. They are to use Beg your pardon appropriately)

* Teaching the sound 'e'
T: (has the students listen to the tape of the pronunciation part of the text looking at the chart)

[e] America remember independence better second celebrate
[i] remember independence declare republic
[i:] meter evening even

T: (has the students listen and repeat.)
S_S: (listen and repeat.)
T: (checks individual student's pronunciation by pointing words randomly)
</td><td></td></tr>
<tr><td></td><td>
* Communication Activities
· Substitution Drill
T: (has the class do the drill following the model below.)

A: <u>When is — New Year's Day?</u>
B: <u>It's the first of [Jan] uary.</u>
1. Children's Day 2. Chusok
3. Christmas

T: (has the students in pairs have a conversation with each other.)
T: (shows a picture card.)
S_1: When is Children's Day?
S_2: It's the fifth of May.
T: (shows a picture cards.)
</td><td></td></tr>
</table>

	S_2: When is Chusok? S_1: It's the 15th day of the 8th lunar month. (with teacher's help if necessary) S_2: (When is April Fool's Day?) S_1: (When is Parents' Day?) S_2: ( )	
Consolidation	T: (has the class listen to and repeat 'Listen and Speak' part.) S_S: (listen and repeat.) T: (writes on the blackboard 'remember', 'meter', 'declare', and has one of the students pronounce them correctly, which is followed by teacher's correction if necessary.) * **Translation** 어린이날은 언제입니까? 5월 5일입니다. T: (has one or two of the class translate the above Korean sentences into English, which is followed by teacher's correction or praise.) * **Assignment** · Reading 'the reading material'. · Practicing the dialogues and the pronunciation learned today enough to recite and pronounce them with their books closed. * **Greeting.**	13

SAMPLE LESSON PLAN (3)

Ⅰ. Subject: Elementary ESL class

Ⅱ. Class Size: Twenty-five to thirty students

Ⅲ. Text: Elementary course in English, Willard D. Sheeler

Ⅳ. Class Period: Fifty minutes

Ⅴ. Equipment: Overhead projector

Ⅵ. Materials:

1. A set of flash cards with magazine cutouts to teach and drill adjectives.
2. a transparency with line drawings for eliciting comparative sentences.
3. A blank overlay for writing sentences describing the drawings in #1.
4. A transparency with a sentence builder using "more" or "less."
5. A transparency with line drawings for eliciting sentences in the superlative.
6. A blank overlay for writing sentences describing the drawings in #5.
7. A transparency with a sentence builder using "the most" and "the least."
8. A transparency containing sentences with irregular comparatives and superlatives: better, best, worse, worst.
9. A transparency showing orthographic changes: y→ie, easy-easier-easiest.

Ⅶ. Previous Lessons: The class has completed Units 18-24 of the text. Unit 19 contains drills on the objectives of color, size, shape, and condition.

Ⅷ. Lesson Objective: To produce comparative and superlative sentences orally and in writing with ninety percent accuracy.

Ⅸ. Activities:

1. Warm up
2. Presentation of the forms of the comparative on an overhead transparency.
3. Oral pattern drill on the comparative.
4. Presentation of the forms of the superlative on an overhead transparency.
5. Oral pattern drill on the superlative.
6. Small group work - Communicative practice.

Ⅹ. Procedures:

1. Warm up

   Vocabulary review of adjectives

   a. Teacher displays the cue cards, one by one, and asks the class to describe them. Students say: *That girl is pretty. That man is tall. That car is old.*

That house is modern. Etc.

b. Teacher asks class if anyone can think of a person who is tall, famous intelligent, pretty, etc. Students may refer to their classmates if they wish.

2. New material

a. Teacher shows transparency with drawings for teaching the comparative.

b. Pattern drill

Teacher: tall

Class: Jack is taller than Bill.

Teacher	Class
fat	
thin	
small	
short	
mean	
nice	
slow	
clean	
dirty	
smart	
dumb	

c. Teacher shows transparency with sentence builder, pronounces a few model sentences and asks the class to practice producing others orally.

		intelligent	
		important	
This man is		comfortable	
This book is	more	expensive	than that one.
This chair is	less	beautiful	
		difficult	
		interesting	
		capable	

d. Generalization: Teacher shows the following transparency:

I	II
Jack is tall.	Jack is taller than Bill.
Fred is short.	Fred is shorter than Bob.
Jane is smart.	Jane is smarter than Joe.
Mary is nice.	Mary is nicer than Jane.

III	IV
Jack is intelligent.	Jack is more intelligent than Bob.
Fred is interesting.	Fred is more interesting than Bill.
Jane is beautiful.	Jane is more beautiful than Mary.
Sue is capable.	Sue is more capable than Lisa.

XI. Teacher's Questions:

1. Look at the underlined words in Column I. How many syllables do you find in each word?
2. When you use these words in comparative sentences (Column II), what ending do you add?
3. Now look at the underlined words in Column III. How many syllables do you find in each word?
4. When you use these words in comparative sentences (Column IV), what other word must you put before each adjective?

e. Teacher shows transparency with drawings for teaching the superlative and follows some procedures used for the comparative lesson.

f. Teacher gives class sentence builders using *better, worse, the best*, and the *worst*.

This	chair dentist car teacher lesson map doctor house book room man	is	better worse	than	that one.

This	chair dentist car teacher lesson map doctor house book man	is	the best. the worst.

g. Teacher shows transparency with orthographic changes. Only the first three examples are completed. The class dictates the other changes and the teacher writes them in.

	Comparative	Superlative
easy	easier than	the easiest
funny	funnier than	the funniest
lonely	lonelier than	the loneliest
pretty		
ugly		
lazy		

3. Small Group Work - Communicative Practice

Divide the class randomly into groups of three. Each group is to find the answers to the following questions:

Who is the tallest?

Who is the youngest?

Who is the richest today? (each person counts the money he or she is carrying)

Then the class reassembles and the groups report their findings.

XII. Homework:

Group A: Students create original sentences.

Write your opinion of the following people or objects by using comparatives or superlatives.

Example: A. Hong-Ik University

Hong-Ik University has the best fine arts college in the country.

B. *American children*

American children are more independent than Korean children.

1. Korean women
2. Korean food
3. The city where we now are
4. Korean men
5. The President of Korea
6. The Minister of Education
7. Korean T.V. programs
8. Korean houses
9. Korean films
10. Your English teacher

Group B: Students write an exercise.
Change each adjective to its opposite and rewrite the sentence (use another piece of paper).

Example: Mary is the tallest girl in the class.
→ Mary is the shortest girl in the class.

1. This is the worst room in the house.
2. I think my English is better than yours.
3. That table is older than mine.
4. Jack is the smartest boy in the class.
5. He married the most beautiful girl in the world.
6. I think that boy is faster than his brother.
7. This lesson is more difficult than that one.
8. This car is cheaper than yours.
9. Mr. Jones is the oldest teacher in our school.
10. Today's lesson is shorter than yesterday's.
11. Her house is smaller than his.
12. I think my country is more beautiful than yours.
13. This problem is simpler than that one.
14. This machine is the most modern in the factory.
15. Her sister is the most intelligent student in the class.
16. Marguerite is the richest woman I know.
17. The earliest you can leave is 6:00.
18. He is the laziest student I know.
19. John is more athletic than Steve.

20. I am healthier than you.

Group C: Students write Exercises 1, 2 and 3 on pages 134 and 135 in the textbook.

Follow-up for the Next Day

Group B and C will be given dittoed sheets with the correct answers so that they may check their assignments. Meanwhile, the teacher is rapidly checking or spot-checking the original sentences written by Group A.

Then the entire class listens to the sentences composed by Group A and indicates whether or not they agree. This becomes the basis for a conversation class.

From Allen, E. D. & Valette, R. M. (1977). *Classroom techniques: foreign languages and English as a second language,* Harcourt Brace Jovannovich, Inc. pp. 403-410.

PART TEN

TEACHERS' ROLE

앞의 장들에서 영어의 각 기능별 지도 및 평가, 그리고 학습지도안 작성에 대해 이론과 실제를 살펴보았지만 어떤 영어교사가 되어야 하는지 교사에 초점을 맞추어 논의하지는 않았다.

이 장은 교사를 중심으로 수업을 이끌어가는 교수기술을 수업환경, 학습활동, 학생참여, 오류수정 등 네 부분으로 나누어 분석기준을 구체적인 예를 들며 설명한 Bailey와 Celce-Murcia의 논문을 소개하는 것으로 시작한다. 이어서 교사의 자질과 관련된 성찰적 교사교육에 대해 Chang은 자세히 설명한다. 자기 평가뿐 아니라 다른 교사의 수업을 평가하는 기준이 될 수 있을 것이다.

마지막으로 결과중심 교수요목에 따라 교과서의 내용을 순서대로 진행해가는 수동적인 교사가 아니고 과정중심 교수를 계획하고 실행하는 능동적인 교사가 요구되는 현 시대를 논해 볼 수 있는 Lee의 글을 다룬다.

38. CLASSROOM SKILLS FOR ESL TEACHERS

INTRODUCTION

Teaching English as a second language has now come to be recognized as a legitimate profession. Many people realize that being an effective ESL teacher demands training and practice. Being a native speaker of English, or a fairly fluent non-native speaker, is not enough. Yet because of credentialing policies and financial pressures on school districts, many ESL teachers in the public schools have gained experience without much formal testing. On the other hand, young teachers just entering the profession may leave their university training with limited practical experience, in spite of strong theoretical preparation.

It is the purpose of this chapter to address both groups of teachers by considering some current research findings and exploring their possible classroom applications. We will first suggest four significant areas of classroom interaction that ESL teachers should be aware of in planning a language lesson and in analyzing their own teaching: the social climate, the variety in learning activities, the opportunity for student participation, and the need for feedback and correction. We will also offer suggestions as to how to implement various teaching strategies related to these important topics. Finally, we will suggest a framework for self-evaluation following a language lesson. It is hoped that the information presented here will provide teachers with ideas for putting currently available theory into useful practice.

SOCIAL CLIMATE

Recent research in language acquisition both in natural environments (Schumann, 1975) and in instructional situations (Stevick, 1976) as well as in teacher effectiveness (Moskowitz, 1976; Moskowitz, Benevento and Furst, 1973; Moskowitz and Hyman, 1974) indicates that the social environment in which a person learns a language is one of the most important facets of the language learning experience. The belief that a good social climate promotes communication is widely accepted in modern language teaching. In research conducted at UCLA the ESL faculty chose social climate as the most important among eleven factors related to language teaching (Bailey, 1976). Hunter (1974) has suggested that the teacher is the single most important variable in the classroom. In reviewing the literature on teacher effectiveness, Brophy and Good (1974) found that teacher warmth and enthusiasm consistently show a positive correlation with student achievement. What the teacher says and does is so significant in establishing classroom atmosphere that it can outweigh the effects of materials, methods, and educational facilities. Given the pressures of curriculum demands, the differing needs of the students, overcrowded classes, and too little time, what can the ESL teacher do to promote a good social climate in the classroom?

The first thing the teacher must do is to learn the students' names, no matter how large the class enrollment is. The teacher should also make it clear that the students will need to know one another's names during the course. Furthermore, the teacher should respect each students' wishes about what s/he will be called in class. For example, a student who is not comfortable with the generally relaxed relationships between teachers and students in the US, or one who is older than the teacher, may prefer to be called Mr. Kim or Mrs. Castillo instead of functioning on a first-name basis. By the same token, a teacher should not undertake to change a child's name from *Ng* to *Henry* unless the child himself expresses a desire for a new name. Our names are such integral parts of ourselves that to forget, mispronounce, or alter a name can be taken as a personal affront.

Learning the students' names can be facilitated by knowing something about the individuals in the class. Many teachers find it useful to solicit information from the students about their background, interests and reasons for taking the course. Using this information, the teacher can compile a class information sheet which gives each student's full name, the name s/he wishes to be called in class, his or her interests, his or her country or origin, the language s/he speaks, etc. If students are intermediate or advanced and can read, distributing copies of the sheet will help the students learn their classmates' names. It will also help to break the ice socially. Furthermore, the class information sheet provides meaningful contexts for many grammar lessons. For example, it can be used in forming *wh*-questions (*Who is from Venezuela? What is Marta's hobby? Where was Hilda born?*), comparatives and superlatives (*Jaime is older than Werner; Jose is taller than Yvonne; Kyung Sook is the youngest person in the class*) or relative clauses (*The student who likes tennis is Fumiko; The student who speaks Persian is Hamid)*. Even in exercises that don't utilize the information on the sheet, the students' names can be used to make them more interesting. Of course, if the students are beginners and/or cannot read, the information on the class sheet will be taught as part of class content, bit by bit.

It is likely that the students will gradually get to know one another during the course, especially if the teacher uses information about members of the class for language practice. However, the teacher can take a more active role in insuring that students get acquainted. An interesting introductory activity during the first class meeting can establish a friendly tone for the course. In one variation of this activity the teacher gives each student a card on which s/he neatly prints his or her name. The teacher collects the cards and redistributes them to different people. Each student must then locate the person whose card s/he holds and prepare to introduce him or her to the class. The teacher can tell the class ahead of time what information is needed (name, country of origin, academic major or profession, favorite food or pastime, etc.) or leave it up to the individuals. Normally this distribution of cards means that each student will talk to at least two new people during the class: the person whose name s/he has, and the person who has his or her name. The students also speak briefly to several other people in the process of finding their person because it is sometimes difficult to tell whether the gender of a foreign name is masculine or feminine. When the students have had time to identify and interview one another, one student comes to the front of the class and introduces another, who in turn introduces another, and so on. This activity helps the students and the teacher to match names with faces, but it also gives the teacher a chance to hear each student speak during the first class period. Normally students find it easier to speak about someone else for a few minutes than to talk about themselves. In the class periods this interviewing activity can be expanded to include other sorts of information. For example, after a lesson on wh-questions, the students can interview one another to get the answers to several questions and have practice in posing them: (*What is your name? Where do you live? How old are you? Where were you born?*). The information learned in the interview is then reported to the class as a follow-up activity.

In intermediate or advanced classes any language activity which involves the entire class cooperating on a specific task can enhance the social climate. For example, a story-sorting activity can provide the impetus for a cooperative problem-solving lesson in which the students must use pronoun reference, adverbial time clues, and verb tenses. In planning this activity, the teacher must first choose an interesting story and divide it into as many sentences as there are students in the class. In order to accommodate late-comers or absent students, the teacher should include a few sentences that can be added or deleted without disrupting the story. The sentences are then printed on index cards, which are shuffled and distributed randomly to the students. Each student has only two or three minutes to memorize his or her sentence. The cards are then collected and the students try to sort themselves into a logical story line. In order to do this, they must listen carefully to one another's recitations and discuss the syntax as well as the content of each sentence. This task usually involves a great deal of positive communication. It also gives the class a feeling of community accomplishment when the finished story is finally presented. In a large group the teacher can split the class into two groups working on the same task by providing a double set of cards. The value of such an activity is that it involves the students using English with one another rather than with the teacher.

The physical environment of a classroom can greatly influence the social climate in an ESL class. Rooms with fixed desks and/or laboratory-like partitions on the tables have an isolating effect on the students. It is difficult, at best, to promote small group interaction in a room full of barriers. Frequently a teacher has little or no control over the facilities, but within certain limits much can be done to improve the environment. First of all is the classroom clean and comfortable? Do the decorations (e. g., bulletin boards, displays, posters, etc.) and the arrangement of the furniture make the students feel at ease? The teacher may not always have time to create bulletin board displays, but students can be given interesting and productive assignments to develop a display around a grammar point, a vocabulary set, minimal pairs, etc. If there are no bulletin boards, the teacher and students can contribute travel posters or drawings to brighten up the room.

Regardless of the classroom layout, the teacher must be aware of the influence the environment can exert on classroom interaction. For example, research has shown that teachers tend to call on people sitting in particular areas of the room (Brophy and Good, ibid.). It is up to the teacher to avoid this pattern by calling on people in the back row or in the corners as often as those in the front or center of the room. The atmosphere of the class can be severely affected if the teacher seems to have "pets" or favor some students over others. The way the teacher manages grouping or the arrangement of desks can prevent the formation of cliques and involve the students in new communicative situations.

Whatever the physical set-up of the classroom may be, the teacher can do much with it to promote learning. Even in a bare classroom one can be imaginative. For example, in a windowless room, the teacher can ask students to imagine a window in a blank wall and then ask individuals to tell the class what they "see" through the window. When no materials are available through the school system, it is up to the teacher to either bring in items of interest or creatively use what little is available to stimulate student interest.

All of these factors — careful attention to names, the students information sheet, introductions and interviews; cooperative learning tasks, and the physical arrangement of the room — can contribute greatly to the social climate of an ESL class. Throughout the course, as well as at the beginning, the teacher should plan activities in which students can pursue and share their own interests. Field trips, oral reports, research projects, and media presentations will be more meaningful if they are in some way related to the students' lives. With adult classes, or in any situation where the curriculum is relatively flexible, the teacher can solicit input from the students about the course content. An informal mid-term evaluation can provide the teacher with valuable feedback about the students' perception of class activities. Using a brief written questionnaire which the students answer anonymously can determine which activities have been most helpful, which have been least helpful, and what there should be more of during the remainder of the course. The social climate can be improved if the students have some voice in what they are learning and feel that the teacher is responsive to their needs.

Ultimately, the responsibility for the classroom atmosphere lies with the teacher. It is important to begin each class period with some expression of interest in the students as individuals: *Maria, is your baby better now? Ahmad, did you get your car fixed? Yoko, the revision of your composition was a big improvement.* Opportunities for humor should be exploited as well. If there is a cartoon, joke, or anecdote that pertains to the lesson, the teacher should share it with the group. In a study that compared outstanding teachers with beginning and "typical" teachers in inner-city schools, Moskowitz and Hayman (ibid.) found that the best teachers used humor in their initial contacts with students. Social climate is affected by the teacher's behavior both inside and outside of class. Whenever time permits, the teacher should be available to discuss problems with students before and after class.

Finally the teacher should project an enthusiastic and positive image. It is unlikely that the students will become actively involved in the material if the teacher doesn't seem to enjoy teaching the course. In another study that compared outstanding and typical language teachers, Moskowitz (ibid.) found that outstanding teachers smiled more than typical teachers, and there was more laughter in their classrooms. In looking at the whole issue of social climate, one must ask whether the teacher's behavior, the physical arrangements, and the class atmosphere work together to create a pleasant learning environment.

VARIETY IN LEARNING ACTIVITIES

Research and common sense suggest that variety makes a language lesson more interesting. A variety of activities can reinforce the teaching point without boring the students. Research by Moskowitz (ibid.) and Politzer (1970) has shown that good language teachers (whether "good teaching" is defined by student achievement records or student evaluations of teaching) use a variety of activities in language lessons. Furthermore, a well-selected variety of activities prevents boredom, minimizes classroom control problems, and even encourages student achievement (Medley and Mitzel, 1963; Moskowitz, ibid; Politzer, 1970; Politzer and Weiss, 1970).

Traditionally ESL teachers have followed the suggested sequence of activities of listening, speaking, reading and writing, because it is thought to parallel the natural language learning process; however, even the validity of this sequence has recently been questioned (Van Syoc, 1977). In using substitution drills, for example, we have often begun with the entire class repeating, then moved to one row at a time, and then individual students. These are certainly good ideas, but the whole question of using variety of activities in a language lesson is much broader and more complex than this. Stevick (1959) was one of the first to recognize this fact in a very useful article on the rhythm of classroom activity and the need for variation in pacing.

At this point it is important to note that here *variety* does not mean a hodgepodge of unrelated activities. In this chapter, variety in learning activities refers to the number and effectiveness (i. e., quality *and* quantity) of the different language tasks the teacher provides for the students to do in mastering the teaching point. In lower level classes, in particular, it is important that these activities be sequenced from easy to difficult, and manipulative to communicative (Prator, 1965). In planning a lesson, the teacher should consider what types of activities would enable the students to understand, practice, and internalize the teaching point.

Nowadays a great deal of variety can be introduced through the use of audiovisual aids. Videotape and audio recordings, filmstrip and movie projectors, overhead projectors and sound-on-slide programs all make the teacher's job easier, but at the same time more challenging and complicated. The thought of coordinating and operating these machines and keeping a language lesson going at the same time can be intimidating. However, with a little practice and some careful planning, the use of such equipment can add variety and interest to a language lesson that would be impossible to achieve in a "one-man show." In fact, Moskowitz and Hayman (ibid.) found that those teachers identified as outstanding by their students used a variety of AV aides, while new and typical teachers did not use many.

Beginning with the traditional sequence of listening, speaking, reading, and writing, we can ask ourselves what variety can be included in these different activities. For example, much of the language lesson involves students in listening, even if, it is just listening to the teacher explain a grammar point. But students quickly become adjusted to their own teacher's voice. They may be able to understand the teacher perfectly well and yet have trouble understanding a neighbor, a bus driver, or a clerk in a store. For this reason, the teacher should provide opportunities for the students to listen to other people speaking English. Tape recordings of live conversations or radio broadcasts are useful, as are videotape recordings of lectures and television programs. Recordings of songs in English can be used with cloze passages of the lyrics to give students guided practice in listening for particular words in context. Films, sound-on-slide programs, or filmstrips with cassette recordings, can provide listening practice reinforced by visual images. Having a guest speaker in class gives the students the chance to hear an entirely new voice. In this situation they can also ask questions of the speaker, which isn't possible with a film, videotape of audio recording. The variety of activities possible in a listening exercise is limited only by the teacher's imagination and the equipment available.

There is also the potential for great variety in speaking activities. In addition to participating in regular live classroom discourse, students can record themselves reading a passage, telling stories, or performing dialogues. Videotaping oral reports or skits provides the students with instant feedback on their pronunciation, fluency, and body language. Such recordings can later be used as student-generated listening materials.

Teletrainers can also be used for a variety of speaking (and listening) activities in the ESL classroom. The teletrainers are a set of two telephones with long cords and a control box which produces a ring and a busy signal. The conversation can be limited to just the two parties on the line, or it can be projected to the entire classroom. Placing the two parties where they can't see each other simulates telephone speech in which the students must get or convey information without the assistance of gestures or facial expressions. The teletrainers also provide a realistic situation for the students to ask questions, rather than just responding to the teacher's questions. Several telephone companies loan the teletrainers to schools free of charge as a public service.

Even when such sophisticate AV equipment is not available, the average teacher has access to thousands of inexpensive items that students can talk about. Pictures cut from magazines can be used in grammar lessons, pronunciation practice, in telling stories or writing dialogues. Common household items can be hidden in a bag while one student describes an item so that his or her classmates can guess its identity.

In introducing more variety into the speaking component of a lesson, the teacher should consider the objectives of the lesson and the language proficiency of the class. Activities should be carefully planned to encourage the students to use the language for communicative purposes. If the proposed activity is too easy, students may become bored, but if it is too difficult, they can get discouraged. In planning a lesson, the teacher should ask him- or herself what communicative activities could be used to get the students talking and give them realistic practice with the teaching point.

Like listening, reading is involved in many language lessons because textbooks are the sources of much of the information students get in class. Research by Politzer (ibid.) has shown that good language teachers are not "book-bound." There are hundreds of things for students to read other than textbooks. Newspapers, magazines, signs, maps, schedules, travel brochures, catalogs, letters, and comic books — in short, anything the students would want to read anyway — can be adapted for use in language lessons. Regardless of the actual material to be read, students may read silently or aloud (to the class, to themselves, to a partner, or on tape). In silent reading, the student can skim for specific information, read to find the main idea, read for entertainment, or do in-depth reading for details. Reading in English is vital, whether it is the main objective of the lesson, or a means to another end.

Sometimes the reading component of a lesson may be as simple as reading the directions to an exercise aloud. In a grammar lesson, students may read what their classmates have written on the blackboard as a lead-in to peer correction. In more advanced classes students can read one another's compositions, which have been duplicated or put on overhead transparencies. Whatever the purpose of the exercise, there are numerous ways in which reading can be used to add variety to a language lesson.

Like the other language skills, writing may be the primary objective of a lesson, or it may be secondary or incidental to the teaching point. For example, grammar and vocabulary lessons often involve some amount of writing in English. But writing can also be a powerful means of adding variety to a language lesson. For instance, even at the early stages of English instruction, stories written by the students themselves can provide reading materials and excellent topics for discussion. Before or after a grammar lesson, a brief writing assignment can provide the teacher with data for error analysis. Students can write as a follow-up to almost any other language activity.

Much has been written about the value of controlled, guided, and free composition. Dicto-comps (Wishon and Burks, 1968) and speed-writing (Celce-Murcia, 1974) can also be used to get students started on writing composition. However, classroom writing should not necessarily be limited to formal expository writing. Students can also use their English in writing short stories, poems, plays, radio dramas, advertisements, dialogues or role-plays, business and personal letters, editorials or jokes. Many teachers find it useful to allow ten minutes of class time for students to write in their own cultural journals, describing their experiences in living in a new place and learning a new language. Keeping a journal not only provides the student with an outlet for personal expression, but also prompts him or her to write about those things which are most important to him or her at the time.

Although independent writing is extremely important, students can also benefit from collaborating on written work. Pairs or groups of students writing a paper together can share ideas, suggest vocabulary, and correct one another's grammar problems. Or the entire class can contribute to one large group composition which is written on the blackboard or an overhead transparency. An anthology of student writings can be produced by the teacher, or it can be edited and developed by the students themselves.

Whatever the particular teaching point may be, in planning the lesson the teacher should consider several ways of making the lesson interesting and stimulating. Careful sequencing of the activities (easy to difficult, manipulative to communicative) will insure that the basic presentation is logical and coherent. Audiovisual equipment, pictures and realia, communication games, student-generated materials, flexible reading and writing assignments, cultural journals and anthologies of the students' work are all means of adding variety to the language classroom. The teacher should utilize whatever activities and equipment will help the students learn the material. However, careful planning and some practice are needed to insure that the activities and AV aids work *with* the lesson and not against it. The objective is to get the students' English out of the textbooks and into the real world. With a little research into the professional journals and a trip to the local educational resource center, the ESL teacher can discover hundreds of useful ideas for adding variety and interest to his or her lessons.

OPPORTUNITY FOR STUDENT PARTICIPATION

It is an axiom of modern language teaching that active use of the language is crucial to good language learning. Yet as ESL teachers we are often faced with anywhere from twenty to sixty students in a class. Given these numbers, how can the teacher involve all the students in the use of the language? Choral repetition has traditionally been used to get many students speaking at once, but can we say students are really *using* the language if they simply repeat en masse?

A possible solution to this dilemma is to increase the opportunity for student participation by cutting back on the amount of "teacher talk" in the lesson. Careful preparation can change the classroom interaction from teacher-dominated activities to teacher/student communication and finally to student/student communication. It stands to reason that planning opportunities for student/student communication will involve a greater number of students in an active, *cognitive* use of the language than does choral repetition or even an mathematically even distribution of turns by the teacher.

How can one plan opportunities for student participation? A simple way to start is to get the students involved in classroom management tasks. Students can call the roll, return corrected papers, develop a bulletin board display, read announcements, etc. Although these are minor details, involving the students in these chores can promote interaction, a sense of teamwork, and the learning of names. The important thing is for the teacher to begin to loosen his or her hold on the total domination/management of the classroom.

Those activities which are teacher-led should be carefully planned to involve all the students. Sometimes teachers are able to call on students randomly, or strike a balance between calling on volunteers and drawing out the quieter students. In a large class it may be helpful for the teacher to use a set of index cards with a student's name on each card. The teacher can flip through the cards, calling on each student as his or her name appears. This simple system can help to ensure a fairer distribution of turns since research (Allwright, 1977) has shown that ESL teachers typically do not distribute turns evenly among students (e. g., we sometimes rely too heavily on bright students or call on those who "look ready").

Another way to involve more students more often is by using a chain-drill approach to grammar. Even at the early stages of language instruction, chain drills can be used to cut down on "teacher talk" and maximize student participation. For example, asking and answering questions has traditionally been a teacher-dominated activity:

Teacher: *Juan, what time do you get up in the morning?*
Juan: *I get up at seven o'clock every morning.*
Teacher: *Very good. Beatriz, what time do you get up in the morning?*

Beatriz: *I get up at six-thirty every day.*
Teacher: *Good...*

When a chain drill is used in the following situation, "teacher talk" is minimized and the students are able to say more:

Teacher: *Juan, what time do you get up in the morning?*
Juan: *I get up at seven o'clock every morning.*
Teacher: *Very good. Find out when Beatriz gets up.*
Juan: *Beatriz, what time do you get up in the morning?*
Beatriz: *I get up at six-thirty every day.*
Juan: *She gets up at six-thirty every day.*

This exchange would be followed by Beatriz finding out when a third student eats breakfast, and so on. With this small change in the teacher's strategy Juan's involvement in the language lesson grew from a simple response to phrasing the question himself (using the *do* auxiliary, rising intonation, and the correct pronoun) and rephrasing the other student's response (employing the correct pronoun, using the third person singular -s marker, and reporting the information). Thus the student was not only given more time to talk, but the opportunity to engage in a much more complicated language task as well. Although it takes careful preparation by the teacher, a chain drill format can be applied to many grammar lessons to increase the opportunity for student participation in the English lesson.

The next logical step in increasing the opportunities for student participation is to ask oneself what *language* activities can be done by the students just as well as by the teacher. Phrased in another way, how can the teacher say less and utilize the students' knowledge more? The opportunities for using such an approach are numerous, even in a lesson that isn't specifically planned to include student/student interaction. For example, teachers are quick to answer questions, when the students themselves could answer many of their peers' questions. Inquiries about vocabulary, spelling, or grammar can easily be thrown back to the class: *That's a good question. Who can answer it?* As opposed to a straightforward teacher response, this strategy involves more people in the use of the language, it keeps the entire class alert and listening, and it provides more chances for hypothesis-testing by the students. Furthermore, it allows the teacher to monitor the production of more students more often.

Taking this idea one step further, the teacher should sometimes plan opportunities for various students to play the part of the teacher. Following presentation and practice of a grammar point, for instance, one student can come to the front of the class and ask questions or distribute the turns in an exercise. Or one student can come to the blackboard and write the answers given by his or her classmates. Those at their desks must speak clearly and the student at the board must listen and write carefully. The entire class must negotiate the spelling of words that are problematic for the "teacher." This sort of activity also works well in using an overhead projector. One student can arrange words or sentences on the screen with directions and feedback from the class. Such a task involves more people more *actively* than if the teacher were simply standing there soliciting the input from one student at a time. This technique can be utilized for almost any word order problem (passive, question formation), practice in paragraph unity (arranging sentences in a logical order, deleting extraneous material), or organization (outlining, grouping by part of speech, etc.).

There are many cases in which students can benefit from working in pairs instead of having the attention of the entire class focused on the teacher. For example, after a lesson on the future tense, students can find out what their partners plan to do that evening or over the weekend. This interview activity is followed by each student reporting the information s/he has learned to the class. During the reporting step, students receive feedback on their use of the future tense. Of course, there is the possibility that some of the questions and answers in this type of activity will involve errors that go uncorrected, even if the teacher circulates and listens during the interviews. But the technique is useful in that the students are utilizing the structures learned in gaining information, a situation which approaches genuine communication.

Pairs of students can also jointly produce information. After studying irregular past tense verbs, for example, students can collaborate on writing a story using those verbs, after which they can read the story to their classmates, who then give them feedback on the correct use of the past tense forms. After working on a pronunciation lesson, pairs of students can write dialogues, then present them before the entire group. There are just a few of the many ways pairs of students can accomplish the same things the teacher would do with individuals or with the entire class.

In using students in pairs, the teacher should first provide the basic information (i. e., the data or rules to work with) and then carefully structure and define the task the students are to perform, so as to give clear and concise directions to the class. In some cases it may be useful for the teacher to determine the pairings in advance (for example, to avoid getting two students from the same language background together, to evenly match English fluency levels, or to put a more advanced student with one who is having problems). Once the pair work begins, the teacher is free to monitor the language production, or respond to questions. Since the idea here is to let the students do most of the talking, the teacher must remember not to interfere, unless the pairs have problems accomplishing the task.

Some language learning or language practicing activities are more appropriate for small group work than for pairs of students. Students can also prepare stories or dialogues in groups of three or four. Many role-playing and problem-solving tasks lend themselves well to groups of three or four students (for example exercises, see Rosensweig, 1974). The well-known "values clarification" exercises (see Simon et al., 1972) and other tasks that involve debatable issues are better suited to groups of three or more than to pairs. Age is also a factor. In elementary classes, students can either complete worksheets individually and then compare answers in small groups, or work in small groups from the start. Some teachers prefer to give only one paper to each group to insure that the students do, in fact, discuss the topic (Allwright, personal communication).

A teacher who decides to try using small groups should consider the effects of various grouping strategies on student participation. It is often helpful to use heterogeneous grouping by language background to guarantee the use of English as the medium of discussion. If students always choose their own groups they may easily come to rely on their friends too much in producing the language. In some language tasks it may be useful to try to have the groups evenly divided between men and women. It may also be desirable to have one talkative person in each group to stimulate discussion. In other cases the teacher may decide to put all the talkative students in one group, so the quieter students will have more opportunity to participate. The method of dividing the class into groups depends largely on the students' background and proficiency and the objective of the lesson. In planning the lesson the teacher should consider which approach would be most appropriate for the activity. As with pair work, during group work the teacher's role is to assist when help is needed, to keep the students working on the task (by offering encouragement, settling disputes, etc.) and to observe the students' use of the language. Normally it is not the teacher's role to interfere or to direct the groups. For this reason it is extremely important that the original explanation of the task, and the students' responsibility for completing the job, be made explicit from the beginning of the exercise. If there is a follow-up activity, for example, the group may choose a spokesperson, or the teacher can choose someone who was relatively passive during the exercise.

Like group cooperation, competition can be used to provide opportunities for student participation. There are many variations on the old spelling bee, which can be used to get the students involved in the language. If the language task is appropriate for the students' ability, adults will enjoy these games as well as children. For example, each student can win points for his or her team by correctly spelling and defining a word with a given prefix. In such a competition, each person is encouraged and coached by his or her teammates. The teacher merely serves as the authority or checks the dictionary. Team competition can be used with hundreds of lesson plans: anything from basic grammatical structures (using the correct preposition, changing a present tense sentence to past tense, etc.) or using a vocabulary item correctly at the lower levels, to asking and answering questions about a classmate's oral report at the upper levels. Whatever type of competitive team activity is used, it is important that the teacher think through the game process and define the rules ahead of time, to insure maximum participation and to prevent confusion.

All of the teaching strategies discussed above — utilizing classroom management chores, name cards and chain drills, turning students' questions back to the class, having a student "play teacher" at the blackboard or overhead projector, pair work, small group work, and team competition — are ways of increasing the opportunity for student participation. The thing to remember is that ESL students need practice in using the language, as well as formal instruction. For the child who speaks no English at home or for the adult learner who works all day among non-English-speaking colleagues, the English class may provide the only opportunity to actively use the language. Keeping this in mind, teachers should learn to minimize the amount of time they spend talking in order to increase the opportunities for the students to utilize their English.

FEEDBACK AND CORRECTION

Although much has been written about feedback and correction in language classrooms, these issues continue to be hotly debated in discussions of methodology. Recent studies have investigated the effectiveness of various feedback and correction strategies (Zahorik, 1968; Lucas, 1975; Fanselow, 1974). Other writers have advocated a policy of non-interference (Castaños and Long, 1976). Others have investigated teacher and learner preferences regarding correction (Cathcart and Olsen, 1976).

The fact remains that many students enroll in ESL classes expecting to be corrected. The teacher is faced with the problem of deciding what to criticize, what to praise, and what to ignore. It is generally accepted that correct responses in a language lesson should be positively reinforced, either by simple confirmation or extended praise, but there is little agreement on what to do with problem utterances. Traditionally, it has been the teacher's role to correct errors in syntax, pronunciation, and vocabulary. But teacher correction may be the least effective form of feedback in terms of student retention and improvement. Students can repeat corrected words or phrases without internalizing them. In fact, when a student is concentrating on conveying a particular message, s/he may not focus on the correctness of the form. It can be frustrating to have an agreement error corrected after struggling to produce the proper vocabulary items in the correct word order.

Should the teacher be concerned with the medium (the form of the utterance) or the message (the content) or both? Certainly severe problems that interfere with communication must be resolved before the listener can interpret the utterance of the speaker. These problems include cases of severe mispronunciation, confusion of minimal pairs in context, or grammatical errors that interfere with the transmission of the message. If the objectives of the class include improving the students' accuracy as well as their communicative competence, then steps should be taken to help the students monitor their own output. In general, it is our feeling that students should only be held responsible for the correct production of material that has already been covered in class (i. e., performance errors rather than competence problems). One other important area for feedback and correction has to do with the question of competence, however. Competence errors can provide a springboard for highly contextualized learning. For example, in a case where the language learner is groping for exactly the right word but is apparently unfamiliar with the appropriate vocabulary item, the teacher can profitably provide the word or lead another student to supply it. Being receptive and alert to this type of error can enable the teacher to meet students' individual needs in the classroom situation. Thus we suggest the teachers concentrate on three different types of errors: those which interfere with communication, those which involve a self-monitoring process in producing structures and vocabulary which have already been studied, and finally, those errors which involve queries — i. e., the student takes a stab at the question but uses rising intonation in his or her response. Whenever possible the teacher should lead the students to self-correct. Allwright (1975) feels that forcing learners back on their own resources all the time may actually give them more precise help than does simple teacher correction. Asking a student to repeat a phrase may be enough of a signal to the speaker to re-process the utterance while checking for errors. The teacher can also give more specific guidance as to the location of the errors:

Student: *After school he go to work.*
Teacher: *After school he* ___________.
Student: *Goes to work.*

Sometimes gestures can be used to help the student identify problems. The students quickly learn to recognize a system of hand signals for indicating errors. For example, pointing with your thumb backward over your shoulder can represent past tense. Teachers who use such gestures report that the visual cue that something is wrong seems to be less disruptive than verbally indicating an error.

Recent research in discourse analysis (Schegloff, Jefferson, and Sacks, 1977) shows that repairs in native-speakers' conversations are often initiated extralinguistically — with body movements, gestures, or changes of facial expression. They also found a preference for self-initiated self-correction. In examining conversational repair strategies among non-native speakers, Schwartz (1977) found that in natural discourse listeners signal confusion or need for correction by leaning forward when seated and/or raising their eyebrows. Although research has not yet determined the effectiveness of teaching such extralinguistic cues, we as teachers should attempt to expose ESL students to the types of feedback they will get in natural conversation.

Another correcting strategy which can be particularly effective with an adult learner who is unable to determine the source of the error is to diagnose the error and then have the student correct the utterance himself. This procedure gives the student guidance as to the location and nature of the error, but also gives him or her the responsibility for correcting it:

> Teacher: *Where did you go last night?*
> Student: *I go to the movies.*
> Teacher: *What tense do you need?*
> Student: *I went to the movies.*

Clearly not every language problem in the classroom is so easily dealt with as this example would indicate. As Allwright points out (ibid.), the language teacher's task is difficult because s/he cannot always wait to see whether or not an error is significantly frequent, developmental, caused by interference, or simply careless. An ESL teacher must be constantly diagnosing and reacting to errors because everything that is said in the language classroom can be considered input. We will learn more about effective feedback strategies as more research is done on language acquisition, classroom interaction, and teacher effectiveness.

Regardless of the way in which it is instigated, we prefer self-correction to other correction strategies because it should eventually contribute to weaning the student away from the need for overt correction. It forces the student to be more responsible for the original output if no one constantly supplies the correct form for him or her.

If a student is not able to self-correct, for whatever reason (forgetting, competence, nervousness, etc.), the teacher can turn the job of correction over to another student. We feel this strategy is preferable to straight teacher correction because it affords another language learner practice at locating, diagnosing, and repairing a problem. Input from peers can be less intimidating than teacher correction, but it must be handled carefully. The teacher should manipulate the distribution of turns so as to avoid embarrassing a student with constant correction from the same classmate. When a student supplies or corrects an answer that another student missed, the teacher should return again to the student who made the error and give him or her another chance, either with the same question or with another question involving the same potential error. Thus peer correction can be utilized in oral work when the self-correction process breaks down or isn't negotiable. Although peer-correction is external and therefore less desirable than self-correction, it has the advantage of giving all the students more opportunities for language production and hypothesis testing. It also promotes communication among students and decreases the teacher's domination of classroom discourse.

Peer correction can also be used effectively with written assignments. In an advanced class a composition can be dittoed and distributed or viewed by the entire group with an overhead projector. The composition could be a composite developed by the teacher to include representative writing problems, or an actual composition written by a student. In correcting the problems it is important that the teacher maintain a constructive atmosphere so that no one feels embarrassed or unduly criticized.

Some teachers find it useful to have the students read one another's compositions before the teacher sees them. Students can actually write their compositions on ditto masters or bring photocopies to class for small group discussions. Some teachers have found that such a filtering process eliminates many of the mechanical errors common in the writing of intermediate students.

Peer correction can also be useful in analyzing spelling, reading, or grammar exercises, even at the more elementary levels. For example, following a homework assignment, groups of three or four students can compare answers without a key to determine points of disagreement. Such small group correction activities promote peer teaching, hypothesis testing, and student talk. The teacher's role becomes one of resolving conflicting ideas and referring students to sources of information rather than being the authority figure (e. g., *Look at the example on page thirty-eight. What does that tell you about your answer to number four?*). And yet, when the authority is needed, the teacher can quickly prevent the spread of misinformation.

The issues of feedback and correction in classroom interaction are extremely complex. Further study of interlanguage, student achievement, and teachers' reacting moves are needed before we can definitively state what ESL teachers should and should not do. However, our experience suggests that leading a student to self-correct, and ultimately to monitor his or her own language production, is an effective means of promoting learning. Peer-correction can also be used to advantage, but must be carefully managed either in a small group or with the entire class. Finally, teacher correction of errors should be selective. Haphazard errors of performance or errors that block communication demand attention but the teacher should also be alert to gaps in the learner's competence. Because everything that is said in the target language can be considered to be input, the way a teacher responds to what the students produce appears to be extremely important, although not enough is known about this area yet.

EIGHT ADDITIONAL SKILLS

In addition to the teacher skills we have discussed above, there are eight others that we should mention. Four of them are fairly self-evident, and four of them are not.

The four self-evident teacher skills that many beginning and experienced teachers find problematic to some degree are:

a. *Volume* level: Does the teacher maintain an appropriate volume level when speaking?
b. *Clarity*: Does the teacher give clear instructions?
c. *Eye contact*: Does the teacher maintain eye contact with the students whenever talking to them or listening to them?
c. *Legibility*: Are the teacher's materials neat and legible (e. g., clear dittoes and overhead transparencies, legible handwriting on the blackboard, etc.)?

A "no" answer to any of the above questions indicates that the teacher's overall effectiveness is probably being compromised due to inattention to the particular skill involved.

Four other important skills which are somehow less self-evident are the following:

e. *Question posing*: Does the teacher pose the question first and then call on a student to respond (a volunteer or someone s/he selects)?
f. *Pause*: Does the teacher allow an appropriate pause between posing the question and calling on the student?
g. *Wait time*: Does the teacher give the student enough time to answer the question before calling on someone else? Are all students given equal time to respond?
h. *Physical movement*: Does the teacher provide an opportunity for appropriate physical movement during the lesson?

In small-group or one-to-one verbal interaction, people instinctively say the addressee's name before posing a question. This gets the person's attention and helps lead up to the question. However, using the same strategy in front of a classroom with twenty to fifty students can be disastrous since many of the students will not even listen to the question if they know that someone else will be responsible for answering it. Posing the question and then pausing appropriately, before calling on someone, encourages each student to listen and to formulate an answer. Also this procedure often encourages students to volunteer whereas the reverse procedure (i. e., name first and then the question) tends to discourage volunteers.

The third question concerning "wait time" is extremely important since previous research involving science and math teachers (Rowe, 1969) and English teachers (McNeil, 1971) indicates that after posing a question, the teachers in these studies instinctively waited *less* for poor students to answer the question than they did for good ones. When the teachers were made aware of this tendency and were properly trained to slow down for all students, the quality of all their students' responses improved.

In many language classes the students sit at their desks the whole hour and the teacher moves along the board or around the room. In some classes even the teacher remains seated at his or her desk or stands in one spot during the course of a lesson. Such a static format is especially unwise in a language class. One of today's highly effective language teaching methodologies is based on the premise that the learner must listen to imperatives (*stand up, sit down,* etc.) and immediately produce the appropriate physical response (i. e., s/he stands up or sits down) (see Asher, 1965 and 1974). Without adopting Asher's methodology completely, the ESL teacher should be appropriately mobile throughout most of the lesson, whether pantomiming or just moving around to monitor different students. The teacher should — as frequently as appropriate — provide individual students, groups of students, and sometimes even the whole class, with an activity that involves the need for some purposeful physical movement (e. g., going to the board, passing out papers, moving into pairs/groups, role-playing in front of the class or in small groups, etc.). Such activities keep students attentive and alert and insure better learning and retention.

The ESL teacher who is interested in knowing how s/he performs regarding the above eight questions should probably write them out on a sheet and ask a fellow ESL teacher to come and observe a class and to rate him or her with respect to these eight skills. Moreover, the areas of legibility and physical movement (if deficient) can usually be improved merely with proper advance planning.

CONCLUSION

Obviously, not even the best ESL teacher can perform all of the skills and behaviors discussed above perfectly and consistently. Also, additional research will reveal other important skills we have not even mentioned here. The essentials for any teacher are : (a) that s/he be aware of effective teaching skills and behaviors; and (b) that s/he know how his or her own performance compares with the ideal — this means knowledge of one's performance on any one particular lesson or of one's performance in general. Doing this also implies (c) the need to keep up with current classroom research applicable to ESL. All three types of information, when coupled with a sincere desire to improve, should facilitate a change for the better.

From Baily, K. M. & Celce-murcia, M. (1979). Classroom skills for ESL teachers, In Celce-Murcia, M. & McIntosh, L. (ed.). *Teaching English as a second or foreign language,* Rowley, MA: Newbury House Publishers, Inc., pp. 315-330.

39. REFLECTIVE TEACHING: A BOTTOM-UP APPROACH TO INSET

Ⅰ. INTRODUCTION

Over the last two decades, we have seen that the focus of language teacher education has shifted from one paradigm to another. Perspectives on language teacher education have shifted from a knowledge or skill-driven, competency-based, trainer-centered, prescriptive and judgemental model to a process, developmental collaborative and reflective model (Freeman, 1993: Richards & Nunan, 1990; Wallace, 1991). The traditional top-down model for transmitting knowledge and skills to trainees has been challenged because it leaves a dilemma that it cannot solve. There has been debate surrounding the competency-based or top-down approach to teacher education, which is linked to a skill-training model. It has been challenged particularly in the sense that it failed to provide teachers with an opportunity to reflect on their actions. The prescriptive nature of the competency-based approach is contrasted with the holistic approach, which stresses the development of personal qualities of creativity, judgement and adaptability (Britten, 1985, p. 113)

In the field of language teacher education, recent years have also witnessed considerable increase in emphasis on in-service teacher education (INSET, henceforth). The reflective or developmental view encourages in-service teachers to assume the responsibility for improving practice through direct action, critical reflection, and evaluation of their own experience. In the bottom-up model, teachers create for themselves a personal understanding of good classroom practice. Teachers become involved in thinking about how they are learning so that they can use their insights to teach more effectively.

In the following discussion, we shall explore the recent overall shift in INSET from trainer-centered to trainee-centered approach. Then, we shall examine reflective teaching more hoping to understand why it might be a viable approach to language teacher's professional development. Finally, we shall look at some implications for in-service teacher education. Throughout the discussion, we often need to look at the issue in a broader educational context.

II. THE SHIFT OF PERSPECTIVES ON TEACHER TRAINING AND EDUCATION

1. Trainee-centered Language Teacher Training

There is a parallel between shifts of perspectives on language teaching and language teacher training leading to learner-centered and trainee-centered approaches. Along with focus on learner perspective in the language classroom there has been increasing emphasis on differences in individual cognitive and learning styles. As Richards and Lockhart (1994, p. 59) note, cognitive styles can be thought as predispositions to particular ways of approaching learning in the language classroom. In addition, they are intimately related to personality types. According to Knowles' (1982, cited by Richards & Lockhart, 1994, p. 6) distinction, some learners with a communicative learning styles prefer a social approach to learning, that is working in groups. On the other hand, learners with an authority-oriented style are said to be responsible and dependent. It is assumed that they prefer the teacher as an authority figure and they are not comfortable with discussion and group activities.

In a similar vein, there has been focus on trainee perspectives in the teacher training context. Emphasis on difference in learning styles has led trainers to the question: What kind of teacher supervisory modes should approximately be taken for different trainees with various cognitive styles? While the learner-centered approach to language teaching calls for teachers' better understanding of learner's needs, beliefs and variety, there is need for trainers' better understanding of trainees' expectations, needs, attitudes and individual difference in learning styles.

2. Multiplication Of Trainer's Roles

The more student-centered communicative language teaching has provided a significant implication for the training classroom in light of roles. As Wright (1987, 1990) indicates, while some roles are defined by the work people do, others are defined by the kind of interpersonal relationships they imply. In the teaching context, it is assumed that teachers interpret their roles in different ways depending on the context in which they work, their teaching methods, personal views, and their cultural assumptions (Richards & Lockhart, 1994). Indeed, there are a variety of factors which reflect different roles of teachers.

It seems to be the case that the roles teachers assume in their own classroom are multiplied in communicative language teaching, including roles as facilitator and organizer of resources (see Gaderer, 1983: Parrott, 1993). As Breen and Candlin (1980, p. 99) note, another role for the teacher in communicative language teaching is that of researcher and learner. There is increasing demand for a teacher as a learner who is aware, self-reliant, better able to learn directly from experience. This multiplication of roles provides important implications for the teacher training classroom: Teachers as trainees are prepared for a wider range of roles in the teaching context and teacher trainers take multiplied roles in the training context as teachers assume in the classroom. Figure 1 shows the varied roles of trainers in the trainee-centered language teacher training classroom.

FIGURE 1

Multi-roles of Trainers

(trainer-centered teacher education)	⟶ (trainee-centered teacher education)
trainer = transmitter of knowledge & skill	facilitator
= dominator of the training course	guide
	understander
	helper
	provider

What we have discussed so far imply that roles trainers assume in the training classroom have become complicated just as those of teachers in the language classroom have.

3. More Responsibility For Teacher Development

Focus on trainee perspectives suggests that trainee teachers take on much of the responsibility for their own learning to teach. As in the language classroom, there has been increasing emphasis on trainees autonomy in the training context. There has been growing demand for in-service teachers to take responsibility for their own development. Traditional approaches to teacher training heavily rely on prescriptive methods. This means that subject knowledge and skills are passed unidirectionally from trainer to trainee with little interaction between them. Given much of responsibility for their own learning, teachers' needs for learning are not fundamentally different from those of students in language learning classroom. As Desforges (1989. p. 18) illustrates, if learning needs to be stimulated by challenging pupils' schema, setting problems and investigations, posing questions and engaging in critical, Socratic conversation, why should not this view be adopted in teacher training? There is no doubt that what is true of the language classroom should be applied to the training classroom.

III. REFLECTIVE TEACHING AND LANGUAGE TEACHER DEVELOPMENT

1. Reflective Teaching

Reflective teaching has a large literature (Cruickshank & Applegate, 1981; Richards, 1991; Schon, 1983; Wallace, 1991; Zeichner & Liston, 1987). Reflection is becoming part of teaching. The conventional model of teaching as a technical process is being challenged, and a very different image of the language teacher is emerging. To fit the reflective model, language teachers need to be more reflective and in control of their own professional lives and so the theme of teacher as reflective practitioner has become an important part of current efforts to improve teaching. According to Richards (1990, p. 9), critical reflection refers to an activity or process in which an experience is recalled, considered, and evaluated, usually in relation to a broader purpose. It involves examination of past experience as a basis for evaluation and decision-making and as a source for planning and action. In a similar vein, there are such terms as 'reflective practitioner' and 'reflection-in-action' (Schon, 1983). Those terms mean that a professional reflects on what he/she does in his/her work context, seeking alternatives, implementing them, and planning further action. Accordingly, as Bartlett (1990) illustrates, becoming a reflective teacher implies moving beyond a primary concern with instructional techniques or 'how to' questions towards asking 'what' and 'why' questions.

We discuss here, in practical terms, how reflective teaching lays a basis for teacher's professional development. Reflective teaching starts by raising questions concerning teaching. Some examples of questions are taken from Richards and Lockhart (1994, pp. 1-2)

- What kind of teacher am I?
- What are my beliefs about teaching and learning, and how do these beliefs influence my teaching?
- What belief do my learners hold about learning and teaching?

In asking and answering these questions it is necessary for a teacher to look at his/her teaching objectively and to reflect critically on what he/she finds out. Reflective teaching goes hand-in-hand with critical self-examination in teaching and allows the teacher to decide which aspects of his/her teaching could be changed, to develop alternative strategies for change and to monitor the effects of those implemented alternatives. One central theme in reflective teaching is awareness-raising. It is achieved through continuing reflection and questioning. Another issue is that reflective teaching is not an on-off activity, but a continuing process throughout a teacher's career. This is how reflective teaching becomes an important component of professional development, which is of concern throughout a career.

2. Language Teachers' Awareness-raising Through Reflection

Contemporary interest in reflective teaching can be traced to Dewey (1933. quoted by Zeichner, 1981-82), who warned against too mechanical focus on teaching technique in the preparation of teachers. He argues that 'immediate skill may be got at the cost of power to go on growing.' Teacher educators (Zeichner, 1981-82; Elbaz, 1988) have acknowledged the importance of reflection if teachers are to be prepared for continuing growth. Zeichner and Liston (1987) argue that self-directed growth and professional development should be addressed within the context of reflective action. The goal of reflective teaching is to enable teachers to develop awareness of their own teaching. That is, teachers acquire professional competence to act critically in various situations through reflection practice. The recent reflective perspective on teacher education brings us to the point that an awareness-raising component or experiential component is becoming significant in INSET. Reflection can only be effective with awareness. Awareness and attitude development is an aspect which has drawn attention recently in teacher training (Freeman, 1989). It is essential to enhance awareness in reflective teaching leading to further professional growth. It should be emphasized again that reflection is strongly linked with awareness development. Appropriate strategies to help language teachers experience self-reflection should be considered further by teacher educators. Within this framework the teachers' ability to reflect in action can be enhanced.

3. Teachers Learn: Turning Experience Into Learning Through Reflection

Teaching is a complex activity which includes making appropriate decisions based on more extensive knowledge and awareness. As Richards and Lockhart (1994) note, experience is the starting point for the decision-making process. However, experience itself is insufficient. As Parker (1984) observes, many classroom routines and strategies are applied more or less automatically and do not involve a great deal of conscious thought or reflection. Here, we need to make a distinction between experiences with or without systematic examination or critical inquiry. The difference between them is whether experience is turned into learning or not. In other words, day-to-day teaching, without reflection, is likely to be a series of automatic occurrences. Reflection acts as a mediator which turns experience into learning (Elliott, 1986). According to Boud et al. (1985, p. 18), reflection is 'a form of response of the learner to experience.' Two main components of the learning process are experience and reflection based on that experience, and reflection works after the experience occurs. Boud, Keogh, and Walker (1985, p. 19) go on to point out that reflection is an important human activity in which people recapture their experience, think about it, mull it over and evaluate it. In Figure 2 the reflection process in context is summarized.

FIGURE 2

The Reflection Process in Context

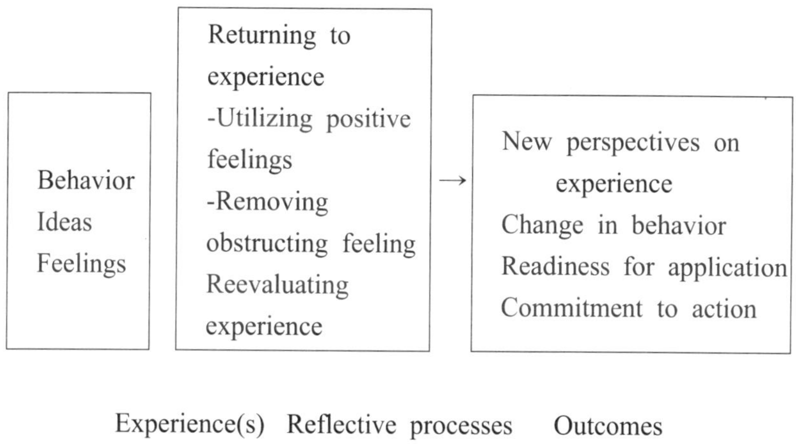

There is a parallel here to Wallace's (1991, p. 15) reflective model of language teacher education. His reflective model shows how professional competence is provided by reflective teaching that integrates received knowledge and experiential knowledge with practice.

FIGURE 3

The Reflective Model of Teacher Education

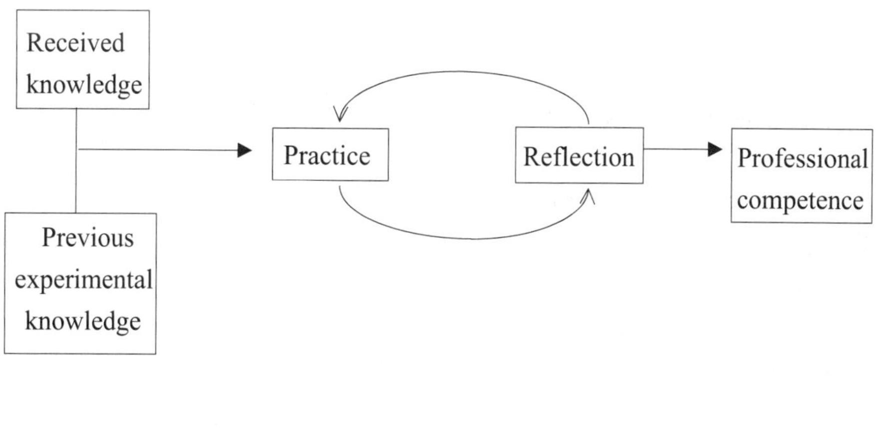

In a similar vein, two models explain that reflection plays a key role in turning experience into competence.

IV. SOME IMPLICATIONS FOR IN-SERVICE LANGUAGE TEACHER EDUCATION

1. The Ownership Of Development And Change

The traditional change process in EFL context is characterized as top-down but the traditional top-down approach has been diagnosed as ineffective in the educational change process. Within the traditional approach, it is very likely that teachers have no sense of ownership of their professional development and change. Much institutional training activity seems so remote from their experience and fails to provide any focus for their professional responsibilities. Teachers' voices are not heard in the decision-making process for change. It is suggested here that the top-down approach should be rejected on the grounds that we cannot achieve the desired outcome, effective change, without teacher-initiated actions. This alternative perspective puts emphasis on the teacher's ownership of professional competence and change.

One of the crucial conditions for a teacher's professional growth is that he/she himself/herself explores his/her own innate potential. This assumption brings us to the key notion that teacher development is in the teacher's own hands. It also raises issues regarding the ownership of change and the bottom-up initiatives, arising from needs that the teacher himself/herself has perceived. We argue, from this point of view, that teachers' professional growth cannot be mandated from the top. It requires the teacher's personal involvement in their own development. It should be clear here that the ownership starts by his/her taking responsibility for his/her own development. In other words, the person who has the greatest influence over his/her personal development as a teacher is the teacher himself/herself and not the university supervisor, nor the headteacher of the school, nor the administrator.

2. Theory In Practice: Bridging The Gap Between Theory And Practice

The gap between theory and practice has been great in the Korean EFL situation. We can link theory and practice through exploratory teaching. That is, reflective teaching is considered as a means of bridging the gap between theory and practice. There is no argument about the view that the gap has been a central concern in the literature of language teacher education. As Ellis (1985, p. 248) states, the problem which language teachers face is a superfluity of theories; the research literature abounds in approaches, theories, methodologies, principles. Richards and Rodgers (1986, p. 166-167) also note that language teaching methodology has evolved a considerable body of techniques, while it is seldom accompanied by a rigorous examination of outcomes or classroom process. Teachers' reactions to this have been to complain about the irrelevance of superfluous theories to their practice. Another issue is that publications concerning the overflowing theories tend to generate a world of their own.

The integration of theory and practice is not a new idea in the field of language teacher education. Efforts have been made by many teacher educators (Brumfit, 1979; Ramani, 1987; Richards & Nunan, 1990). As Ramini (1987) emphasizes, the main underpinning of those efforts can be summarized as follows; it is essential to raise awareness between practice and theoretical principles. This means that theory must be seen to be rooted practice, and teachers should inquire into theoretical principles through practice. Therefore there is no separation between theory and practice. In Taylor's (1985) words, we should talk about 'theory of practice,' not 'theory and practice.' Likewise, emphasis should be put on the concept of theory in practice. It should be recognized that a teacher's practical knowledge does not come directly out of a knowledge of theoretical principles about teaching; the reverse is the case.

EFL teachers' reflection is seen as one of approaches to integrating theory with practice by encouraging classroom teachers to look into their own classroom teaching and learning process. By doing so, language teachers take an important role in classroom research. This helps them to make instructional decisions within a context of practical activity instead of seeking applications for educational theories which have often been grounded on pure scientific tradition and lack stringency or the power to influence practice.

3. Teacher-initiated Classroom Research

The central idea of language teacher as reflective practitioner is the belief that research, to be valuable as well as relevant to teachers, needs to be undertaken hand in hand with teachers in classroom contexts. As emphasized before, language teaching should not be seen as the technical practice of passing on subject knowledge. Teacher-centered classroom investigation leads teachers to the 'why' behind certain teaching methodologies (Bowers, 1987). Further, teachers are able to make full use of opportunity for their own learning. Through the classroom research, teachers apply research and theory to their own class. They are involved in critical reflection on their daily teaching, which leads to awareness raising. Therefore, teachers' professional development can be promoted by taking a more active role in the process of educational change (Elliott, 1991a, 1991b).

In the Korean EFL context, these days there is much talk of the need for teachers to encourage their pupils to engage in genuine communication in the language class. The question is how to satisfy the need with a number of local constraints. Classroom research conducted by teachers themselves is one way of improving the teaching in the given situation. Teachers should be encouraged through the classroom research to develop alternatives and assess their usefulness. Given a variety of alternative teaching strategies, teachers should be particularly concerned with changing teaching methods. Teacher research can provide a means for teachers to examine the effects of new ideas implanted by teacher education programs. The significant movement toward teacher research is one that holds promise for bridging the theory-practice gap. Widdowson (1984, p. 90) summarizes the rationale for the movement of teacher as researcher; 'Teachers are not consumers of research, but researchers in their own right.'

V. CONCLUSION

We have seen the shift of perspective from the competency-based, or prescriptive view to a holistic, developmental, reflective one in the field of INSET. Technical skills and subject knowledge are required, but these are not enough in the long term. There has been an on-going demand for teachers as empowered and reflective decision makers in their own teaching context. Reflective decision makers are seen as teachers who are thoughtful persons intrinsically motivated to analyze situations, set goals, plan and monitor actions, and evaluate results.

Focus on trainee perspectives also suggest that trainee teachers take on much of the responsibility for their own learning to teach through reflective teaching. As in the language classroom, there has been increasing emphasis on trainee autonomy in the in-service teacher training context. There has been also growing demand for in-service teachers to take responsibility for their own teacher development. Given much of responsibility for their own learning, teachers' needs for learning are not fundamentally different from those of students in language learning classroom. It is a truism to say that language teachers work in very different situations, with different teaching methods, and different experience and skill. However, behind various aspects of local differences, individual or cultural context, we can find a common thread of teacher development: 'Teachers learn from experience through reflection.'

■ References

Barlett, L. (1990). Teacher development through reflective teaching. In J. C. Richards & D. Nunan (Eds.), *Second language teacher education*. Cambridge: Cambridge University Press. pp. 202-214.

Boud, D., Keogh, R. & Walker, D. (1985). Promoting reflection in learning: A model. In D. Boud, R. Keogh & D. Walker (Eds.), *Reflection: Turning experience into learning*. London: Kogan Page. pp. 18-40.

Bowers, R. (1987). Developing perceptions of the classroom. In R. Bowers (Ed.), *Language teacher education: An integrated programme for ELT teacher training*. ELT Documents 125, Oxford: Modern English Publications/British Counsil. pp. 138-179.

Breen, M., & Candlin, C. N. (1980). The essentials of a communicative curriculum in language teaching. *Applied Linguistics, 1*(2). pp. 89-112.

Britten, D. (1985). State of the art: Teacher training in ELT 1. *Language Teaching, 18*(2). pp. 112-128.

Brumfit, C. (1979). Integrating theory and practice. In S. Holden (Ed.), *Teacher Training*. London: Modern English Publications. pp. 1-8.

Cruickshank, D. R. & Applegate, J. H. (1981). Reflective teaching as a strategy for teacher growth. *Educational Leadership, 38*. pp. 553-554.

Desforges, C. (1989). Understanding learning for teaching. *Westminster Studies in Education*, *12*. pp. 17-19.

Dewey, J. (1933). How we think: A restatement of the relation of reflective thinking to the educative process. Chicage: Henry Regnery.

Elbaz, F. (1988). Critical reflection on teaching: Insights from Freire. *Journal of Educaion for Teaching, 14*(2). pp. 171-181.

Elliott, J. (1986). How do teachers learn: In D. HOpkins (Ed.), *Inservice training and educational development: An international survey*. London: Croom Helm. pp. 138-145.

Elliott, J. (1991a). *Action research for educational change*. Milton Keynes: Open University Press.

Elliott, J. (1991b). a model of professionalism and its implications for teacher education. *British Educational Research Journal, 17*(4). pp. 309-318.

Ellis, R. (1985). *Understanding second language acquisition*. Oxford: Oxford University Press.

Freeman, D. (1989). Teacher training, development, and decision making: A model of teaching and relative strategies for language teacher education. *TESOL Quarterly, 23*(1). pp. 27-45.

Freeman, D. (1993). *New ways in teacher education*. Alexandria, VA: TESOL.

Gaderer, H. K. (1983). Learning by doing: Multiplier systems in the training of EFL teachers in Austria. In J. E. Alatis, H. H. Stern & P. Strevens (Eds.), *Applied linguistics and the preparation of second language teachers: Toward a rationale*. Georgetown University Round Table on Language and Linguistics. Washington, DC: Georgetown University Press. pp. 193-210.

Knowles, L. (1982). *Teaching and reading*. London: National Council on Industrial Language Training.

Parker, W. C. (1984). Developing teacher's decision making. *Journal of Experimental Education, 52*(4). pp. 220-226.

Parrott, M. (1993). *Tasks for language teachers*. Cambridge: Cambridge University Press.

Ramani, E. (1987). Theorizing from the classroom. *ELT Journal, 41*(1). pp. 3-11.

Richards, J. C. (1990). What happened to methods? *The Language Teacher, 15*(6). pp. 9-10.

Richards, J. C. (1991). Towards reflective teaching. *The Teacher Trainer, 5*(3). pp. 4-8.

Richards, J. C., Lockhard, C. (1994). *Reflective teaching in second language classrooms.* Cambridge: Cambridge University Press.

Richards, J. C., & Nunan, D. (Eds.), (1990). *Second language teacher education.* Cambridge: Cambridge University Press.

Richards, J. C., & Rodgers, T. S. (1986). *Approaches and methods in language teaching: A description and analysis.* Cambridge: Cambridge University Press.

Schon, D. (1983). *The reflective practitioner.* London: Temple Smith.

Taylor, D. S. (1985). The place of methodology in the training of language teachers and the integration of theory and practice. *System, 13*(1). pp. 37-41.

Wallace, M. J. (1991). *Training foreign language teacher: A reflective approach.* Cambridge: Cambridge University Press.

Widdowson, H. G. (1984). The incentive value of theory in teacher education. *ELT Journal, 38*(2). pp. 86-90.

Wright, T. (1987). *Roles of teachers and learners.* Oxford: Oxford University Press.

Wright, T. (1990). Understanding classroom role relationships. In J. C. Richards & D. Nunan (Eds.), *Second language teacher education.* Cambridge: Cambridge University Press. pp. 82-97.

Zeichner, K. M. (1981-82). Reflective teaching and field-based experience in teacher education. *Interchange, 12*(4). pp. 1-22.

Zeichner, K. M., & Liston, D. P. (1987). Teaching student teachers to reflect. *Havard Educational Review, 57*(1). pp. 23-48.

From Chang, K. S. (1998). Reflective teaching: A bottom-up approach to INSET, *영어교육, 53.* pp. 25-40.

40. APPROACHES TO LANGUAGE SYLLABUS DESIGN AND SOME IMPLICATIONS FOR ENGLISH LANGUAGE TEACHING IN KOREA

INTRODUCTION

'Syllabus' is generally distinguished from 'curriculum'. Candlin (1987: 6) suggests 'curriculum' as general guidelines, and 'syllabus' as accounts of classroom works. A curriculum is concerned with making general statements about language learning, learning purpose and experience, evaluation, roles of teachers and learners. It also includes banks of learning items and suggestions about how these might be used in class. To be more specific, a language curriculum typically consists of objectives (which reflects the value system underlying curriculum, [White 1983: 78]), content (What is to be learned), method (the means by which the objectives will be achieved, and the content will be taught), and evaluation procedures. These components are seen to be basically interrelated, not independent of each other, in the realization of the aims of the curriculum.

A syllabus is primarily concerned with content and method components of a curriculum. So it is rather localized and based on accounts and records of what actually happens at the classroom level as a teacher and learners are involved in teaching and learning in their own situation. These accounts can provide feedback to make subsequent modifications to the curriculum, and consequently make further adjustments of the syllabus itself. Although 'syllabus' can be seen as a hyponym to 'curriculum', the relationship between them is 'ongoing and circular' (Nunan 1988: 3). Recently as communicative language teaching methodology develops and introduces the notion of 'learner-centeredness' in language teaching, 'syllabus design' is seen from rather a different perspective from the conventional one. Widdowson (1987: 65) defines syllabus as:

> ... The specification of teaching programme or pedagogic agenda which defines a particular subject for a particular group of learners. Such specification provides not only a characterization of content, the formalization in pedagogic terms of an area of knowledge or behaviour, but also arranges this content as a succession of interim objectives.

Breen (1983: 58) also suggests his definition of syllabus:
a particular specification of the content upon which teaching and learning would act.

> Typically, a syllabus further specifies the pedagogic organization of such content in terms of its sequencing, subdivision and continuity.

With this distinction between curriculum and syllabus, and their definitions in mind, this paper attempts to discuss two basic approaches to syllabus design: a **product-oriented syllabus** and a **process-oriented syllabus**, and underlying ideas behind each approach, and finally to seek implication for the Korean English teaching/learning situation, especially for secondary level schools. It is assumed that two different approaches to syllabus design can best be accounted for by discussing from the perspective of the views of the nature of language and language learning.

A PRODUCT-ORIENTED SYLLABUS

Grammatical/Structural Syllabus

Development

Traditionally the grammatical/structural syllabus for language teaching, whether it was explicit or implicit, was considered as logical and natural. The assumption was that, if a teacher taught a language, learners should naturally have the knowledge after the teaching. The achievement of a certain degree of knowledge and skills of the language was the objectives of language teaching (course). So teachers or syllabus designers were interested in defining what knowledge and skills learners should have as a result of their teaching. In other words, they attempted to define the objectives of language teaching (which were termed 'terminal behaviours') in terms of the possession of grammatical knowledge and skills of, primarily, reading. One of the easiest and logical ways of deciding the terminal behaviours was to analyze the would-be terminal behaviours in terms of grammar and structures. Such analysis was possible because they thought language could be divided into parts and could be most successfully learned one by one, one point at a time. That is to say, their view of the nature of language and language learning was that language consisted of a finite set of rules which could be combined in various ways to make meaning, and that the discretely divided language items could be learned in an additive and linear manner.

This tendency became firm in designing a language teaching syllabus, due to the influence of behaviourism in psychology and structuralism in linguistics. People who were under the influence of the behaviourism and structuralism assumed that "once learners have internalized the formal aspects of a given piece of language, they will automatically be able to use it in genuine communication outside the classroom" (Rutherford 1987). So the grammatical/

structural syllabus was organized centering around grammar and structures which learners were to acquire after the teaching. The organizing principle was the notion of grammatical simplicity and complexity, which turned out to be lacking explanatory power. Along this principle, grammatical points or structures were graded and sequenced with an earlier step becoming prerequisite for a next step. In brief, the role of grammatical/structural syllabus was to divide the terminal behaviours into "pedagogically manageable items" and to select the items for coverage in the language course, and to rate the order in which these items would be covered (Johnson 1983: 55). In other words, the grammatical/structural syllabus was composed of sequenced linguistic items, all of which were meant to teach learners to master, in the hope that those language items would automatically be able to be used in genuine communication.

Evaluation

The grammatical/structural syllabus is viewed as suitable for developing basic language knowledge and skills. Crawford-Lange (1982: 125) argues that "the identification of specific learning units and objectives makes this design particularly suitable to remediation [sic] of an individual student's weaknesses as well as to building and strengthening basic language skills".

However, this syllabus has some serious drawbacks: First, the assumption that a series of discrete items can be combined into a whole (i. e. communication) is largely faulty, because it implies that all learners will arrive at the same result (i. e. the same product) at the same rate. This is not true because different learners learn the same thing in different ways at different rates, because of their individual differences in intelligence, aptitude, interest, needs, learning strategy, sociocultural background and motivation, etc. That is, not all learners learn a language in a linear and cumulative fashion (Ellis 1986: 190-214, Long 1987: 297). As Candlin & Murphy (1987: 1) point out, "something next to impossible" might have been attempted in that this syllabus attempted to predict learning outcomes, and covertly to prescribe the learning process.

Second, in this syllabus, it is implied that what is exposed to the learners (i. e. input) is not the same, in its nature, as what they are expected to do after the teaching. In other words, learners are provided with linguistic items (i. e. discrete language items), but are expected to communicate using the language (i. e. a whole) in actual situations. Here is an inherent difficulty of this type of syllabus. As is clear, communication is inherently dynamic and unpredictable, requiring the communication participants to employ Halliday's three types of knowledge (i. e. ideational, interpersonal and textual knowledge) at the same time. However, in this syllabus, only one type of knowledge (i. e. textual knowledge) is over-emphasized, with the other two neglected.

Third, it is not very helpful to make learners use the learnt language effectively and appropriately in actual communication. That seems to be because grading and sequencing of grammatical items tend to distort the language available to the learners, and because separating form from meaning misrepresents or distorts the true nature of language as communication. In fact, attempts to systematize the exposure to the target language can easily make learners confused about the nature of the target language (Allwright 1979: 170).

Functional/Notional Syllabus

Development

As society changes economically and scientifically and whatever, opportunities for communication with a language other than one's first language have certainly increased: communication (interpersonal/transactional) has become vital in language function. So the communicative functions and purposes of language have become to be regarded as one of the most important aspects of the essential nature of language. The concept of 'communicative competence' introduced by Hymes (1972) seems to have had a great impact on the subsequent developments of theories of language and language learning.

Accordingly serious doubts, particularly in the area of foreign/second language teaching, have arisen about the decontextualized grammar/structure-focused teaching, because learners who had learned the target language very often turned out not to be able to use effectively the linguistic knowledge for actual communication.

With a fresh awareness of communicative functions of language, van Ek (1975), Wilkins (1976) and Munby (1978) suggested specifications of content which are more socially sensitive than in the grammatical/structural syllabus. van Ek (1975: 8-9) specified, in his *threshold level English,* necessary components of a language syllabus, such as the situations (including topics), the language activities, the language functions, the general notions, topic-related specific notions, the language forms and the targeted degree of skill (Nunan 1988: 7).

Wilkins (1976) suggested the distinction between synthetic syllabus and analytic syllabus. The former syllabus was assumed to refer to, roughly, the grammatical/structural syllabus as discussed above, and the latter one, to refer to the notional syllabus, of which the discussion follows: He recognized the importance of communication in the nature of language and the importance for learners to have opportunities to engage in genuine communication activities (Wilkins 1983: 26). He also relied on learners' own analyzing ability. He believed that learners had their own ability to set an order to a chaosed input, which derived from their prior knowledge and experience of their first language. He suggested a categorization of functions and notions in the form of taxonomy, and recognized the need to integrate grammar in order to realize a complete syllabus (referenced in Crawford-Lange 1982:129). However, he assumed that "priority must be given to the mastery of the linguistic elements, structures and systems" (Wilkins 1983: 42) in language teaching and in its syllabus. He argued, "In short, the linguistic content is planned according to the semantic demands of the learner" (Wilkins 1976: 19). This is seen to suggest that there is a hidden grammatical syllabus behind his notional syllabus idea.

Munby (1978) assumed that "the selection of communicative units for inclusion in the content involves the analysis at the level of human interaction" (i. e. how language is used for different purposes), and that "if communicative competence is truly a goal, then the usual structure of syllabuses must be redefined to include that concern" (referenced in Crawford-Lange 1982: 129). However, his attempts have often ended up by atomizing communicative competence and with linear ordering of discrete functions of language (Long 1978: 299-300).

All of these attempts are generally regarded as a fail, because none of them are faithfully reflecting the true nature of language as communication. It seems that their attempts might have been heavily affected by practical and pedagogical purposes, and certain meaning/functions and their assumed linguistic exponents (Breen 1983: 60).

This way of organizing syllabus so as to be sensitive to functions of language is usually termed 'functional', 'notional', or 'functional/notional' syllabus. For this syllabus, Finocchiaro & Brumfit (1983: 17) enumerate a variety of merits, such as "it provides for the teaching of everyday, real-world language", and "it recognizes that the speaker must have a real purpose for speaking and something to talk about" (quoted in Nunan 1988: 36).

Evaluation

However, the functional/notional syllabus has some drawbacks, which are not significantly different from those of the grammatical/structural syllabus.

First, there is a danger of encouraging the view that there is one-to-one correspondence between form and function. Language use is not predictable, so it is clear that we can not find any consistent one-to-one relationship between form and function, because one form can serve a variety of functions, and on the other hand, one function can be realized in a variety of forms.

Second, selecting and grading, even roughly, of functional/notional items are much more complex than in the grammatical/structural syllabus.

Third, there is no guarantee for learners to use effectively and appropriately what they have learned in actual communication situations which may be similar to, but actually different from those in classroom. That is, there is doubt about the transferability, or deployability of classroom learning to outside world situations.

Fourth, it is not fundamentally different from the grammatical/structural syllabus, in that whatever the notion or function is, they look for the linguistically most salient realizations" (Long 1987: 297-298). As Widdowson (1979) suggests, it seems obvious that dividing language into discrete units of whatever types misrepresents/distorts the nature of language as communication.

Prabhu (1987) termed the product-oriented syllabus of these kinds 'illuminative construct', and viewed the underlying view of language acquisition as a planned process of input-assimilation (Prabhu 1984), while Johnson (1983: 47) termed these an 'ends-driven syllabus'.

A PROCESS-ORIENTED SYLLABUS

Development

The view of language as communication, to be more accurate, the change of view of the nature of language and language learning has brought about the introduction of a variety of new binary concepts, such as 'use' and 'usage' (Widdowson 1978), 'fluency' and 'accuracy ' (Brumfit 1984), and 'acquisition' and 'learning' (Krashen 1982). Moreover, various interlanguage studies have provided a new perspective on how language is learned or acquired. Interlanguage researchers such as Corder (1967, 1971), Selinker (1972) and Tarone (1979), etc. viewed language as basically communication, and attempted to integrate the behaviourists' view and the cognitivists' view of language and language learning. Briefly, behaviourists viewed language as a series of discrete items, and language learning as a habit-formation by imitation and reinforcement, totally neglecting factors internal to learners. On the other hand, cognitivists viewed language as a system of finite sets of rules, and language acquisition as rule-governed behaviour achieved by the language acquisition device innate in learners, neglecting factors external to learners such as language input, learning environment and learner background, etc. However, interlanguage researchers viewed language development as a continual revision/elaboration for a transitional competence prompted by new conflicting language data. They hypothesized that learners slowly created, by hypotheses-testing, the rule system of the target language in a manner similar to L1 acquisition (this is the Recreating Continuum Hypothesis of interlanguage development which is generally supported, as opposed to the Restructuring continuum Hypothesis [Tarone 1979, referenced in Mclaughlin 1987: 64, Ellis 1986: 53, Stern 1983: 396]).

Thus, interlanguage studies seem to have provided a very important perspective on the language learning process, consequently influencing language teaching methodology and syllabus design. That is to say, interlanguage studies seem to have triggered the change of the view of the language learning from "the 'product' orientation of the morpheme studies and error analysis to the 'process' orientation that focuses on form-function mappings and on the role of discourse in language acquisition" (Mclaughlin 1987: 76)

Another very important perspective comes from Hatch (1978), when she suggested the opposite direction of understanding of language learning. Instead of the conventional bottom-up approach, which is characterized by the order of structure-manipulation and then conversation/communication, she suggested the top-down approach. She states:

> One learns how to do conversation. One learns how to interact verbally, and out of this interaction, syntactic structures are developed (Hatch 1978: 404).

She argues that structure evolves from discourse, not because of some magic acquisition device which operates automatically on input, but because of the conscious desire of the learner to say something or to talk about something (Hatch 1978: 405). This perspective also emphasizes the process of language learning rather than the product.

As a result, subsequent second language acquisition researches (e. g. Krashen's (1982) acquisition/learning hypothesis, input hypothesis, etc) and the communicative language teaching methodology put more emphasis on the process than on the product.

From the perspective derived from the change of viewpoints of language and language learning, has arisen the Communicative Language Teaching (=CLT) methodology, or communicative approach to language teaching, of which the basic principle is to teach language by letting learners communicate in the target language. Communication is inherently a process rather than a set of products. It is always dependent on the participants, situations and purposes. Nobody can predict exactly what the communicative outcome will be, because it is heavily dependent upon the interaction and negotiation between the participants in a given situation. The interaction and negotiation is, by their nature, a process, not a product.

CLT sees language learning as learning how to communicate as a member of a particular sociocultural group. The social conventions governing language forms and behaviour within the group are, therefore, central to the process of language learning. That is, for effective communication, the participants should understand *ideational* (=a system of ideas and concepts), *textual* (=how these ideas and this interpersonal behaviour can be realized in language) knowledge altogether. This allows us to participate in a creative meaning-making process and to express or interpret the potential meanings within spoken or written texts (Breen & Candlin 1980: 90). Thus, language learning is basically viewed as "a process which grows out of the communicative interaction involving learners, teachers, texts (=materials) and activities all together" (Breen & Candlin 1980: 95).

As Breen (1983: 60) suggests, communication is inherently dynamic and unpredictable. It is always subject to the situations, topics, and participants of communication. Breen (1983) argues:

> Communication is typified by a continually dynamic and relatively unpredictable relationship between structures and the many possible functions which they may achieve. Also, within communication, form and meaning are inextricably linked and in ways in which we cannot predict the one from the other (Breen 1983: 60).

To teach language effectively as communication, accommodating this complex, dynamic and unpredictable nature of communication, recent studies suggest some conditions, which seem to be generally agreed upon. Those conditions are roughly as follows:

- There must be exposure to the target language.
- There must be opportunities to use the target language for as genuine communication as possible.
- There must be motivation to exploit these two essential conditions. (Brumfit 1985: 152)

These conditions are seen to strongly imply learners' active involvement, or learners' responsibility in language learning. This implication seems to coincide with Breen & Candlin's (1980) view of the learner's communicative ability, which they claim consists of interpretation, expression and negotiation.

Seen from this perspective of the CLT, there seems to emerge another possibility for organizing a syllabus; by not separating form from meaning, structure from function, but by combining together forms/structures and meaning/ideas and interpersonal behaviours (Breen 1983: 61). Breen (1983) suggests two interrelated syllabuses: the learner's internal syllabus (=the learner's capacity to imposes his/her own order upon the apparent chaos of input made available to him) and the procedural syllabus (in which the focus is on the selection and sequencing of learner tasks, not on the selection and sequencing of the content which those tasks act upon). He suggests the main function of the latter as the providing of the conditions for application and refinement of the former (Breen 1983: 62-64).

The term and notion of 'procedural syllabus' are seen to come from Prabhu (1984, 1987). He did an experiment entitled as 'the communicational Teaching Project', which is better known as 'the Bangalore Project', from 1979 in India. Dissatisfied with the ineffectiveness of what is called the S-O-S pedagogy (Structural-Oral-Situational), i. e. with the learners' inability to deploy what they have learned in the classroom in actual communication situations, he attempted to test his hypothesis that "language structure is best acquired when the learner's attention is on meaning". He assumed that learner's prime attention on meaning could only be achieved when the learner was given communicative tasks (consisting of pre-tasks and tasks) which involved them in meaning-focused activity (not meaningful activity; he made a distinction between them, 1987: 27). He reported that he did not use any vocabulary- or structure-based syllabus, nor employ any practice of language items and sentence-contredness in classroom activity. Anyway, he emphasized the process of, not the product of, language learning, in which learners were actively involved in interaction with the teacher and/or other learners by carrying out the given tasks. From this, task-based language teaching seems to have been termed. The notion of process-oriented syllabus seems to have come from the concept of Prabhu's procedural syllabus.

In the process-oriented syllabus, the focus is, by definition, given on the **process** of language learning, i. e. on the language learning experiences themselves. So a syllabus is organized around 'tasks' rather than grammar, structure, vocabulary, function or notion. In other words, it consists of the specifications of the tasks and activities that learners will actually engage in class. In this regard, Widdowson (1981: 100) is quite helpful in getting a clearer picture about process-orientedness. He states that "process-oriented approach focuses on the presentation of language by reference to the means of learning and allows the ends to be achieved by the learner by exercising the ability he/she has acquired. The aim of process-oriented instruction is to develop a capacity to learn: it does not itself realize any special purpose, but provides the learner with the potential for its realization". Thus, process-oriented teaching based on process-oriented syllabus always tries to create conditions which **force**, in a sense, **learners to use the target language** in order to accomplish the given tasks. In this process of teaching, 'learning' on the side of learners can not avoid being emphasized rather 'teaching' from the side of teachers, i. e. learner-centeredness naturally emerges.

On seed of the CLT which emphases learner's active involvement in language learning process can be found in Brumfit's (1979) 'deep-end strategy'. Instead of the traditional procedure of 'presentation-practice -production', he suggests the procedure of 'production-presentation-practice', in which the teacher lets learners communicate as far as possible with all available resources, and then teacher presents language items felt to be essential for effective communication, and finally the teacher lets them drill if necessary. In this process, learners are thrown into a deep-end because they are asked to do something he/she has not yet been taught to do (Brumfit 1979: 183-191).

Prabhu (1987) termed the process-oriented syllabus 'operational construct', and viewed the underlying idea of language acquisition as a process of organic development, furthered by the learner's effect to deploy his/her communicative resources (Prabhu 1984), and Johnson (1983: 47) termed this a 'means-driven syllabus'.

Evaluation

Despite Allwright's (1979: 170) strong claim that "if the language teacher's management activities are directed exclusively at involving the learners in solving communication problems in the target language, then language learning will take care of itself", process-oriented language teaching, which is seen to be based on the claim of this kind seems not free from drawbacks. First, it is very difficult to monitor the occurrence of different items of language (in terms of structural and lexical units), especially in speaking activities. Thus, assessment of learners' progress is much more difficult than in the grammatical/structural stimulus. The criteria of assessment should be changed, and the method and procedures of assessment, as well. However, it is clear that there is a long way to go before any reliable criteria, method, and procedures are established.

Second, it is also difficult to ensure the coverage of language items (i. e. whether all or necessary language items/structures are covered, or not), because the process-oriented teaching and its syllabus are seen to be totally or heavily dependent upon learners' interaction/activities, which are not known until they have performed. On what criteria should the content be selected, graded and sequenced for teaching? Although a variety of criteria were suggested (Candlin 1987: 19-20, Prabhu 1987: 87-88), none of them is clear about dealing with the coverage of language items. Since communication consists of both code and message, code should not be neglected or dealt with randomly, even though we admit that message is primary, because it is the code (i. e. grammar) that represents the essential resource for making meanings in language use (Widdowson1983: ii).

Third, it is difficult to prevent learners from developing 'fossilization' and 'pidginization' during their communicative verbal interactions, especially in EFL situations where learners have generally homogeneous cultural backgrounds. In such situations, learners may be able to understand/express what they want to communicate (in their classroom activities), for example, with an incorrect single word or incorrect structures/word-order (most probably influenced by their mother tongue). Their feeling of repeated success in communicability in the target language achieved in this manner, may give them the impression that they have become capable of effective communication. Then, learners may end up with fossilized and pidginized English, which may be incommunicable with English native speakers. This is a serious problem.

In recent years, syllabus design by negotiation among teachers, learners and administrators has been suggested on grounds of the different interests of different people existing within the social system of the school (White 1983: 79), but space does not allow further discussion of it.

Finally, as the idea of process-orientedness is such that syllabus design and methodology have become rather vague in its distinction, Prabhu (1984) argues that a clear distinction between them is not necessary, and that the relationship between syllabus and methodology should be that of harmony, not that of tension. However, it seems to be premature, both in theory and practice, to discard one type of syllabus in favour of the other. Both have respectively their own merits and demerits. Those merits and demerits will depend on each language teaching situation and the purposes of language teaching. So efforts to integrate them in actual teaching seems to be crucial.

IMPLICATION

Korea has a national curriculum for secondary education which is characteristically product-oriented. The curriculum has been revised every five years in order to meet the demands for revision raised both by academics and by practical teaching situations. As of 1993, the fifth revised version of the national curriculum is being implemented. It is generally regarded as having reflected much of the trends of CLT. But, it can safely be regarded as a mixture of grammatical/structural syllabus and functional-notional syllabus. The sixth revised version awaiting to be implemented from 1995-1996 seems to be regarded as being oriented towards the functional-notional syllabus approach, scaling down the features of the grammatical/structural syllabus [See Lee 1992]. This is also not without problems. Since education is a practical enterprise which can always not be free from the practical constraints, an educated or informed compromise is always necessary. This is because however theoretically good an approach or a method may be, it is useless if it does not fit the practical situations.

In discussing language teaching syllabus, it should be appreciated that the teacher's perception of the syllabus has a vital influence on the actual teaching and learning, and that no single approach, method or technique is a panacea for a variety of teaching/learning situations. Especially in such situations as Korea's where many teachers have less professional training and less confident in the command of spoken English, teachers may not be aware very well of a variety of approaches to language teaching, syllabus design and methodology, etc. In this sense, it is necessary that Korea have a national curriculum/syllabus as general direction-setting guidelines for the teacher's teaching and evaluation. So it seems that, in Korea, the national curriculum, even if it is quite heavily product-oriented, is indispensable. In this situation it seems premature to discard the product-oriented syllabus in total favour of the process-oriented syllabus, however effective the latter may be in teaching language and in enhancing learner motivation.

Then, what implication can we find from the foregoing discussion for Korea's present actual situation? First, teachers' professional qualities should remarkably be enhanced by further professional training both in terms of learner-centered, task-based teaching methodology. By being better informed of the theory underlying their teaching, and by being enabled to integrate the theory and the constraints that their practical teaching situations inevitably involve, teachers should be provided with some solid grounds for their confident judgements, moment by moment, in the process of their teaching, in terms of both the use of the most appropriate teaching method for the given content, and the management of learners' learning. That is, they should be (re)trained/(re)educated so as to find the best solutions for each of their situations. Every effort is to be made to get teachers properly and adequately trained/educated.

Second, it should be fully appreciated that teachers have professional expertise. They know much better and more than anyone else about their own teaching and learning conditions, and, more importantly, about their learners. So they are advised to be given some freedom to interpret the curriculum, the given syllabus, textbooks and their actual situation, and to employ their expertise, with the national curriculum as guide, without being too much discouraged by the national curriculum. No matter how elaborate the curriculum may be, it would be of no great value if the actual realization of the curriculum in the classroom is poor. That is because it is teachers that make the greatest contribution to the effective realization of the curriculum. However, a great difficulty lies in their way: the higher-school entrance-related examinations always discourage teachers from exercising their freedom in interpreting and implementing the curriculum. This difficulty can hardly be eased without the improvement of such examinations. With every effort directed to the improvement of the examinations, teachers at the same time should be made fully aware of the greatness of their part to be played in achieving the objectives of the curriculum.

In this sense, it seems crucially important that teacher-training course (whether pre-service or in-service) should be organized so as for 'theory' (such as approaches to syllabus design and learner-centered CLT, etc) to be fully integrated with 'practice' (such as small group teaching, task-based teaching, task design, and other teaching techniques, etc). The integration of theory and practice can be achieved in the way theory is induced by teachers themselves from their practice, not in the way theory is presented first, being followed by some seemingly grudging demonstration of theory. Any innovations or changes in practical teaching situations are not likely to be successful unless those are fully understood and accepted by the teachers themselves first. The quality of teaching is obviously heavily dependent upon the teacher's quality in terms not only of his/her awareness of theory and but also of his/her actual teaching techniques.

Finally, in this situation where learners are not very familiar with taking responsibility for their own learning, and thus less independent of their teacher, it is very necessary for learners to be made responsible for their own learning, i. e. to learn how to learn on their own. Especially, in this regard, the process-oriented syllabus has its own value. If learners are gradually made to be familiar with active involvement in interaction and negotiation with other learners, using the target language in order to achieve a given task, by a well-trained teacher, it will work, despite the difficulties involved in the situation, and despite the risk of developing pidginization and fossilization. Since the process-oriented syllabus is theoretically tenable, it seems to be important to apply it, even limitedly, within the bounds of the national curriculum of Korea, and then adjust it to be fitted into the actual situation. For this, adequate teacher training should be preceded with the efforts for improving the actual teaching situations.

■ References

Allwright, R. (1979). *Language Learning through Communication Practice,* in C. J. Brumfit & K. Johnson (eds.).

Breen, M. (1983). *Prepared Comments on Syllabus Design: Possible Future Trends,* presented by K. Johnson 1983, in K. Johnson & D. Porter (eds).

Breen, M. & C. N. Candlin. (1980). The Essentials of a Communicative Curriculum in Language Teaching. *Applied Linguistics,* 1-2.

Brumfit, C. J. (1979). *Communicative Language Teaching: An Educational Perspective*, In C. J. Brumfit & K. Johnson(eds.).

Brumfit, C. J. (1984). *Communicative Methodology in Language Teaching: The Roles of Fluency and Accuracy.* Cambridge University Press.

Brumfit, C. J. (1985). *Creativity and Constraints in the Language Classroom*, in R. Quirk & H. G. Widdowson (eds.).

Brumfit, C. J. & K. Johnson (eds.). (1979). *The Communicative Approach to Language Teaching,* Oxford University Press.

Candlin, C. N. (1987). *Toward Task-based Language Learning*, in C. N. Candlin & M. Murphy (eds.).

Candlin, C. N. & M. Murphy (eds). *Language Learning Tasks,* Prentice Hall.

Corder, S. P. (1967). The Significance of Learners' Errors. *International Review of Applied Linguistics, 5.*

Corder, S. P. (1971). Idiosyncratic Dialect and Error Analysis. *International Review of Applied Linguistics, 9.*

Crawford-Lange, L. M. (1982). *Curricular Alternatives for Second Language Learning*, in M. Long & J. C. Richards (eds.).

Ellis, R. (1986). *Understanding Second Language Acquisition,* Oxford University Press.

Finocchiaro, M. & C. J. Brumfit. (1983). *The Notional/Functional Approach: From Theory to Practice to Practice*, Oxford University Press.

Hatch, E. M. (1978). *Discourse Analysis and Second Language Acquisition*, in E. M. Hatch (ed.).

Hatch, E. M. (ed.). (1978). *Second Language Acquisition: a Book of Readings,* Newbury House.

Hymes, D. (1972). *On Communicative Competence*, in C. J. Brumfit & K. Johnson (eds.). 1979.

Johnson, K. (1983). *Syllabus Design: Possible Future Trends*, in K. Johnson & D. Porter (eds)

Johnson, K. & D. Porter (eds.). (1983). *Perspectives in Communicative Language Teaching,* Academic Press.

Krashen, S. D. (1982). *Principles and Practice in Second Language Acquisition*, Pergamon Oxford.

Lee, W. K. (1992). An Evaluation of the 6th Revised Edition of the Middle School English Curriculum. *Educational Development, 14-6.*

Long, M. H. (1987). Second Language Acquisition & the Language Curriculum. *Prospect, 2-3.*

Mclaughlin, B. (1987). *Theories in Second Language Learning*, Edward Arnold.

Munby, J. (1978). *Communicative Syllabus Design*, Cambridge University Press.

Nunan, D. (1988). *Syllabus Design,* Oxford University Press.

Prabhu, N. S. (1984). *Procedural Syllabuses,* in J. A. S. Read (ed.).

Prabhu, N. S. (1985). *Coping with the Unknown in Language Pedagogy*, in R. Quirk & H. G. Widdowson (eds.).

Prabhu, N. S. (1987). *Second Language Pedagogy,* Oxford University Press.

Quirk, R. & H. G. Widdowson (eds.). (1985). *English In The World*, Cambridge University Press.

Richards, J. C. & Long (eds.) (1987). *Methodology in TESOL: a Book of Readings,* Newbury House.

Read, J. A. S. (ed.) (1984). *Second Language Grammar: Learning & Teaching,* Longman.

Selinker, L. (1972). Interlanguage. *International Review of Applied Linguistics, 10.*

Stern, H. H. (1983). *Fundamental Concepts of Language Teaching*, Oxford University Press.

Tarone, E. (1979). Interlanguage as Chameleon. *Language Learning, 29.*

Tickoo, M. (ed.). (1987). *Syllabus Design*, The state of the Art. R. E. L. C.

van, Ek. (1975). *Threshold Level English,* Pergamon Oxford.

White, R. (1983). *Curriculum Development & English Language Syllabus Design,* in K. Johnson & D. Porter (eds.).

Widdowson, H. G. (1978). *Teaching Language As Communication*, Oxford University Press.

Widdowson, H. G. (1981). *ESP: Criteria for Course Design,* in J. C. Richards & M. Long (eds.),

Widdowson, H. G. (1987). *Aspects of Syllabus Design*, in M. Tickoo (ed.).

Wilkins, D. (1976). *Notional Syllabus,* Oxford University Press.

Wilkins, D. (1983). *Some Issues in Communicative Language Teaching & Their Relevance to the Teaching of Language in Secondary Schools*, in K. Johnson & D. Porter (eds.)

From Lee, W. (1994). Approaches to language syllabus design and some implications for English language teaching in Korea, *응용언어학*, 7, pp. 73-93.

PART ELEVEN

TEXTBOOK EVALUATION

영어 교과서는 검인정이어서 각 학교는 교육부의 심사를 거친 5종 이상의 교과서 중에서 선택할 수 있다. 물론 일단 심사에서 통과를 했기 때문에 일정한 기준은 충족시킨다고 보아야 하지만 대상 (일반학교, 상업학교 등)에 따라 달라지는 경우도 있을 것이다.

여기에 제시된 네 가지 기준에서는 서로 중복되는 부분이 많지만 한편 상호 보완되고 보충되어야 할 내용 또한 찾을 수 있을 것이다. 따라서 각자 어느 하나를 선택하거나 또는 전체를 통합하고 보충하여 자신의 기준을 다시 만들거나 함으로서 각 학교에서 사용하는 영어 교과서 또는 앞으로 사용할 영어 교과서를 그 기준에 맞춰 평가하는 연습을 하기를 제안한다.

41. CHECKLIST FOR TEXTBOOK EVALUATION

1. On what method is the book based?
   Is this method appropriate for your purposes?
   Is this method carried through well in the unit design?

2. Is the material of a kind which would interest junior high school or senior high school students?
   Is it too juvenile? Is it too dull? Does it make too obvious an effort to amuse?

3. Does the unit design allow for progressive development of and practice in listening comprehension? speaking? reading? writing?

4. Is provision made for the presentation of new work in oral form first?
   Can this material be presented in oral form first in any case?

5. If there are dialogues, are they realistic, authentic in language and situation, with sentences which are not too long for memorization?
   Are the dialogues too long to be useful?

6. Is reading introduced early or late?
   Does the reading material provide for progressive teaching of the reading skill? Is it interesting and written in language which is appropriate for the content, and for your students?

7. Is writing introduced early or late?
   Do the writing exercises provide for progressive development of this skill?

8. What is the proportion of working time which is allotted to each skill in the unit design?
   Is this proportion right for the objectives of your course?

9. Is the language in the lesson authentic (not stilted or artificial; not old-fashioned; correct for the persons and relationships for which it is used)?

10. How is pronunciation dealt with? Is this satisfactory? Is attention paid to distinctions between near-equivalents in the native and foreign languages, and within the foreign

language? Is the sound system taught as an interdependent whole? Are stress and intonation considered?

11. Is the grammar presented through structures? Some other way? Does this suite your purposes?
    Is the grammar summarized from time to time? Are the grammatical descriptions sound? Do you think the number of structures (or the amount of grammar) is sufficient for this level? Too much? Are there significant omissions? Is provision made for thorough drilling before new structures are introduced? Are the structures reintroduced systematically through the different units?
    Are verb forms drilled sufficiently for this level? Are there summaries of verb forms (paradigms, conjugations) somewhere in the book?

12. How much is the native language used in the exercises (or other sections of the book)? Could the foreign language have been used instead?

13. Is there variety in the types of exercises? Do they give adequate practice in what they purport to teach? Do they test instead of teaching? Are the exercises interesting? Do the grammatical exercises and drills emphasize the contrasts which are most likely to cause native-language interference?
    Are the drills well designed (programmed)?
    Are there enough (too many) exercises and (or) drills in each unit for practical use?

14. Is the vocabulary well presented? How much per lesson? Is the vocabulary reintroduced sufficiently within the unit and in successive units? Is it summarized in some way? At the end of the book? In a foreign-language dictionary section or in a bilingual list? Does the way it is summarized suit your teaching approach? Is attention paid to roots, cognates, synonyms, antonyms, thematic groupings?
    Is choice of vocabulary based on a frequency count? If so, is the level of the count for this book sufficient, or too advanced, for your purposes?

15. Are there indications of ways in which students can be encouraged to use what they have learned in actual communication (in speech and writing)?

16. Does the material give a fair, balanced picture of life in the foreign country? Does it bring out contrasts between the foreign culture and the culture of your students? Are there pictures, maps, diagrams?

17. Are the illustrations in a style which is likely to make the book seem old-fashioned

or ridiculous to your students?

18. Are indications given of extra activities (games, songs, poems, crossword puzzles) which would add variety to the lessons?
    Does the publisher provide a teacher's manual with indications on how to use the book and suggestions for extra activities?

19. Are tapes, films, slides, filmstrips, or flashcards available with this book? If so, are they well constructed methodologically and effectively produced?
    Are there practice records for the students? Are these aids reasonably priced?

20. Are supplementary readers, workbooks, or tests available with the book?
    Are they satisfactory for the standard of your class? Do they correspond precisely with what is in the textbook?

21. Is the book printed in an interesting style?
    Is the type clear?
    Is the work set out so that it is easy to find what you want?
    Are the binding, cover, quality of paper, and general spacing satisfactory?
    Is there a detailed index?

22. Would you enjoy working with this book at this level?
    Is it hard on the teacher in any way?
    Could the other teachers (particularly the inexperienced ones) work with it?

23. Is the price reasonable for your school situation?

24. Is the book part of a series which would be adequate for the sequence of classes in your school?
    Are the later books in the series satisfactory for the purposes of your higher classes?

25. Has the book been pre-tested in schools and revised before being printed in its final form?

From Rivers, W. M. (1968). *Teaching foreign language skills*, Chicago, Ill: The University of Chicago Press, pp. 368-371.

42. 영어교과서 평가 기준

A: 목 표

1. 교과서의 목표가 문교부 규정 영어교육 목표 (학년별 목표)와 부합되는가?
2. 교과서는 문법을 중시하는가?
3. 교과서는 의사소통 기능을 중시하는가?

B: 주 제

4. 학습자의 흥미에 맞는가?
5. 학습자의 수준에 맞는가?
6. 다양한 주제를 다루는가?
7. 주제가 영어사용 국민들의 문화를 적절히 소개하려 하는가?

C: 방 법

8. 다양한 교수방법을 사용할 수 있는가?
9. 다양한 집단 학습 (개별학습, 소집단학습 등)을 할 수 있는가?
10. 학생 중심의 학습방법이 많이 사용될 수 있는가?

D. 발음지도

11. 발음이 체계적으로 전 교과서를 통하여 다루어지고 있는가?
12. 우리언어와 영어에서의 유사한 발음의 차이에 관심을 두는가?
13. 한국학생들에게 어려운 발음에 충분한 주의를 하고 있는가?
14. 발음을 문맥 속에서 다루는가? (독립적으로 다루어지지 않음)
15. 강세와 억양이 체계적으로 다루어지는가?
16. unstressed vowels의 발음을 가르치는가?

E. 문법지도

17. 영어문법이 단순한 것에서 복잡한 것으로 진행하며 제시되는가?
18. 학년에서 다루어지는 문법의 양이 적당한가?
19. 새 문법이 제시되기 전에 충분한 학습이 되도록 배려하는가?
20. 이미 학습된 문법사항이 새 문법사항과 적절히 배합되면서 강화되는가?
21. 문법이 교과서에서 효율적으로 요약되는가?

22. 문법을 의미 있는 상황에서 적용할 기회가 충분히 주어지는가?

F. 어휘지도

23. 각 단원에서 소개되는 어휘 량이 적당한가?
24. 소개되는 어휘의 종류가 학습자의 흥미와 수준에 맞는가?
25. 어근, 어원, 동의어, 반의어 지도가 병행하도록 배려하고 있는가?
26. 소개된 어휘는 새 어휘와 함께 적절히 반복되는가?
27. 어휘가 문맥 안에서 의미 있게 사용되도록 하는가?

G: 듣기지도

28. 듣기자료가 교과서 전체에 있는가?
29. 듣기자료의 양이 적당한가?
30. 표현이 짧고 자연스러운가?
31. 표현이 일상생활에서 자주 사용되는 것들인가?
32. 듣기지도를 위한 특별한 방법이 제시되는가?
33. 듣기능력이 점진적으로 향상되도록 하는가?
34. 영어교육 목표의 듣기부분을 충족시킬 수 있겠는가?

H: 말하기 지도

35. 말하기 자료가 교과서 전체에 있는가?
36. 말하기 자료의 양이 적당한가?
37. 표현이 짧고 자연스러운가?
38. 표현이 일상생활에서 자주 사용되는 것들인가?
39. 실제와 유사한 상황에서 말하기 연습을 하게 하는가?
40. 자유롭게 학습자의 의사를 표현할 기회가 주어지는가?
41. 교육목표의 말하기 부분을 충족시킬 수 있다고 생각하는가?

I: 읽기 지도

42. 읽기 자료는 과 전체와 서로 유기적인 관계를 가지는가?
43. 각과에서의 읽기 자료는 양에 있어서 적당한가?
44. 내용이 학습자의 흥미에 맞는가? (학습자의 경험과 밀접한 관계가 있는가?)
45. 내용이 현대의 것을 주로 다루는가?
46. 적당한 양의 어휘를 대체로 포함하고 있는가?
47. 내용에 관한 단편적인 암기보다 전체적인 이해를 중요시하는가?
48. 내용에 관하여 개인적인 의사를 표현하게 하는가?

49. 자료의 문장구조가 과에서 중점을 두는 문법을 충분히 활용하는가?
50. 교육목표의 읽기 부분을 충족시킬 수 있다고 생각하는가?

J: 쓰기 지도

51. 쓰기 연습은 교과서 전체를 통하여 점진적으로 발전해 가는가?
52. 쓰기 기술의 향상을 위한 연습활동이 다양한가? (문장완성, 통제작문등)
53. 쓰기 연습은 수준에 맞는 어느 정도의 자기표현을 하게 하는가?
54. 교육목표의 쓰기 부분을 충족시킬 수 있다고 생각하는가?

K: 문화지도

55. 대화가 영어사용 국민들의 여러 가지 일상생활 모습을 보여주는가?
56. 읽기 자료가 영어사용 국민들의 여러 가지 일상생활 모습을 나타내주는가?
57. 읽기 자료가 영어사용국의 위인이나 예술작품 등 역사적인 사실들을 적당히 소개하는가?
58. 교과서의 적당한 부분에서 대화시 사용해서는 안되는 표현이라든가 그밖에 학습자가 지녀야할 영어사용국의 문화적 지식을 소개 또는 요약하고 있는가?
59. 교육목표의 문화부분을 충족시킬 수 있는가?
60. 문화지식에 대한 평가를 연습문제에서 다루고 있는가?

L: 연습문제

61. 연습문제의 분량이 적절한가?
62. 문제의 종류가 다양한가?
63. 다루어지는 문제가 단원에 따라 순서 등에서 약간씩 차이가 있는가?
64. 기계적으로 반복하거나 답을 거의 기계적으로 할 수 있는 문제보다 현실적인 상황을 다루어 의미 있는 의사소통을 하게 하는 문제에 비중이 큰가?
65. 전에 배운 학습내용을 새 학습내용과 적절히 배합하여 보강해주고 있는가?

K: 분 량

66. 한 학년에 끝낼 수 있도록 전 교과서의 분량이 적당한가?
67. 각과의 양은 적절한가? (흥미 유지와 학습향상 면에서)
68. 순서가 잘 짜여져 있어 단원 혹은 전체를 재구성할 필요가 없다고 생각하는가?

O: 삽화 (그림, 도표 등)

69. 내용을 이해하는 데 대체로 도움이 되고 불필요한 것은 없는가?
70. 삽화의 위치가 대체로 적절한가?
71. 삽화가 필요한 만큼 있는가?

P: 보충활동

72. 게임, 노래, 편지 쓰기, 시 등의 보충자료나 활동이 포함되는가?
73. 이러한 보충활동이 충분하다고 생각하는가?
74. 이러한 보충활동이 적절하다고 생각하는가?

Q: 보충자료

75. 교사용 교본은 있는가?
76. 교사용 교본은 교수방법 및 다양한 학습활동 등에 관한 충분한 지시를 하고 있는가?

R: 기 타

77. 활자의 크기나 모양에 있어서 문제가 있는가?
78. 표지나 제본, 종이질이 마음에 드는가?
79. 경험 없는 교사가 사용하기에도 무리가 없는가?
80. 모국어의 사용이 꼭 필요한가?

From 박상옥. (1991). 중학교 영어 교과서 분석. *영어교육, 41, 2,* pp. 111-115.

43. EVALUATIVE CRITERIA FOR BEGINNING FOREIGN-LANGUAGE TEXTBOOKS

1. **SKILL DEVELOPMENT:** Is provision made for learning all four skills?
   Yes-Students practice all four skills though not necessarily to the same degree.
   No-One (or more) of the four skills is largely neglected.

2. **LISTENING COMPREHENSION:** Does the text contain appropriate listening comprehension material?
   Yes-Specific listening comprehension material is present throughout the text; utterances are short, natural, and of high frequency in English.
   No-Specific listening comprehension material is sporadic or missing; utterances are too long, unnatural, or uncommon.

3. **PRONUNCIATION:** Is pronunciation dealt with satisfactorily?
   Yes-Pronunciation and the sound system are dealt with explicitly, either in a pronunciation unit or a unit by unit basis throughout the text; sufficient attention is paid to close "equivalents" in Korean and English and to those sounds which are difficult for Koreans; stress and intonation are considered.
   No-Pronunciation and the sound system are to be learned indirectly, they are never dealt with explicitly; the sound system is dealt with, but insufficient attention is paid to near-equivalents in Korean and English and to problem sounds in English; stress and intonation are not considered.

4. **SPEAKING:** Is appropriate conversational material present?
   Yes-Oral practice material is available throughout the text; utterances are short, natural, and concentrate on basic English structures.
   No-Material for developing oral skills is sporadic or missing, material contains lengthy or seldom-used utterances and structures.

5. **WRITING:** Is adequate opportunity provided for practicing the writing skill?
   Yes-Writing exercises develop progressively through the book; exercises are varied and emphasize recombination of previously learned material; exercises lead

to a degree of self-expression appropriate to the instructional level.

No-Writing exercises do not develop progressively; very few different types of exercises are available; exercises call for excessive amount of new vocabulary or structures; exercises do not lead to self-expression.

6. READING: Is adequate opportunity provided for practicing the reading skill?

Yes-Reading material derives organically from the unit; reading material is not overburdened with new vocabulary; reading material aims at comprehension of the written word rather than translation.

No-Reading material does not relate to the unit; reading material demands learning too much vocabulary; reading material is largely an exercise in translating rather than direct comprehension of the written word.

7. GRAMMAR: Is grammar dealt with satisfactorily?

Yes-Basic English grammar is accurately presented; provision is made for sufficient drilling before proceeding to new structures; the amount of grammar is about right for the students.

No-Grammar is described incompletely or faultily; grammatical principles are seldom or never summarized; insufficient drill opportunity is afforded before introducing new structures; there is too much or too little grammar.

8. VOCABULARY: Is the vocabulary in the text appropriate and adequately presented?

Yes-Vocabulary is appropriate to the needs and interests of the students; vocabulary is introduced in context, vocabulary is summarized by chapter in the form of lists, glossaries, or indexes.

No-Vocabulary is too difficult for the students or too irrelevant to their interests; vocabulary is presented without context; vocabulary items are inadequately summarized by chapter.

9. CULTURE: Does the book present suitable cultural material?

Yes-Examples of culture both in the fine arts sense and the anthropological sense are presented; the material is organically related to the rest of the unit.

No-There is a one-sided emphasis on culture; the material does not relate to the rest of the unit.

10. DRILLS AND EXERCISES: Are drills and exercises varied and numerous?

Yes-The book contains a wide variety of drills and exercises; drills and exercises are numerous to minimize the need for teacher-devised material.

No-The book utilizes the same types of practice material throughout the text; the kinds of exercises are so few in number and so limited in scope that teacher-written material is necessary.

11. LENGTH: Are the text and its units realistic in terms of the amount of material presented?

Yes-The text can be completed by most middle school or high school students in one year; the units are short enough to maintain student interest and afford a feeling of progress.

No-One or more of the above is missing.

12. CONSTRUCTION: Is the book well-constructed?

Yes-Hardbound; drawings and/or photographs; variety of type style and sizes; clearly arranged; detailed index; error-free in language, cultural information, and printing.

No-One or more of the above is missing.

13. FLEXIBILITY: Is the text flexible and adaptable?

Yes-The text makes provision for a variety of student interests, abilities, and learning styles.

No-The text makes no such provision.

14. SUPPLEMENTARY MATERIALS: Are basic supplementary materials available?

Yes-Teacher's edition or manual; workbook; audio materials; visuals; tests and quizzes.

No-One or more of the above is missing.

15. SUGGESTED SUPPLEMENTARY ACTIVITIES: Are suggestions made for supplementary activities?

Yes-Suggestions are made for supplementing the text with such things as films, games, songs, slides, crossword puzzles, field trips, student-created skits, letter writing, and English cooking.

No-No such suggestions are made.

From Grittner F. M. & Welty, S. (1974). Beginning German textbooks for the high school level (1969-73): A descriptive evaluation, *The Modern Language Journal,* 58, 7, pp. 314-322.

44. EVALUATION OF FOREIGN LANGUAGE TEXTBOOKS

EVALUATIVE CRITERIA

A body of criteria for textbook evaluation can be organized in numerous ways. For the system suggested here, the criteria have been divided into four categories: Pronunciation, Grammar, Content, and General.

Pronunciation Criteria

Evaluation of the presentation of pronunciation requires attention to three important criteria:

1. Completeness of presentation. A Complete presentation of the pronunciation of English requires two essential ingredients: the sounds, and the suprasegmental signals (stress, pitch, intonation, juncture).

Presentation of the sound system must include the full range of vowels and diphthongs. Present in practically every syllable, they are probably best presented first. Where the age of the learner permits, information about the point and manner of articulation should accompany the subsequent presentation of the consonants. Hopefully, some systematic grouping will be evident in presentation of the consonants. Grouping such as stops, fricatives, and nasal resonants, with the voiced/voiceless distinction made wherever it applies, is better than a presentation in terms of alphabetical position. Again, where the age of the learner makes it practical, the presentation of a suitable system of phonetic or phonemic symbols may facilitate both text and chalkboard display.

Since the suprasegmental signals are so extensive in English and contribute so much to meaning as well as to correct rhythm and pronunciation, they should be presented as fully as the age of the learners permits. This presentation should include information, examples, and practice on basic sentence intonation patterns, word and sentence stress, coincidence of pitch and stress, and juncture.

A complete presentation of English pronunciation will include considerable attention as well to the practice of reducing unstressed vowels and the consequent substitution of schwa /ə/ or barred-*i* /ɨ/ in unstressed positions. Since the rhythm of spoken English depends so much upon a correct application of this concept, its presentation is an important item.

Some texts leave far too many of the problems of English pronunciation to the teacher. Often the teacher is not capable of supplying this information adequately. If the book is designed for learners too young to benefit from the more complicated aspects of the pronunciation system, they should be included in a teacher's text, guide, or handbook.

2. Appropriateness of presentation. The book must be evaluated in terms of the appropriateness of the presentation of pronunciation for the situation in which it is to be used. Beginning texts will divide into at least four categories in terms of their presentation of the sound system.

First, they will divide into two groups based on the background of the student. If the book is for students from a single language background, it should present a contrastive analysis of the sound system of English and that of the native language. It should emphasize drill sequences of minimal-pair words and utterances that illustrate the sounds and combinations most difficult for the student because of interference from his native language. But if the book is for students from a heterogeneous background, its presentation of the sound system must be based on an analysis of English, with special emphasis on those sounds that have been found to be especially difficult for most learners of English.

Second, beginning texts can present the sound system in one of two ways, depending on the age of the student. The book for younger students can leave more to the teacher and to the technique of imitation in presenting linguistic and phonetic details and terminology. If diagrams or drawings of the voice mechanism are included, they should be appropriate to the age and level of the learner and clearly and simply labeled. On the other hand, if the text is for learners who are literate in a common background language, much of the information about pronunciation can be given to them in their native language, especially in the earlier parts of the text.

3. Adequacy of practice. Materials for pronunciation practice must be adequate in both quality and quantity. Vocabulary lists to be pronounced after the teacher do not insure adequate pronunciation practice because such lists may not take into account the learner's difficulties with pronunciation. Beginning with the initial presentation of the sounds and continuing throughout the text, all pronunciation practice should be presented in a context. That is, individual sounds should be practiced in words and words should be practiced in sentences.

Sounds that are difficult for most learners or for learners from a specific language background should be initially presented for practice in series of minimally different words. Subsequently, such practice may be in sentences, conversations, or dialogs. Similarly, problems of word stress and vowel reduction, along with sentence rhythm and intonation, require a great number of illustrating and contrasting sentences for practice. The pronunciation materials presented in, or accompanying, the text should include a sufficient number of drill words and sentences related to the vocabulary and structures presented in the lessons.

In summary, it is particularly important that the various aspects of pronunciation be *practiced* — not merely talked about — and further, that pronunciation drill materials be provided in the book rather than left to the teacher.

Grammar Criteria

In applying grammar criteria, the evaluator is concerned with how much of the structure of the language is presented, how well it is presented, and how readily the student may be able to benefit from the presentation.

4. Adequacy of pattern inventory. The variety, extent, and quality of language patterns presented should be carefully considered. The text should include the basic patterns necessary for using the language up to whatever level of complexity the book achieves, and the structural features introduced should contribute to that goal. While a quick look at the table of contents may suggest the extent of the pattern inventory, a careful examination of the lessons might reveal that the presentation and practice of patterns is clumsy, obscure, fragmented, or faulty.

If the level of sentence complexity presented in the text does not go beyond simple sentences, there is obviously little need for a full presentation of the conjunction system. But, in any beginning text, a fairly full range of prepositions, along with adverbs, adjectives, and possessives, is necessary. The function of nouns as modifiers distinguished from compound nouns, as in *gold ring* versus *gold mine,* and a clear distinction between mass and count nouns are examples of additional desirable patterns.

In summary, the pattern inventory is adequate to the extent that it presents the patterns possible within the limits of the book's terminal level. And the patterns presented are of adequate quality if they reveal the forms and characteristics of the various systems of which they are members.

5. Appropriate sequencing. Since organization is so necessary to language learning, a primary function of instruction is to present the language in a way that helps the student either to understand the textbook's organization or to develop his own. In the case of a beginning textbook, these purposes are best served by a careful sequencing of the levels of structure so that the introduction of new structures or patterns rests upon a foundation of simpler patterns and structures already mastered.

Except where functional load would indicate otherwise, presentation of sentence patterns, modifier structures, and vocabulary should move gradually from the simple to the more difficult. Simple sentence patterns like Subject — Verb — Noun are suitable for early lessons and should be thoroughly learned before more complicated patterns are introduced and before modifying structures are attached to them.

In a similar way, question transformations should be presented in a graded sequence.

Probably the simplest form of question is the inversion of *That is a clock* to form *Is that a clock?* Other types of questions, involving more complex transformations, should be presented subsequently according to the order of difficulty.

Regular verbs are best dealt with first, except where functional load requires the use of high-frequency irregular verbs. *To be*, of course, must be presented very early in the course despite its irregularity. The present continuous is probably the most functional tense for early use.

Among the pronouns, subject pronouns are needed first. Depending on the sequencing of related structures, the other pronouns may be taught in almost any order.

6. Adequacy of drill model and pattern displays. An evaluation of the book in terms of this criterion involves making a judgment about how readily the student can discern the form and content of a new pattern and can discover what is expected of him in the various drills and pattern practices. If the book is to be easy for him to follow in this respect, it must present simple, self-explanatory initial displays of each new pattern. Also, it must show him the kind of pattern substitution, alteration, or response required of him in a drill.

These displays are best understood by the student of a beginning text if they make use of boxes, arrows, contrasting colors and type faces, and other graphic devices rather than lengthy explanations. Also, the age or level of the learner must determine the appropriate level of complexity of such displays. Labels and grammatical identifications should be kept to a practical minimum. Wherever necessary, they should be expressed in simple terms, and a term once used should be consistently adhered to.

7. Adequacy of practice. Genuinely adequate practice of patterns and structures requires drills and practice exercises which are meaningful, appropriate for their purpose, and sufficiently diverse. A book that parades a wide variety of drill types in each lesson may include among these drills many that require of the student only the tiresome repetition of a single word or phrase in a long list of sentence contexts. In such cases, quantity does not guarantee adequacy. The student should be practicing what he is expected to learn, and while it may be true that elementary language learning is more a matter of habit formation than of problem solving, mere repetition in a number of unlikely or ridiculous contexts is apt to prove unproductive.

Good drills frequently require the student to make a variety of responses and discriminations which are representative of the decisions and productions necessary in actual speech. Appropriate drills provide the variety necessary to permit student practice of the range of behavior that is relevant to the structure or structures being practiced. On the other hand, exercises which test knowledge of the language should not be mistaken for exercises which give practice in using the language; testing exercises are not practice exercises.

Content Criteria

Lessons in pronunciation and grammar require the use of the language as content. The actual vocabulary presented, the situations discussed, and the semantic contexts used to impart additional meaning within the lesson comprise an important element of the book.

8. Functional load. The problem of functional load is, actually, a problem created by the extent to which certain difficult and complex words and structures are essential to the manipulation of the language or to its minimal use in communication. Some irregular forms, complex structures, or patterns which are hard to explain, such as greeting formulas, must be presented early in the book. They should be presented as formulas to be learned without explanation. For example, the introduction of *to be* presents many problems to the learner because of its irregularity, even in the simple present. But, because one cannot say *I am the teacher* or *How are you*? without it, the functional load of 'to be' justifies its presence very near the beginning of the course.

Similarly, the introduction of vocabulary must conform to the requirements of functional load. Complex expressions used in telling time, counting money, the naming the days and months are necessary very early, if dialogs and drills are to approximate real conversations. The same justification can be extended to the inclusion of such idiomatic expressions *as I feel fine and All right.*

The textbook which is prepared for an adult learner in specialized circumstances may exhibit special functional load requirements for technical vocabulary of a trade or profession.

In summary, the presentation of vocabulary and patterns of the language should follow a scheme of logical sequencing, derived from the basic structure of the language, unless the special requirement of functional load dictates otherwise.

9. Rate and manner of entry and re-entry. Application of this criterion should be extended to both vocabulary and grammatical structures. Suitable entry involves economy and timing. Both vocabulary and structures should probably be introduced sparingly in early lessons. Some texts introduce six words and one or two structures in the first lesson. The optimal number depends upon the age of the learner and the length of the lesson in terms of class minutes or hours. The number may increase in later lessons. The number of structures presented may increase somewhat, too. However, for most beginning learners, a one-hour lesson probably cannot effectively present more than three structures, depending upon their complexity.

The concept of economy also applies to re-entry. Once a word or structure has been introduced, it should continue to play an active role. Some vocabulary and some structures are capable of much more frequent use than others. However, even the less adaptable items should reappear from time to time. Although introduction formulas need not be a part of every lesson, they can occasionally reappear in different dialog and narrative contexts. A verb tense, once introduced, can play a very steady part in the majority of the lessons. In particular, a given tense may reappear as an aid to practicing a subsequent new verb tense.

Timing of entry and re-entry is deserving of some scrutiny. Suitable entry is, like sequencing, a matter of careful arrangement with special attention to the adjacent items. Confusingly similar vocabulary or structures should not be introduced in close proximity. For example, the introduction of *they are* and *there are* in the same lesson is very confusing to most students.

Common to most current methodology is the audio-lingual approach to the sequencing of language skills. According to this approach, all new material should be presented first in an oral practice, a dialog, or a narrative portion of a lesson, so that the student hears and repeats it before he looks at the printed words. A book organized in such a way that this kind of presentation is difficult or impossible does not lend itself to the audio-lingual approach to language teaching.

When items reappear, they should often do so in somewhat different contexts and situations in order to facilitate learning their range of applicability in English. The uses of verbs like *make* and *have*, and of prepositions, for example, can be gradually expanded by re-entry in slightly different contexts which exemplify new environments. Re-entry is closely related to sequencing. Re-entry in new contexts, therefore, usually presupposes re-entry in more complex structures and in larger patterns. The re-presentation of a word or simple structure always in the same kind of sentence or frame is inconsistent with the concept of a sequential increase of difficulty.

10. Appropriateness of contexts and situations. The content of the text can be evaluated in terms of both pedagogical and cultural appropriateness. The context of an oral practice, narrative, or dialog should be prepared in such a way that a variety of natural English utterances can be used to introduce the vocabulary and structures to be taught in that lesson. Certainly, a dialog format provides better opportunity for introduction of a new question pattern than a narrative oral practice would. Also, the content of narratives, dialogs, etc., can help to establish the meanings of the words and phrases that are introduced.

Content material should be suited to the age, level, background, and interests of the students. Young children are easily bored with "talky" narratives, while older students may intellectually reject childish dialog. In general, interesting material presented in vocabulary and structures that the student can control with a steady rate of increment will likely prove to be the most appropriate pedagogically.

The contents of oral practices and dialogs and the situations discussed therein can contribute meaningfully to the general presentation of the culture of English-speaking peoples. If the learners are likely to live in, or visit, an English-speaking country, an expanding cultural insight should be one goal of instruction. And since effective control of the language requires at least a minimum of knowledge of the cultural implications in formulas, idioms, etc., presentation of the culture is really inescapable.

However, if the text is designed for an area where English is taught as a second language for use as a medium of instruction, the learner is likely to need and want considerably less of the target culture. Rather, the content will be more appropriate for him if it is developed from a contrastive analysis of the two cultures and gives considerable weight to his native culture. Also, if the text is designed for learners from a single language background, its contents should be carefully controlled to avoid situations which offend local sensitivities or violate cultural taboos.

General Criteria

The remainder of the criteria require a broader view of the book and frequently involve assessing factors that are external to the volume itself.

11. Authenticity of language. The language used in a beginning text must, for simplicity's sake, be confined to a narrow range of style and functional variation. Since the language which is being taught is the spoken language, the tone of language used in the text should be that of standard spoken English. Idioms and idiomatic usage are necessary and advisable, but sub-standard dialects, slang, and obscure regional idioms should be avoided in a beginning text.

12. Availability of supplementary materials. If a language lab, tape recorder, or record player is available, supplementary pronunciation and pattern-drill tapes or discs might be very helpful. If available teachers are not adequate models of spoken English, such audio supplements become even more advisable. Also, pictorial display materials for picture practice may be available. Other things being equal, the text whose publisher offers these and similar supplementary aids may offer some advantages over competing volumes.

13. Adequate guidance for non-native teachers. Quite apart from supplementary materials is the problem of sufficient guidance for the non-native teacher. If the teachers are unlikely to have native competence in English or sufficient training in modern methodology, the text should be accompanied by a teacher's edition or guide with adequate simplified guidance for presenting the varied ingredients of the text. In some cases, the guide or handbook may include some background on current methodology and suggestions for classroom activities and techniques. For some teachers, assistance in point and manner of articulation of English sounds and exposure to a phonetic alphabet may be helpful. Where a variety of texts are available and roughly comparable, tailoring the choice to the needs of the teachers in terms of teacher guidance may serve to increase the quality and decrease the burden of the teaching.

14. Competence of the author. The question of the author's competence is largely answered through an examination of his product, the textbook. However, knowledge of an author's reputation and previous works may be helpful in the following ways: 1) If the evaluator has rated the book highly on a significant number of important criteria, then the name of a recognized and respected author tends to confirm this favorable assessment. 2) If the evaluator believes the author to have previously produced some unsound works, this should point to a more rigorous scrutiny of the judgments made. If the author is unknown to the evaluator, a bit of investigation will reveal his standing in the field. In the final analysis, of course, the book should be accepted on its own merits. The name of a highly esteemed author is of little value on the jacket of a book that appears to be unsuitable.

15. Appropriate level for integration. If the text under consideration is not part of a series, all of which is being considered, then the question of how well it will fit with the text for the following course must be asked. An examination of the early lessons in the following course will give a good indication of what competency in English is assumed there as entering behavior for the students. This assumed competence then becomes the measure of a suitable level of instruction which this text should contribute to. For example, if in the beginning of the text for the next course, the present perfect tense is used in dialogs and is not taught, then that tense should have been taught in the preceding text. A similar comparison of the complexity of sentences, level of vocabulary, and emphasis on composition and reading will serve to indicate how well the text being evaluated will contribute to the necessary entering behavior for the following course. A certain amount of overlap is desirable. The initial lessons in a second course may profitably represent material covered late in the previous course. However, if this overlap is too extensive, little learning and considerable boredom may result.

16. Durability. The more expensive hard-cover text is often considered to be the most durable type. A careful examination may reveal weak o r wide-spaced stitching in the binding, lightweight or easily breakable hard board in the covers, or shoddy fabric used as cover material. The best of the hard covers reveal their durability through the absence of these shortcomings. Plastic-impregnated fabrics provide the most durable covers because they are stain and dirt resistant, as well as washable.

A good soft-cover (paperback) text may be much more durable than a poorly bound hard cover. Although the cover will inevitably show use faster than a hard cover, the soft-cover text may stand many a semester's use. The most durable soft-cover book has a sewn or stapled binding with a sturdy fabric backbinding. Such books do not lose their pages like the texts with a glued binding. A gazed paper stock provides a better and more durable cover. For hard- or soft-cover texts being considered for use in very humid areas, additional attention needs to be given to the quality of paper. Some paper stock warps and discolors badly in extreme humidity. For either type of text, the smaller octavo size tends to be more durable than the larger sizes.

17. Quality of editing and publishing. It may require a rather careful examination to discover the quality of editing. Quality, here, is revealed through such things as effective choices of type face, absence of typographical errors, and removal of the author's oversights. Effective use of light and dark type and contrasting type sizes and styles can add considerably to the ease with which the student discerns the organization within the book. Misprints which are obvious to a native speaker may be confusing or misleading to a student. And even the best authors may make an occasional slip in small details.

The quality of publishing, quite apart from matters of durability, can be seen in attention to details of interest and attractiveness in the book. The cost of color is no longer as prohibitive as it once was. Its effective use in illustrations and diagrams can produce a lively and attractive volume. The inclusion of maps, even on the end sheets, may make the book more interesting. Such maps should be simple enough to be read easily and uncluttered by trivial details. Occasionally, student aids such as phonetic display of the sound system are printed inside the cover. A colorful, well-designed cover reflects the skill and interest of the publisher in packaging his product.

18. Price and value. Price is often an extremely significant criterion. Frequently, choices must be made within certain price limits. Sometimes, unfortunately, such limits may remove from consideration one or more of the best available texts. If so, then the matter of price and value comes down to the question: Is this the best for the price within our limits? Making such a decision involves consideration of the evaluator's cumulative judgments about the suitability of the text for its intended use, its promise of durability, and its price. Then, a judgment should be made about the relationship of its value to its price; in other words, "How much of what we hoped for are we getting for our money?" Comparison of several books in this way should help to reveal the best bargain among them. Perhaps, if one text demonstrably offers a much greater value, a prior decision about price limits may be amended to permit its purchase.

From Madson, H. S. & Bowen, J. D.(1978). *Adaptation in language teaching*, Rowley, MA: Newbury House Publishers, Inc., pp. 220-232.

찾아보기

A

B

C

D

E

U

V

W

저 자

박상옥(朴商玉, Sang Ok Park)

성균관 대학교 영어영문학과 졸업
미국 켄트 주립대학교 대학원 석사
미국 인디애나 대학교 대학원 박사
現 홍익대학교 사범대학 영어교육과 교수

저서: 한국인을 위한 영어학습지도 (신아사, 2004)
American Reader (편저) (신아사, 2001)
American Culture in Daily life (편저) (신아사, 2000)
Current Laboratory English for Communication (신아사, 2000)
English Language Teaching Techniques (편저) (신아사, 2000)

논문: 영어 교사교육, 조기 영어교육, 영어 읽기교육, 문화교육, 대학 교양
영어교육 등 영어교육 관련 논문 外

영어교수기법

ENGLISH LANGUAGE TEACHING TECHNIQUES

초판 1쇄 발행 _ 2000년 2월 25일
2판 2쇄 발행 _ 2011년 9월 10일

저 자 | 박 상 옥
발 행 인 | 정 현 걸
발 행 | 신 아 사
인 쇄 | 예지인쇄
출판등록 | 1956년 1월 5일 (제9-52호)
주 소 | 서울특별시 은평구 녹번동 28-36번지 2F
전 화 | 02)382-6411 • 팩스 02)382-6401
홈페이지 | www.shinasa.co.kr
E-MAIL | shinasa@chol.com

ISBN 978-89-8396-639-1(93740)

정가 *17,000* **원**